THE
SACRED BOOKS OF THE BUDDHISTS

SACRED BOOKS OF THE BUDDHISTS

TRANSLATED

BY VARIOUS ORIENTAL SCHOLARS

AND EDITED BY

F. MAX MÜLLER

PUBLISHED IN 1899 UNDER THE PATRONAGE OF
HIS MAJESTY KING CHULĀLANKARANA,
KING OF SIAM

VOL. II

Published by
THE PALI TEXT SOCIETY, LONDON

Distributed by
ROUTLEDGE & KEGAN PAUL LTD.
LONDON, HENLEY AND BOSTON
1977

DIALOGUES OF THE BUDDHA

TRANSLATED FROM THE PALI

BY

T. W. RHYS DAVIDS

PART I

First published	.	.	.	1899
Reprinted	.	.	.	1956
Reprinted	.	.	.	1969
Reprinted	.	.	.	1973
Reprinted	.	.	.	1977

ISBN 0 7100 7629 0
© PALI TEXT SOCIETY

Printed in Great Britain by
REDWOOD BURN LIMITED
Trowbridge and Esher

CONTENTS.

PREFACE.

—•—

THE Dialogues of the Buddha, constituting, in the
Pâli text, the Dîgha and Ma*ggh*ima Nikâyas, contain
a full exposition of what the early Buddhists considered the teaching of the Buddha to have been.
Incidentally they contain a large number of references
to the social, political, and religious condition of India
at the time when they were put together. We do not
know for certain what that time exactly was. But
every day is adding to the number of facts on which
an approximate estimate of the date may be based.
And the ascertained facts are already sufficient to give
us a fair working hypothesis.

In the first place the numerous details and comparative tables given in the Introduction to my translation of the Milinda show without a doubt that
practically the whole of the Pâli Pi*t*akas were known,
and regarded as final authority, at the time and place
when that work was composed. The geographical
details given on pp. xliii, xliv tend to show that the
work was composed in the extreme North-West of
India. There are two Chinese works, translations
of Indian books taken to China from the North of
India, which contain, in different recensions, the intro-

duction and the opening chapters of the Milinda[1].
For the reasons adduced (*loco citato*) it is evident
that the work must have been composed at or about
the time of the Christian era. Whether (as M. Sylvain
Lévy thinks) it is an enlarged work built up on the
foundation of the Indian original of the Chinese books;
or whether (as I am inclined to think) that original is
derived from our Milinda, there is still one conclusion
that must be drawn—the Nikâyas, nearly if not quite
as we now have them in the Pâli, were *known at a very
early date in the North of India.*

Then again, the Kathâ Vatthu (according to the
views prevalent, at the end of the fourth century A. D.,
at Kâñkipura in South India, and at Anurâdhapura
in Ceylon; and recorded, therefore, in their commentaries, by Dhammapâla and Buddhaghosa) was
composed, in the form in which we now have it, by
Tissa, the son of Moggalî, in the middle of the third
century B. C., at the court of Asoka, at Pâtaliputta, the
modern Patna, in the North of India.

It is a recognised rule of evidence in the courts of
law that, if an entry be found in the books kept by
a man in the ordinary course of his trade, which entry
speaks *against* himself, then that entry is especially
worthy of credence. Now at the time when they
made this entry about Tissa's authorship of the Kathâ
Vatthu the commentators believed, and it was an
accepted tenet of those among whom they mixed—
just as it was, *mutatis mutandis,* among the theologians
in Europe, at the corresponding date in the history of
their faith—that the whole of the canon was the word
of the Buddha. They also held that it had been
actually recited, at the Council of Râgagaha, immediately after his decease. It is, I venture to submit,
absolutely impossible, under these circumstances, that
the commentators can have invented this information

---

[1] See the authors quoted in the Introduction to vol. ii of my
translation. Professor Takakusu, in an article in the J. R. A. S. for
1896, has added important details.

about Tissa and the Kathâ Vatthu. They found it in the records on which their works are based. They dared not alter it. The best they could do was to try to explain it away. And this they did by a story, evidently legendary, attributing the first scheming out of the book to the Buddha. But they felt compelled to hand on, as they found it, the record of Tissa's authorship. And this deserves, on the ground that it is evidence against themselves, to have great weight attached to it.

The text of the Kathâ Vatthu now lies before us in a scholarly edition, prepared for the Pâli Text Society by Mr. Arnold C. Taylor. It purports to be a refutation by Tissa of 250 erroneous opinions held by Buddhists belonging to schools of thought different from his own. We have, from other sources, a considerable number of data as regards the different schools of thought among Buddhists—often erroneously called 'the Eighteen Sects[1].' We are beginning to know something about the historical development of Buddhism, and to be familiar with what sort of questions are likely to have arisen. We are beginning to know something of the growth of the language, of the different Pâli styles. In all these respects the Kathâ Vatthu fits in with what we should expect as possible, and probable, in the time of Asoka, and in the North of India.

Now the discussions as carried on in the Kathâ Vatthu are for the most part, and on both sides, an appeal to authority. And to what authority? Without any exception as yet discovered, to the Pi*t*akas, and as we now have them, in Pâli. Thus on p. 339 the appeal is to the passage translated below, on p. 278, § 6; and it is quite evident that the quotation is from our Suttanta, and not from any other passage where

---

[1] They are not 'sects' at all, in the modern European sense of the word. Some of the more important of these data are collected in two articles by the present writer in the 'Journal of the Royal Asiatic Society' for 1891 and 1892.

the same words might occur, as the very name of the
Suttanta, the Kevaddha (with a difference of reading
found also in our MSS.), is given. The following are
other instances of quotations :—

Katha Vatthu.	The Nikâyas.	Katha Vatthu.	The Nikâyas.
p. 344 = A. II, 50.		p. 505 = M. I, 490.	
345 = S. I, 33.		506 = M. I, 485 = S. IV, 393 (nearly).	
345 = A. II, 54.		513 = A. I, 197.	
347 = Kh. P. VII, 6, 7.		522 = M. I, 389.	
348 = A. III, 43.		525 = Dhp. 164.	
351 = Kh. P. VIII, 9.		528 = M. I, 447.	
369 = M. I, 85, 92, &c.		549 = S. N. 227 = Kh. P. VI, 6.	
404 = M. I, 4.		554 = S. I, 233.	
413 = S. IV, 362.		554 = Vim. V. XXXIV, 25–27.	
426 = D. I, 70.		565 = D. I, 156.	
440 = S. I, 33.		588, 9 = P. P. pp. 71, 72.	
457 = D. (M. P. S. 23).		591 = M. I, 169.	
457 = A. II, 172.		597, 8 = A. I, 141, 2.	
459 = M. I, 94.		602 = Dh. C. P. Sutta, §§ 9–23.	
481 = D. I, 83, 84.			
483 = D. I, 84.			
484 = A. II, 126.			
494 = S. I, 206 = J. IV, 496.			

There are many more quotations from the older
Pi*t*aka books in the Kathâ Vatthu, about three or
four times as many as are contained in this list.
But this is enough to show that, *at the time when
the Kathâ Vatthu was composed, all the Five Nikâyas
were extant; and were considered to be final authorities
in any question that was being discussed.* They must
themselves, therefore, be considerably older.

Thirdly, Hofrath Bühler and Dr. Hultsch have
called attention [1] to the fact that in inscriptions of
the third century B.C. we find, as descriptions of donors
to the dâgabas, the expressions dhammakathika,
pe*t*akî, suttantika, suttantakinî, and pa*ñk*a-nekâ-

---
[1] 'Epigr. Ind.,' II, 93, and 'Z. D. M. G.,' xl, p. 58.

yika. The Dhamma, the Pitakas, the Suttantas, and
the five Nikâyas must have existed for some time
before the brethren and sisters could be described as
preachers of the Dhamma, as reciters of the Pitaka,
and as guardians of the Suttantas or of the Nikâyas
(which were not yet written, and were only kept alive
in the memory of living men and women).

Simple as they seem, the exact force of these
technical designations is not, as yet, determined.
Dr. K. Neumann thinks that Petaki does not mean
'knowing the Pitakas,' but 'knowing the Pitaka,' that
is, the Nikâyas—a single Pitaka, in the sense of the
Dhamma, having been known before the expression
'the Pitakas' came into use [1]. As he points out, the
title of the old work Petakopadesa, which is an
exposition, not of the three Pitakas, but only of the
Nikâyas, supports his view. So again the Dialogues
are the only parts or.passages of the canonical books
called, in our MSS., suttantas. Was then a suttantika one who knew precisely the Dialogues by heart?
This was no doubt the earliest use of the term. But
it should be recollected that the Kathâ Vatthu, of
about the same date, uses the word suttanta also for
passages from other parts of the scriptures.

However this may be, the terms *are conclusive proof
of the existence, some considerable time before the date of
the inscriptions, of a Buddhist literature called either
a Pitaka or the Pitakas, containing Suttantas, and
divided into Five Nikâyas.*

Fourthly, on Asoka's Bhabra Edict he recommends
to the communities of the brethren and sisters of the
Order, and to the lay disciples of either sex, frequently
to hear and to meditate upon seven selected passages.
These are as follows :—

1. Vinaya-samukkamsa.
2. Ariya-vâsâni from the Dîgha (Samgîti Suttanta).
3. Anâgata-bhayâni from the Anguttara III, 105–108.
4. Muni-gâthâ from the Sutta Nipâta 206–220.

---

[1] 'Reden des Gotamo,' pp. x, xi.

5. Moneyya Sutta from the Iti Vuttaka 67 = A.
I, 272.

6. Upatissa-pasina.

7. Râhulovâda = Râhulovâda Suttanta (M. I, 414–420).

Of these passages Nos. 1 and 6 have not yet been satisfactorily identified. The others may be regarded as certain, for the reasons I have set out elsewhere [1] No. 2 also occurs in the tenth book of the Anguttara. It is clear that in Asoka's time there was acknowledged to be an authoritative literature, probably a collection of books, containing what was then believed to be the words of the Buddha : and that it comprised passages already known by the titles given in his Edict. Five out of the seven having been found in the published portions of what we now call the Pitakas, and in the portion of them called the Five Nikâyas, raises the presumption that when the now unpublished portions are printed the other two will also, probably, be identified. We have no evidence that any other Buddhist literature was in existence at that date.

What is perhaps still more important is the point to which M. Senart [2] has called attention, and supported by numerous details :—the very clear analogy between the general tone and the principal points of the moral teaching, on the one hand of the Asoka edicts as a whole, and on the other of the Dhammapada, an anthology of edifying verses taken, in great part, from the Five Nikâyas. The particular verses selected by M. Senart, as being especially characteristic of Asoka's ideas, include extracts from each of the Five.

Fifthly, the four great Nikâyas contain a number of stock passages, which are constantly recurring, and in which some ethical state is set out or described. Many of these are also found in the prose passages

---

[1] 'Journal of the Pâli Text Society,' 1896 ; 'Journal of the Royal Asiatic Society,' 1898, p. 639. Compare 'Milinda' (S. B. E., vol. xxxv), pp. xxxvii foll.

[2] 'Inscriptions de Piyadasi,' II, 314–322.

of the various books collected together in the Fifth,
the Khuddaka Nikâya. A number of them are found
in each of the thirteen Suttantas translated in this
volume. There is great probability that such passages
already existed, as ethical sayings or teachings, not
only before the Nikâyas were put together, but even
before the Suttantas were put together.

There are also entire episodes, containing not only
ethical teaching, but names of persons and places and
accounts of events, which are found, in identical terms,
at two or more places. These should be distinguished
from the last. But they are also probably older than
our existing texts. Most of the parallel passages,
found in both Pâli and Sanskrit Buddhist texts, come
under one or other of these two divisions.

Sixthly, the Samyutta Nikâya (III, 13) quotes one
Suttanta in the Dialogues by name; and both the
Samyutta and the Aṅguttara Nikâyas quote, by name
and chapter, certain poems now found only in a particular chapter of the Sutta Nipâta. *This Suttanta,
and these poems, must therefore be older, and older in
their present arrangement, than the final settlement of
the text of these two Nikâyas.*

Seventhly, several of the Dialogues purport to
relate conversations that took place between people,
cotemporaries with the Buddha, but *after the Buddha's
death.* One Sutta in the Aṅguttara is based on the
death of the wife of Muṇḍa, king of Magadha, who
began to reign about forty years after the death of the
Buddha. There is no reason at all to suspect an
interpolation. It follows that, not only the Sutta
itself, but *the date of the compilation of the Aṅguttara,
must be subsequent to that event.*

There is a story in Peta Vatthu IV, 3, 1 about
a King Pingalaka. Dhammapâla, in his commentary,
informs us that this king, of whom nothing is otherwise
known, lived two hundred years after the Buddha. It
follows that this poem, and also the Peta Vatthu in
which it is found, and also the Vimâna Vatthu, with
which the Peta Vatthu really forms one whole work,

are later than the date of Pingalaka. And there is no reason to believe that the commentator's date, although it is evidently only a round number, is very far wrong. These books are evidently, from their contents, the very latest compositions in all the Five Nikâyas.

There is also included among the Thera Gâthâ, another book in the Fifth Nikâya, verses said, by Dhammapâla the commentator [1], to have been composed by a *thera* of the time of King Bindusâra, the father of Asoka, and to have been added to the collection at the time of Asoka's Council.

Eighthly, several Sanskrit Buddhist texts have now been made accessible to scholars. We know the real titles, given in the MSS. themselves, of nearly 200 more [2]. And the catalogues in which the names occur give us a considerable amount of detailed information as to their contents. No one of them is a translation, or even a recension, of any one of the twenty-seven canonical books. They are independent works; and seem to bear to the canonical books a relation similar, in many respects, to that borne by the works of the Christian Fathers to the Bible. But though they do not reproduce any complete texts, they contain numerous verses, some whole poems, numerous sentences in prose, and some complete episodes, found in the Pâli books. And about half a dozen instances have been already found in which such passages are stated, or inferred, to be from older texts, and are quoted as authorities. Most fortunately we may hope, owing to the enlightened liberality of the Academy of St. Petersburg, and the zeal and scholarship of Professor d'Oldenbourg and his co-workers, to have a considerable number of Buddhist Sanskrit Texts in the near future. And this is just what, in the present state of our knowledge of the history of Buddhist writings, is so great a *desideratum*.

---

[1] Quoted by Prof. Oldenberg at p. 46 of his edition.
[2] Miss C. Hughes is preparing a complete alphabetical list of all these works for the 'Journal of the Royal Asiatic Society,' 1899.

It is possible to construct, in accordance with these facts, a working hypothesis as to the history of the literature. It is also possible to object that the evidence dràwn from the Milinda may be disregarded on the ground that there is nothing to show that that work, excepting only the elaborate and stately introduction and a few of the opening chapters, is not an impudent forgery, and a late one, concocted by some Buddhist in Ceylon. So the evidence drawn from the Kathâ Vatthu may be disregarded on the ground that there is nothing to show that that work is not an impudent forgery, and a late one, concocted by some Buddhist in Ceylon. The evidence drawn from the inscriptions may be put aside on the ground that they do not explicitly state that the Suttantas and Nikâyas to which they refer, and the passages they mention, are the same as those we now have. And the fact that the commentators point out, as peculiar, that certain passages are nearly as late, and one whole book quite as late, as Asoka, is no proof that the rest are older. It may even be maintained that the Pâli Pitakas are not therefore Indian books at all: that they are all Ceylon forgeries, and should be rightly called 'the Southern Recension' or 'the Simhalese Canon.'

Each of these propositions, taken by itself, has the appearance of careful scruple. And a healthy and reasonable scepticism is a valuable aid to historical criticism. But can that be said of a scepticism that involves belief in things far more incredible than those it rejects? In one breath we are reminded of the scholastic dulness, the sectarian narrowness, the literary incapacity, even the senile imbecility of the Ceylon Buddhists. In the next we are asked to accept propositions implying that they were capable of forging extensive documents so well, with such historical accuracy, with so delicate a discrimination between ideas current among themselves and those held centuries before, with so great a literary skill in expressing the ancient views, that not only did

B

they deceive their contemporaries and opponents, but European scholars have not been able to point out a single discrepancy in their work[1]. It is not unreasonable to hesitate in adopting a scepticism which involves belief in so unique, and therefore so incredible, a performance.

The hesitation will seem the more reasonable if we consider that to accept this literature for what it purports to be—that is, as North Indian[2], and for the most part pre-Asokan—not only involves no such absurdity, but is really just what one would *a priori* expect, just what the history of similar literatures elsewhere would lead one to suppose likely.

The Buddha, like other Indian teachers of his time, taught by conversation. A highly educated man (according to the education current at the time), speaking constantly to men of similar education, he followed the literary habit of his time by embodying his doctrines in set phrases, sûtras, on which he enlarged on different occasions in different ways. In the absence of books—for though writing was widely known, the lack of writing materials made any lengthy written books impossible[3]—such sûtras were the recognised form of preserving and communicating opinion. These particular ones were not in Sanskrit, but in the ordinary conversational idiom of the day, that is to say, in a sort of Pâli.

---

[1] As is well known, the single instance of such a discrepancy, which Prof. Minayeff made so much of, is a mare's nest. The blunder is on the part of the European professor, not of the Ceylon pandits. No critical scholar will accept the proposition that because *the commentary on* the Kathâ Vatthu mentions the Vetulyakâ, therefore *the Kathâ Vatthu itself* must be later than the rise of that school.

[2] North Indian, that is, from the modern European point of view. In the books themselves the reference is to the *Middle Country* (Magghima Desa). To them the country to the south of the Vindhyas simply did not come into the calculation. How suggestive this is as to the real place of origin of these documents!

[3] Very probably memoranda were used. But the earliest records of any extent were the Asoka Edicts, and they had to be written on stone.

When the Buddha died these sayings were collected together by his disciples into the Four Great Nikâyas. They cannot have reached their final form till about fifty years afterwards. Other sayings and verses, most of them ascribed not to the Buddha himself, but to the disciples, were put into a supplementary Nikâya. We know of slight additions made to this Nikâya as late as the time of Asoka. And the developed doctrine found in certain short books in it—notably in the Buddhavamsa and Kariyâ Pitaka, and in the Peta- and Vimâna-Vatthus—show that these are later than the four old Nikâyas.

For a generation or two the books as originally put together were handed down by memory. And they were doubtless accompanied from the first, as they were being taught, by a running commentary. About 100 years after the Buddha's death there was a schism in the community. Each of the two schools kept an arrangement of the canon—still in Pâli (or possibly some allied dialect). Sanskrit was not used for any Buddhist works till long afterwards, and never used at all, so far as we know, for the canonical books. Each of these two schools broke up, in the following centuries, into others; and several of them had their different arrangements of the canonical books, differing also no doubt in minor details. Even as late as the first century after the Christian Era, at the Council of Kanishka, these books, among many others then extant, remained the only authorities[1]. But they all, except only our present Pâli Nikâyas, have been lost in India. Of the stock passages of ethical statement, and of early episodes, used in the composition of them, and of the Suttas now extant, numerous fragments have been preserved in the Hînayâna Sanskrit texts. And some of the Suttas, and of the separate books, as used in other schools, are represented in Chinese translations of the fourth and

---

[1] On the often repeated error that a Sanskrit canon was established at Kanishka's Council, see my 'Milinda,' vol. ii, pp. xv, xvi.

fifth centuries A. D. A careful and detailed comparison
of these remains with the Pâli Nikâyas, after the
method adopted in Windisch's ' Mâra und Buddha,'
cannot fail to throw much light on the history, and on
the method of composition, of the canonical books,
which in style and method, in language and contents
and tone, bear all the marks of so considerable an
antiquity.

Hofrath Dr. Bühler, in the last work he published,
expressed the opinion that these books, as we have
them in the Pâli, are good evidence, certainly for the
fifth, probably for the sixth, century B.C. Subject to
what has been said above, that will probably become,
more and more, the accepted opinion. And it is this
which gives to all they tell us, either directly or by
implication, of the social, political, and religious life of
India, so great a value [1].

It is necessary, in spite of the limitations of our
space, to add a few words on the method followed in
this version. We talk of Pâli *books*. They are not
books in the modern sense. They are memorial
sentences intended to be learnt by heart; and the
whole style, and method of arrangement. is entirely
subordinated to this primary necessity. The leading
ideas in any one of our Suttantas, for instance, are
expressed in short phrases not intended to convey to
a European reader the argument underlying them.
These are often repeated with slight variations. But
neither the repetitions nor the variations—introduced,
and necessarily introduced, as aids to memory—help
the modern reader very much. That of course was
not their object. For the object they were intended

---

[1] No reference has been made, in these slight and imperfect
remarks, to the history of the Vinaya. There is nothing to add,
on that point, to the able and lucid exposition of Prof. Oldenberg in
the Introduction to his edition of the text.

to serve they are singularly well chosen, and aptly introduced.

Other expedients were adopted with a similar aim. Ideas were formulated, not in logically co-ordinated sentences, but in numbered groups; and lists were drawn up such as those found in the tract called the Sîlas, and in the passage on the rejected forms of asceticism, both translated below. These groups and lists, again, must have been accompanied from the first by a running verbal commentary, given, in his own words, by the teacher to his pupils. Without such a comment they are often quite unintelligible, and always difficult.

The inclusion of such *memoria technica* makes the Four Nikâyas strikingly different from modern treatises on ethics or psychology. As they stand they were never intended to be read. And a version in English, repeating all the repetitions, rendering each item in the lists and groups as they stand, by a single English word, without commentary, would quite fail to convey the meaning, often intrinsically interesting, always historically valuable, of these curious old documents.

It is no doubt partly the result of the burden of such *memoria technica*, but partly also owing to the methods of exposition then current in North India, that the leading *theses* of each Suttanta are not worked out in the way in which we should expect to find similar theses worked out now in Europe. A proposition or two or three, are put forward, re-stated with slight additions or variations, and placed as it were in contrast with the contrary proposition (often at first put forward by the interlocutor). There the matter is usually left. There is no elaborate logical argument. The choice is offered to the hearer; and, of course, he usually accepts the proposition as maintained by the Buddha. The statement of this is often so curt, enigmatic, and even —owing not seldom simply to our ignorance, as yet, of the exact force of the technical terms used—so

ambiguous, that a knowledge of the state of opinion
on the particular point, in North India, at the time, or
a comparison of other Nikâya passages on the subject,
is necessary to remove the uncertainty.

It would seem therefore most desirable that
a scholar attempting to render these Suttantas into
a European language—evolved in the process of
expressing a very different, and often contradictory,
set of conceptions—should give the reasons of the
faith that is in him. He should state *why* he
holds such and such an expression to be the least
inappropriate rendering : and quote parallel passages
from other Nikâya texts in support of his reasons.
He should explain the real significance of the thesis
put forward by a statement of what, in his opinion,
was the point of view from which it was put forward,
the stage of opinion into which 'it fits, the current views
it supports or controverts. In regard to technical terms,
for which there can be no exact equivalent, he should
give the Pâli. And in regard to the mnemonic lists
and groups, each word in which is usually a *crux*, he
should give cross-references, and wherever he ventures
to differ from the Buddhist explanations, as handed
down in the schools, should state the fact, and give
his reasons. It is only by such discussions that we
can hope to make progress in the interpretation of the
history of Buddhist and Indian thought. Bare versions
are of no use to scholars, and even to the general
reader they can only convey loose, inadequate, and
inaccurate ideas.

These considerations will, I trust, meet with the
approval of my fellow workers. Each scholar would
of course, in considering the limitations of his space,
make a different choice as to the points he regarded
most pressing to dwell upon in his commentary, as
to the points he would leave to explain themselves.
It may, I am afraid, be considered that my choice in
these respects has not been happy, and especially that
too many words or phrases have been left without
comment, where reasons were necessary. But I have

endeavoured, in the notes and introductions, to emphasise those points on which further elucidation is desirable; and to raise some of the most important of those historical questions which will have to be settled before these Suttantas can finally be considered as having been rightly understood.

T. W. Rhys Davids.

'Nâlandâ,' *April,* 1899.

ABBREVIATIONS.

1. BUDDHIST CANONICAL BOOKS.

A.	Aṅguttara Nikâya.
B. V.	Buddha Vamsa.
D.	Dîgha Nikâya.
Dhp.	Dhammapada.
Gât.	Gâtaka.
Kh. P.	Khuddaka Pâtha.
M.	Magghima Nikâya.
M. P. S.	Mahâparinibbâna Sutta.
S.	Samyutta Nikâya.
S. N.	Sutta Nipâta.
Ud.	Udâna.
Vim. V.	Vimâna Vatthu.
V. or Vin.	Vinaya.

2. OTHER BOOKS.

Abh. Pad.	Abhidhâna Padîpikâ.
Asl.	Attha Salinî.
Ath. V.	Atharva Veda.
Brîhad.	Brîhadâranyaka Upanishad.
Dhp. Cy.	Dhammapada commentary.
Divy.	Divyâvadâna.
Ep. Ind.	Epigraphia Indica.
J. P. T. S.	Journal of the Pâli Text Society.
J. R. A. S.	Journal of the Royal Asiatic Society.
Khând.Up.	Khândogya Upanishad.
M. B. V.	Mahâ Bodhi Vamsa.
Mil.	Milinda Pañha.
Pàr. Dîp.	Paramattha Dîpanî.
S. B. E.	Sacred Books of the East.
Sum.	Sumangala Vilâsinî.
Sat. Br.	Satapatha-Brâhmana.
Tait.	Taittirîya Upanishad.
Z.D.M.G.	Zeitschrift der deutschen morgenländischen Gesellschaft.

INTRODUCTION

BRAHMA-GÂLA SUTTA.

THE phase of beliefs which this Suttanta is intended to meet, into which its argument fits, has been set out in some detail in the opening chapter of my 'American Lectures.' As there pointed out[1], the discussion which thus opens this series of dialogues forms also the first question in the Kathâ Vatthu, and the first question in the Milinda. We cannot be far wrong if, in our endeavours to understand the real meaning of the original Buddhism, we attach as much weight to this question as did the author or authors of these ancient and authoritative Buddhist books.

The Suttanta sets out in sixty-two divisions[2] various speculations or theories in which the theorisers, going out always from various forms of the ancient view of a 'soul'—a sort of subtle manikin inside the body but separate from it, and continuing, after it leaves the body, as a separate entity—attempt to reconstruct the past, or to arrange the future. All such speculation is condemned. And necessarily so, since the Buddhist philosophy is put together without this ancient idea of 'soul.'

The Buddhist scheme endeavours, in other words, to include all the truth which previous thinkers had grafted on to the old savage theories of a semi-material, subtle, permanent entity inside the body, while rejecting those theories themselves; it endeavours to retain all the philosophic truth which previous thinkers had grafted on to the theosophies—the corollaries of the soul theories—while rejecting those theosophies themselves. The reasons given for this position are threefold : firstly, that such speculators about ultimate things,

---

[1] 'American Lectures on Buddhism.' London, 1896, pp. 38–43.

[2] Summed up below, pp. 52, 53 ; and set out more fully in the list in the 'American Lectures,' pp. 31–33.

either in the past or the future, have insufficient evidence,
see only one side of the shield [1] ; secondly, that such speculations do not lead to emancipation, to Arahatship [2] ; and
thirdly, that such theories are really derived from the hopes,
the feelings, and the sensations arising from evanescent
phenomena [3]—they belong, in other words, to the realm of
hastily formed, empirical opinion (ditthi), not to that of the
higher wisdom (paññâ). So that Buddhism, in the first place,
holds a position somewhat similar to the modern Agnostic
position. Secondly, while acknowledging the importance of
feeling and of intellect, it lays special stress upon the regulation,
the cultivation, of the will [4]. And thirdly, it distinguishes
between a lower and a higher wisdom [5].

Several scholars, and especially—with more knowledge
and detail—Dr. Karl Neumann, have maintained that the
position of Buddhism in the history of Indian philosophy is
analogous to that of Schopenhauer in European philosophy.
On the other hand, it is maintained by Professor Deussen
that Schopenhauer's position is analogous to that of the
Upanishads. The reconciliation will probably be found
to be that what Buddhism took over, with more or less of
modification, from the Upanishads, is about the same as that
part of the Upanishad doctrine which is found, in European
phraseology, in Schopenhauer; and what Buddhism rejected
altogether is not to be found in Schopenhauer. He himself,
who however knew both systems only from second-hand and
inaccurate authorities, says, ' If I am to take the results of
my own philosophy as the standard of truth, I should be
obliged to concede to Buddhism the pre-eminence over other
(systems of philosophy).'

However this question may be decided—and its discussion,
at the necessary length, by a competent student of philosophy,
is a very pressing want—it is certain from the details given
in our Suttanta that there were then current in Northern
India many other philosophic and theosophic speculations
besides those the priests found it expedient to adopt, and
have preserved for us in the Upanishads. And who can
doubt but that some, if not all of them, may also have had
their influence on the new doctrine ? There was always much
philosophising in India outside the narrow and inexact limits

---

[1] See the fable quoted below, pp. 187, 188.
[2] See below, pp. 44, 188.
[3] See for instance below, pp. 53, 54.
[4] See the paper on ' The Will in Buddhism,' J. R. A. S., 1898.
[5] See below, p. 42, &c., of this Suttanta.

of the so-called six Darsanas; and we have to thank Buddhist scholars for preserving, in their Pâli and Sanskrit works, the evidences of such philosophy as the priests wished to exclude from notice [1].

---

[1] Professor Cowell has been good enough to inform me that, in his opinion, the attempted restriction of all philosophy to the six Darsanas, and the very use of the term, is late mediaeval. The six are of course not mutually exclusive; and this, and the omissions in the classification of philosophy under these six heads, render it rather like a classification of animals into men, horses, birds, ghosts, beetles, and sparrows.

DIALOGUES OF THE BUDDHA.

—◦—

DÎGHA NIKÂYA.

[COLLECTION OF LONG DIALOGUES.]

—◦—

I. BRAHMA-*G*ÂLA SUTTA [1].

[THE PERFECT NET.]

I. 1. Thus have I heard. The Blessed One was once going along the high road between Râ*g*agaha and Nâlandâ [2] with a great company of the brethren, with about five hundred brethren. And Suppiya the mendicant [3] too was going along the high road between Râ*g*agaha and Nâlandâ with his disciple the youth Brahmadatta. Now just then Suppiya the mendicant was speaking in many ways in dispraise of the Buddha, in dispraise of the Doctrine, in dispraise of the Order. But young Brahmadatta, his pupil, gave utterance, in many ways, to praise of the Buddha, to praise of the Doctrine, to praise of the Order. Thus they two, teacher and pupil, holding opinions in direct contradiction one to the other, were following, step by

---

[1] The whole of this Sutta was translated into English by the Rev. Daniel Gogerly, Wesleyan missionary in Ceylon, in the Journal of the Ceylon Branch of the Royal Asiatic Society for 1846 (reprinted by P. Grimblot in his 'Sept Suttas Palis,' Paris, 1876).

[2] Nâlandâ, afterwards the seat of the famous Buddhist university, was about seven miles north of Râ*g*agaha, the capital of Magadha, the modern Ra*g*-gir (Sum. p. 35).

[3] Suppiya was a follower of the celebrated teacher Sa*ñ*gaya, whose views are set out and controverted in the next Sutta.

step, after the Blessed One and the company of the brethren.

2. Now the Blessed One put up at the royal rest-house in the Ambala*tth*ikâ pleasance [1] to pass the night, and with him the company of the brethren. And so also did Suppiya ùie mendicant, and with him his young disciple Brahmadatta. And there, at the rest-house, these two carried on the same discussion as before.

[2] 3. And in the early dawn a number of the brethren assembled, as they rose up, in the pavilion ; and this was the trend of the talk that sprang up among them, as they were seated there. 'How wonderful a thing is it, brethren, and how strange that the Blessed One, he who knows and sees, the Arahat, the Buddha Supreme, should so clearly have perceived how various are the inclinations of men! For see how while Suppiya the mendicant speaks in many ways in dispraise of the Buddha, the Doctrine, and the Order, his own disciple young Brahmadatta, speaks, in as many ways, in praise of them. So do these two, teacher and pupil, follow step by step after the Blessed One and the company of the brethren, giving utterance to views in direct contradiction one to the other.'

4. Now the Blessed One, on realising what was the drift of their talk, went to the pavilion, and took his seat on the mat spread out for him. And when he had sat down he said : 'What is the talk on which you are engaged sitting here, and what is the subject of the conversation between you?' And they told him all. And he said :

---

[1] Ambala*tth*ikâ, 'the mango sapling.' It was, says Buddhaghosa (pp. 41, 42), a well-watered and shady park so called from a mango sapling by the gateway. It was surrounded with a rampart, and had in it a rest-house adorned with paintings for the king's amusement.

There was another garden so named at Anurâdhapura in Ceylon, to the east of the Brazen Palace (Sum. I, 131). This was so named, no doubt, after the other which was famous as the scene of the 'Exhortation to Râhula starting with falsehood,' mentioned in Asoka's Bhabra Edict (see my 'Buddhism,' pp. 224, 225).

5. 'Brethren, if outsiders should speak against me, or against the Doctrine, [3] or against the Order, you should not on that account either bear malice, or suffer heart-burning, or feel illwill. If you, on that account, should be angry and hurt, that would stand in the way of your own self-conquest. If, when others speak against us, you feel angry at that, and displeased, would you then be able to judge how far that speech of theirs is well said or ill?'

'That would not be so, Sir.'

'But when outsiders speak in dispraise of me, or of the Doctrine, or of the Order, you should unravel what is false and point it out as wrong, saying: "For this or that reason this is not the fact, that is not so, such a thing is not found among us, is not in us."

6. 'But also, brethren, if outsiders should speak in praise of me, in praise of the Doctrine, in praise of the Order, you should not, on that account, be filled with pleasure or gladness, or be lifted up in heart. Were you to be so that also would stand in the way of your self-conquest. When outsiders speak in praise of me, or of the Doctrine, or of the Order, you should acknowledge what is right to be the fact, saying: "For this or that reason this is the fact, that is so, such a thing is found among us, is in us."

7. 'It is in respect only of trifling things, of matters of little value, of mere morality, that an unconverted man, when praising the Tathâgata, would speak. And what are such trifling, minor details of mere morality that he would praise?'

[4] [THE MORALITIES [1]. PART I.]

8. '" Putting away the killing of living things, Gotama the recluse holds aloof from the destruction

---

[1] These titles occur, in the MSS., at the end of the sections of the tract that now follows. It forms a part of each of the Suttas in the first division, the first third, of this collection of Suttas. The division is called therefore the Sîla Vagga or Section containing the Sîlas. The tract itself must almost certainly have existed as a separate work

of life. He has laid the cudgel and the sword aside, and ashamed of roughness, and full of mercy, he dwells compassionate and kind to all creatures that have life." It is thus that the unconverted man, when speaking in praise of the Tathâgata, might speak [1].

'Or he might say: "Putting away the taking of what has not been given, Gotama the recluse lived aloof from grasping what is not his own. He takes only what is given, and expecting that gifts will come [2], he passes his life in honesty and purity of heart."

'Or he might say: "Putting away unchastity, Gotama the recluse is chaste. He holds himself aloof, far off, from the vulgar practice, from the sexual act [3]."

9. 'Or he might say: "Putting away lying words, Gotama the recluse holds himself aloof from falsehood. He speaks truth, from the truth he never swerves; faithful and trustworthy, he breaks not his word to the world."

'Or he might say: "Putting away slander, Gotama the recluse holds himself aloof from calumny. What he hears here he repeats not elsewhere to raise a quarrel

---

before the time when the discourses, in each of which it recurs, were first put together.

Certain paragraphs from this tract occur also elsewhere. So in Magghima I, 179 we have the whole of the short paragraphs; in Magghima, Nos. 76 and 77, and in Mahâvagga V, 8, 3, we have § 17; in Magghima II, 3 we have most of § 18; and so on. The whole of this tract has been translated into English by Gogerly (in Grimblot, see page 1, note), into French by Burnouf (also in Grimblot, pp. 212 foll.), and into German by Dr. Neumann (in his Buddhistische Anthologie, pp. 67 foll.).

[1] This refrain is repeated at the end of each clause. When the Sîlas recur below, in each Sutta, the only difference is in the refrain. See, for instance, the translation of p. 100 in the text.

[2] Neumann has 'waiting for a gift' which is a possible rendering: but pâtikankhati has not yet been found elsewhere in the sense of 'waiting for.' The usual meaning of the word expresses just such a trifling matter as we have been led, from the context, to expect.

[3] Gâma-dhammâ, 'from the village habit, the practice of country folk, the "pagan" way.' One might render the phrase by 'pagan' if that word had not acquired, in English, a slightly different connotation. It is the opposite of porî, urbane (applied to speech, below, § 9). Dr. Neumann misses the point here, but has 'höflich' below.

against the people here; what he hears elsewhere he repeats not here to raise a quarrel against the people there. Thus does he live as a binder together of those who are divided, an encourager of those who are friends, a peacemaker, a lover of peace, impassioned for peace, a speaker of words that make for peace."

'Or he might say: "Putting away rudeness of speech, Gotama the recluse holds himself aloof from harsh language. Whatsoever word is blameless, pleasant to the ear, lovely, reaching to the heart, urbane[1], pleasing to the people, beloved of the people —such are words he speaks."

'Or he might say: "Putting away frivolous talk[2], Gotama the recluse holds himself aloof from vain conversation. In season he speaks, in accordance with the facts, words full of meaning, on religion, on the discipline of the Order. He speaks, and at the right time, words worthy to be laid up in one's heart, [6] fitly illustrated, clearly divided, to the point."

10. 'Or he might say: "Gotama the recluse holds himself aloof from causing injury to seeds or plants[3].

He takes but one meal a day, not eating at night, refraining from food after hours (after midday).

He refrains from being a spectator at shows at fairs, with nautch dances, singing, and music.

He abstains from wearing, adorning, or ornamenting himself with garlands, scents, and unguents.

He abstains from the use of large and lofty beds.

He abstains from accepting silver or gold.

He abstains from accepting uncooked grain.

He abstains from accepting raw meat.

He abstains from accepting women or girls.

He abstains from accepting bondmen or bond-women.

---

[1] Porî. See note above on § 8.

[2] Sampha-ppalâpa. Sampha occurs alone in the Hemavata Sutta, and at Gât. VI, 295; A. II, 23.

[3] Samârambhâ cannot mean 'planting' as Dr. Neumann renders it.

He abstains from accepting sheep or goats.

He abstains from accepting fowls or swine.

He abstains from accepting elephants, cattle, horses, and mares.

He abstains from accepting cultivated fields or waste.

He abstains from the acting as a go-between or messenger.

He abstains from buying and selling.

He abstains from cheating with scales or bronzes [1] or measures.

He abstains from the crooked ways of bribery, cheating, and fraud.

He abstains from maiming, murder, putting in bonds, highway robbery, dacoity, and violence."

'Such are the things, brethren, which an unconverted man, when speaking in praise of the Tathâgata, might say.'

Here ends the *K*ûla Sîla [the Short Paragraphs on Conduct].

11. 'Or he might say: "Whereas some recluses and Brahmans, while living on food provided by the faithful, continue addicted to the injury of seedlings and growing plants whether propagated from roots or cuttings or joints or buddings or seeds [2]—Gotama the

---

[1] Ka*m*sa-kû*t*a. The context suggests that ka*m*sa (bronze) may here refer to coins, just as we say in English 'a copper,' and the word is actually so used in the 11th and 12th Bhikkhunî Nissaggiya Rules —the oldest reference in Indian books to coins. The most ancient coins, which were of private (not state) coinage, were either of bronze or gold. Buddhaghosa (p. 79) explains the expression here used as meaning the passing off of bronze vessels as gold. Gogerly translates 'weights,' Childers *sub voce* has 'counterfeit metal,' and Neumann has 'Maass.' Buddhaghosa is obliged to take ka*m*sa in the meaning of 'gold pot,' which seems very forced; and there is no authority for ka*m*sa meaning either weight or mass. On the whole the coin explanation seems to me to be the simplest.

[2] Buddhaghosa gives examples of each of these five classes of the vegetable kingdom without explaining the terms. But it is only the fourth which is doubtful. It may mean 'graftings,' if the art of grafting was then known in the Ganges valley.

recluse holds aloof from such injury to seedlings and growing plants."

12. [6] 'Or he might say: "Whereas some recluses and Brahmans, while living on food provided by the faithful, continue addicted to the use of things stored up; stores, to wit, of foods, drinks, clothing, equipages, bedding, perfumes, and curry-stuffs[1]—Gotama the recluse holds aloof from such use of things stored up."

13. 'Or he might say: "Whereas some recluses and Brahmans, while living on food provided by the faithful, continue addicted to visiting shows[2]; that is to say,

(1) Nautch dances (na*kk*a*m*)[3].

(2) Singing of songs (g*î*ta*m*).

(3) Instrumental music (v*â*dita*m*).

(4) Shows at fairs (pek-kha*m*)[4].

---

[1] Âmisa. Buddhaghosa (p. 83) gives a long list of curry-stuffs included under this term. If he is right then Gogerly's 'raw grain' is too limited a translation, and Neumann's 'all sorts of articles to use' too extensive. In its secondary meaning the word means 'something nice, a relish, a dainty.'

[2] Vis*û*ka-dassana*m*. This word has only been found elsewhere in the phrase di*tt*hi-vis*û*ka*m*, 'the puppet shows of heresy' (Mag*gh*ima I, pp. 8, 486; and Serissaka Vim*â*na LXXXIV, 26). The Sinhalese renders it wipar*î*ta-dar*s*a*n*a.

[3] Dancing cannot mean here a dancing in which the persons referred to took part. It must be ballet or nautch dancing.

[4] Literally 'shows.' This word, only found here, has always been rendered 'theatrical representations.' Clough first translated it so in his Sinhalese Dictionary, p. 665, and he was followed by Gogerly, Burnouf, myself (in 'Buddhist Suttas,' p. 192), and Dr. Neumann (p. 69),—and Weber (Indian Literature, pp. 199, 319) seems to approve this. But it is most unlikely that the theatre was already known in the fifth century B.C. And Buddhaghosa (p. 84) explains it, quite simply, as na*t*a-sama*gg*â. Now sama*gg*o is a very interesting old word (at least in its P*â*li form). The Sanskrit sama*g*y*â*, according to the Petersburg Dictionary, has only been found in modern dictionaries. The P*â*li occurs in other old texts such as Vinaya II, 107; IV, 267 (both times in the very same context as it does here); ibid. II, 150; IV, 85; Sig*â*lovada Sutta, p. 300; and it is undoubtedly the same word as sam*â*g*a* in the first of the fourteen Edicts of Asoka. In the Sig*â*lovada there are said to be six dangers at such a sama*gg*o; to wit, dancing, singing, music, recitations, conjuring tricks, and acrobatic shows. And in the Vinaya passages we

(5) Ballad recitations (akkhânam) [1].

(6) Hand music (pânis-saram) [2].

(7) The chanting of bards (vetâlam) [3].

(8) Tam-tam playing (kumbhathûnam) [4].

learn that at a samaggo not only amusements but also food was provided; that high officials were invited, and had special seats; and that it took place at the top of a hill. This last detail of 'high places' (that is sacred places) points to a religious motive as underlying the whole procedure. The root ag (ἄγω, ago, whence our 'act') belongs to the stock of common Aryan roots, and means carrying on. What was the meaning of this 'carrying on together'? Who were the people who took part? Were they confined to one village? or have we here a survival from old exogamic communistic dancings together? Later the word means simply 'fair,' as at Gâtaka III, 541:

'Many the bout I have played with quarterstaves at the fair,'
with which Gâtaka I, 394 may be compared. And it is no doubt this side of the festival which is here in the mind of the author; but 'fair' is nevertheless a very inadequate rendering. The Sinhalese has 'rapid movement in dance-figures' (ranga-mandalu).

[1] These ballad recitations in prose and verse combined were the source from which epic poetry was afterwards gradually developed. Buddhaghosa has no explanation of the word, but gives as examples the Bhârata and the Râmâyana. The negative anakkhânam occurs Magghima I, 503.

[2] Buddhaghosa explains this as 'playing on cymbals'; and adds that it is also called pânitâlam. The word is only found here and at Gâtaka V, 506, and means literally 'hand-sounds.'

[3] Buddhaghosa says 'deep music, but some say raising dead bodies to life by spells.' His own explanation is, I think, meant to be etymological; and to show that he derives the word from vi + tâla. This would bring the word into connection with the Sanskrit vaitâlika, 'royal bard.' The other explanation connects the word with vetâla, 'a demon,' supposed to play pranks (as in the stories of the Vetâla-panka-vimsati) by reanimating corpses. Dr. Neumann adopts it. But it does not agree so well with the context; and it seems scarcely justifiable to see, in this ancient list, a reference to beliefs which can only be traced in literature more than a thousand years later. Gogerly's rendering 'funeral ceremonies,' which I previously followed, seems to me now quite out of the question.

[4] It is clear from Gâtaka V, 506 that this word means a sort of music. And at Vinaya IV, 285 kumbhathûnikâ are mentioned in connection with dancers, acrobats, and hired mourners. Buddhaghosa is here obscure and probably corrupt, and the derivation is quite uncertain. Gogerly's guess seems better than Burnouf's or Neumann's. The Sinhalese has 'striking a drum big enough to hold sixteen gallons.'

(9) Fairy scenes (Sobhanagaraka*m*)[1].

(10) Acrobatic feats by *K*and*â*las (*K*and*â*la-va*m*sa-dhopana*m*)[2].

(11) Combats of elephants, horses, buffaloes, bulls, goats, rams, cocks, and quails.

(12) Bouts at quarter-staff[3], boxing, wrestling[4].

(13-16) Sham - fights, roll-calls, manoeuvres, reviews[5]—

Gotama the recluse holds aloof from visiting such shows."

14. 'Or he might say: "Whereas some recluses and Brahmans, while living on food provided by the faithful, continue addicted to games and recreations[6]; that is to say,

(1) Games on boards with eight, or with ten, rows of squares[7].

(2) The same games

---

[1] Buddhaghosa seems to understand by this term (literally 'of Sobha city') the adornments or scenery used for a ballet-dance. (Pa*t*ibhâ*n*a-*k*itta*m* at Vinaya II, 151; IV, 61, 298, 358; Sum. I, 42 is the nude in art.) Weber has pointed out (Indische Studien, II, 38; III, 153) that Sobha is a city of the Gandharvas, fairies much given to music and love-making. It is quite likely that the name of a frequently used scene for a ballet became a proverbial phrase for all such scenery. But the Sinhalese has 'pouring water over the heads of dancers, or nude paintings.'

[2] Buddhaghosa takes these three words separately, and so do all the MSS. of the text, and the Sinhalese version. But I now think that the passage at *G*âtaka IV, 390 is really decisive, and that we have here one of the rare cases where we can correct our MSS. against the authority of the old commentator. But I follow him in the general meaning he assigns to the strange expression '*K*and*â*la-bamboo-washings.'

[3] See *G*âtaka III, 541.

[4] Nibbuddha*m*. The verbal form nibbu*gg*/*h*ati occurs in the list at Vinaya III, 180 (repeated at II, 10); and our word at Milinda 232.

[5] All these recur in the introductory story to the 50th Pâ*k*ittiya (Vinaya IV, 107). On the last compare Buddhaghosa on Mahâvagga V, 1, 29.

[6] All these terms recur at Vinaya III, 180 (repeated at II, 10).

[7] Chess played originally on a board of eight times ten squares was afterwards played on one of eight times eight squares. Our text cannot be taken as evidence of real chess in the fifth century B.C., but it certainly refers to games from which it and draughts must have been developed. The Sinhalese Sanna says that each of these games

played by imagining such boards in the air .

(3) Keeping going over diagrams drawn on the ground so that one steps only where one ought to go [2].

(4) Either removing the pieces or men from a heap with one's nail, or putting them into a heap, in each case without shaking it. He who shakes the heap, loses

(5) Throwing dice [4].

(6) Hitting a short stick with a long one [5].

(7) Dipping the hand with the fingers stretched out in lac, or red dye, or flour-water, and striking the wet hand on the ground or on a wall, calling out ' What shall it be ? ' and showing the form required —elephants, horses, &c. [6]

(8) Games with balls [7].

(9) Blowing through toy pipes made of leaves [8].

(10) Ploughing with toy ploughs [9].

(11) Turning summersaults [10].

(12) Playing with toy windmills made of palm-leaves [11].

---

was played with dice and pieces such as kings and so on. The word for pieces is poru (from purisa)—just our ' men.'

[1] Âkâsam. How very like blindfold chess !

[2] Parihâra-patham. A kind of primitive ' hop-scotch.' The Sinhalese says the steps must be made hopping.

[3] Santikâ. Spellicans, pure and simple.

[4] Khalikâ. Unfortunately the method of playing is not stated. Compare Eggeling's note as in his Satapatha-Brâhmana III, 106, 7. In the gambling-scene on the Bharhut Tope (Cunningham, Pl. XLV, No. 9) there is a board marked out on the stone of six times five squares (not six by six), and six little cubes with marks on the sides visible lie on the stone outside the board.

[5] Ghatikam. Something like 'tip-cat.' Sim-kelîmaya in Sinhalese.

[6] Salâka-hattham. On flour-water as colouring matter, see Gâtaka I, 220.

[7] Akkham. The usual meaning is ' a die.' But the Sinhalese translator agrees with Buddhaghosa. Neither gives any details.

[8] Pangakîram. The Sinhalese for this toy is pat-kulal. Morris in J. P. T. S., 1889, p. 205, compares the Marathî pungî.

[9] Vankakam. From Sanskrit vrika. See Journal of the Pâli Text Society, 1889, p. 206.

[10] Mokkhakikâ. So the Sinhalese. Buddhaghosa has an alternative explanation of turning over on a trapeze, but gives this also. See Vinaya I, 275, and J. P. T. S., 1885, p. 49.

[11] Kingulikam. See Morris in the J. P. T. S., 1885, p. 50, who compares kingulâyitvâ at Anguttara III, 15, 2.

(13) Playing with toy measures made of palm-leaves.

(14, 15) Playing with toy carts or toy bows[1].

(16) Guessing at letters

[7] Gotama the recluse holds aloof from such games and recreations."

traced in the air, or on a playfellow's back[2].

(17) Guessing the play-fellow's thoughts.

(18) Mimicry of deform-ities—

15. 'Or he might say: "Whereas some recluses and Brahmans, while living on food provided by the faithful, continue addicted to the use of high and large couches; that is to say[3],

(1) Moveable settees, high, and six feet long (Âsandi)[4].

(2) Divans with animal figures carved on the sup-ports (Pallanko)[5].

---

[1] All these six, from No. 10 inclusive, are mentioned in the Magghima, vol. i, p. 266, as children's games.

[2] Akkharikâ. It is important evidence for the date at which writing was known in India that such a game should be known in the fifth century B.C.

[3] The following list recurs Vinaya I, 192 = II, 163 = Anguttara I, 181, &c.

[4] Âsandî. Buddhaghosa merely says 'a seat beyond the allowed measure,' but that must refer to height, as the only rule as to measure in seats is the 87th Pâkittiya in which the height of beds or chairs is limited to eight 'great' inches (probably about eighteen inches). The Sinhalese Sanna adds 'a long chair for supporting the whole body.' At Gât. I, 208 a man lies down on an âsandî so as to be able to look up and watch the stars. At Dîgha I, 55 = Magghima I, 515 = Samyutta III, 307 (where the reading must be corrected), the âsandî is used as a bier. The âsandî is selected as the right sort of seat for the king in both the Vâgapeya and Inauguration ceremonies because of its height (Eggeling, Sat.-Brâh. III, 35, 105). It is there said to be made of common sorts of wood, and perforated; which probably means that the frame was of wood and the seat was of interlaced cane or wickerwork. The diminutive âsandiko, with short legs and made square (for sitting, not lying on), is allowed in the Buddhist Order by Vinaya II, 149. And even the âsandî is allowed, if the tall legs be cut down, by Vinaya II, 169, 170 (where the reading khinditvâ seems preferable, and is read in the quotation at Sum. I, 88). The renderings 'large cushion' at 'Vinaya Texts,' II, 27 and 'stuffed couch' at III, 209 must be accordingly corrected. Gogerly translates 'large couch,' Burnouf 'une chaise longue,' and Neumann 'bequeme Lehnstuhl.'

[5] Pallanko. It is noteworthy that, in spite of the use of a divan

(3) Goats' hair coverlets with very long fleece (Gonako) [1].

(4) Patchwork counterpanes of many colours (Kittakâ).

(5) White blankets (Paṭikâ).

(6) Woollen coverlets embroidered with flowers (Paṭalikâ).

(7) Quilts stuffed with cotton wool (Tûlikâ).

(8) Coverlets embroidered with figures of lions, tigers, &c. (Vikatikâ).

(9) Rugs with fur on both sides (Uddalomî).

(10) Rugs with fur on one side (Ekantalomî).

(11) Coverlets embroidered with gems (Kaṭṭhissam).

(12) Silk coverlets (Koseyyam).

(13) Carpets large enough for sixteen dancers (Kuttakam).

(14–16) Elephant, horse, and chariot rugs.

(17) Rugs of antelope skins sewn together (Aginapaveni).

(18) Rugs of skins of the plantain antelope.

(19) Carpets with awn-

---

with animals carved on its supports being here objected to, it is precisely the sort of seat on which the Buddha himself, or Buddhist personages of distinction, are often, in later sculptures, represented as sitting (Grünwedel, 'Buddhistische kunst,' pp. 111, 124, 137; Mitra, 'Budh Gayâ,' Plates XI, XX, &c. &c.). At Mahâvamsa 25 sîhâsana and pallanko are used of the same seat (Asoka's throne), and sîhâsana is used of Duṭṭha Gamini's throne, ibid. 157. But the Lion throne of Nissanka Malla, found at Pollonnaruwa, is not a pallanko, but an actual stone lion, larger than life size ('Indian Antiquary,' vol. i, p. 135. Compare the similar seat in Grünwedel, p. 95).

By Vinaya II, 170 the possession of a pallanka was allowed to the Order if the animal figures were broken off (the translation in 'Vinaya Texts,' III, 209, must be altered accordingly, reading vâle for vale, as at Vinaya IV, 312). By Vinaya II, 163 it is laid down that members of the Order were not to use a complete pallanko even in laymen's houses, so that Nigrodha's action in the passage just quoted (Mahâvamsa 25) was really a breach of the regulations.

[1] The words from gonako down to kaṭṭhissam inclusive, and also kuttakam, are found only in this list, and Buddhaghosa seems to be uncertain as to the exact meaning of some of them. All except No. 7 might be used in laymen's houses ('Vinaya Texts,' III, 197), and all might be possessed by the Order if used only as floorcoverings (ibid. III, 209); except again No. 7, the cotton wool of which might be utilised for pillows. As there is a doubt about the spelling it may be noticed that the Sanna reads goṇakam and

ings above them (Sa-uttara-*kkha*da*m*). | (20) Sofas with red pillows for the head and feet."

16. 'Or he might say: "Whereas some recluses and Brahmans, while living on food provided by the faithful, continue addicted to the use of means for adorning and beautifying themselves; that is to say,—

Rubbing in scented powders on one's body, shampooing it, and bathing it. Patting the limbs with clubs after the manner of wrestlers [1]. The use of mirrors, eye-ointments, garlands, rouge, cosmetics, bracelets, necklaces, walking-sticks, reed cases for drugs, rapiers, sunshades, embroidered slippers, turbans, diadems, whisks of the yak's tail, and long-fringed white robes—

Gotama the recluse holds aloof from such means of adorning and beautifying the person [2]."

17. 'Or he might say: "Whereas some recluses and Brahmans, while living on food provided by the faithful, continue addicted to such low conversation as these:

Tales of kings, of robbers, of ministers of state; tales of war, of terrors, of battles; talk about foods and drinks, clothes, beds, garlands, perfumes; talks about relationships, equipages, villages, town, cities, and countries; tales about women [8], and about heroes; gossip at street corners [3], or places whence

---

uddalomi*m*: and the MS. in the R. A. S. (which repeats each sentence) has gonaka*m* and uddalomi*m* both times.

[1] Sambâhana*m*. Perhaps rubbing the limbs with flat pieces of wood. See Buddhaghosa here and at 'Vinaya Texts,' III, 60.

[2] This is not quite accurate. Out of the twenty items here objected to, three (shampooing, bathing, and the use of sunshades) were allowed in the Order, and practised by Gotama himself. Bathrooms, and halls attached to them, are permitted by 'Vinaya Texts,' III, 189; shampooing by ibid. III, 68, 297. There are elaborate regulations for the provision of hot steam baths and the etiquette to be observed in them; and instances of the use of the ordinary bath in streams or rivers are frequent. The use of sunshades is permitted by 'Vinaya Texts,' III, 132–3, and is referred to ibid. III, 88, 274.

[3] Visikhâ-kathâ. Buddhaghosa (p. 90) takes this word (literally 'street-talk') in the sense of talk about streets, whether ill or well situate, and whether the inhabitants are bold or poor, &c.

water is fetched; ghost stories [1]; desultory talk [2];
speculations about the creation of the land or sea [3],
or about existence and non-existence [4]—

Gotama the recluse holds aloof from such low conversation."

18. 'Or he might say: "Whereas some recluses
and Brahmans, while living on food provided by the
faithful, continue addicted to the use of wrangling
phrases [5]: such as—

"You don't understand this doctrine and discipline,
I do."

"How should you know about this doctrine and
discipline?"

"You have fallen into wrong views. It is I who
am in the right."

"I am speaking to the point, you are not [6]."

"You are putting last what ought to come first,
and first what ought to come last [7]."

"What you've excogitated so long, that's all quite
upset."

---

[1] Pubba-peta-kathâ. The commentator confines this to boasting
talk about deceased relatives or ancestors.

[2] Nânatta-katham, literally 'difference-talk.' The expression
seems somewhat forced, if taken as meaning 'desultory'; but I see
no better explanation.

[3] Lokakkhâyikâ. Buddhaghosa refers this specially to such
speculations as are put forth according to the Lokâyata system
by the Vitandas (also called Lokâyatikas). These are materialistic
theorisers, of whose system very little is, so far, known. See the note
at 'Vinaya Texts,' vol. iii, p. 151. I have collected other references
to them in my 'Milinda,' vol. i, p. 7; and to these Dîgha I, 11,
114, 120, and Attha Sâlinî, p. 3, may now be added. They are
probably referred to below in chap. iii of this Sutta, §§ 10, 20.

[4] This list of foolish talks recurs in Suttas 76–78 in the Magghima,
and at Vinaya I, 188.

[5] These expressions all recur at Magghima II, 3.

[6] Sahitam me, literally 'the put together is to me,' &c. The
idiom is only found here, and may mean either as rendered above, or
'the context is on my side,' or 'the text (of the Scriptures) is on my
side,' or merely 'that which is of use is on my side.' This last, given
by the Sanna, amounts to the same as the version adopted above.

[7] Putting the cart before the horse.

"Your challenge has been taken up[1]."
"You are proved to be wrong[2]."
"Set to work to clear your views[3]."
"Disentangle yourself if you can[4]"—
Gotama the recluse holds aloof from such wrangling phrases."

19. 'Or he might say: "Whereas some recluses and Brahmans, while living on food provided by the faithful, continue addicted to taking messages, going on errands, and acting as go-betweens; to wit, on kings, ministers of state, Kshatriyas, Brahmans, or young men, saying: 'Go there, come hither, take this with you, bring that from thence'—
Gotama the recluse abstains from such servile duties."

20. 'Or he might say: "Whereas some recluses and Brahmans, while living on food provided by the faithful, are tricksters[5], droners out (of holy words for pay)[6],

---

[1] Âropito te vâdo. On the use of this idiom compare the Commentary on the Therî Gâthâ, p. 101. There is a misprint here in the text, aropito for âropito. 'Issue has been joined against you' would be a possible rendering. It is the phrase used, when some one has offered to hold debate (maintain a thesis) against all comers, by an opponent who takes up the challenge.

[2] Niggahîto si. On this idiom compare the opening paragraphs of the Kathâ Vatthu and the Commentary on them (especially pp. 9, 10). It is literally 'you are censured.'

[3] Kara vâda-pamokkhâya. So Buddhaghosa. But Gogerly renders, 'Depart, that you may be freed from this disputation;' and the only parallel passage seems to support this view. It is Magghima I, 133, where it is said to be wrong to learn the Scriptures for the sake of the advantage of being freed from discussion or debate where texts are quoted against one. Pamokkha occurs besides at Samyutta I, 2, Gâtaka V, 30, 31, and Mahâvamsa 158, but not in this connection.

[4] So the author of Milinda in making his hero Nâgasena use just such a phrase (Mil. p. 27) is making him commit a breach of propriety.

[5] Kuhakâ. 'Astonish the world with the three sorts of trickery,' says Buddhaghosa. These are also referred to without explanation at Gâtaka IV, 297 (where we should, I think, read kuhana).

[6] Lapakâ. Compare Itivuttaka, No. 99 = Anguttara I, 165, 168; and also Milinda 228, Gâtaka III, 349.

diviners [1], and exorcists [2], ever hungering to add gain to gain [3]—Gotama the recluse holds aloof from such deception and patter." '

Here ends the Ma*gghi*ma Sîla [the Longer Paragraphs on Conduct].

[9] 21. 'Or he might say : " Whereas some recluses and Brahmans, while living on food provided by the faithful, earn their living by wrong means of livelihood, by low arts, such as these :—

(1) Palmistry—prophesying long life, prosperity, &c. (or the reverse), from marks on a child's hands, feet, &c.[4]

(2) Divining by means of omens and signs [5].

(3) Auguries drawn from thunderbolts and other celestial portents [6].

---

[1] Nemittakâ, 'interpreters of signs and omens.' See the note on nimitta*m* in the next paragraph. Compare Milinda 299; *G*ât. IV, 124.

[2] Nippesikâ, 'scarers away' (? of ghosts, or bad omens). But the Commentary and Sanna give no help, and the word has only been found in this list.

[3] All the five words in this list recur at A. III, 111, but the context there is as undecisive as it is here, and the Commentary (fol. *di* of the Turnour MS. at the India Office), though slightly different, gives no better help.

[4] A*n*ga*m*, literally 'limbs.' Buddhaghosa distinguishes this from lakkha*n*a*m* (No. 5 in this list), and from anga-vi*gg*â (No. 16). It is not found, in this sense, anywhere in the texts.

[5] Nimitta*m*, literally 'marks,' or 'signs.' Buddhaghosa tells a story in illustration. King Pa*nd*u, they say (Pâ*nd*i in the Sanna), took three pearls in his closed hand, and asked a diviner what he had in it. The latter looked this way and that for a sign; and seeing a fly which had been caught by a house-lizard (the Sanna says 'by a dog,' perhaps the meaning is simply 'in sugar') getting free (muttâ), said at once 'pearls' (also muttâ in Pâli). 'How many?' says the king. The diviner, hearing a dog bark thrice, answered 'three.' Compare Mil. 178, and the note to the last section on nemittikâ, and the story at Mahâva*m*sa 82.

[6] Uppâdo, 'the portents of the great ones, thunderbolts falling, and so on,' says Buddhaghosa. The Great Ones here mean, I think, the spirits or gods presiding over the sun, moon, and planets (see the note on § 26). The word corresponds to the Sanskrit Utpâta, though the d is vouched for by overwhelming authority. But this is only another instance of a change not infrequent (as Ed. Müller has shown,

(4) Prognostication by interpreting dreams [1].

(5) Fortune-telling from marks on the body [2].

(6) Auguries from the marks on cloth gnawed by mice [3].

(7) Sacrificing to Agni [4].

(8) Offering oblations from a spoon [5].

(9–13) Making offerings to gods of husks, of the red powder between the grain and the husk, of husked grain ready for boiling, of ghee, and of oil [6].

(14) Sacrificing by spewing mustard seeds, &c., into the fire out of one's mouth [7].

(15) Drawing blood from one's right knee as a sacrifice to the gods [8].

Pâli Grammar, p. 37); and the one or two cases where Burmese scribes have (wrongly) corrected to uppâta is another instance to be added to those referred to in the Introduction to Sum. I of their habit of putting an easier reading where the more difficult one is really right. Childers should therefore have kept this word separate from the other uppâdo. Comp. Gât. I, 374.

[1] Supinam. On the theory of dreams compare Mil., pp. 297–301. At Gât. I, 374 the word is masculine. Perhaps charms to avert bad dreams (Ath.-veda VI, 46; XVI, 5 and 6) are included in this 'low art.' Gât. No. 77 mocks at the dream interpreters.

[2] Lakkhanam. The commentator on this word as used in the very same connection at Gât. I, 374 adds that it means also the knowledge of good and bad marks on such persons and things as are mentioned here in our next paragraph. Buddhaghosa confines its meaning to that given above. This contradiction is another confirmation of the opinion expressed by me in 1880 in 'Buddhist Birth Stories,' pp. lxiii foll., that Childers was wrong in ascribing the Gâtaka Commentary to Buddhaghosa. The word occurs in Buddhaghosa's sense at D. I, 114, 120 = A. I, 163, &c.; Gât. I, 56.

[3] Musikâkkhinnam. The allied superstition of thinking it unlucky to wear clothes gnawed by mice is laughed out of court in the Mangala Gâtaka, No. 87.

[4] Aggi-homam. Telling people that a sacrifice, if offered in a fire of such and such a wood, will have such and such a result.

[5] Dabbi-homam. Telling people that an oblation of such and such grains, butter, or so on, poured into the fire from such and such a sort of spoon, will have such and such a result.

[6] See Hillebrandt, 'Neu und Vollmondsopfer,' pp. 31, 171, and 'Ritual-literatur' in Bühler's 'Grundriss,' pp. 71, 72, 114, 176. The nine homas here objected to may also be compared with the seven at Ath.-veda VIII, 9, 18.

[7] No instance of this can be traced in the books of the Brahmans.

[8] Compare the passage in Hillebrandt, in Bühler's 'Grundriss,'

(16) Looking at the knuckles, &c., and, after muttering a charm, divining whether a man is well born or lucky or not [1].

(17) Determining whether the site, for a proposed house or pleasance, is lucky or not [2].

(18) Advising on customary law [3].

(19) Laying demons in a cemetery [4].

(20) Laying ghosts [5].

(21) Knowledge of the charms to be used when lodging in an earth house [6].

(22) Snake charming [7].

p. 176, on the use of blood for sorcery. In one passage, Rig-vidh. III, 18, 3, it is one's own blood that is to be used. But the specific interpretation given here by Buddhaghosa cannot be paralleled from the Brahmanical books.

[1] Anga-viggâ. Buddhaghosa thus separates this from the angam of No. 1. In both the passages Gât. II, 200, 250 the knowledge is simply that of judging from a man's appearance that he is rough or bad, and it is the good man in the story (in the second case the Bodisat himself) who is the anga-viggâ-pâthako. So at Gât. V, 458 it is by anga-viggâ that the Bodisat prophesies that a man will be cruel.

[2] Vatthu-viggâ. Childers (Dict., p. 559) has 'pool' instead of 'house,' having misread sara for ghara (s and gh are nearly alike in Sinhalese). The craft is further explained by Buddhaghosa in his comment on the Mahâ-parinibbâna Sutta I. 26. Its success depended on the belief that the sites were haunted by spirits. See further below, § 27.

[3] Khatta-viggâ. The Burmese MSS. correct the rare khatta into the familiar khetta. Khetta-viggâ indeed occurs at Ud. III, 9, and may just possibly there (in connection with writing, arithmetic, tables, &c.) be correct in the meaning of 'land-surveying, mensuration.' Buddhaghosa, though his explanation is corrupt, evidently understands the phrase in a sense similar to that of khatta-dhamma at Gât. V, 489, 490; Mil. 164 (see also 178); and his gloss nîti-sattham is probably nearer the mark than Sankara's (on Khând. Up. VII, 1, 2), which is dhanur-veda. It is the craft of government, then lying in great part in adhering to custom.

The Sutta only follows the Upanishad in looking at all these crafts as minor matters, but it goes beyond it in looking upon them as a 'low' way, for a Brahman, of gaining a livelihood.

[4] Siva-viggâ. It is clear that siva is used euphemistically, and we may here have an early reference to what afterwards developed into the cult of the god Siva. Buddhaghosa gives an alternative explanation as knowledge of the cries of jackals.

[5] Bhûta-viggâ. Also in the Khândogya list (loc. cit.).

[6] Bhûri-viggâ. It is the same as bhûri-kammam, explained in the same way by Buddhaghosa on § 27 below.

[7] Ahi-viggâ. One method is described at Gât. IV, 457, 8.

(23) The poison craft [1]. | number of years that a
(24) The scorpion craft [2]. | man has yet to live.
(25) The mouse craft [2]. | (29) Giving charms to
(26) The bird craft [3]. | ward off arrows [5].
(27) The crow craft [4]. | (30) The animal
(28) Foretelling the | wheel [6]—

Gotama the recluse holds aloof from such low arts."

22. 'Or he might say: " Whereas some recluses and Brahmans, while living on food provided by the faithful, earn their living by wrong means of livelihood, by low arts, such as these—

Knowledge of the signs of good and bad qualities in the following things and of the marks in them denoting the health or luck of their owners :—to wit, gems [7], staves, garments, swords, arrows, bows, other weapons, women [8], men [8], boys [8], girls [8], slaves, slave-girls, elephants, horses, buffaloes, bulls, oxen, goats [9], sheep [9], fowls [9], quails [9], iguanas [9], earrings [10], tortoises, and other animals—

Gotama the recluse holds aloof from such low arts."

23. 'Or he might say: " Whereas some recluses

Perhaps such charms against snake bite as Ath.-v. V, 13 ; VI, 12, 56 ; VII, 88, are included.

[1] Buddhaghosa says curing or giving poison, or poison spells (compare Ath.-v. VI, 90, 93, 100).

[2] These are explained to mean simply curing the bites of these creatures.

[3] Understanding their language.

[4] Divining by the appearance and the cawings of crows.

[5] Compare the Ambattha-viggâ at Sum. 255 and below, p. 96 of the text, § 23.

[6] Miga-kakkam.   Understanding the language of all creatures.

[7] The whole of this ' low art' as applied to gems has been collected in a series of manuals now edited by L. Finot in his 'Lapidaires Indiens,' Paris, 1896.

[8] The art in these four cases is to determine whether the marks on them show they will bring good (or bad) luck to the houses in which they dwell.

[9] The art in these five cases is to say whether it is unclean or not to eat them.

[10] This comes in here very oddly.   But the old commentator had the same reading, and takes the word in its ordinary senses, not even as amulet.

and Brahmans, while living on food provided by the faithful, earn their living by wrong means of livelihood, by low arts, such as soothsaying, to the effect that—

[10] The chiefs will march out.

The chiefs will march back.

The home chiefs will attack, and the enemies' retreat.

The enemies' chiefs will attack, and ours will retreat.

The home chiefs will gain the victory, and the foreign chiefs suffer defeat.

The foreign chiefs will gain the victory, and ours will suffer defeat [1]—

Thus will there be victory on this side, defeat on that—

Gotama the recluse holds aloof from such low arts."

24. 'Or he might say : " Whereas some recluses and Brahmans, while living on food provided by the faithful, earn their living by wrong means of livelihood, by such low arts as foretelling—

(1) There will be an eclipse of the moon.

(2) There will be an eclipse of the sun.

(3) There will be an eclipse of a star (Nak-shatra) [2].

(4) There will be aber-ration of the sun or the moon.

(5) The sun or the moon will return to its usual path.

(6) There will be aber-rations of the stars.

(7) The stars will return to their usual course [3].

---

[1] Throughout these paragraphs the plural is used. This cannot be honorific, as the few great kings of that time are always spoken of in the singular. Yet all the previous translators, except Burnouf, trans-late by the singular—'the king will march out,' &c. It is evident that we have to understand 'chiefs,' and not the 'king': and that not absolute monarchies, but republican institutions of a more or less aristocratic type, were in the mind of the composer of the paragraph.

[2] Nakkhatta, translated by Gogerly and Neumann a 'planet.' Buddhaghosa explains it by 'Mars and so on.' This may apply to planets, but also to stars in general, and I know no other passage where the meaning of the word is confined to planets. Burnouf has 'constellation,' but what can the eclipse of a constellation mean?

[3] Patha-gamana and uppatha-gamana. Prof. Kielhorn says (in a note he has been kind enough to send me on this section): 'What the author means by these words I do not know. But

(8) There will be a fall of meteors [1].

(9) There will be a jungle fire [2].

(10) There will be an earthquake.

(11) The god will thunder.

(12–15) There will be rising and setting, clearness and dimness, of the sun or the moon or the stars [3], or foretelling of each of these fifteen phenomena that they will betoken such and such a result " [11]

25. 'Or he might say : "Whereas some recluses and Brahmans, while living on food provided by the faithful, earn their living by wrong means of livelihood, by low arts, such as these :—

Foretelling an abundant rainfall.

Foretelling a deficient rainfall.

Foretelling a good harvest.

Foretelling scarcity of food.

Foretelling tranquillity.

Foretelling disturbances.

Foretelling a pestilence.

Foretelling a healthy season.

Counting on the fingers [4].

---

uppatha-gamana would be literally "aberration, the going away from one's proper path"; and patha-gamana therefore should be "following one's proper course." I am sure the two words could not mean conjunction and opposition; nor, I think, ascension and declension. It is curious that Buddhaghosa has not explained them.'

[1] Ukkâ-pâto. See Gât. I, 374; Mil. 178.

[2] Disâ-dâho. 'Thunder and lightning,' according to Neumann; 'fiery corruscations in the atmosphere,' according to Gogerly, whom Burnouf follows. But Buddhaghosa's words are only explicable of a jungle fire. Compare Gât. I, 212, 213, 374.

[3] Burnouf takes these four words to refer to four occurrences. Gogerly and Neumann take them as only two. Buddhaghosa seems to imply four.

[4] Muddâ. There has been great diversity in the various guesses made at the meaning in this connection of muddâ, which usually means 'seal' or 'seal-ring.' Gogerly has 'conveyancing,' and so also Childers; Burnouf takes this word and the next as one compound in the sense of foretelling the future 'by calculating diagrams'; and Neumann has 'Verwaltungsdienste,' administrative services. Buddhaghosa is very curt. He says only hattha-muddâ gananâ. Hattha-muddâ is found elsewhere only at Gât. III, 528, where hattha-

Counting without using the fingers [1].
Summing up large totals [2].
Composing ballads, poetizing [3].
Casuistry, sophistry [4]—
Gotama the recluse holds aloof from such low arts."

26. 'Or he might say: "Whereas some recluses and Brahmans, while living on food provided by the faithful, earn their living by wrong means of livelihood, by low arts, such as—

---

muddam karoti means 'to beckon,' and at Vin. V, 163, where it is said of the polite member of the Order that he makes no sign with his hand, nor beckons. (On hattha-vikâra compare Mil. I, 207, 547 = Vin. I, 157 = Vin. II, 216.) Both these passages are much later than our text, and the sense of beckoning is here impossible. But muddâ is mentioned as a craft at Vin. IV, 7 (where it is called honourable), at M. I, 85, and several times in the Milinda (pp. 3, 59, 78, 178 of the Pâli text), and muddiko as the person who practises that craft at D. I, 51 and Vin. IV, 8. The Sinhalese comment on this (quoted in my translation of the Milinda, I, 91) shows that the art there was simply arithmetic, using the joints or knuckles of the fingers as an aid to memory. And this is no doubt the meaning in our paragraph.

[1] Gananâ. Buddhaghosa's comment on this is akkhiddakâ-gananâ, in contradistinction to the last. It is evidently calculation not broken up by using the fingers, mental arithmetic pure and simple. The accountant who uses this method is called ganako (D. I, 51; Vin. IV, 8). Buddhaghosa's comment on the latter passage is given by Minayeff at Pat. 84, but with a wrong reading, akkhimtaka.

[2] Samkhânam, literally 'counting up.' He who has the faculty of doing this can, on looking at a tree, say how many leaves it has, says Buddhaghosa. But the first words of his comment are doubtful. He may perhaps mean calculating masses by means of the rosary. Burnouf skips this word, and Neumann has simply 'counting.'

[3] Kâveyyam. The word recurs, in a bad sense, at A. I, 72 = III, 107, and also at S. I, 110 in the phrase kâveyya-matto, 'drunk with prophecy, inspired.' Buddhaghosa enumerates, in the words of A. II, 230, four kinds of poetry, and explains them in nearly the same words as found in the Manoratha Pûranî on that passage. None of the four refer to sacrificial hymns. Impromptu rhyming, ballad singing, and the composition of poems are meant.

[4] Lokâyatam. Usually rendered 'materialism.' But it is quite clear that this meaning is impossible in this connection. See Milinda 174.

(1) Arranging a lucky day for marriages in which the bride or bridegroom is brought home [1].

(2) Arranging a lucky day for marriages in which the bride or bridegroom is sent forth [2].

(3) Fixing a lucky time for the conclusion of treaties of peace [or using charms to procure harmony] [3].

(4) Fixing a lucky time for the outbreak of hostilities [or using charms to make discord] [3].

(5) Fixing a lucky time for the calling in of debts [or charms for success in throwing dice] [3].

(6) Fixing a lucky time for the expenditure of money [or charms to bring ill luck to an opponent throwing dice] [3].

(7) Using charms to make people lucky [4].

(8) Using charms to make people unlucky.

(9) Using charms to procure abortion.

(10) Incantations to bring on dumbness.

(11) Incantations to keep a man's jaws fixed.

(12) Incantations to make a man throw up his hands.

(13) Incantations to bring on deafness [5].

---

[1] Compare the Sinhalese bîna marriage in which the bridegroom is brought into the house of the bride's family.

[2] Compare the Sinhalese dîga marriage in which the bride is sent out to live in the bridegroom's family. We have no words now in English to express this difference between marrying and giving in marriage.

[3] Samvadanam. Childers calls this a magic art, following Burnouf who calls it sorcery. Buddhaghosa explains it as astrology. The fact is all these expressions are technical terms for acts of astrology or sorcery, they none of them occur elsewhere either in Pâli or Sanskrit, and the tradition preserved by Buddhaghosa may be at fault in those cases in which the use of the word had not survived to later times. The general sense may be sufficiently clear, but for absolute certainty of interpretation we must wait till examples are found in Indian books of the actual use of the words, not in mere lists, but in a connection which shows the meaning. Ath.-v. III, 30 is a charm to secure concord in a family, compare VII, 52; and there are several charms in the Atharva-veda for success in gambling.

[4] Subhaga-karanam. Many such charms are preserved in the Atharva-veda (for instance, X, 3; 5; XVI, 4; 9).

[5] It would be useless to seek in the Atharva-veda, which (with the one exception mentioned in the notes to the next section) gives only the charms which are supposed to bring benefits, for instances of

(14) Obtaining oracular answers by means of the magic mirror [1].

(15) Obtaining oracular answers through a girl possessed [2].

(16) Obtaining oracular answers from a god [3].

(17) The worship of the Sun [4].

(18) The worship of the Great One [5].

(19) Bringing forth flames from one's mouth.

(20) Invoking Sirî, the goddess of Luck [6]—

Gotama the recluse holds aloof from such low arts."

---

these malevolent practices. But we have here direct evidence that black magic, as was indeed inevitable, was as fully trusted in the sixth century B.C. in the valley of the Ganges as white. We need not be surprised that the malevolent charms are not recorded.

[1] Âdâsa-pañho. Buddhaghosa says they made a god appear in the mirror and answer questions put. It is a later conception to discard the god, and make the mirror itself give pictures of the hidden events. The mirror is of metal (Par. Dîp. 235).

[2] Kumârî-pañho. Through a girl of good family and repute.

[3] Deva-pañho. Also obtained through a girl, but this time a deva-dâsî or temple prostitute. It is instructive to find, even under the patriarchal régime of the sixth century B. c., that men thought they could best have communications from the gods through the medium of a woman.

[4] Âdikkupatthânam. Such sun-worship is ridiculed in the Gâtaka of the same name, No. 173.

[5] Buddhaghosa explains the Great One as Mahâ Brahmâ. This seems to me very doubtful. It is at least odd to find Brahmâ introduced in this connection. We may grant that the Buddhists might have put sun-worship into a list of sorceries, but there was no ceremonial cult of Brahma and little or none of Brahmâ. And however much the new gospel might hold the speculations of the dominant theosophy in contempt, that would scarcely explain their being ranked as privates in this regiment. Burnouf avoids this by rendering the phrase generally 'serving the great,' and Neumann has 'practising sorcery.' Neither of these guesses seems happy. Mahat in composition is elsewhere always mahâ in Pâli, and we possibly have here a sandhi for mahatî-upatthânam, in the sense of worship of the Great Mother, the Earth, with covert allusion to mahî. This would give excellent sense, as the worship of the Mother Earth was closely associated in the popular mind with witchcraft. A god or goddess is certainly meant, and one so associated would be best in place here. It is perhaps worthy of note that in the oldest portion of the Taittirîya Upanishad, Sun, Moon, Earth, and Srî occur together in a set of mystic groups, and Sun, Moon, Brahma, and food are all identified by a word-play with Mahas (Sîksâ-vallî 4–7).

[6] See Milinda 191, and Gât. II, 410.

[12] 27. 'Or he might say : " Whereas some recluses and Brahmans, while living on food provided by the faithful, earn their living by wrong means of livelihood, by low arts, such as these :—

(1) Vowing gifts to a god if a certain benefit be granted.

(2) Paying such vows.

(3) Repeating charms while lodging in an earth house [1].

(4) Causing virility [2].

(5) Making a man impotent [2].

(6) Fixing on lucky sites for dwellings [3].

(7) Consecrating sites [3].

(8) Ceremonial rinsings of the mouth.

(9) Ceremonial bathings [4].

(10) Offering sacrifices.

(11–14) Administering emetics and purgatives.

(15) Purging people to relieve the head (that is by giving drugs to make people sneeze).

(16) Oiling people's ears (either to make them grow or to heal sores on them).

(17) Satisfying people's eyes (soothing them by dropping medicinal oils into them).

(18) Administering drugs through the nose [5].

(19) Applying collyrium to the eyes.

(20) Giving medical ointment for the eyes.

(21) Practising as an oculist.

(22) Practising as a surgeon.

(23) Practising as a doctor for children.

---

[1] Bhûri-kamma*m*. Is this a place sacred to Mother Earth? The ceremony referred to is the carrying out of the vi*gg*â or craft mentioned in the list at § 21.

[2] Vassa- and vossa-kamma*m*. Morris discusses the etymology of these words, only found in this list, in the J. P. T. S., 1889, p. 208. The idea of the second is not, of course, castration, but making a man's desire to fail by a spell. Several such are preserved in the Atharva (IV, 4 ; VI, 101 to give virility ; VI, 138 ; VII, 113 to cause impotence).

[3] Vatthu-kamma*m* and -parikira*n*a*m*. These constitute the vatthu-vi*gg*â of § 21.

[4] Bathings, that is, of other people.

[5] See Mil. I, 511 and the rules laid down in 'Vinaya Texts,' II, 53–55.

(24) Administering	(25) Administering me-
roots and drugs.	dicines in rotation [1]—

Gotama the recluse holds aloof from such low arts."

'These, brethren, are the trifling matters, the minor details, of mere morality, of which the unconverted man, when praising the Tathâgata, might speak.'

Here end the Long Paragraphs on Conduct.

28. 'There are, brethren, other things, profound, difficult to realise, hard to understand, tranquillising, sweet, not to be grasped by mere logic, subtle, comprehensible only by the wise [2]. These things the Tathâgata, having himself realised them and seen them face to face, hath set forth; and it is of them that they, who would rightly praise the Tathâgata in accordance with the truth, should speak.

'And what are they?

29. 'There are recluses and Brahmans, brethren, who reconstruct the ultimate beginnings of things, whose speculations are concerned with the ultimate past [3], and who on eighteen grounds put forward various

---

[1] The Buddhist view of Nos. 11–25 must not be mistaken. It is sufficiently clear from the numerous examples in the Vinaya (see especially 'Vinaya Texts,' II, pp. 41–144), and from the high praise accorded to Gîvaka and other physicians, that the objection was to recluses and Brahmans practising medicine as a means of livelihood. They might do so gratis for themselves or for their coreligionists, and laymen might do so for gain.

The use of paṭimokkha in No. 25 is curious. It is when, for instance, a purgative is first given and then a tonic to counteract the other, to set free from its effect. Compare Gât. V, 25.

[2] The corresponding Sanskrit terms occur at Divyâvadâna, p. 492. No doubt the reading there ought to be nipuno.

[3] These phrases recur S. III, 45. On anuddiṭṭhi see also Gogerly in the 'Ceylon Friend,' 1875, p. 133, and Morris in the J. P. T. S., 1886, p. 113; and compare attânuddiṭṭhi at Mil. 146, 160, 352; S. N. 1119. As in our colloquial expression a 'viewy man,' diṭṭhi almost always, and anudiṭṭhi in all the seven passages where it occurs, have a connotation of contempt—a mere view, an offhand ill-considered opinion, a delusion. The Greek δόξα has had a similar history, and dogma or speculation is a better rendering than view or belief.

assertions regarding it. [13] And about what, with reference to what, do those venerable ones do so?

30. 'There are, brethren, some recluses and Brahmans who are Eternalists [1], and who, on four grounds, proclaim that both the soul and the world are eternal. And about what, with reference to what, do those venerable ones do so?

31. 'In the first place, brethren, some recluse or Brahman by means of ardour, of exertion, of application, of earnestness, of careful thought, reaches up to such rapture of heart that, rapt in heart, he calls to mind his various dwelling-places in times gone by—in one birth, or in two, or three, or four, or five, or ten, or twenty, or thirty, or forty, or fifty, or a hundred, or a thousand, or in several hundreds or thousands or laks of births—to the effect that "There I had such and such a name, was of such and such a lineage [2] and caste [3], lived on such and such food, experienced such and such pains and pleasures, had such and such a span of years. And when I fell from thence I was reborn in such and such a place under such and such a name, in such and such a lineage and caste, living on such and such food, experiencing such and such pains and pleasures, with such and such a span of years. And when I fell from thence I was reborn here." Thus does he recollect, in full detail both of condition and of custom, his various dwelling-

---

[1] Sassata-vâdâ.

[2] Gotra, literally 'cow-stall.' The history of this word has yet to be written. It probably meant at the time this Sutta was written a family or lineage traced through the father. On the meaning of gotraga (the gentiles of Roman Law) in the later law-books see West and Bühler, 'Hindu Law of Inheritance,' p. 171.

[3] Vanna, literally 'colour.' Gogerly renders it 'appearance,' and Neumann 'Beruf.' I have chosen caste (though it is not caste in its strictest sense) because it no doubt refers to the kattâro vannâ mentioned so often in the Suttas. It is true that these—Khattiyas, Brahmans, Vessas, and Suddas—were not castes, but four divisions of the people, each consisting of many subdivisions (by customs as to connubium and commensality) which afterwards hardened into castes. See J. R. A. S., 1897, pp. 180–190.

places in times gone by. [14] And he says to himself:
"Eternal is the soul; and the world, giving birth to
nothing new, is stedfast as a mountain peak, as a pillar
firmly fixed; and though these living creatures transmigrate and pass away, fall from one state of existence
and spring up in another, yet they are for ever and
ever. And why must that be so? Because I, by
means of ardour of exertion of application of earnestness of careful thought, can reach up to such rapture
of heart that, rapt in heart, I can call to mind, and in
full detail both of condition and of custom, my various
dwelling-places in times gone by—by that is it that
I know this—that the soul is eternal; and that the
world, giving birth to nothing new, is stedfast as
a mountain peak, as a pillar firmly fixed; and that
though these living creatures transmigrate and pass
away, fall from one state of existence and spring up in
another, yet they are for ever and ever."

'This, brethren, is the first state of things on
account of which, starting from which, some recluses
and Brahmans are Eternalists, and maintain that both
the soul and the world are eternal.

32. [The second case put is in all respects the same
save that the previous births thus called to mind extend over a still longer period up to ten world aeons[1].]

33. [15] [The third case put is in all respects the
same save that the previous births thus called to mind
extend over a still longer period up to forty world aeons.]

34. [16] 'And in the fourth place, brethren, on what
ground is it, starting from what, that those venerable
ones are Eternalists, and maintain that the soul and the
world are eternal.

'In this case, brethren, some recluse or Brahman

---

[1] Samvatta-vivattam (rolling up and evolution, from vatt, to turn).
It is the period of the gradual disintegration and conformation of a
world. Needless to add that the length of this period cannot be
expressed in figures.

Neither the idea nor the word occurs in books known to be before
the Buddha. But both are Indian rather than Buddhist. Samvarta
is found in the Mahâ Bhârata and the Râmâyana; and the later Sânkhya
notion of pralaya is closely allied.

is addicted to logic and reasoning. He gives utterance to the following conclusion of his own, beaten out
by his argumentations and based on his sophistry [1];
"Eternal is the soul; and the world, giving birth to
nothing new, is stedfast as a mountain peak, as a pillar
firmly fixed; and these living creatures, though they
transmigrate and pass away, fall from one state of
existence and spring up in another, yet they are for
ever and ever."

'This, brethren, is the fourth state of things on the
ground of which, starting from which, some recluses
and Brahmans are Eternalists, and maintain that the
soul and the world are eternal.'

35. 'These, brethren, are those recluses and Brahmans who are Eternalists, and in four ways maintain
that both the soul and the world are eternal. For
whosoever of the recluses and Brahmans are such and
maintain this, they do so in these four ways, or in one
or other of the same, and outside these there is no way
in which this opinion is arrived at.

36. 'Now of these, brethren, the Tathâgata knows
that these speculations thus arrived at, thus insisted on,
will have such and such a result, such and such an
effect on the future condition of those who trust in
them. [17] That does he know, and he knows also
other things far beyond (far better than those speculations) [2]; and having that knowledge he is not puffed
up, and thus untarnished he has, in his own heart [3],
realised the way of escape from them [4], has understood,
as they really are, the rising up and passing away of
sensations, their sweet taste, their danger, how they
cannot be relied on; and not grasping after any (of

---

[1] This phrase recurs below, chap. iii, §§ 14, 20.

[2] Sîla, for instance, and samâdhi, and all the other things known
to a Buddha, says Buddhaghosa, p. 108.

[3] Pakkattam. See the common phrases A. II, 198=S. I, 9, 10,
117; M. I, 188=422; M. I, 251, 252=S. III, 54, &c.; and S. N.
611, 906; Mil. 96, 347; Sum. 182. 'Without depending on any one
else, himself by himself,' says Buddhaghosa.

[4] Nirvâna, says Buddhaghosa.

those things men are eager for) he, the Tathâgata, is quite set free[1].

37. 'These[2], brethren, are those other things, profound, difficult to realise, hard to understand, tranquillising, sweet, not to be grasped by mere logic, subtle, comprehensible only by the wise, which the Tathâgata, having himself realised and seen face to face, hath set forth ; and it is concerning these that they who would rightly praise the Tathâgata in accordance with the truth, should speak.'

Here ends the First Portion for Recitation.

CHAPTER II.

1. 'There are, brethren, some recluses and Brahmans who are Eternalists with regard to some things, and in regard to others Non-Eternalists ; who on four grounds maintain that the soul and the world are partly eternal and partly not.

'And what is it that these venerable ones depend upon, what is it that they start from, in arriving at this conclusion ?

2. 'Now there comes a time, brethren, when, sooner or later, after the lapse of a long long period, this world-system passes away. And when this happens beings have mostly been reborn in the World of Radiance, and there they dwell made of mind, feeding on joy, radiating light from themselves, traversing the air, continuing in glory ; and thus they remain for a long long period of time.

3. 'Now there comes also a time, brethren, when,

---

[1] Gogerly (pp. 77, 78 in Grimblot) has made a sad mess of this paragraph, misunderstanding the grammatical construction of the first clause, and misinterpreting parâmasati in the second, and nissaranam in the third.

[2] Not of course the four speculations, but the higher knowledge which has led him to reject them.

sooner or later, this world-system begins to re-evolve. When this happens the Palace of Brahmâ appears, but it is empty. And some being or other, either because his span of years has passed or his merit is exhausted, falls from that World of Radiance, and comes to life in the Palace of Brahmâ. And there also he lives made of mind, feeding on joy, radiating light from himself, traversing the air, continuing in glory ; and thus does he remain for a long long period of time.

4. ' Now there arises in him, from his dwelling there so long alone, a dissatisfaction and a longing : " O ! would that other beings might come to join me in this place ! " And just then, either because their span of years had passed or their merit was exhausted, other beings fall from the World of Radiance, and appear in the Palace of Brahmâ as companions to him, and in all respects like him. [18]

5. ' On this, brethren, the one who was first reborn thinks thus to himself : " I am Brahmâ, the Great Brahmâ, the Supreme One, the Mighty, the All-seeing, the Ruler, the Lord of all, the Maker, the Creator, the Chief of all, appointing to each his place, the Ancient of days, the Father of all that are and are to be [1]. These other beings are of my creation. And why is that so ? A while ago I thought, ' Would that they might come ! ' And on my mental aspiration, behold the beings came."

'And those beings themselves, too, think thus : " This must be Brahmâ, the Great Brahmâ, the Supreme, the Mighty, the All-seeing, the Ruler, the Lord of all, the Maker, the Creator, the Chief of all, appointing to each his place, the Ancient of days, the Father of all that are

---

[1] This string of epithets recurs at M. I, 327 in the course of the story of the Brahmâ, named Baka, who is represented as coming to the very conclusion set out in our section. The story was a favourite one, and three recensions of it have been preserved (M. I, 326–331 ; S. I, 142–144, and *Gât.* No. 405). Mr. Crow evidently considered himself the Mahâ Brahmâ of the period.

The omission in the Dialogue of all reference to the Kesava Birth Story may be a sign of greater age or it may be due simply to the fact that it is not required for the argument there.

and are to be. And we must have been created by
him. And why? Because, as we see, it was he who
was here first, and we came after that."

6. 'On this, brethren, the one who first came into
existence there is of longer life, and more glorious, and
more powerful than those who appeared after him.
And it might well be, brethren, that some being on his
falling from that state, should come hither. And having
come hither he might go forth from the household life
into the homeless state. And having thus become a
recluse he, by reason of ardour of exertion of application of earnestness of careful thought, reaches up to
such rapture of heart that, rapt in heart, he calls to
mind his last dwelling-place, but not the previous ones.
He says to himself: "That illustrious Brahmâ, the
Great Brahmâ, the Supreme One, the Mighty, the
All-seeing, the Ruler, the Lord of all, the Maker, the
Creator, the Chief of all, appointing to each his place,
the Ancient of days, the Father of all that are and are
to be, he by whom we were created, he is stedfast
immutable eternal, of a nature that knows no change,
and he will remain so for ever and ever. But we who
were created by him have come hither as being impermanent mutable limited in duration of life.

[19] 'This, brethren, is the first state of things on
account of which, starting out from which, some recluses
and Brahmans, being Eternalists as to some things, and
Non-eternalists as to others, maintain that the soul and
the world are partly eternal and partly not.

7. 'And what is the second?

'There are, brethren, certain gods called the "Debauched by Pleasure[1]." For ages they pass their time
in the pursuit of the laughter and sport of sensual lusts.
In consequence thereof their self-possession is corrupted,
and through the loss of their self-control they fall from
that state[2].

---

[1] Khiddâ-padosikâ. They are not mentioned elsewhere except
in the list of gods in the Mahâ Samaya (p. 287).

[2] Buddhaghosa on this has a curious note. The gods, though of
great glory, are delicate in body. A man, having gone without food

8. ' Now it might well be, brethren, that some being, on his falling from that state, should come hither. And having come hither he should, as in the last case, become a recluse, and acquire the power of recollecting his last birth, but only his last one.

9. ' And he would say to himself: " Those gods who are not debauched by pleasure are stedfast, immutable, eternal, of a nature that knows no change, and they will remain so for ever and ever. [20] But we—who fell from that state, having lost our self-control through being debauched by pleasure—we have come hither as being impermanent, mutable, limited in duration of life."

10. ' And what is the third?

' There are, brethren, certain gods called " the De-bauched in Mind [1]." They burn continually with envy[2] one against another, and being thus irritated, their hearts become ill-disposed towards each other, and being thus debauched, their bodies become feeble, and their minds imbecile. And those gods fall from that state.

11. ' Now it might well be, brethren, that some

---

for seven days even, may restore his strength by the use of clear broth and so on. But the gods can't play tricks with themselves; and if they lose their heads and forget their meal-times, they die—pass away from that state. The poor gods! Whether this be really implied in the text or not, it is at least in harmony with the irony of the Buddha's talk.

[1] Mano-padosikâ. Only found here and in the list in the Samaya Sutta. Even there it is almost certainly merely taken from this passage, so that it looks very much as if both these classes or titles of gods were simply invented, in irony, for the sake of the argument. Buddhaghosa identifies this class with the retinue of the Four Great Kings—that is the regents of the four quarters.

[2] Upanigghâyanti, from ghâyati, to burn. Elsewhere found only at Vin. I, 193; II, 269; III, 118, in all which passages it has the connotation of 'covet, lust after.' Buddhaghosa takes it here in the sense of envy, and tells a tale, too long to quote, to show the quarrelsome nature of these gods. In the sense of 'consider' (from ghâyati, to think) the word has only been found at S. N., p. 143. There may have been confusion between the two homonyms, so that ours got to mean 'to consider in such a way as to be excited, to burn.'

being, on his falling from that state, should come
hither; and having become a recluse should, as in the
other cases, acquire the power of recollecting his last
birth, but only his last one.

12. 'And he would say to himself: "Those gods
who are not debauched in mind do not continually burn
with envy against each other, so their hearts do not
become evil disposed one towards another, nor their
bodies feeble and their minds imbecile. Therefore
they fall not from that state; they are stedfast, immutable, eternal, of a nature that knows no change, and
they will remain so for ever and ever. [21] But we
were corrupted in mind, being constantly excited by
envy against one another. And being thus envious
and corrupt our bodies became feeble, and our minds
imbecile, and we fell from that state, and have come
hither as being impermanent, mutable, limited in
duration of life."

'This, brethren, is the third case.

13. 'And what is the fourth?

'In this case, brethren, some recluse or Brahman is
addicted to logic and reasoning. He gives utterance
to the following conclusion of his own, beaten out by
his argumentations and based on his sophistry: "This
which is called eye and ear and nose and tongue and
body is a self which is impermanent, unstable, not
eternal, subject to change. But this which is called
heart, or mind, or consciousness is a self which is permanent, stedfast, eternal, and knows no change, and it
will remain for ever and ever [1]."

'This, brethren, is the fourth state of things, on the
ground of which, starting from which, some recluses

---

[1] Buddhaghosa explains that these speculators perceive how the
organs of sense break up (and sense impressions pass away); but
they fail to see that the same thing holds even more strongly in the
case of thoughts, since no sooner has each mental impression given
rise to the succeeding one than it passes away. Not perceiving that,
and depending on the analogy of birds, who fly away from one tree
only to alight on another, they conclude that the mind, when this
individuality is broken up, goes (as a unity) elsewhere.

and Brahmaṇs are Semi-eternalists, and in four ways maintain that the soul and the world are in some respects eternal, and in some not.

14. 'These, brethren, are those recluses and Brahmans who are Semi-éternalists, and in four ways maintain that the soul and the world are etérnal in some cases and not in others. For whosoever of the recluses and Brahmans are such and maintain this, they do so in these four ways or in one or other of the same; and outside these there is no way in which this opinion is arrived at.

[22] 15. 'Now of these, brethren, the Tathâgata knows that these speculations thus arrived at, thus insisted on, will have such and such a result, such and such an effect on the future condition of those who trust in them. That does he know, and he knows also other things far beyond (far better than those speculations); and having that knowledge, he is not puffed up, and thus untarnished he has, in his own heart, realised the way of escape from them, has understood, as they really are, the rising up and passing away of sensations, their sweet taste, their danger, how they cannot be relied on, and not grasping after any (of those things men are eager for) he, the Tathâgata, is quite set free.

'These, brethren, are those other things, profound, difficult to realise, hard to understand, tranquillising, sweet, not to be grasped by mere logic, subtle, comprehensible only by the wise, which the Tathâgata, having himself realised and seen face to face, hath set forth; and it is concerning these that they who would rightly praise the Tathâgata in accordance with the truth, should speak.'

---

16. 'There are, brethren, certain recluses and Brahmans who are Extensionists[1], and who in four ways set forth the infinity or finiteness of the world. And

---

[1] Antânantikâ.

on what ground, starting out from what, do these venerable ones maintain this?

17. 'In the first case, brethren, some recluse or Brahman, by means of ardour of exertion of application of earnestness of careful thought, reaches up to such rapture of heart that he, rapt in heart, dwells in the world imagining it finite. And he says thus to himself: "Finite is the world, so that a path could be traced round it[1]. And why is this so? Since I, by means of ardour of exertion of application of earnestness of careful thought, can reach up to such rapture of heart that, rapt in heart, I dwell in the world perceiving it to be finite—by that I know this."

'This, brethren, is the first case.

18. 'The second case is similar, only that the conclusion is: [23] "Infinite is the world without a limit. Those recluses and Brahmans who say it is finite, so that a path could be traced round it, are wrong[2]."

19. 'The third case is similar, only that the conclusion is that he imagines the world limited in the upward and downward directions, but infinite across; he declares both the former conclusions to be wrong.

20. 'In the fourth case, brethren, some recluse or Brahman is addicted to logic and reasoning. He gives utterance to the following conclusion of his own, beaten out by his argumentations and based on his sophistry: "This world is neither finite nor yet infinite. Those recluses and Brahmans who maintain either the first, or the second, or the third conclusion, are wrong. [24] Neither is the world finite, nor is it infinite."

'This, brethren, is the fourth case.

---

[1] Parivatumo. Only found here. Buddhaghosa says nothing.

[2] According to Buddhaghosa (Ats. 160) there are four things that are infinite—space, the number of world-systems, the number of living creatures, and the wisdom of a Buddha. Had this doctrine formed part of the original Buddhism we should expect to find these *kattâri anantâni* in the chapter on the 'Fours' in the Anguttara, but I do not find them there.

21. 'These, brethren, are those recluses and Brahmans who are Extensionists, and in four ways maintain that the world is finite or infinite. For whosoever of the recluses and Brahmans are such, and maintain this, they do so in these four ways or in one or other of the same ; and outside these there is no way in which this opinion is arrived at.

22. 'Now of these, brethren, the Tathâgata knows that these speculations thus arrived at, thus insisted on, will have such and such a result, such and such an effect on the future condition of those who trust in them. That does he know, and he knows also other things far beyond (far better than those speculations) ; and having that knowledge he is not puffed up, and thus untarnished he has, in his own heart, realised the way of escape from them, has understood, as they really are, the rising up and passing away of sensations, their sweet taste, their danger, how they cannot be relied on, and not grasping after any (of those things men are eager for) he, the Tathâgata, is quite set free.

'These, brethren, are those other things, profound, difficult to realise, hard to understand, tranquillising, sweet, not to be grasped by mere logic, subtle, comprehensible only by the wise, which the Tathâgata, having himself realised and seen face to face, hath set forth ; and it is concerning these that they who would rightly praise the Tathâgata in accordance with the truth, should speak.'

23. 'There are, brethren, some recluses and Brahmans who wriggle like eels ; and when a question is put to them on this or that they resort to equivocation, to eel-wriggling, and this in four ways.

'Now on what ground, starting out from what, do those venerable ones do so ?

24. 'In the first place, brethren, some recluse or Brahman does not understand the good in its real nature, nor the evil. And he thinks : " I neither know

E

the good, as it really is, nor the evil.   [**25**] That being
so, were I to pronounce this to be good or that to be
evil, I might be influenced therein by my feelings or
desires, by illwill or resentment.   And under these
circumstances I might be wrong; and my having been
wrong might cause me the pain of remorse; and the
sense of remorse might become a hindrance to me [1]."
Thus fearing and abhorring the being wrong in an
expressed opinion, he will neither declare anything
to be good, nor to be bad; but on a question being
put to him on this or that, he resorts to eel-wriggling,
to equivocation, and says: "I don't take it thus.   I don't
take it the other way.   But I advance no different
opinion.   And I don't deny your position.   And I don't
say it is neither the one, nor the other [2]."

 ' This is the first case.
 ' And what is the second?
   25. [The same, reading] '..." Under these circumstances I might fall into that grasping condition of heart
which causes rebirth; and my so falling might cause
me the pain of remorse; and the sense of remorse
might become a hindrance to me."   [**26**] Thus fearing and abhorring the falling into that state [3], he will
neither declare (&c., as in § 24).

 ' This is the second case.
 ' And what is the third?
   26. [The same, reading] ' And he thinks : " I neither
know the good, as it really is, nor the evil.   Now
there are recluses and Brahmans who are clever,
subtle, experienced in controversy, hair-splitters, who
go about, methinks, breaking to pieces by their wisdom

---

 [1] 'Either in self-training or in the attainment of bliss in heaven,'
says Buddhaghosa (p. 115).
 [2] Buddhaghosa gives examples of these five equivocations.
 [3] Buddhaghosa explains that if, in his ignorance, he should, by
chance, declare the good to be good, he will be puffed up by the
approval of the wise.   But if he should blunder, he will be filled with
vexation and illwill when his error is pointed out.   Either of these
states of mind will be the fuel to keep the fire burning, the state
technically called Upâdâna, 'grasping.'

the speculations of others. Were I to pronounce this to be good, or that to be evil, these men might join issue with me, call upon me for my reasons, point out my errors. And on their doing so, I might be unable to explain [1]. And that might cause me the pain of remorse; and the sense of remorse might become a hindrance to me." Thus fearing and abhorring the joinder of issue, he will neither declare (&c., as in § 24).

'This is the third case. [**27**]

'And what is the fourth?

27. 'In this case, brethren, some recluse or Brahman is dull, stupid. And it is by reason of his dullness, his stupidity, that when a question on this or that is put to him, he resorts to equivocation, to wriggling like an eel—" If you ask me whether there is another world,—well, if I thought there were, I would say so. But I don't say so. And I don't think it is thus or thus. And I don't think it is otherwise. And I don't deny it. And I don't say there neither is, nor is not, another world." Thus does he equivocate, and in like manner about each of such propositions as the following [2]:—

α. (2) There is not another world.

(3) There both is, and is not, another world.

(4) There neither is, nor is not, another world.

β. (1) There are Chance Beings (so called because they spring into existence, either here or in another world, without the intervention of parents, and seem therefore to come without a cause).

(2) There are no such beings.

(3) There both are, and are not, such beings.

(4) There neither are, nor are not, such beings.

γ. (1) There is fruit, result, of good and bad actions.

---

[1] Sampâyati. See the note at 'Vinaya Texts,' III, 317, and compare M. I, 85, 96, 472.

[2] Such questions are called elsewhere the common basis of discussions among Brahmans.

(2) There is not.

(3) There both is, and is not.

(4) There neither is, nor is not.

δ. (1) A man who has penetrated to the

truth [1] continues to exist after death.

(2) He does not.

(3) He both does, and does not.

(4) He neither does, nor does not.

'This, brethren, is the fourth case [2].

[28] 28. 'These, brethren, are those recluses and Brahmans who wriggle like eels; and who, when a question is put to them on this or that, resort to equivocation, to eel-wriggling; and that in four ways. For whosoever do so, they do so in these four ways, or in one or other of the same; there is no other way in which they do so.

29. 'Now of these, brethren, the Tathâgata knows that these speculations thus arrived at, thus insisted on, will have such and such a result, such and such an effect on the future condition of those who trust in them. That does he know, and he knows also other things far beyond (far better than those speculations); and having that knowledge he is not puffed up, and thus untarnished he has, in his own heart, realised the way of escape from them, has understood, as they really are, the rising up and passing away of sensations, their sweet taste, their danger, how they cannot be relied on, and not grasping after any (of those things men are eager for) he, the Tathâgata, is quite set free.

'These, brethren, are those other things, profound, difficult to realise, hard to understand, tranquillising,

---

[1] The word here used is Tathâgata, 'he who has gone, or perhaps come, to the truth.' See Chalmers in the J. R. A. S., Jan., 1898, and compare S. III, 111, 116–118; M. I, 140, 171, 486; S. N. 467. The use of sammaggato (D. I, 55, &c.) and of gatatto (D. I, 57, &c.) shows that gata was used elliptically in the sense of 'gone to the furthest point aimed at' among the followers of the other sects that arose at the same time as Buddhism. The exact derivation and history of the word Tathâgata may be doubtful, but its meaning is, on the whole, clear enough.

[2] This is the identical answer put below (p. 57 of the text) into the mouth of Sañgaya Belatthaputta.

sweet, not to be grasped by mere logic, subtle, comprehensible only by the wise, which the Tathâgata, having himself realised and seen face to face, hath set forth ; and it is concerning these that they who would rightly praise the Tathâgata in accordance with the truth, should speak.'

30. ' There are, brethren, some recluses and Brahmans who are Fortuitous-Originists [1], and who in two ways maintain that the soul and the world arise without a cause. And on what ground, starting out from what, do they do so ?

31. ' There are, brethren, certain gods called Unconscious Beings [2]. As soon as an idea occurs to them they fall from that state. Now it may well be, brethren, that a being, on falling from that state, should come hither ; and having come hither he might go forth from the household life into the homeless state. And having thus become a recluse he, by reason of ardour and so on (as in the other cases) reaches up to such rapture of heart that, rapt in heart, he calls to mind how that idea occurred to him, but not more than that. He says to himself : " Fortuitous

---

[1] Adhikka-samuppannikâ. This adhikka (which must be distinguished from the other adhikka, derived from adhîyati, occu..ing at Gât. III, 218=IV, 301) recurs at M. I, 443, where it is opposed in the sense of 'occasional' to abhinha at M. I, 442 in the sense of 'habitual.' Udâna VI, 5 throws light on its use here. It is there associated with words meaning 'neither self-originated, nor created by others.' It is explained by Buddhaghosa on our passage (Sum. I, 118) as 'springing up without a cause.' The derivation is doubtful.

[2] Asañña-sattâ. They spring into being in this wise. Some one of the Brahman ascetics having practised continual meditation and arrived at the Fourth Ghâna, sees the disadvantage attached to thinking, and says to himself: ' It is by dwelling on it in thought that physical pain and all sorts of mental terrors arise. Have done with this thinking. An existence without it were better.' And dying in this belief he is reborn among the Unconscious Ones, who have form only, and neither sensatlons nor ideas nor predispositions nor consciousness. So long as the power of the Ghâna lasts, so long do they last. Then an idea occurs to them—the idea of rebirth in this world—and they straightway die.

in origin are the soul and the world. And why so? Because formerly I was not, but now am. Having not been, I have come to be." [29]

'This, brethren, is the first state of things on account of which, starting out from which, some recluses and Brahmans become Fortuitous-Originists, and maintain that the soul and the world arise without a cause.

32, 33. 'And what is the second?

' In this case, brethren, some recluse or Brahman is addicted to logic and reasoning. He gives utterance to the following conclusion of his own, beaten out by his argumentations, and based on his sophistry: " The soul and the world arose without a cause."

' This, brethren, is the second case.

34. ' Now of these, brethren, the Tathâgata knows that these speculations thus arrived at, thus insisted on, will have such and such a result, such and such an effect on the future condition of those who trust in them. That does he know, and he knows also other things far beyond (far better than those speculations); and having that knowledge he is not puffed up, and thus untarnished he has, in his own heart, realised the way of escape from them, has understood, as they really are, the rising up and passing away of sensations, their sweet taste, their danger, how they cannot be relied on, and not grasping after any (of those things men are eager for) he, the Tathâgata, is quite set free.

' These, brethren, are those other things, profound, difficult to realise, hard to understand, tranquillising, sweet, not to be grasped by mere logic, subtle, comprehensible only by the wise, which the Tathâgata, having himself realised and seen face to face, hath set forth; and it is concerning these that they who would rightly praise the Tathâgata in accordance with the truth, should speak.'

---

[30] 35. ' These, brethren, are the recluses and Brahmans who reconstruct the ultimate beginnings of things, whose speculations are concerned with the

ultimate past, and who on eighteen grounds put forward various assertions regarding the past [1]. And those who do so, all of them, do so in one or other of these eighteen ways. There is none beside.

36. 'Now of these, brethren, the Tathâgata knows that these speculations thus arrived at, thus insisted on, will have such and such a result, such and such an effect on the future condition of those who trust in them. That does he know, and he knows also other things far beyond (far better than those speculations); and having that knowledge he is not puffed up, and thus untarnished he has, in his own heart, realised the way of escape from them, has understood, as they really are, the rising up and passing away of sensations, their sweet taste, their danger, how they cannot be relied on, and not grasping after any (of those things men are eager for) he, the Tathâgata, is quite set free.

'These, brethren, are those other things, profound, difficult to realise, hard to understand, tranquillising, sweet, not to be grasped by mere logic, subtle, comprehensible only by the wise, which the Tathâgata, having himself realised and seen face to face, hath set forth; and it is concerning these that they who would rightly praise the Tathâgata in accordance with the truth, should speak.'

---

37. 'There are, brethren, recluses and Brahmans who arrange the future, whose speculations are concerned with the future, and who on forty-four grounds put forward various assertions regarding the future. And on account of what, starting out from what, do they do so?

38. 'There are, brethren, recluses and Brahmans who [31] hold the doctrine of a conscious existence after death [2], and who maintain in sixteen ways that

---

[1] See I, 1, 29 (p. 12 of the text).
[2] Literally 'who are After-deathers, Conscious-maintainers.' These summary epithets are meant to be contemptuous, and the word chosen for death adds to the force of the phrase. It is not the usual word,

the soul after death is conscious. And how do they do so ?

'They say of the soul: " The soul after death, not subject to decay, and conscious,

(1) has form [1],

(2) is formless [2],

(3) has, and has not, form,

(4) neither has, nor has not, form,

(5) is finite,

(6) is infinite,

(7) is both,

(8) is neither,

(9) has one mode of consciousness,

(10) has various modes of consciousness,

(11) has limited consciousness,

(12) has infinite consciousness,

(13) is altogether happy,

(14) is altogether miserable,

(15) is both,

(16) is neither."

39. 'These, brethren, are those recluses and Brahmans who hold the doctrine of a conscious existence after death, and who maintain in sixteen ways that the soul after death is conscious. And those who do so, all of them, do so in one or other of these sixteen ways. There is none beside.

40. 'Now of these, brethren, the Tathâgata knows that these speculations thus arrived at, thus insisted on, will have such and such a result, such and such an effect on the future condition of those who trust in them. That does he know, and he knows also other things far beyond (far better than those speculations); and having that knowledge he is not puffed up, and thus untarnished he has, in his own heart, realised the way of escape from them, has understood, as they really are, the rising up and passing away of sensations, their sweet taste, their danger, how they cannot be relied on, and not grasping after any (of those things men are eager for) he, the Tathâgata, is quite set free.

but âghâtana (so read in the text), meaning literally 'shambles, place of execution.' The ordinary phrase would have been parammaranikâ.

[1] So the Agîvakas, says Buddhaghosa.

[2] So the Niganthas, says Buddhaghosa.

'These, brethren, are those other things, profound, difficult to realise, hard to understand, tranquillising, sweet, not to be grasped by mere logic, subtle, comprehensible only by the wise, which the Tathâgata, having himself realised and seen face to face, hath set forth ; and it is concerning these that they who would rightly praise the Tathâgata in accordance with the truth, should speak.'

Here ends the Second Portion for Recitation. [32]

Chapter III.

1. ' There are, brethren, recluses and Brahmans who hold the doctrine of an unconscious existence after death, and who maintain in eight ways that the soul after death is unconscious. And how do they do so ?

2. ' They say of the soul : " The soul after death, not subject to decay, and unconscious,

(1) has form,	not, form,
(2) is formless,	(5) is finite,
(3) has, and has not, form,	(6) is infinite,
	(7) is both,
(4) neither has, nor has	(8) is neither."

3. ' These, brethren, are those recluses and Brahmans who hold the doctrine of an unconscious existence after death, and who maintain in eight ways that the soul after death is unconscious. And those who do so, all of them, do so in one or other of those eight ways. There is none beside.

4. ' Now of these, brethren, the Tathâgata knows that these speculations thus arrived at, thus insisted on, will have such and such a result, such and such an effect on the future condition of those who trust in them. That does he know, and he knows also other things far beyond (far better than those speculations) ; and having that knowledge he is not puffed up, and thus untarnished he has, in his own heart, realised the

way of escape from them, has understood, as they really are, the rising up and passing away of sensations, their sweet taste, their danger, how they cannot be relied on, and not grasping after any (of those things men are eager for) he, the Tathâgata, is quite set free.

'These, brethren, are those other things, profound, difficult to realise, hard to understand, tranquillising, sweet, not to be grasped by mere logic, subtle, comprehensible only by the wise, which the Tathâgata, having himself realised and seen face to face, hath set forth; and it is concerning these that they who would rightly praise the Tathâgata in accordance with the truth, should speak.

5–8. [**33**] [Similar sections for those who maintain in eight ways that the soul after death is neither conscious nor unconscious.]

[1] 9. [**34**] 'There are, brethren, recluses and Brahmans who are Annihilationists, who in seven ways maintain the cutting off, the destruction, the annihilation of a living being [2]. And on account of what, starting out from what, do they do so?

10. 'In the first place, brethren, some recluse or Brahman puts forth the following opinion, the following view: "Since, Sir, this soul has form, is built up of the four elements, and is the offspring of father and mother, it is cut off, destroyed, on the dissolution of the body; and does not continue after death; and then, Sir, the soul is completely annihilated." Thus is it that some maintain the cutting off, the destruction, the annihilation of a living being.

11. 'To him another says: "There is, Sir, such a soul as you describe. That I do not deny. But the whole soul, Sir, is not then completely annihilated. For there is a further soul—divine, having form, belonging to the sensuous plane, feeding on solid food. That you neither know of nor perceive. But I know

---

[1] §§ 9–18 are discussed by James D'Alwis in 'Buddhist Nirvana,' p. 47. Comp. Jacobi, 'Jaina Sûtras,' II, 236, 339.

[2] Sato sattassa. Insert the word sato in the text (as in §§ 17, 19, 41, 42). The Katha Upanishad I, 20 alludes to such belief.

and have experienced it. And since this soul, on the dissolution of the body, is cut off and destroyed, does not continue after death, then is it, Sir, that the soul is completely annihilated." Thus is it that some maintain the cutting off, the destruction, the annihilation of a living being.

12. 'To him another says: "There is, Sir, such a soul as you describe. That I do not deny. But the whole soul, Sir, is not then completely annihilated. For there is a further soul—divine, having form, made of mind, with all its major and minor parts complete, not deficient in any organ. This you neither know of nor perceive. But I know and have experienced it. And since this soul, on the dissolution of the body, is cut off and destroyed, does not continue after death, then is it, Sir, that the soul is completely annihilated." Thus is it that some maintain the cutting off, the destruction, the annihilation of a living being.

13. 'To him another says: "There is, Sir, such a soul as you describe. That I do not deny. But the whole soul, Sir, is not then completely annihilated. For there is a further soul, which by passing beyond ideas of form, by the dying out of ideas of resistance, by paying no heed to ideas of difference, conscious that space is infinite, reaches up to the plane of the infinity of space[1]. This you neither know of nor perceive. [35] But I know and have experienced it. And since this soul, on the dissolution of the body, is cut off and destroyed, does not continue after death, then is it, Sir, that the soul is completely annihilated." Thus is it that some maintain the cutting off, the destruction, the annihilation of a living being.

14. 'To him another says: "There is, Sir, such a soul as you describe. That I do not deny. But the whole soul, Sir, is not then completely annihilated.

---

[1] Compare the 4th Vimokha. See Rh. D. 'Buddhist Suttas,' pp. 52, 213. The idea of resistance, pa/igha, is here not ethical, but refers to the senses. Having no sense of reaction to touch, of opposition to muscular effort. It appears from M. I, 164 that this was pretty much the view put forth by Gotama's first teacher Â/âra Kâlâma.

For there is a further soul, which having passed beyond the plane of the infinity of space, knowing that consciousness is infinite, reaches up to the plane of the infinity of consciousness [1]. This you neither know of nor perceive. But I know and have experienced it. And since this soul, on the dissolution of the body, is cut off and destroyed, does not continue after death, then is it, Sir, that the soul is completely annihilated." Thus is it that some maintain the cutting off, the destruction, the annihilation of a living being.

15. 'To him another says: "There is, Sir, such a soul as you describe. That I do not deny. But the whole soul, Sir, is not then completely annihilated. For there is a further soul, which by passing quite beyond the plane of the infinity of consciousness, knowing that there is nothing, reaches up to the plane of no obstruction [2]. This you neither know of nor perceive. But I know and have experienced it. And since this soul, on the dissolution of the body, is cut off and destroyed, does not continue after death, then is it, Sir, that the soul is completely annihilated." Thus is it that some maintain the cutting off, the destruction, the annihilation of a living being.

16. 'To him another says: "There is, Sir, such a soul as you describe. That I do not deny But the whole soul, Sir, is not then completely annihilated. For there is a further soul, which by passing quite beyond the plane of no obstruction, realises 'This is good, this is excellent,' and reaches up to the plane of neither ideas nor the absence of ideas [3]. This you

---

[1] Compare the 5th Vimokha. This seems from M. I, 165 to have been much the same as the view held by Râma, whose son and pupil, Uddaka, was Gotama's second teacher.

[2] Compare the 6th Vimokha.

[3] Though it is not explicitly so stated, this last of these seven theorisers is no doubt to be considered as believing in all the sorts of soul held by the others, so that he believes in seven. One may compare the five souls each more subtle than the last, made respectively of anna, prâna, manas, vigñâna, and ânanda (food, breath, mind, consciousness, and joy), described in the Taittirîya Upanishad II, 1–5. The Buddhist modification of these theories omits the souls, and

neither know of, nor perceive. But I know and have experienced it. And since this soul, on the dissolution of the body, is cut off, destroyed, does not continue after death, then is it, Sir, that the soul is completely annihilated." Thus is it that some maintain the cutting off, the destruction, the annihilation of a living being.

17. 'These, brethren, are the recluses and Brahmans who are Annihilationists and in seven ways maintain the cutting off, the destruction, the annihilation of a living being. [86] And whosoever do so they, all of them, do so in one or other of these seven ways. There is none beside.

18. [Repetition of § 40, above p. 44, setting forth that other, higher, knowledge of a Tathâgata, for which alone he can be rightly praised.]

---

19. 'There are, brethren, recluses and Brahmans who hold the doctrine of happiness in this life, who in five ways maintain the complete salvation, in this visible world, of a living being. And relying on what, starting out from what, do they do so ?

20. 'Hereon, brethren, some recluse or Brahman may have the following opinion, the following view : " Whensoever the soul, in full enjoyment and posses-

---

treats instead of various states of mind (produced by stages of meditation), the attainment of which, during this life, leads to rebirth in corresponding worlds, or planes of existence, named after those stages of meditations. But the oldest Piṭaka texts say very little about it, and the history of Buddhist speculation on the matter has yet to be formulated.

Centuries afterwards we find a somewhat analogous conception in the gradually ascending series of seven, each more subtle than the last (Sthûla-sarîra, liṅga-sarîra, indriya, manas, ahaṅkara, buddhi, and âtman), set out in the Sâṅkhya texts, and the later Vedânta has a similar series. There is sufficient truth in the idea of the series of seven set out in our text to explain the persistence of the general idea in all the Indian systems, but the details and the application are strikingly different.

The text shows that the four Arûpa Vimokhas of the Buddhist theory were regarded by the early Buddhists as derived from closely allied speculations, older than Buddhism, and expressed in almost identical phraseology.

sion of the five pleasures of sense, indulges all its
functions, then, Sir, the soul has attained, in this visible
world, to the highest Nirvâna [1]." Thus do some
maintain the complete happiness, in the visible world,
of a living being.

21. 'To him another says: "There is, Sir, such
a soul as you describe. That I do not deny. But the
soul does not by that alone attain to the highest
Nirvâna. And why not? Sensuous delights, Sir, are
transitory, they involve pain, their very nature is to
fluctuate. And grief, lamentation, pain, sorrow, and
loathing arise out of their inconstancy and change.
[37] But whensoever the soul, putting away sensuous
delights and evil dispositions, enters into and abides in
the First Ghâna, the state of joy and ease, born of
seclusion, accompanied by reflection, accompanied by
investigation, then, Sir, has the soul attained, in this
visible world, to the highest Nirvâna." Thus do
some maintain the complete happiness, in the visible
world, of a living being.

22. 'To him another says: "There is, Sir, such
a soul as you describe. That I do not deny. But the
soul does not by that alone attain to the highest
Nirvâna. And why not? Because inasmuch as that
state involves reasoning and investigation it is stamped
as being gross. But whensoever, Sir, the soul, suppressing both reasoning and investigation, enters into
and abides in the Second Ghâna, the state of joy and
ease, born of serenity, without reflection or investigation, a state of elevation of mind, internal calm of
heart, then, Sir, has the soul attained, in this visible
world, to the highest Nirvâna." Thus do some maintain the complete happiness, in the visible world, of
a living being.

---

[1] Buddhaghosa here (Sum. I, 121) explains Nirvâna as the suppres-
sion of pain; pain, dukha, being bodily, as opposed to domanassa,
mental. 'In this visible world' means in whatever world the particular soul happens to be at the time. On parikâreti compare
V. II, 290 râgâ uyyâne parikâresi, 'the king indulged himself,
enjoyed himself, in the garden.' 'All its functions' is added from the
Commentary.

23. 'To him another says: "There is, Sir, such a soul as you describe. That I do not deny. But the soul does not by that alone attain to the highest Nirvâna. And why not? Because inasmuch as that state involves the sense of joy, of exhilaration of heart, it is stamped as being gross. But whensoever, Sir, the soul, by absence of the longing after joy remains in equanimity, mindful and self-possessed, and experiences in the body that ease of which the Arahats speak (when they say) 'the man serene and thoughtful dwells at ease,' and so enters into and abides in the Third Ghâna—then, Sir, has the soul attained, in this visible world, to the highest Nirvâna." Thus do some maintain the complete happiness, in the visible world, of a living being.

24. 'To him another says: "There is, Sir, such a soul as you describe. That I do not deny. But the soul does not by that alone attain to the highest Nirvâna. And why not? Because inasmuch as that state involves a constant dwelling of the mind on the ease it has enjoyed it is stamped as gross. [38] But whensoever, Sir, the soul, by putting away ease, by putting away pain, by the previous dying away both of joys and griefs has entered into and abides in the Fourth Ghâna [1]—a state made pure by self-possession and equanimity, without pain and without ease—then, Sir, has the soul attained, in this visible world, to the highest Nirvâna." Thus do some maintain the complete happiness, in the visible world, of a living being.

25. 'These, brethren, are the recluses and Brahmans who hold the doctrine of happiness in this life, who in five ways maintain the complete salvation, in this visible world, of a living being. And those who do

---

[1] The text shows that the four Ghânas were regarded by the early Buddhists as older than Buddhism. The very words used are identical; the only modification introduced in Buddhism being the omission of the 'souls.' These four, together with the four Arûpa Vimokhas (see note on § 19), make up the Eight Attainments (Samâpattiyo), often mentioned in the Gâtaka commentary as practised by pre-Buddhistic recluses.

so, all of them, do so in one or other of these five ways. There is none beside.

26. [Repetition of § 40, above p. 44, setting forth that other, higher, knowledge of a Tathâgata, for which alone he can be rightly praised.]

27. 'These, brethren, are the recluses and Brahmans who arrange the future, whose speculations are concerned with the future, and who on forty-four grounds put forward various assertions regarding the future. And those who do so, all of them, do so in one or other of these forty-four ways. There is none beside.

28. [Repetition of § 40, above p. 44, setting forth that other, higher, knowledge of a Tathâgata, for which alone he can be rightly praised.]

[39] 29. 'These, brethren, are the recluses and Brahmans who reconstruct the past, and arrange the future, or who do both, whose speculations are concerned with both, and who in sixty-two ways put forward propositions with regard to the past and to the future, and those who do so, all of them, do so in one or other of these sixty-two ways. There is none beside.

30. [Repetition of § 40, above p. 44, setting forth that other, higher, knowledge of a Tathâgata, for which alone he can be rightly praised.]

[40] 32. 'Of these, brethren, those recluses and Brahmans who are Eternalists, who in four ways maintain that the soul and the world are eternal:

(2) those who are Semi-eternalists, who in four ways maintain that the soul and the world are partly eternal and partly not:

(3) those who are Extensionists, who in four ways maintain the infinity or the finiteness of the world:

(4) those who are Eel-wrigglers, who when a question is put to them on this or that resort, in four ways, to equivocation, to wriggling like eels:

(5) those who are Fortuitous-Originists, who in two ways maintain that the soul and the world arose without a cause:

(6) those who in any of these eighteen ways reconstruct the past :

(7) those who hold the doctrine of a conscious existence after death, who maintain in sixteen ways that the
soul after death is conscious :

(8) those who hold the doctrine of an unconscious
existence after death, who maintain in eight ways that
the soul after death is unconscious :

(9) those who maintain in eight ways that the soul
after death is neither conscious nor unconscious:

(10) those who are Annihilationists, who maintain in
seven ways the cutting off, the destruction, the annihilation of a living being :

(11) those who hold the doctrine of happiness in this
life, who in five ways maintain the complete salvation,
in this visible world, of a living being—

That opinion of theirs is based only on the personal
sensations, on the worry and writhing consequent
thereon [1], of those venerable recluses and Brahmans,
who know not, neither perceive, and are subject to all
kinds of craving :

45 foll. [**41, 42**] 'Those opinions of theirs are therefore
based upon contact (through the senses).

58 foll. [**43**] 'That they should experience those sensations without such contact, such a condition of things
could not be.

71. [**44**] 'They, all of them, receive those sensations
through continual contact in the spheres of touch. To
them on account of the sensations arises craving, on
account of the craving arises the fuel (that is, the
necessary condition, the food, the basis, of future
lives), from the fuel results becoming, from the tendency to become arises rebirth, and from rebirth
comes death, and grief, lamentation, pain, sorrow, and
despair. It is, brethren, when a brother understands,

---

[1] On paritasita compare M. I, 36 na asati paritassati, 'is
not worried at what is not': paritassanâ, 'fidgetiness' or 'worry,'
at M. I, 136; S. III, 15-19; and Mil. 253, 400. On vipphandita,
M. I, 8, 486; Dh. S. 381 (Asl. 253); Gât. IV, 495.

as they really are, the origin and the end, the attraction,
the danger, and the way of escape from the six realms
of contact, that he gets to know what is above, beyond,
them all [1].

72. [45] 'For whosoever, brethren, whether recluses
or Brahmans, are thus reconstructors of the past or
arrangers of the future, or who are both, whose speculations are concerned with both, who put forward
various propositions with regard to the past and to the
future, they, all of them, are entrapped in the net of
these sixty-two modes; this way and that they plunge
about, but they are in it; this way and that they may
flounder, but they are included in it, caught in it.

'Just, brethren, as when a skilful fisherman or fisher-
lad should drag a tiny pool of water with a fine-meshed
net he might fairly think: "Whatever fish of size may
be in this pond, every one will be in this net; flounder
about as they may, they will be included in it, and
caught"—just so is it with these speculators about the
past and the future, in this net, flounder as they may,
they are included and caught. [46]

73. 'The outward form, brethren, of him who has
won the truth [2], stands before you, but that which binds
it to rebirth is cut in twain. So long as his body shall
last, so long do gods and men behold him. On the
dissolution of the body, beyond the end of his life,
neither gods nor men shall see him.

'Just, brethren, as when the stalk of a bunch of mangoes has been cut, all the mangoes that were hanging
on that stalk go with it; just so, brethren, though the
outward form of him who has won the truth stands
before you, that which binds it to rebirth has been cut
in twain. So long as his body shall last, so long do
gods and men behold him. On the dissolution of the
body, beyond the end of his life, neither gods nor men
shall see him.'

---

[1] In the text the first three of these four propositions are repeated
of each of the eleven classes of theorisers. The fourth is put in the
form which, to avoid repetition, I have adopted for all the four.

[2] Tathâgata, that is the speaker himself, the Buddha.

74. When he had thus spoken, the venerable Ânanda said to the Blessed One: 'Strange, Lord, is this, and wonderful! And what name has this exposition of the truth?'

'Ânanda, you may remember this exposition as the Net of Advantage, and as the Net of Truth, and as the Supreme Net, and as the Net of Theories; remember it even as the Glorious Victory in the day of battle!'

Thus spake the Blessed One, and glad at heart the brethren exalted his word. And on the delivery of this discourse the thousandfold world-system shook.

Here ends the Brahma-*g*âla Sutta.

INTRODUCTION

SÂMAÑÑA-PHALA SUTTA.

THE first Dialogue deals with the most fundamental conceptions that lay at the root of the Buddha's doctrine, his Dharma, his ethical and philosophical view of life—the second puts forth his justification for the foundation of the Order, for the enunciation of the Vinaya, the practical rules of canon law by which life in the Order is regulated. The Rules themselves are not discussed. It is only certain ethical precepts that are referred to in so many words. The question is a larger and wider one than the desirability of any particular injunction. It is as to the advantage, as to the use, of having any Order at all.

King Agâtasattu of Magadha, after pointing out the advantages derived from their occupations by a long list of ordinary people in the world, asks whether the members of the Order, who have given up the world, derive any corresponding advantage, visible in this life, from theirs. The answer is a list of such advantages, arranged in an ascending scale of importance, each one mentioned being said to be better and sweeter than the one just before described.

The list of ordinary occupations given in the question is interesting evidence, especially as compared with the later lists of a similar kind referred to in the notes, of social conditions in the Ganges valley at the time when this Dialogue was composed. And the introductory story, in which the king explains how he had put a similar question to the founders of six other orders, and gives the six replies he received, is interesting evidence of the views held by the authors of the Dialogue as to beliefs current at the time.

The replies are no less interesting from the fact, pointed out by the king, that they are not to the point. Each of the six teachers goes off into a general statement of his theory instead of answering the question put. But as the works, if any, of all these teachers save one—Nigantha Nâta-putta—have been irretrievably lost, the summary here given of their doctrines is of great importance as evidence of the sort of speculation they favoured. The six paragraphs are short and obscure, and this is just what we should expect. As is the case with the accounts given by early Catholic writers of opinions they held to be heretical, the versions of these six sets of belief are neither adequate nor clear. But a number of other references to these six theories are found, as pointed out in the notes, both in the Buddhist and in the *G*ain records. And it would be premature to discuss our six paragraphs until the whole of the available evidence is made accessible to scholars. It is noteworthy that in at least two of these answers some of the expressions used seem to be in a Prâkrit differing in dialect from the Pâli of the Pi*t*akas. And these are not the only instances of the preservation in the Pi*t*akas of ancient dialectical varieties.

The answer which the Buddha is represented to have given, in his turn, to the question raised by the king, takes (as is so often the case) the form of a counter-question. 'The very man whom, under ordinary circumstances, you would treat as slave or servant—what treatment would you mete out to him after he had joined an Order?' The king confesses that he would treat him as a person worthy of honour and respect. And neither in question nor answer is there any reference specially to the Buddhist Order. It is taken for granted, alike by the Buddha and the king, that any one who had devoted himself to the religious life, whatever the views or opinions he held, or the association he had joined, would, in accordance with the remarkable tolerance of that age and country, be treated with equal respect and courtesy. And the same note runs all through the Dialogue. The Buddha shows the advantages of the 'life of a recluse,' not necessarily of a follower of his own. And most of what he says would apply as much to his strongest opponents as to the members of his own Order.

The following, in a constantly ascending order of merit, are the advantages, visible in this life, which he claims for such a recluse:—

1. The honour and respect shown to a member of a religious order.

2. The training in all those lower kinds of mere morality set out in the very ancient document called 'The Sîlas.' The importance of this document has been discussed above, in the Introduction to the Brahma-*g*âla. The details of it may be summarised here as follows:—

a. Mercy and kindness to all living things; § 43[1].

---

[1] Details *a–d* (though the fact is not referred to here) are the

b. Honesty.

c. Chastity.

d. Truthfulness, peacefulness, courtesy, and good sense in speech; § 44.

e. Abstinence from luxury of twelve different kinds, and freedom from trickery and violence; § 45.

f. Not injuring plants; § 46.

g. Not laying up treasure, of seven kinds; § 47.

h. Not frequenting shows, of twenty-six specified kinds; § 48.

i. Not playing games, eighteen being mentioned by name; § 49.

j. Not using luxurious rugs, &c., of twenty different kinds; § 50.

k. Not using toilet luxuries, of which twenty-two are specified; § 51.

l. Not talking vain things, of which twenty-seven instances are given; § 52.

m. Not using sophistical and rude phrases when talking of higher things; § 53.

n. Not acting as go-between; § 54.

o. Not practising trickery and mystery under the guise of religion; § 55.

p. Not gaining a living by low arts, such as auguries (§ 56); advising as to the best sorts of various things (§ 57); prophesying as to war and its results (§ 58); astrology (§ 59); foretelling famine or plague or the reverse (§ 60); arranging marriages, using spells, or worshipping gods (§ 61); various sorts of medical trickery (§ 62).

3. The confidence of heart, absence of fear, resulting from the consciousness of right doing; § 63.

4. The habit of keeping guarded the door of his senses; § 64.

5. The constant self-possession he thus gains; § 65.

6. The power of being content with little, with simplicity of life; § 66.

7. The emancipation of heart from the Five Hindrances to self-mastery—covetousness, ill-temper, laziness, worry and flurry, and perplexity; §§ 68–74.

8. The joy and peace that, as a result of the sense of this emancipation, fills his whole being; § 75.

---

opposites of the three bad acts of the body, and the four bad acts of speech, kâya- and vakî-dukkaritâni, so often referred to in the Suttas, and in the Abhidhamma. The three others (of the mind), making up the ten given in my manual, p. 142, are omitted here because they belong to the higher morality.

9. The practice of the Four *Gh*ânas ; §§ 75–82[1].

10. The Insight arising from knowledge (*ñ*âna-dassana) ; §§ 83, 84.

11. The power of projecting mental images ; §§ 85, 86.

12. The five modes of mystic Insight (abhi*ññ*â) ; §§ 87–96—
a. The practice of Iddhi.
b. The Heavenly Ear—hearing heavenly sounds.
c. Knowledge of others' thoughts.
d. Memory of his own previous births.
e. Knowledge of other people's previous births (the Heavenly Eye).

13. The realisation of the Four Truths, the destruction of the Âsavas, and attainment of Arahatship ; §§ 97, 98.

Now it is perfectly true that of these thirteen consecutive propositions, or groups of propositions, it is only the last, No. 13, which is exclusively Buddhist. But the things omitted, the union of the whole of those included into one system, the order in which the ideas are arranged, the way in which they are treated as so many steps of a ladder whose chief value depends on the fact that it leads up to the culminating point of Nirvâ*n*a in Arahatship—all this is also distinctively Buddhist. And further, the whole statement, the details of it, the order of it, must have soaked very thoroughly into the minds of the early Buddhists. For we find the whole, or nearly the whole, of it repeated (with direct reference by name to our Sutta as the oldest and most complete enumeration of it) not only in all the subsequent dialogues translated in this volume, but also in many others.

In these repetitions the order is always the same, and the details (so far as they occur) are the same. But one or other of the thirteen groups is often omitted, and the application of those of them that remain is always different—that is to say, they are enumerated in support, or in illustration, of a different proposition.

A comparison of some of these other applications of the list is full of suggestion as to its real meaning here.

In the Amba*tth*a the point is as to caste. The Kshatriya caste is the most honourable, but wisdom and conduct are higher still. What then is the right conduct, what the right

---

[1] Buddhaghosa (p. 219) says that though the Four Arûpa Vimokkhas are not explicitly mentioned they are to be understood (thus making up the Eight Samâpattis). This may be so : but it looks like a later writer reading his own opinion into the older text. They are put into the text at Po*tth*apâda, pp. 183, 184, and it is difficult to see why they should not have been also inserted here, if they were really implied.

wisdom? The conduct (*karana*) is all the above paragraphs from 2–9 inclusive; the wisdom (*viggâ*) is the rest, 10–13 [1].

In the Soṇadaṇḍa the question is: 'What is the true Brahman?' After, by his usual Socratic method, leading Soṇadaṇḍa to acknowledge that the only two essential requisites are goodness and intelligence, these last are explained as above (2–9 and 10–13).

In the Kûṭadanta the question is as to the right sort of sacrifice. After rejecting animal sacrifice we have generosity (of various kinds, each better than the last), faith, training in the precepts, and 2–13, set forth as each of them a better sacrifice than the last.

In the Gâliya the question is whether the soul is the same as, or is other than, the body. The answer is a counter-question. Repeating our sections 2–13 (omitting 11 and 12) the Buddha asks, at the end of each subdivision, whether men who do *that* would be likely to trouble themselves as to speculations about the soul? And the answer being, of course, 'No,' rejoins that neither does he.

In the Poṭṭhapâda the question is as to the way in which various recluses attain to mystic trance. The Buddha's answer is that it is by training; and the training should be first in morals (our groups 2 and 3) then in the things mentioned in our groups 4–9, and then in the Four Arûpa Vimokkhas. The Dialogue then takes up other questions, omitting our groups 10–13.

In the Kevaddha the talk is on miracles, mystic powers. And the Buddha, disparaging all others, calls attention to our groups 2–13.

In the Lohikka the question is as to who is the right sort of teacher; and the answer is that it is the one whose pupil carries out our groups 2–13.

In the Tevigga the question is as to the way by which one can attain to union with God (Brahmâ-sahavyatâ). The answer gives our groups 1–8, and then adds the Four Brahma-vihâras.

In the shorter of the two Hatthipadopama Suttas

---

[1] Possibly Nos. 11 and 12 are meant, both here and in all the other Suttas, to be omitted. The wording is ambiguous. Buddhaghosa, who talks here (see p. 268) of Nos. 10–13 as the Eightfold paññâ, apparently means to include them (he could not otherwise get eight). But the argument of the Mahâli seems to exclude them. The texts always jump from the last words of 10 to the last words of 13. Now as in the Mahâli No. 12 is excluded, it is clear that at least there only Nos. 10 and 13 are meant. And there is no difference between the phraseology in the Mahâli and that used in the other Suttas.

(No. 27 in the Magghima), the question discussed between a Brahman and an ascetic is as to the ascendancy of the Buddha over the other teachers of the time. The Buddha himself giving afterwards the full reason, repeats our group 2 (omitting however clauses *f* to *p* inclusive[1]), then repeats our groups 6, 3, 4, 5, 7, 8, 9, then omitting groups 10 and 11, quotes two only, the last two (omitting the first three)[2] of the five Abhiññâs in group 12, and concludes with group 13 in full.

In the Mahâ Tanhâ-sankhaya Sutta (No. 38 in the Magghima), we have the same sequence—our group 2 (omitting *f* to *p*), then 6, 3, 4, 5, 7, 8, and 9. The rest is omitted.

In the next Sutta, the longer of the Assapuras, after a summary in different words of most of the contents of our group 2, we have our group 4, then two paragraphs not in our Sutta, then our groups 5, 7, 8, 9, and the last two only out of group 12, and then (as a climax) our group 13—all enumerated to show what is the true Brahman, the true samana.

Then again in the Sakuludâyi, No. 79 of the Magghima, it is declared to be not for the sake of realising happiness that recluses take up the celibate life in the Order under the Buddha, but for the sake of those matters set forth in our groups 2–9 inclusive[3], of the two last of the Abhiññâs, and above all for the sake of the attainment of Arahatship.

Besides the differences pointed out above between the Suttas preserved in the Dîgha, and in the Magghima, respectively—differences due, I think, solely to the difference in the subjects under discussion—there are also a few verbal differences, amounting to scarcely more than 'various readings,' due, perhaps, to the divergent traditions of the Dîgha-bhânakâ and the Magghima-bhânakâ (the students and repeaters of the two collections in which the Dialogues are handed down to us).

However this may be, it is clear that the sum and the sequence of the paragraphs in our Sutta is regarded as of

---

[1] From which we may infer that, as respects those matters, he saw no difference between himself and the other teachers.

[2] So that the power of Iddhi, of hearing heavenly sounds, and of knowing other people's thoughts, are apparently supposed to be common ground between the Buddhists and the other sects. They are included in our Sutta because they are supposed to be part of the advantage of life in an Order—in any Order, that is, not only the Buddhist.

[3] Magghima II, 37, 38. Perhaps the pe is meant to be supplied from the twenty-seventh Sutta just quoted—the difference, however, as we have seen, is not of great importance.

great importance, not as a statement of Buddhist ethics, or of Buddhist philosophy, or of the Buddhist religion, but as a statement of the advantages that may be looked for as the result of life in an Order. And further that the statement has to be slightly modified and shortened when the question is the narrower one of life in the particular community which we call the Buddhist Order.

The difference is interesting—in the scheme for the Buddhist Order the ñâna-dassana, the power of projecting a mental image (apparently of oneself, which seems like the earliest germ of the modern Yoga ideas about the astral body), the powers of Iddhi, the power of hearing heavenly sounds (something like hearing the music of the spheres), and the power of knowing the thoughts of others, are all omitted.

In the abstract given above, I have called these last three, together with the power of calling to mind one's own, and other peoples', previous births, the Five Abhiññâs, or Intuitions. And this is in accord with the passages on which Childers's article *sub voce* is based. But these powers are not so called either in our text, or in any other Dialogue yet published. The use of the word abhiññâ in this technical sense would seem therefore (to judge from the published texts) to be a sign of the later date of the book in which it occurs [1]. In the oldest portions of the Pitakas the word is always used in the general sense of insight, and if any special limitation is hinted at, it is simply the insight of Arahatship that is emphasised (as in Dhammapada 423, which is a quotation from Iti-Vuttaka, No. 99, and is quoted also at Anguttara I, 165) [2].

The Eightfold Path is not mentioned in our Sutta. This is not merely because it is not possible always to mention

---

[1] The oldest case of the technical use of the word, so far as I know, is in the introductory story of the Mahâ Vibhanga on the fourth Pârâgika (Vin. III, 87). This is later than the Old Commentary on the Pâtimokkha, from which it incorporates many passages, and this again is later, of course, than the Pâtimokkha itself.

Neither the Five nor the Six Abhiññâs are given as groups among the groups of Fives and Sixes in the Anguttara. The word Abhiññâ is used in the divisions containing the Fives and Sixes exclusively in its ordinary sense (III, 277, 451; comp. IV, 348). And this is the more instructive as what were afterwards called the Six Abhiññâs are actually given in full (IV, 17-19, §§ 6-11) in the same words as in the Âkankheyya Sutta (No. 6 of the Magghima, translated in my 'Buddhist Suttas'), and very nearly as in our Sutta, here under discussion. But they are not called Abhiññâs.

[2] Compare also A. I, 100; II, 249; III, 3, 9, 277.

everything. The Path does not come within the special advantages of life in the Order. To enter upon the Path to Arahatship, to walk along it, is not peculiar to members of the Order. A bhikshu might reach the goal either along that path, open also to laymen [1], or by the process set out in our Sutta. They are two quite distinct methods of training, of which our Sutta deals only with one

It is essential, in order to understand Buddhist ethics, to bear in mind that there are (and must be in such a system) several different lines along which both speculation and edifying teaching run. These are :

1. The course of conduct laid down for the ordinary Buddhist layman, contained in the Gahapati-vaggas found in the various nikâyas [2].

2. The rules as to the outward conduct of the members of the Order, laid down in the Pâtimokkha and in the Khandhakas [3].

3. The system of self-training in higher things prescribed for members of the Order. Of this our present Sutta is a striking example.

4. The method of self-training laid down for those who have entered upon the Path to Arahatship. (The Four Truths, the Eightfold Path, and the Âsavas.)

In the first of these Buddhism goes very little beyond the current ethics of the day. In the second a very great deal has been simply incorporated from the rules found expedient by previous recluses, both Brahman and non-Brahman, though there are numerous differences, both of the positive regulations included, and also of things deliberately omitted. Even the third, as we have seen, cannot be considered, except in a very limited sense, as exclusively Buddhist. It is in the fourth that the essential doctrines of Buddhism are to be found. All four have, no doubt, become welded together into a more or less consistent whole. But to understand the whole, the relation of its various parts has to be kept constantly in view.

This will explain an apparent contradiction. The last Sutta quoted, the Sakuludâyi, states that the aim of the religious or celibate life as led in the Buddha's Order, is the attainment, in order, of the various things set out in our Sutta (groups 2-9, 12 and 13).

---

[1] For a list of twenty-one laymen Arahats see A. III, 451; and there are other instances recorded.

[2] A good summary of this is in the Sigâlovada Sutta, an abstract of which is given in my Manual, pp. 143 foll.

[3] Translated in 'Vinaya Texts' (S. B. E.).

Now in other passages other things are stated to be the aim. Thus in the Samyutta (IV, 51) the Buddha himself is represented as explaining that the celibate life (the brahma-kariyâ)[1] is led by his followers for the sake of the complete understanding of pain (dukkha-pariññâ). Further on in the same book (VI, 253 = V, 6, 27) this is three times repeated, with the suggestive addition that there is one way to this, to wit, the Noble Eightfold Path.

Again, in the Anguttara (IV, 7) the higher life is said to be for the sake of getting rid of, of cutting through, seven Bonds which prevent one from attaining Arahatship. The argument on pp. 88, 99 (though the word brahma-kariyâ does not occur) comes to much the same thing. And further on in the same book (IV, 272) the object is stated to be for the sake of getting rid of five particular sorts of envy.

Nâgasena is therefore quite right when he says that the object of renouncing the world to live in the Order is for the sake of righteousness and peace[2]; and in another place that it is to the end that sorrow may pass away[3]. All these explanations belong to the Path, not to the rules of the Order. They are not really inconsistent with the other aim that our Sutta sets out. And they are only additional proof, if such were needed, that it is no more possible to sum up in a single phrase (as some writers have tried to do) the aim of Buddhism, or the object of life in the Order, than it would be to sum up in a similar way the aim of Christianity, or the object for which men enter a Christian Order. The aims are necessarily as various as the character and circumstances of the various individuals who take them up. And Nâgasena does not hesitate to add—and to add in speaking to a king—that some had joined the Order in terror at the tyranny of kings, some in fear of robbers, some because they were harassed by debt, and some perhaps merely to gain a livelihood.

This also would apply to other Orders both in India and elsewhere, and is quite consistent with our Sutta, which only purports to set forth the advantages the early Buddhists held to be the likely results of joining, from whatever motive, such an Order as their own.

---

[1] That is, of course, 'the best course of life' with the connotation of celibacy. The German 'Wandel' is a good rendering of Kariyâ. We have no expression so good. See Samyutta V, 16, 17.

[2] Milinda I, 31 (of my translation).

[3] Ibid. I, 51; compare I, 101.

II. SÂMAÑÑA-PHALA SUTTA.

[THE FRUITS OF THE LIFE OF A RECLUSE[1].]

[47] 1. Thus have I heard. The Blessed One was once dwelling at Râgagaha in the Mango Grove of Gîvaka the children's physician[2], with a great company of the brethren, with twelve hundred and fifty of the brethren. Now at that time the king of Magadha, Agâtasattu, the son of the Videha princess[3], on the Uposatha day, held on the fifteenth, on Komudi (white

---

[1] Gogerly's translation of the first part of this Sutta, and Burnouf's translation of the whole of it, have been reprinted in Grimblot's 'Sept Suttas Palis.' These versions, of remarkable merit for the time when they were made, are full of mistakes which the since-published editions of the Commentary, and of numerous allied texts, enable us now to avoid. I have not thought it necessary to point out the numerous passages, occurring indeed in nearly every sentence, in which the present translation differs from theirs. It should be mentioned here, however, that Burnouf has missed the whole point of the dialogue by misunderstanding the constantly repeated phrase sanditthikam sâmañña-phalam from which this title is taken. He renders it throughout as meaning 'foreseen and general fruit' which is grammatically impossible as regards sanditthikam, and rests on a false derivation as regards sâmañña. This last word means, of course, 'samanaship, being a samana, living as a samana, a recluse, a religieux.'

[2] Gîvakassa komârabhakkassa. Buddhaghosa (Sum. I, 133) naturally follows the compilers of the Khandakas (V. I, 269) in interpreting the adjective as 'brought up by the Prince.' But see the note at 'Vinaya Texts,' II, 174; which shows that the more likely meaning is 'the bringer-up of children' (child-doctor). Several cures, however, wrought by him are recorded; and the patients are always adults. There is no other reference at all to his being a child-doctor, and the Khandaka which gives the other interpretation is a very ancient document.

[3] See the note in my 'Buddhist Suttas,' p. 1. Buddhaghosa (p. 139) says she was the daughter of the king of Kosala.

water-lily), the full moon day of the fourth month[1], at
night, when the moon was full, was seated on the upper
terrace roof of his palace surrounded by his ministers.
And the king, on that sacred day, gave utterance to
a hymn of joy, saying:

'How pleasant, friends, is the moonlight night!
How beautiful, friends, is the moonlight night!
How lovely, friends, is the moonlight night!
How soothing, friends, is the moonlight night!
How grand a sign, friends, is the moonlight night!
'Who is the recluse or Brahman whom we may call
upon to-night, who, when we call upon him, shall be
able to satisfy our hearts[2]?'

2. When he had thus spoken, a certain minister said
to the king: 'There is, Sire, Pûraṇa Kassapa, the head
of an order, of a following, the teacher of a school, well
known and of repute as a sophist, revered by the people,
a man of experience, who has long been a recluse, old
and well stricken in years. Let your Majesty pay
a visit to him. It may well be[3] that, on calling upon
him, your heart, Sire, shall find peace.' But when he
had thus spoken Agâtasattu the king kept silence.

3–7. Then other five ministers spake in the same
terms of Makkhali of the cow-pen, [48] of Agita of the
garment of hair, of Pakudha Kakkâyana, of Sañgaya
of the Belaṭṭha clan, and of the Nigaṇṭha of the Nâta
clan. And still, to each, Agâtasattu the king kept
silence.

---

[1] This is interesting, as it shows that the year, for the compilers
of our Sutta, began in Sâvana (middle of July to middle of August),
that is, with the rainy season. There were three Uposatha days in
each month, on the 7th, 14th, and 15th day of the month. The
full moon night of Kattika (middle of October to middle of Novem-
ber) is called Komudi (from Kumuda, a white water-lily), because
that flower is supposed to bloom then. Burnouf is wrong in trans-
lating Komudi as the name of the month.

[2] The same lines recur, but in a different order, at Gât. I, 105.
Dosinâ, the etymology of which puzzled Childers and also Buddhaghosa (p. 141), is gyotsnâ.

[3] Appeva nâma. Both Gogerly and Burnouf take this to mean
'to a certainty,' but compare D. I, 179, 205; V. II, 85, 262.

8. [49] Now at that time *G*īvaka the physician was
seated, in silence, not far from A*g*âtasattu the king.
And the king said to him: 'But you, friend *G*īvaka,
why do you say nothing?'

'The Blessed One, Sire, the Arahat, the all-awakened-
one, is now lodging in our Mango Grove, with a great
company of the brethren, with twelve hundred and fifty
brethren. And this is the good report that has been
noised abroad as to Gotama the Blessed One: "An
Arahat, fully awakened, is the exalted One, abounding
in wisdom and goodness, happy, with knowledge of
the worlds, unsurpassed as a guide to mortals willing
to be led, the teacher of gods and men, a blessed
Buddha." Let your Majesty pay a visit to him. It
may well be that, on calling upon him, your heart, Sire,
shall find peace.'

'Then, friend *G*īvaka, have the riding-elephants made
ready.'

9. 'Very good, Sire!' said *G*īvaka the physician in
assent to the words of the king. And he had five
hundred she-elephants made ready, and the state
elephant the king was wont to ride, and had word
brought to the king: 'The elephants, Sire, are
caparisoned. Do now what seemeth to you meet.'
Then the king had five hundred of his women mounted
on the she-elephants, one on each; and himself mounted
the state elephant; and he went forth, the attendants
bearing torches, in royal pomp, from Râ*g*agaha to
*G*īvaka the physician's Mango Grove.

10. And the king, when close upon the Mango Grove,
was seized with a sudden fear and consternation, and
the hairs on his body stood erect. And anxious and
excited, he said to *G*īvaka: [50] 'You are playing me
no tricks, *G*īvaka? You are not deceiving me? You
are not betraying me to my foes? How can it be
that there should be no sound at all, not a sneeze nor
a cough, in so large an assembly of the brethren,
among twelve hundred and fifty of the brethren?'

'Fear not, O king. I play no trick, neither deceive
you; nor would I betray you to the foe. Go on, O king,

go straight on! There, in the pavilion hall, the lamps are burning.'

11. Then the king went on, on his elephant as far as the path was passable for elephants, and then on foot, to the door of the pavilion; and then said to *G*îvaka: 'But where, *G*îvaka, is the Blessed One?'

'That is he, O king, sitting against the middle pillar, and facing the East, with the brethren around him.'

12. Then the king went up, and stood respectfully on one side. And as he stood there and looked on the assembly, seated in perfect silence, calm as a clear lake, he broke out: 'Would that my son, Udâyi Bhadda, might have such calm as this assembly of the brethren now has!'

'Do your thoughts then go where love guides them?'

'I love the boy, and wish that he, Udâyi Bhadda, might enjoy such calm as this assembly has.'

13. Then the king bowed to the Blessed One, and stretching forth his joined palms in salutation to the Order took his seat aside, [51] and said to the Blessed One: 'I would fain question the Blessed One on a certain matter, if he give me opportunity to set forth the question.'

'Ask, O king, whatsoever you desire.'

14. 'There are, Sir, a number of ordinary crafts :— mahouts, horsemen, charioteers, archers, standard bearers, camp marshalls, camp followers, high military officers of royal birth, military scouts[1], men brave as elephants, champions, heroes, warriors in buckskin, home-born slaves, cooks, barbers, bath attendants, confectioners, garland-makers, washermen, weavers, basket-makers, potters, arithmeticians, accountants, and whatsoever others of like kind there may be. All

---

[1] Pakkhandino, 'rushers forth.' The exact meaning of some of these military terms is still uncertain, and was apparently uncertain to Buddhaghosa. They all recur, with some differences of reading, in the Milinda (p. 331, in a later and much longer list), and also in the Aṅguttara (IV, 107), as the names of the constituent elements of a standing army.

these enjoy, in this very world, the visible fruits of their craft. They maintain themselves, and their parents and children and friends, in happiness and comfort. They keep up gifts, the object of which is gain on high, to recluses and Brahmans,—gifts that lead to rebirth in heaven, that redound to happiness, and have bliss as their result. Can you, Sir, declare to me any such immediate fruit, visible in this very world, of the life of a recluse[1]?'

15. 'Do you admit to us, O king, that you have put the same question to other recluses or to Brahmans?'

'I do, Lord.'

'Then tell us how they answered it, if you do not mind.'

'I have no objection where the Blessed One, or others like him, are.'

[52] 'Then speak, O king.'

16. 'Once I went to Pûrana Kassapa[2]. And after exchanging with him the greetings and compliments of friendship and courtesy, I seated myself beside him, and put to him the same question as I have now put, Lord, to you.

17. 'Then Pûrana Kassapa said to me: "To him who acts, O king, or causes another to act, to him who mutilates or causes another to mutilate, to him who punishes or causes another to punish, to him who causes grief or torment, to him who trembles or causes others to tremble, to him who kills a living creature, who takes what is not given, who breaks into houses, who commits dacoity, or robbery, or highway robbery, or adultery, or who speaks lies, to him thus acting there is no guilt. If with a discus with an edge sharp as

---

[1] Burnouf has made a sad mess of this important and constantly repeated clause. He has 'Is it then possible, Sir, that one should declare to them (that is, to the craftsmen just mentioned) in this world, such a result (of their actions) as foreseen and as the general fruit of their conduct?' But the king asks the Buddha to tell him (the king himself) whether the members of the Order derive from their life any benefit corresponding to that which the craftsmen derive from theirs.

[2] According to Buddhaghosa (p. 142) he was one of the teachers who went about naked.

G

a razor he should make all the living creatures on the earth one heap, one mass, of flesh, there would be no guilt thence resulting, no increase of guilt would ensue.   Were he to go along the south bank of the Ganges striking and slaying, mutilating and having men mutilated, oppressing and having men oppressed, there would be no guilt thence resulting, no increase of guilt would ensue.   Were he to go along the north bank of the Ganges giving alms, and ordering gifts to be given, offering sacrifices or causing them to be offered, there would be no merit thence resulting, no increase of merit.   [53] In generosity, in self-mastery, in control of the senses, in speaking truth there is neither merit, nor increase of merit." Thus, Lord, did Pûra*n*a Kassapa, when asked what was the immediate advantage in the life of a recluse, expound his theory of non-action [1].   Just, Lord, as if a man, when asked what a mango was, should explain what a bread fruit is, just so did Pûra*n*a Kassapa, when asked what was the fruit, in this present state of being, of the life of a recluse, expound his theory of non-action.   Then, Lord, it occurred to me : "How should such a one as I think of giving dissatisfaction to any recluse or Brahman in my realm?"   So I neither applauded nor blamed what he said, and though dissatisfied I gave utterance to no expression of dissatisfaction, and neither accepting nor rejecting that answer of his, I arose from my seat, and departed thence.

19. ['In the same manner I went to five other teachers, and receiving to this same question put an answer not to the point, I behaved in each case as just set forth.   And the answers of the five were thus :][2]

---

[1] A kiriya*m* vyâkâsi. Gogerly interprets this 'he replied by affirming that there are no future rewards and punishments.' Burnouf has simply 'm'a donné une réponse vaine.' But the corresponding word in the subsequent sections summarises the theory of the teacher questioned. On this theory compare A. I, 62; V. I, 235.

[2] In the text the framework of the interview is repeated each time in the same words as above. Only the answers differ. The answers all recur in the Magg*h*ima I, 513 foll.

20. 'When one day I had thus asked Makkhali of the cow-pen [1], he said: "There is, O king, no cause, either ultimate or remote, for the depravity of beings: they become depraved without reason and without cause. There is no cause, either proximate or remote, for the rectitude of beings; they become pure without reason and without cause. The attainment of any given condition, of any character, does not depend either on one's own acts, or on the acts of another, or on human effort. There is no such thing as power or energy, or human strength or human vigour. All animals, all creatures (with one, two, or more senses), all beings (produced from eggs or in a womb), all souls (in plants) [2] are without force and power and energy of their own. They are bent this way and that by their fate, by the necessary conditions of the class to which they belong, by their individual nature: and it is according to their position in one or other of the six classes that they experience ease or pain.

---

[1] There is a good deal in both the Buddhist and the Gain texts about this Makkhali Gosâla, whose followers were called Âgîvakas, and who was regarded, from the Buddhist point of view, as the worst of the sophists. Some of the Gaina passages, and also Buddhaghosa here, are referred to by Hoernle, 'Uvâsaka dasâo,' pp. 108 foll.: and in the Appendixes. The principal Pitaka passages are M. I, 31, 198, 238, 250, 483, 516, 524. S. I, 66, 68; III, 69, 211; IV, 398. A. I, 33, 286; III, 276, 384. V. I, 8, 291; II, 111, 130, 165, 284; IV, 74. See also Gât. I, 493 and G. V, 68. As the sect is thrice mentioned in the Asoka Edicts as receiving royal gifts it is certain that it retained an important position for several centuries at least. See Senart, 'Inscriptions de Piyadasi,' II, 82, 209.

From the beginning of the answer down to the end of p. 53 recurs at S. III, 211, and the rest of it at ibid. 212, and the first part of the answer is ascribed at ibid. p. 69 to Pûrana Kassapa.

[2] Sabbe sattâ, sabbe pânâ, sabbe bhûtâ, sabbe gîvâ. Buddhaghosa gives details of these four classes of living beings, showing how they are meant to include all that has life, on this earth, from men down to plants. The explanation is very confused, and makes the terms by no means mutually exclusive. They are frequently used in the same order in the Gaina-Sûtras, and Professor Jacobi renders them accordingly 'Every sentient being, every insect, every living thing, whether animal or vegetable.' 'Gaina-Sûtras,' II, xxv. This is much better; but we have, in our version, to give the sense in which the Buddhists supposed Gosâla to have taken the words.

[54] ' " There are fourteen hundred thousands of the
principal sorts of birth, and again six thousand others,
and again six hundred.   There are five hundred sorts
of Karma, and again five (according to the five senses),
and again three (according to act, word, and thought);
and there is a whole Karma and a half Karma (the
whole being a Karma of act or word, the half a Karma
of thought).

' " There are sixty-two paths (or modes of conduct),
sixty-two periods, six classes (or distinctions among
men)[1], eight stages of a prophet's existence[2], forty-nine
hundred sorts of occupation[3], forty-nine hundred sorts
of wandering mendicants, forty-nine hundred regions
dwelt in by Nâgas, two thousand faculties, three
thousand purgatories, thirty-six places where dust accu-
mulates, seven sorts of animate and seven of inanimate
production, and seven of production by grafting, seven
sorts of gods, and of men, and of devils, and of great
lakes, and seven principal and again seven hundred
minor sorts of Pakutas[4] of precipices, and of dreams.

' " There are eighty-four hundred thousand periods
during which both fools and wise alike, wandering in
transmigration, shall at last make an end of pain.
Though the wise should hope : ' By this virtue or
this performance of duty, or this penance, or this
righteousness will I make the Karma (I have inherited),
that is not yet mature, mature '—though the fool should
hope, by the same means, to get gradually rid of Karma
that has matured—neither of them can do it.   The
ease and pain, measured out, as it were, with a measure,
cannot be altered in the course of transmigration ; there

---

[1] Compare the corresponding theory of the Gains as given in the
Uttarâdhyâyana Sûtra in Jacobi's Gaina-Sûtras, vol. ii, p. 213 : and
that of Pûrana Kassapa quoted in Añguttara III, 383.

[2] Buddhaghosa gives the details ' babyhood, playtime, trial time,
erect time, learning time, ascetic time, prophet time, and prostrate
time' with (very necessary) comments on each.   One may compare
Shakspere's ' Seven Ages of Man.'

[3] Âgîva.   The Siamese edition reads âgîvaka.

[4] I think this is the right reading, but don't know what it means.

can be neither increase nor decrease thereof, neither excess nor deficiency. Just as when a ball of string is cast forth it will spread out just as far, and no farther, than it can unwind, just so both fools and wise alike, wandering in transmigration exactly for the allotted term, shall then, and only then, make an end of pain."

'Thus, Lord, did Makkhali of the cow-pen, when asked what was the immediate advantage in the life of a recluse, expound his theory of purification through transmigration.

[55] 23. 'When, one day, I had thus asked Agita of the garment of hair, he said[1]: " There is no such thing, O king, as alms or sacrifice or offering. There is neither fruit nor result of good or evil deeds. There is no such thing as this world or the next. There is neither father nor mother, nor beings springing into life without them. There are in the world no recluses or Brahmans who have reached the highest point[2], who walk perfectly, and who having understood and realised, by themselves alone, both this world and the next, make their wisdom known to others.

'" A human being is built up of the four elements. When he dies the earthy in him returns and relapses to the earth, the fluid to the water, the heat to the fire, the windy to the air, and his faculties[3] pass into space. The four bearers, on the bier as a fifth, take his dead body away; till they reach the burning-ground men utter forth eulogies, but there his bones are bleached,

---

[1] This answer recurs S. III, 307, M. I, 515 (compare Dh. S. 1215, 1362, 1364), as the view of a typical sophist.

[2] Sammag-gato. Buddhaghosa gives here no explanation of this word, but the Gâtaka Commentary on Gât. III, 305 says it means the man who has attained the highest fruit; that is, Arahatship. Gato is used here in the same sense as it has in Tathâgato, in gatatto (in the Nigantha paragraph below), and in viggâ-gato (S. N. 730, 733, 743), that is, who has not only attempted to go to, but has actually reached, the aim (common alike to the orthodox Vedântist Brahmans and to each of the various schools of independent, dissenting, thinkers and recluses) of the conquest over ignorance, of the grasp of truth.

[3] Indriyâni, the five senses, and the mind as a sixth.

and his offerings[1] end in ashes. It is a doctrine of
fools, this talk of gifts. It is an empty lie, mere idle
talk, when men say there is profit therein. Fools and
wise alike, on the dissolution of the body, are cut off,
annihilated, and after death they are not."

'Thus, Lord, did A*g*ita of the garment of hair, when
asked what was the immediate advantage in the life of
a recluse, expound his theory of annihilation.

[56] 26. 'When, one day, I had thus asked Pakudha
Ka*kk*âyana, he said: "The following seven things,
O king, are neither made nor commanded to be made,
neither created nor caused to be created, they are
barren (so that nothing is produced out of them),
stedfast as a mountain peak, as a pillar firmly fixed.
They move not, neither do they vary, they trench not
one upon another, nor avail aught as to ease or pain or
both. And what are the seven? The four elements—
earth, water, fire, and air—and ease, and pain, and the
soul as a seventh. So there is neither slayer nor
causer of slaying, hearer or speaker, knower or ex-
plainer. When one with a sharp sword cleaves a head
in twain, no one thereby deprives any one of life,
a sword has only penetrated into the interval between
seven elementary substances."

'Thus, Lord, did Pakudha Ka*kk*âyana, when asked
what was the immediate advantage in the life of
a recluse, expound the matter by expounding something else.

[57] 28. 'When, one day, I had thus asked the
Niga*nth*a of the Nâta *e*lan, he said: "A Niga*nth*a,
O king (a man free from bonds), is restrained with a
fourfold self-restraint. He lives restrained as regards
all water; restrained as regards all evil; all evil has
he washed away; and he lives suffused with the
sense of evil held at bay. Such is his fourfold self-
restraint. And since he is thus tied with· this fourfold

---

[1] Âhutiyo. See Buddhava*m*sa XXVII, 10; Kathâ Vatthu 550. The
phrase is omitted in the parallel passage in the *G*aina 'Sûtrak*ri*tânga'
pointed out by Jacobi, '*G*aina-Sûtras,' II, xxiv.

bond, therefore is he, the Niga*nth*o (free from bonds), called G atatto (whose heart has gone ; that is, to the summit, to the attainment, of his aim) Yatatto (whose heart is kept down ; that is, is under command), and *Th*itatto (whose heart is fixed)[1]."

'Thus, Lord, did the Niga*nth*a of the Nâta clan, when asked what was the immediate advantage in the life of a recluse, expound his theory of the fourfold bond.

[58] 31. 'When, one day, I had thus asked Sa*ñg*aya of the Bela*tth*a clan, he said : " If you ask me whether there is another world—well, if I thought there were, I would say so. But I don't say so. And I don't think it is thus or thus. And I don't think it is otherwise. And I don't deny it. And I don't say there neither is, nor is not, another world. And if you ask me about the beings produced by chance ; or whether there is any fruit, any result, of good or bad actions ; or whether a man who has won the truth continues, or not, after death—to each or any of these questions do I give the same reply[2]."

[59] 33. 'Thus, Lord, did Sa*ñg*aya of the Bela*tth*a clan, when asked what was the immediate advantage in the life of a recluse, show his manner of prevarication. And to him, as to all the others, I expressed neither approval nor dissatisfaction, but neither accepting nor

---

[1] The series of riddles in this difficult passage is probably intended to be an ironical imitation of the Niga*nth*a's way of talking. Gogerly has caught the general sense fairly enough, but his version is very free, and wrong as to two of the words, and it gives no idea of the oracular form in which the original is couched. Burnouf's rendering is quite wide of the mark.

The first of the 'Four Restraints' is the well-known rule of the *G*ains not to drink cold water, on the ground that there are 'souls' in it. See the discussion in the Milinda (II, 85–91 of my translation).

Professor Jacobi ('*G*aina-Sûtras,' II, xxiii) thinks the 'Four Restraints' are intended to represent the four vows kept by the followers of Pars*v*a. But this surely cannot be so, for these vows were quite different.

[2] The text repeats the whole paragraph put above (p. 27 of the text) into 'the mouth of the Eel-wriggler.

rejecting what was said, I arose from my seat, and departed thence[1].

34. 'And now, Lord, I put the same question to the Blessed One. Can you show me any immediate fruit, in this world, of the life of a recluse, such as those who follow each of the occupations I have mentioned are, each of them, able to show?'

'I can, O king. And to that end I would fain put a question to you. Answer it as you may think most fit.

[60] 35. 'Now what do you think, O king. Suppose among the people of your household there were a slave who does work for you, rises up in the morning before you do and retires later to rest, who is keen to carry out your pleasure, anxious to make himself agreeable in what he does and says, a man who watches your every look. Suppose he should think, "Strange is it and wonderful, this issue of meritorious deeds, this result of merit! Here is this king of Magadha, Agâta-sattu, the son of the Videha princess—he is a man, and so am I. But the king lives in the full enjoyment and possession of the five pleasures of sense—a very god, methinks—and here am I a slave, working for him, rising before him and retiring later to rest, keen to carry out his pleasure, anxious to make myself agreeable in deed and word, watching his very looks. Would that I were like him, that I too might earn merit. Why should not I have my hair and beard shaved off,

---

[1] Of these six teachers Pûrana denies the evil Karma in a bad act and *vice versa;* Agita, in preaching annihilation at death, shuts out the possibility of any effect to be worked by Karma; and Makkhali rejects both Karma and its effect. The theory of Pakudha seems to exclude responsibility; the Nigantha simply begs the question, by asserting that a Nigantha has attained the end; and Sañgaya gives no answer at all.

The only one of these six theories of life on which independent evidence is at present accessible is that of the Nigantha (the Gain theory). But no attempt has yet been made to summarise it, or set it out in a manner intelligible to Western readers. It is very much to be hoped that this want may soon be supplied by one or other of the excellent scholars familiar with the texts.

and don the yellow robes, and going forth from the household state, renounce the world?"   And suppose, after a time, he should do so. And having been admitted into an Order, should dwell restrained in act and word and thought, content with mere food and shelter, delighting in solitude.   And suppose your people should tell you of this, saying: "If it please your majesty, do you know that such a one, formerly your slave, who worked for you, and so on (all as before) has now donned the yellow robes, and has been admitted into an Order, and dwells restrained, content with mere food and shelter, delighting in solitude?" Would you then say : "Let the man come back ; let him become a slave again, and work for me"?'

36. 'Nay, Lord, rather should we greet him with reverence [61], and rise up from our seat out of deference towards him, and press him to be seated. And we should have robes and a bowl, and a lodging place, and medicine for the sick—all the requisites of a recluse—made ready, and beg him to accept of them. And we should order watch and ward and guard to be kept for him according to the law.'

' But what do you think, O king. That being so, is there, or is there not, some fruit, visible in this world, of the life of a recluse?'

'Certainly, Lord, that is so.'

'This then, O king, is the first kind of the fruit, visible in this world, which I maintained to arise from the life of a recluse.'

37. 'Can you, Lord, show me any other fruit, visible in this world, of the life of a recluse ?'

'I can, O king. And to that end I would fain put a question, &c. [as before, to the end of § 36, the case now put being that of a free man who cultivates his land, a householder, who pays taxes and thus increases the king's wealth, but gives up his little property and his position in his clan, and enters an Order.]'

[62] 39. 'Can you, Lord, show me any other fruit, visible in this world, of the life of a recluse, a fruit higher and sweeter than these ?'

'I can, O king. Give ear therefore, O king, and give good heed, and I will speak.

40. 'Suppose, O king, there appears in the world one who has won the truth, an Arahat, a fully awakened one, abounding in wisdom and goodness, happy, who knows all worlds, unsurpassed as a guide to mortals willing to be led, a teacher for gods and men, a Blessed One, a Buddha. He, by himself, thoroughly knows and sees, as it were, face to face this universe,—including the worlds above of the gods, the Brahmas, and the Mâras, and the world below with its recluses and Brahmans, its princes and peoples,—and having known it, he makes his knowledge known to others. The truth, lovely in its origin, lovely in its progress, lovely in its consummation, doth he proclaim, both in the spirit and in the letter, the higher life doth he make known, in all its fullness and in all its purity [1].

41. 'A householder [2] or one of his children, or a man of inferior birth in any class listens to that truth ; and on hearing it he has faith in the Tathâgata (the one who has found the truth); and when he is possessed of that faith, he considers thus within himself :

'" Full of hindrances is household life, a path for the dust of passion. Free as the air is the life of him who has renounced all worldly things. How difficult is it for the man who dwells at home to live the higher life in all its fullness, in all its purity, in all its bright perfection ! Let me then cut off my hair and beard, let me clothe myself in the orange-coloured robes, and let me go forth from the household life into the homeless state."

'Then, before long, forsaking his portion of wealth, be it great or small, forsaking his circle of relatives, be they many or be they few, he cuts off his hair and beard, he clothes himself in the orange-coloured robes,

---

[1] Buddhaghosa applies these last two adjectives to the truth, not to the life. But it seems more in accord with the next paragraph to refer them to the life.

[2] Gahapati, which Buddhaghosa takes here in the sense of peasant, ryot.

and he goes forth from the household life into the homeless state.

42. 'When he has thus become a recluse he lives self-restrained by that restraint that should be binding on a recluse [1]. Uprightness is his delight, and he sees danger in the least of those things he should avoid. He adopts, and trains himself in, the precepts. He encompasses himself with good deeds in act and word. Pure are his means of livelihood, good is his conduct, guarded the door of his senses. Mindful and self-possessed he is altogether happy.

43. 'And how, O king, is his conduct good?

'In this, O king, that the Bhikshu, putting away the killing of living things, holds aloof from the destruction of life. The cudgel and the sword he has laid aside, and ashamed of roughness, and full of mercy, he dwells compassionate and kind to all creatures that have life.

'This is part of the goodness that he has.

[Here follow the whole of the Sîlas (the paragraphs on minor morality), in the words already translated above in the Brahma-*g*âla Sutta, §§ 8 to 27. Only for 'Gotama the recluse' one should read 'the Bhikshu'; and alter in each case the words of the refrain accordingly.]

[69] 63. 'And then that Bhikshu, O king, being thus master of the minor moralities, sees no danger from any side; that is, so far as concerns his self-restraint in conduct. Just, O king, as a sovereign, duly crowned, whose enemies have been beaten down, sees no danger from any side; [70] that is, so far as enemies are concerned, so is the Bhikshu confident. And endowed with this body of morals, so worthy of honour, he experiences, within himself, a sense of ease without alloy. Thus is it, O king, that the Bhikshu becomes righteous.

64. 'And how, O king, is the Bhikshu guarded as to the doors of his senses [2]?'

---

[1] Pâtimokkha-sa*m*vara-sa*m*vuto. Buddhaghosa, I think, takes this to mean 'restrained according to the rules of the Pâtimokkha.'

[2] On the following important and constantly repeated paragraph compare M. I, 180, 268; K. V. 424-6, 463-4; Mil. 367; Asl. 400, &c.

'When, O king, he sees an object with his eye he is
not entranced in the general appearance or the details
of it[1]. He sets himself to restrain that which might
give occasion for evil states, covetousness and dejection, to flow in over him so long as he dwells unrestrained as to his sense of sight. He keeps watch
upon his faculty of sight, and he attains to mastery
over ·it. And so, in like manner, when he hears a
sound with his ear, or smells an odour with his nose,
or tastes a flavour with his tongue, or feels a touch with
his body, or when he cognises a phenomenon with his
mind he is not entranced in the general appearance or
the details of it. He sets himself to restrain that
which might give occasion for evil states, covetousness
and dejection, to flow in over him so long as he
dwells unrestrained as to his mental (representative)
faculty. He keeps watch upon his representative
faculty, and he attains to mastery over it. And endowed with this self-restraint, so worthy of honour, as
regards the senses, he experiences, within himself, a
sense of ease into which no evil state can enter[2]. Thus
is it, O king, that the Bhikshu becomes guarded as to
the doors of his senses.

65. 'And how, O king, is the Bhikshu mindful and
self-possessed ?

'In this matter, O king, the Bhikshu in going forth
or in coming back keeps clearly before his mind's eye
(all that is wrapt up therein—the immediate object of

---

[1] Na nimittaggâhî hoti nânuvyañganaggâhî. The phrase
nimittam ganhâti means either to seize upon anything as the
object of one's thought to the exclusion of everything else (see, for
instance, Vin. I, 183, and Buddhaghosa's note on it given in the
'Vinaya Texts,' II, 9), or to seize upon the outward sign of anything
so keenly as to recognise what it is the mark of (Vin. III, 17). And
when the object is a person of the other sex this phrase is the idiom
used for our 'falling in love with.' Buddhaghosa gives, as an instance
of the nimitta, the general conclusion that the object seen, heard, &c.,
is a man or woman; of the anuvyañgana, the perception of the
detail that he or she is smiling, talking, &c.

[2] Avyâseka, literally 'with no besprinkling' (of evil, says Buddhaghosa).

the act itself, its ethical significance, whether or not it
is conducive to the high aim set before him, and the
real facts underlying the mere phenomenon of the outward act). And so also in looking forward, or in looking round; in stretching forth his arm, or in drawing it
in again; in eating or drinking, in masticating or
swallowing, in obeying the calls of nature, in going or
standing or sitting, in sleeping or waking, in speaking
or in being still, he keeps himself aware of all it really
means [1]. Thus is it, O king, that the Bhikshu becomes
mindful and self-possessed.

[71] 66. 'And how, O king, is the Bhikshu content?
'In this matter, O king, the Bhikshu is satisfied with
sufficient robes to cherish his body, with sufficient food
to keep his stomach going. Whithersoever he may go
forth, these he takes with him as he goes—just as
a bird with his wings, O king, whithersoever he may
fly, carries his wings with him as he flies. Thus is it,
O king, that the Bhikshu becomes content [2].

---

[1] A small volume might be written on the various expansions
of this text in the Pi/akas. Several whole Dialogues are devoted to
it, and various Suttas in others of the oldest texts. Buddhaghosa
has many pages upon it here, and deals with it also at length in the
Visuddhi Magga and elsewhere. What is above added in brackets
explains the principal points of what is implied, according to the
Pi/akas, in this famous passage,—the Buddhist analogue to St. Paul's:
'Whether therefore ye eat or drink, or whatsoever ye do, do all to
the glory of God' (1 Cor. x. 31).

By the real fact underlying any action is meant that, in the
Buddhist theory, behind the action (going, seeing, &c.) there is no
ego, no actor (goer, seer, &c.), that can be called a 'soul'
(Abbhantare attâ nâma âloketâ vâ viloketâ vâ n' atthi), but
that there is a psychological explanation sufficient, of itself, without
the soul-theory.

[2] 'Consider the fowls of the air,' &c. (Matt. vi. 26).

> No man can call me servant, and I wander—
> So said the Exalted One—
> At will, o'er all the earth, on what I find
> I feel no need of wages, or of gain,
> So let the rain pour down now, if it likes, to-night.
> (Dhaniya Sutta 8.)

And see the context in my 'American Lectures,' p. 168.

67. 'Then, master of this so excellent body of moral precepts, gifted with this so excellent self-restraint as to the senses, endowed with this so excellent mindfulness and self-possession, filled with this so excellent content, he chooses some lonely spot to rest at on his way—in the woods, at the foot of a tree, on a hill side, in a mountain glen, in a rocky cave, in a charnel place, or on a heap of straw in the open field. And returning thither after his round for alms he seats himself, when his meal is done, cross-legged, keeping his body erect, and his intelligence alert, intent.

68. ' Putting away the hankering after the world [1], he remains with a heart that hankers not, and purifies his mind of lusts. Putting away the corruption of the wish to injure, he remains with a heart free from ill-temper, and purifies his mind of malevolence. Putting away torpor of heart and mind [2], keeping his ideas alight [3], mindful and self-possessed, he purifies his mind of weakness and of sloth. Putting away flurry and worry, he remains free from fretfulness, and with heart serene within, he purifies himself of irritability and vexation of spirit. Putting away wavering, he remains as one passed beyond perplexity; and no longer in suspense as to what is good, he purifies his mind of doubt.

69. ' Then just, O king, as when a man, after contracting a loan [4], should set a business on foot, and his

---

[1] Abhiggham loke pahâya. Gogerly renders 'banishes desire from him,' leaving out loke altogether, and rendering abhigghâ in defiance both of the derivation and of the traditional explanation of the word. Even Burnouf (who frequently uses 'desire' for words in the Pâli meaning 'lusts' or 'excitement') has here 'cupidité.'

[2] So Buddhaghosa here (p. 211). But the Dhamma Sangani 1156, 1157 explains it as torpor of mind and body.

[3] Âloka-saññî, literally 'whose ideas are light.' Neumann ('Reden des Gotamo,' I, 434, &c.) translates 'loving the light,' which may be the right connotation. Burnouf has 'being aware of his visual sensation' (de son regard), which is certainly wrong.

[4] Inam âdâya. Neumann has 'oppressed by debt,' but Buddhaghosa (p. 212) says 'taking goods on interest'; and this is confirmed by Gât. IV, 256, V, 436.

business should succeed, and he should not only be able to pay off the old debt he had incurred, but there should be a surplus over to maintain a wife. Then would he realise [72]: "I used to have to carry on my business by getting into debt, but it has gone so well with me that I have paid off what I owed, and have a surplus over to maintain a wife." And he would be of good cheer at that, would be glad of heart at that :—

70. 'Then just, O king, as if a man were a prey to disease, in pain, and very ill, and his food would not digest, and there were no strength left in him; and after a time he were to recover from that disease, and his food should digest, and his strength come back to him; then, when he realised his former and his present state, he would be of good cheer at that, he would be glad of heart at that :—

71. 'Then just, O king, as if a man were bound in a prison house, and after a time he should be set free from his bonds, safe and sound, and without any confiscation of his goods; when he realised his former and his present state, he would be of good cheer at that, he would be glad of heart at that :—

72. 'Then just, O king, as if a man were a slave, not his own master, subject to another, unable to go whither he would; and after a time he should be emancipated from that slavery, become his own master, not subject to others, a free man, free to go whither he would; then, on realising his former and his present state, he would be of good cheer at that, he would be glad of heart at that :—

[73] 73. 'Then just, O king, as if a man, rich and prosperous, were to find himself on a long road, in a desert, where no food was, but much danger; and after a time were to find himself out of the desert, arrived safe, on the borders of his village, in security and peace; then, on realising his former and his present state, he would be of good cheer at that, he would be glad of heart at that :—

74. 'Just so, O king, the Bhikshu, so long as these

five Hindrances are not put away within him looks
upon himself as in debt. diseased, in prison, in slavery,
lost on a desert road. But when these five Hindrances
have been put away within him, he looks upon himself as freed from debt, rid of disease, out of jail, a free
man, and secure;

75. 'And gladness springs up within him on his
realising that, and joy arises to him thus gladdened,
and so rejoicing all his frame becomes at ease, and
being thus at ease he is filled with a sense of peace,
and in that peace his heart is stayed[1].

75 A. 'Then estranged from lusts, aloof from evil
dispositions, he enters into and remains in the First
Rapture—a state of joy and ease born of detachment[2],
reasoning and investigation going on the while.

'His very body does he so pervade. drench, permeate,
and suffuse with the joy and ease born of detachment,
that there is no spot in his whole frame not suffused
therewith.

[74] 76. 'Just, O king, as a skilful bathman or his
apprentice will scatter perfumed soap powder in a metal
basin, and then besprinkling it with water, drop by
drop, will so knead it together that the ball of lather,
taking up the unctuous moisture, is drenched with it,
pervaded by it, permeated by it within and without,
and there is no leakage possible.

---

[1] From the beginning of § 68 the text, though here split up into
paragraphs for the convenience of the reader, is really one long
sentence or paragraph of much eloquence and force in the Pâli; and
the peroration, leading on to the Ghânas, is a favourite passage
recurring M. I, 71; Vin. I, 294; Mil. 84. The five similes are to
be taken, in order, as referring to the Five Hindrances (Nîvaranâ)
given in § 68. The Dhamma Sangani 1152 gives six hindrances,
and M. I. 360–3 gives eight.

[2] Viveka, 'separation'—physically of the body, 'seclusion'; intellectually, of the objects of thought, 'discrimination'; ethically, of the
heart, 'being separate from the world.' We have no word in English
suggesting these three. all of which are implied. The stress is upon
separation from the world, taking 'world' in the sense of all the
hindrances to spiritual progress, and especially of the five chief
Hindrances (Nîvaranâ) just above set out. Buddhaghosa has
nothing here, but compare Asl. 166.

'This, O king, is an immediate fruit of the life of
a recluse, visible in this world, higher and sweeter than
the last.

77. 'Then further, O king, the Bhikshu suppressing
all reasoning and investigation enters into and abides
in the Second *Gh*âna, a state of joy and ease, born of
the serenity of concentration, when no reasoning or
investigation goes on,—a state of elevation[1] of mind,
a tranquillisation of the heart within.

'And his very body does he so pervade, drench,
permeate, and suffuse with the joy and ease born of
concentration, that there is no spot in his whole frame
not suffused therewith.

78. 'Just, O king, as if there were a deep pool, with
water welling up into it from a spring beneath, and
with no inlet from the east or west, from the north or
south, and the god should not from time to time send
down showers of rain upon it.   Still the current of cool
waters rising up from that spring would pervade, fill,
permeate, and suffuse the pool with cool waters, and
there would be no part or portion of the pool unsuffused
therewith.

[75] 'This, O king, is an immediate fruit of the life
of a recluse, visible in this world, and higher and
sweeter than the last.

79. 'Then further, O king, the Bhikshu, holding
aloof from joy, becomes equable[2]; and mindful and
self-possessed he experiences in his body that ease
which the Arahats talk of when they say: "The man
serene and self-possessed is well at ease," and so he
enters into and abides in the Third *Gh*âna.

'And his very body does he so pervade, drench,

---

[1] Ekodibhâva.   Compare Asl. 169, Senart in Mahâvastu I, 554,
and the notes in J. P. T. S., 1884, p. 32 foll.

[2] Upekhako, literally 'looking on,' that is, looking on rival
mental states with equal mind.   Imperturbable, impartial, tolerant,
unsusceptible, stoical, composed, are all possible renderings, and all
unsatisfactory.   The ten kinds of Upekkhâ, 'equanimity,' translated
into English from Sinhalese by Spence Hardy (Manual, p. 505), can
now be corrected from the Pâli at Asl. 172.

H

permeate, and suffuse with that ease that has no joy
with it, that there is no spot in his whole frame not
suffused therewith.

80. 'Just, O king, as when in a lotus tank the
several lotus flowers, red or white or blue, born in the
water, grown up in the water, not rising up above
the surface of the water, drawing up nourishment from
the depths of the water, are so pervaded, drenched,
permeated, and suffused from their very tips down to
their roots with the cool moisture thereof, that there
is no spot in the whole plant, whether of the red lotus,
or of the white, or of the blue, not suffused therewith.

'This, O king, is an immediate fruit of the life of
a recluse, visible in this world, and higher and sweeter
than the last.

81. 'Then further, O king, the Bhikshu, by the
putting away alike of ease and of pain, by the passing
away alike of any elation, any dejection, he had
previously felt, enters into and abides in the Fourth
Ghâna, a state of pure self-possession and equanimity,
without pain and without ease.

[76] 'And he sits there so suffusing even his body
with that sense of purification, of translucence, of heart,
that there is no spot in his whole frame not suffused
therewith.

82. 'Just, O king, as if a man were sitting so wrapt
from head to foot in a clean white robe, that there were
no spot in his whole frame not in contact with the clean
white robe—just so, O king, does the Bhikshu sit there,
so suffusing even his body with that sense of purification, of translucence, of heart, that there is no spot in
his whole frame not suffused therewith.

'This, O king, is an immediate fruit of the life of
a recluse, and higher and sweeter than the last.

83. 'With his heart thus serene, made pure, translucent, cultured, devoid of evil, supple, ready to act,
firm, and imperturbable, he applies and bends down
his mind to that insight that comes from knowledge.
He grasps the fact: "This body of mine has form, it
is built up of the four elements, it springs from father

and mother, it is continually renewed by so much boiled
rice and juicy foods, its very nature is impermanence,
it is subject to erasion, abrasion, dissolution, and disintegration[1]; and therein is this consciousness[2] of
mine, too, bound up, on that does it depend."

84. 'Just, O king, as if there were a Veluriya gem,
bright, of the purest water, with eight facets, excellently
cut, clear, translucent, without a flaw, excellent in every
way. And through it a string, blue, or orange-coloured,
or red, or white, or yellow should be threaded. If
a man, who had eyes to see, were to take it into his
hand, he would clearly perceive how the one is bound
up with the other[3].

[77] 'This, O king, is an immediate fruit of the
life of a recluse, visible in this world, and higher and
sweeter than the last.

85. 'With his heart thus serene, made pure, translucent, cultured, devoid of evil, supple, ready to act,
firm, and imperturbable, he applies and bends down
his mind to the calling up of a mental image. He
calls up from this body another body, having form,

---

[1] This is a favourite description of the body. (See M. I, 500;
II, 17; S. IV, 83; Gât. I, 146, &c.) The words for erasion, abrasion,
are cunningly chosen (ukkhâdana, parimaddana). They are also
familiar technical terms of the Indian shampooer, and are so used
above (p. 7, § 16 of the text). The double meaning must have been
clearly present to the Indian hearer, and the words are, therefore,
really untranslatable.

[2] Viññâna. 'The five senses, sensations arising from objects, and
all emotions and intellectual processes,' says Buddhaghosa (p. 221).

[3] In spite of this and similar passages the adherents of the soul
theory (having nothing else to fasten on) were apt to fasten on to
the Buddhist Viññâna as a possible point of reconciliation with
their own theory. Even an admirer of the Buddha (one Sâti, a
member of the Order) went so far as to tell the Buddha himself
that he must, as he admitted transmigration, have meant that the
Viññâna did not really depend upon, was not really bound up with,
the body, but that it formed the link in transmigration. In perhaps the
most earnest and emphatic of all the Dialogues (M. I, 256 foll.), the
Buddha meets and refutes at length this erroneous representation of his
view. But it still survives. I know two living writers on Buddhism
who (in blissful ignorance of the Dialogue in question) still fasten upon
Buddha the opinion he so expressly refused to accept.

made of mind, having all (his own body's) limbs and
parts, not deprived of any organ [1].

86. 'Just, O king, as if a man were to pull out
a reed from its sheath. He would know: "This is
the reed, this the sheath. The reed is one thing, the
sheath another. It is from the sheath that the reed
has been drawn forth [2]." And similarly were he to take
a snake out of its slough, or draw a sword from its
scabbard [3].

'This, O king, is an immediate fruit of the life of
a recluse, visible in this life, and higher and sweeter
than the last.

87. 'With his heart thus serene, made pure, translucent, cultured, devoid of evil, supple, ready to act,
firm and imperturbable, he applies and bends down his
mind to the modes of the Wondrous Gift [4]. [78] He
enjoys the Wondrous Gift in its various modes—
being one he becomes many, or having become many
becomes one again; he becomes visible or invisible;
he goes, feeling no obstruction, to the further side
of a wall or rampart or hill, as if through air; he
penetrates up and down through solid ground, as if
through water; he walks on water without breaking

---

[1] Buddhaghosa explains that, if the Bhikshu have his ears un-
pierced, so will the image, and so on.

[2] This old simile occurs already in the Satapatha-Brâhmana IV,
3, 3, 16.

[3] The point is the similarity. Buddhaghosa explains that the
Karanda is not a basket (as Burnouf renders it), but the skin which
the snake sloughs off; and that the scabbard is like the sword,
whatever the sword's shape. He adds that of course a man could
not take a snake out of its slough with his hand. He is supposed
in the simile to do so in imagination.

[4] Iddhi, literally 'well-being, prosperity.' The four Iddhis of a
king are personal beauty, length of life, strong health, and popularity
(M. Sud. Sutta in my 'Buddhist Suttas,' pp. 259–261). The Iddhis
of Gotama when at home, as a boy, were the possession of a beautiful
garden, soft clothing, comfortable lodging, pleasant music, and good
food (A. I, 145). Worldly Iddhi is distinguished from spiritual
at A. I, 93. Buddhaghosa gives nine sorts of Iddhi, mostly intellectual, at Asl. 91, and compare 237. There are no examples in the
Pitakas of concrete instances of any of these except the last; but see
S. IV, 289, 290; A. III, 340, 341; M. P. S. 43.

through, as if on solid ground ; he travels cross-legged
in the sky, like the birds on wing ; even the Moon and
the Sun, so potent, so mighty though they be, does he
touch and feel with his hand ; he reaches in the body
even up to the heaven of Brahmâ.

88. ' Just, O king, as a clever potter or his apprentice
could make, could succeed in getting out of properly
prepared clay any shape of vessel he wanted to have—
or an ivory carver out of ivory, or a goldsmith out of
gold.

[79] ' This, O king, is·an immediate fruit of the life
of a recluse, and higher and sweeter than the last.

89. ' With his heart thus serene, made pure, translucent, cultured, devoid of evil, supple, ready to act,
firm and imperturbable, he applies and bends down his
mind to the Heavenly Ear. With that clear Heavenly
Ear surpassing the ear of men he hears sounds both
human and celestial, whether far or near.

90. ' Just, O king, as if a man were on the high road
and were to hear the sound of a kettledrum or a tabor
or the sound of chank horns and small drums he would
know: " This is the sound of a kettledrum, this is the
sound of a tabor, this of chank horns, and of drums [1]."

' This, O king, is an immediate fruit of the life of a
recluse, visible in this life, and higher and sweeter than
the last.

91. ' With his heart thus serene (&c. as before), he
directs and bends down his mind to the knowledge
which penetrates the heart. Penetrating with his own
heart the hearts of other beings, of other men, he
knows them. He discerns—

The passionate mind to be passionate, and the calm
mind calm ;

[80] The angry mind to be angry, and the peaceful
mind peaceful ;

The dull mind to be dull, and the alert mind alert ;

---

[1] The point of the comparison, says Buddhaghosa (223), is that
if he is in trouble and has lost his way he might be in doubt. But
if calm and secure he can tell the difference.

The attentive mind to be attentive, and the wandering mind wandering;

The broad mind to be broad, and the narrow mind narrow;

The mean mind to be mean, and the lofty mind lofty [1];

The stedfast mind to be stedfast, and the wavering mind to be wavering;

The free mind to be free, and the enslaved mind enslaved.

92. 'Just, O king, as a woman or a man or a lad, young and smart, on considering attentively the image of his own face in a bright and brilliant mirror or in a vessel of clear water would, if it had a mole on it, know that it had, and if not, would know it had not.

[81] 'This, O king, is an immediate fruit of the life of a recluse, visible in this world, and higher and sweeter than the last.

93. 'With his heart thus serene (&c. as before), he directs and bends down his mind to the knowledge of the memory of his previous temporary states. He recalls to mind his various temporary states in days gone by—one birth, or two or three or four or five births, or ten or twenty or thirty or forty or fifty or a hundred or a thousand or a hundred thousand births, through many an aeon of dissolution, many an aeon of evolution, many an aeon of both dissolution and evolution [2]. " In such a place such was my name, such my family, such my caste [3], such my food, such my experience of discomfort or of ease, and such the limits of my life. When I passed away from that state, I took form again in such a place. There I had

---

[1] Sa-uttara and anuttara. Unless the interpretation given in the Dhamma Saṅgaṇi 1292, 1293, 1596, 1597 ('occupied with rebirth in heaven, and occupied with Arahatship') reveals a change in the use of terms, the evil disposition, in this case only, is put first.

[2] This is based on the Indian theory of the periodic destruction and renovation of the universe, each of which takes countless years to accomplish.

[3] Vaṇṇa, 'colour.'

such and such a name and family and caste and food
and experience of discomfort or of ease, such was the
limit of my life. When I passed away from that state
I took form again here"—thus does he call to mind
his temporary state in days gone by in all their details,
and in all their modes.

94. 'Just, O king, as if a man were to go from his
own to another village, and from that one to another,
and from that one should return home. Then he
would know: "From my own village I came to that
other one. There I stood in such and such a way,
sat thus, spake thus, and held my peace thus. Thence
I came to that other village; and there I stood in
such and such a way, sat thus, spake thus, and held
my peace thus. And now, from that other village,
I have returned back again home [1]."

[82] 'This, O king, is an immediate fruit of the life
of a recluse. Visible in this world, and higher and
sweeter than the last.

95. 'With his heart thus serene (&c. as before), he
directs and bends down his mind to the knowledge of
the fall and rise of beings. With the pure Heavenly
Eye [2], surpassing that of men, he sees beings as they
pass away from one form of existence and take shape
in another; he recognises the mean and the noble, the
well favoured and the ill favoured, the happy and the
wretched, passing away according to their deeds:
"Such and such beings, brethren, evil in act and word
and thought, revilers of the noble ones, holding to
wrong views, acquiring for themselves that Karma
which results from wrong views, they, on the dissolution
of the body, after death, are reborn in some unhappy
state of suffering or woe. But such and such beings,
my brethren, well doers in act and word and thought,
not revilers of the noble ones, holding to right views,

---

[1] The three villages correspond to the three stages of being, the
three Bhûmis,—the world of lust, the world of form, and the
formless worlds (the Kâma, Rûpa, and Arûpa Lokas).

[2] Dibba-*k*akkhu. See the note below on § 102 at the end of
this Sutta.

acquiring for themselves that Karma that results from right views, they, on the dissolution of the body, after death, are reborn in some happy state in heaven." Thus with the pure Heavenly Eye, surpassing that of men, [83] he sees beings as they pass away from one state of existence, and take form in another ; he recognises the mean and the noble, the well favoured and the ill favoured, the happy and the wretched, passing away according to their deeds [1].

96. 'Just, O king, as if there were a house with an upper terrace on it in the midst of a place where four roads meet, and a man standing thereon, and with eyes to see, should watch men entering a house, and coming forth out of it, and walking hither and thither along the street [2], and seated in the square in the midst. Then he would know : "Those men are entering a house, and those are leaving it, and those are walking to and fro in the street, and those are seated in the square in the midst."

'This, O king, is an immediate fruit of the life of a recluse, visible in this world, and higher and sweeter than the last.

97. 'With his heart thus serene (&c. as before), he directs and bends down his mind to the knowledge of the destruction of the Deadly Floods [3]. He knows

---

[1] This paragraph forms the subject of the discussion in the Kathâ Vatthu III, 9 (p. 250). The mere knowledge of the general fact of the action of Karma is there distinguished from the Dibba-*k*akkhu, the Heavenly Eye; and the instance of Sâriputta is quoted, who had that knowledge, but not the Heavenly Eye. As he was an Arahat it follows that the possession of the Heavenly Eye was not a necessary consequence of Arahatship. Buddhaghosa adds (p. 224) that the sphere of vision of the Heavenly Eye did not extend to the Formless Worlds. On the Dhamma-*k*akkhu, 'the Eye for the Truth,' see below, p. 110, § 21 of the text.

[2] Vîtisa*ñk*arante is Buddhaghosa's reading. The Siamese has Vithi*m*. Compare M. I, 279.

[3] Âsavas, Deadly Floods, another untranslatable term. Neumann has Illusion (Wahn); Burnouf has defilement (souillures). They are sometimes the three here mentioned (M. I, 23, 155; A. I, 167; S. IV, 256, &c.); but speculation, theorising (Di*tth*i) is added as a fourth in the M. P. S. and elsewhere. Unfortunately,

as it really is: "This is pain." [84] He knows as it really is: "This is the origin of pain." He knows as it really is: "This is the cessation of pain." He knows as it really is: "This is the Path that leads to the cessation of pain." He knows as they really are: "These are the Deadly Floods." He knows as it really is: "This is the origin of the Deadly Floods." He knows as it really is: "This is the cessation of the Deadly Floods." He knows as it really is: "This is the Path that leads to the cessation of the Deadly Floods." To him, thus knowing, thus seeing, the heart is set free from the Deadly Taint of Lusts[1], is set free from the Deadly Taint of Becomings[2], is set free from the Deadly Taint of Ignorance[3]. In him, thus set free, there arises the knowledge of his emancipation, and he knows: "Rebirth has been destroyed. The higher life has been fulfilled. What had to be done has been accomplished. After this present life there will be no beyond!"

98. 'Just, O king, as if in a mountain fastness there were a pool of water, clear, translucent, and serene; and a man, standing on the bank, and with eyes to see, should perceive the oysters and the shells, the gravel and the pebbles and the shoals of fish, as they move about or lie within it: he would know: "This

---

the word has not been yet found in its concrete, primary, sense; unless indeed Buddhaghosa's statement (at Asl. 48) that well-seasoned spirituous liquors were called âsavâ be taken literally. It is therefore impossible to be sure what is the simile that underlies the use of the word in its secondary, ethical sense. Perhaps after all it is the idea of overwhelming intoxication, and not of flood or taint or ooze, that we ought to consider.

Subhûti in quoting the above passage from Buddhaghosa (in the Abhidhâna Padîpikâ Sûki, p. 43) reads părivas° throughout for pârivâs°.

[1] Kamâsavâ, with special reference to the taint of hankering after a future life in the sensuous plane (Kâma Loka); that is, in the world.

[2] Bhavâsavâ, with special reference to the taint of hankering after a future life in the plane of form and the formless plane (the Rûpa and Arûpa Lokas); that is, in heaven.

[3] Aviggâsavâ, with special reference to ignorance of the Four Great Truths, just above summarised.

pool is clear, transparent, and serene, and there within it are the oysters and the shells, and the sand and gravel, and the shoals of fish are moving about or lying still[1]."

[85] 'This, O king, is an immediate fruit of the life of a recluse, visible in this world, and higher and sweeter than the last. And there is no fruit of the life of a recluse, visible in this world, that is higher and sweeter than this[2].'

99. And when he had thus spoken, Agâtasattu the king said to the Blessed One : 'Most excellent, Lord, most excellent! Just as if a man were to set up that which has been thrown down, or were to reveal that which is hidden away, or were to point out the right road to him who has gone astray, or were to bring a lamp into the darkness so that those who have eyes could see external forms—just even so, Lord, has the truth been made known to me, in many a figure, by the Blessed One. And now I betake myself, Lord, to the Blessed One as my refuge, to the Truth, and to the Order. May the Blessed One accept me as a disciple, as one who, from this day forth, as long as life endures, has taken his refuge in them. Sin has overcome me, Lord, weak and foolish and wrong that I am, in that, for the sake of sovranty, I put to death my father, that righteous man, that righteous king! May the Blessed One accept it of me, Lord, that do so acknowledge it as a sin, to the end that in future I may restrain myself.'

100. 'Verily, O king, it was sin that overcame you in acting thus. But inasmuch as you look upon it as sin, and confess it according to what is right, we accept your confession as to that. For that, O king, is custom in the discipline of the noble ones[3], that whosoever

---

[1] The simile recurs M. I, 279; A. I, 9. Compare for the words sippi-sambuka Gât. V, 197; A. III, 395; Trenckner, 'Pali Miscellany,' p. 60.

[2] Because, as Buddhaghosa points out, this is really Arahatship, Nirvâna; and it was to this, to Arahatship, that all the rest led up.

[3] Ariyânam. That is, either of previous Buddhas, or perhaps of the Arahats.

looks upon his fault as a fault, and rightfully confesses it, shall attain to self-restraint in future.'

101. When he had thus spoken, Agâtasattu the king said to the Blessed One: 'Now, Lord, we would fain go. We are busy, and there is much to do.'

'Do, O king, whatever seemeth to thee fit.'

Then Agâtasattu the king, pleased and delighted with the words of the Blessed One, arose from his seat, and bowed to the Blessed One, and keeping him on the right hand as he passed him, departed thence.

102. Now the Blessed One, not long after Agâtasattu the king had gone, addressed the brethren, and said: 'This king, brethren, was deeply affected, he was touched in heart. If, brethren, the king had not put his father to death, that righteous man, and righteous king, then would the clear and spotless eye for the truth have arisen in him, even as he sat there [1].'

Thus spake the Blessed One. The brethren were pleased and delighted at his words.

Here ends the Discourse on the Fruits of the Life of a Recluse.

Sâmañña-phala Sutta is ended.

---

[1] The Dhamma-kakkhu (Eye for the Truth) is a technical term for conversion, for entering on the Path that ends in Arahatship. It is higher than the Heavenly Eye (dibba-kakkhu, above, p. 82 of the text, § 95) which sees other people's previous births, and below the Eye of Wisdom (paññâ-kakkhu) which is the wisdom of the Arahat (Itivuttaka, p. 52, § 61).

INTRODUCTION

AMBA*TTH*A SUTTA.

THIS is one of several Suttas (mentioned in the notes to the celebrated verse quoted at the end of Chapter I) which deal with the subject of caste.

It is sufficiently evident from the comparative frequency of the discussions on the matter of Brahman pretensions that this was a burning question at the time when the Dialogues were composed. No other social problem is referred to so often; and Brahmans would not be so often represented as expressing astonishment or indignation at the position taken up regarding it by the early Buddhists unless there had really been a serious difference on the subject between the two schools. But the difference, though real, has been gravely misunderstood.

Some writers on Buddhism do not hesitate to ascribe to Gotama the rôle of a successful political reformer, by representing him as having fought for the poor and despised against the rich and privileged classes, and as having gone far to abolish caste. Other writers gird at the Buddha because most of the leaders of this Order were drawn from the ranks of the respectable and the well-to-do, with an education in keeping with their social position; and disparage him for neglecting the humble and the wretched, for not using his influence to abolish, or to mitigate, the harshness of caste rules.

Both views are equally unhistorical. It is well known that the population of India is now divided into a number of sections (we call them 'castes'), the members of which are debarred from the right of intermarriage (from the *connubium*) with those outside their caste, and also, but in constantly varying degrees, from the right of eating together (of *commensality*) with the members of other sections. Each such 'caste' has also a council or committee by which it is governed, and which settles all disputes regarding the caste.

The disastrous effects, from the ethical, social, and political points of view, of these restrictions, and of caste as a whole, have been often grossly exaggerated, and the benefits of the system ignored. And we are entirely unwarranted in supposing the system, as it now exists, to have been in existence also at the time when Buddhism arose in the valley of the Ganges. Our knowledge of the actual facts of caste, even as it now exists, is still confused and inaccurate. The theories put forward to explain the facts are loose and irreconcilable. And an accurate statement of the corresponding facts, if any, at the time of Gotama, has yet to be drawn up.

We have long known that the *connubium* was the cause of a long and determined struggle between the patricians and the plebeians in Rome. Evidence has been yearly accumulating on the existence of restrictions as to intermarriage, and as to the right of eating together, among other Aryan tribes— Greeks, Germans, Russians, and so on. Even without the fact of the existence, now, of such restrictions among the modern successors of the ancient Aryans in India, it would have been almost certain that they also were addicted to similar customs. It is certain that the notion of such usages was familiar enough to some at least of the tribes that preceded the Aryans in India. It is quite a mistake to look upon all these tribes as far below the Aryans in culture. Both the Kolarians and the Dravidians were probably quite the equals of the Aryans in social organisation. And the Aryans probably adopted much from them, especially in matters relating to land tenure, village community, government, taxation, and so on. Their custom of endogamy and exogamy, their ideas as to purity and the reverse, may have differed from those of the Aryans, but were similar in kind. Rules of endogamy and exogamy ; privileges, restricted to certain classes, of eating together, are not only Indian or Aryan, but world-wide phenomena. Both the spirit, and to a large degree the actual details, of modern Indian caste usages, are identical with these ancient, and no doubt universal, customs. It is in them that we have *the key to the origin of caste*.

At any moment in the history of a nation such customs seem, to a superficial observer, to be fixed and immutable. As a matter of fact they are never quite the same in successive centuries, or even generations. A man's visible frame, though no change is at any moment perceptible, is really never the same for two consecutive moments, and the result of constant minute variations becomes clear after the lapse of time. The numerous and complicated details which we sum up under the convenient (but often misleading) single name of caste are solely dependent for their sanction on public opinion. That opinion seems stable. But it is always tending to vary as to the degree of importance attached to some particular one of the details, as to the size and complexity of the particular groups in which each detail ought to be observed.

This last statement may be illustrated by the case of the Chaliyas. When the Dutch started cinnamon cultivation in Ceylon on a large scale, they wanted labourers. The peasantry, who belonged almost exclusively to one caste, the Goigamas, regarded it as unworthy of a free man to work for hire. Some of them, however, in the struggle of motives, found the pressure of poverty too strong for them, and accepted service as coolies. The others, thinking this bad form, became averse to giving their daughters in marriage to such coolies. These feelings were naturally stronger at first among the Goigamas of good social position, and it became a mark of superiority not to have a relative married to a worker in the cinnamon gardens. And such workers were called Chaliyas. By the time that the families of Chaliyas were numerous enough to afford mates for the male or female coolies, the Chaliyas found it impossible to find wives elsewhere. And thus, under the very eyes of Europeans, the size of one group had been diminished by the very considerable number of persons engaged in a new and despised trade. In other words, what we call a new caste had arisen, the caste of the Chaliyas. When the English took Ceylon they gave up the government cultivation of cinnamon. The gardens were carried on, in ever lessening numbers, by private individuals. The number of the Chaliyas consequently declined. Numbers of them, as they gradually returned to ordinary peasant work, became reabsorbed among the Goigamas. This was an instance of a change precisely contrary to that which happened when the caste gradually arose. But all did not succeed in returning ; and there are, therefore, still some Chaliyas left. And the caste survives though the members of it are now no longer exclusively, or even largely, employed in cinnamon gardens ; and many of them have become wealthy and honoured.

What had happened in this case was, not two separate and striking revolutions, but a long series of slight changes in public opinion, no doubt quite imperceptible at the time to the very people among whom the changes were taking place. And after all the changes were not so very slow. Three or four generations were enough to cover the whole series with the consequent results. Who can doubt but that the history of ancient India, if we had only access to the necessary evidence, would be found to cover, in its two thousand five hundred years, and through its wide territory, a constant succession of similar variations ; and that similar variations are recurring still to-day.

Owing to the fact that the particular set of people who worked their way to the top based its claims on religious grounds, not on political power or wealth, the system has, no doubt, lasted longer in India than in Europe. But public opinion still insists in considerable circles, even in Europe, on restrictions of a more or less defined kind, both as to marriage and as to eating together. And in India the problem still remains to trace in the literature the gradual growth of the system—the gradual formation of new sections among the people, the gradual extension of the institution to the families of people engaged in certain trades, belonging to the same sect or tribe, tracing their ancestry (whether rightly or wrongly) to the same source. All these factors, and others besides, are real factors. But *they are phases of the extension and growth*, not explanations of the origin, of the system.

There is no evidence to show that at the time when the conversations recorded in the Dialogues took place (that is to say, in the sixth century B.C.) there was any substantial difference, as regards the barriers in question, between the peoples dwelling in the valley of the Ganges and their contemporaries dwelling on the shores of the Mediterranean. The point of greatest weight in the establishment of the great difference in the subsequent development—the supremacy, in India, of the priests—was still being hotly debated. And all our evidence tends to show that at least in the wide extent of territory covered by the Pi/akas—countries close upon a hundred thousand square miles in area—the struggle was being decided rather against the Brahmans than for them. There were distinctions as to marriage; endogamous and exogamous groups. In a few instances, all among the lower classes of the people, these amounted, probably, to what would now be called caste-divisions. But of castes, in the modern sense, among the preponderating majority there is little or no conclusive evidence.

There was a common phrase current among the people, which divided all the world into four va*nn*â (colours or complexions)—the nobles, the priests. the other Aryan people, and the non-Aryan *S*ûdras (Khattiyâ, Brâhma*n*â, Vessâ, and Suddâ). The priests put themselves first, and had a theological legend in support of their contention. But it is clear from the Pi/akas that this was not admitted by the nobles. And it is also clear that no one of these divisions was a caste. There was neither *connubium* nor commensality between all the members of one va*nn*a, nor was there a governing council for each. The fourth was distinguished from the others by race. The remaining three were distinguished from each other by social position. And though in a general rough way the classification corresponded to the actual facts of life, there were insensible gradations within the four classes, and the boundary between them was both variable and undefined.

And this enumeration of the populace was not complete. Outside these classes there were others, resembling in many points the modern low castes, and always when mentioned in the Pi*t*akas following after the above four. Thus in Aṅguttara I, 162 [1], the argument is that just as there is no real difference in oxen, in spite of the fact that they can be arranged in classes by difference of colour (va*nn*a), and the strong, active, well-trained ox is selected by preference, without regard to his colour (va*nn*a); so also, when presenting gifts, the man of strong, active, well-trained mind should be selected as donee —without reference to the fact of his belonging to any one of the four classes of society (va*nn*â), or of his being a *K*a*nd*âla or a Pukkusa. It is plain that this passage distinguishes the last two from the four va*nn*â and therefore from the *S*ûdras.

Other old texts [2] insert between these two three further names—the Ve*n*as, the Nesâdas, and the Rathakâras, that is to say, the workers in rushes [3], bird-catchers, and cart-makers. By these are meant aboriginal tribesmen who were *hereditary* craftsmen in these three crafts; for they are called hîna-gâtiyo, low tribes. They no doubt formed castes in the modern sense, though we have no information as to their marriage customs. They are represented in the *G*âtaka book as living in villages of their own, outside the towns in which ordinary people dwelt, and formed evidently a numerically insignificant portion of the populace.

In the last passage quoted in the previous note there are mentioned, as distinct from these low tribes (the hîna-gâtiyo), certain low occupations (hîna-sippâni)—mat-makers, potters, weavers, leather-workers, and barbers. As they are excluded from the list of those distinguished by birth (*g*âti), it is implied that there was no hard and fast line, determined by birth, for those who gained their living by these trades. There would be a natural tendency for the son to follow the father's craft [4];

---

[1] Compare Petavatthu II, 6, 12.

[2] Assalâyana (No. 93 in the Ma*ggh*ima); Aṅguttara II, 85=P. P. IV, 19; Sa*m*yutta I, 93; Vinaya IV, 6–10, &c.

[3] Sometimes explained as carpenters, sometimes as basket-makers, sometimes as makers of sunshades.

[4] Further exemplified by the number of people described as keva*tt*a-putto, assâroha-putto, na*t*a-putto, sûda-putto, &c.

centuries afterwards they had become castes, and they were then on the border line. But they were not castes as yet.

Besides the above, who were all freemen, there were also slaves. We only hear of them quite occasionally, as domestic servants, in the houses of the very rich. Individuals had been captured in predatory raids, and reduced to slavery (Gât. IV, 220); or had been deprived of their freedom as a judicial punishment (Gât. I, 200); or had submitted to slavery of their own accord ('Vinaya Texts,' I, 191 ; Sum. I, 168). Children born to such slaves were also slaves, and the emancipation of slaves is often referred to. But we hear nothing of such later developments of slavery as rendered the Roman *latifundia*, or the plantations of some Christian slave-owners, scenes of misery and oppression. For the most part the slaves were household servants, and not badly treated, and their numbers seem to have been insignificant [1].

What we find then, in the Buddha's time, is caste in the making. The great mass of the people were distinguished quite roughly into four classes—social strata—of which the boundary lines were vague and uncertain. At the one end of the scale certain outlying tribes, and certain hereditary crafts of a dirty or despised kind, were already, probably, castes. At the other end of the scale Brahmans by birth (not necessarily sacrificial priests, for they followed all sorts of occupations) were putting forward caste claims that were not yet universally admitted. There were social customs about the details of which we know very little (and dependent probably, more exactly upon the gotta rather than upon the gâti), which raised barriers, not seldom broken through, as to intermarriage of people admittedly belonging to the same va*nn*a, and *a fortiori* of others. And there was a social code, based on the idea of impurity, which prevented familiar intercourse (such as commensality) between people of different rank ; and rendered disgraceful the use of certain foods. We find, however, no usages which cannot be amply paralleled in the history of other peoples throughout the world in similar stages of social evolution. The key-stone of the arch of the peculiarly Indian caste organisation—the absolute supremacy of the Brahmans —had not yet been put in position, had not, in fact, been yet made ready. *The caste-system, in any proper or exact use of the term, did not exist.*

In the face of this set of circumstances Gotama took up

---

[1] See also A. I, 145, 206; II, 67 ; III, 36, 132, 217 ; Vin. IV, 224 ; D. I, 5, 60, 72, 93, 141 (translated above); Gât. I, 226, 385; III, 343, 437; Dhp. Cy. 238, &c.

I

a distinct position.   It meets us, it is true, in two phases; but it forms one consistent and logical whole.

In the first place, as regards his own Order, over which alone he had complete control, he ignores completely and absolutely all advantages or disadvantages arising from birth, occupation, and social status, and sweeps away all barriers and disabilities arising from the arbitrary rules of mere ceremonial or social impurity.

One of the most distinguished members of his Order, the very one of them who was referred to as the chief authority, after Gotama himself, on the rules of the Order, was Upâli, who had formerly been a barber, one of the despised occupations. So Sunita, one of the brethren whose verses are chosen for insertion in the Thera Gâthâ, was a Pukkusa, one of the low tribes. Sâti, the propounder of a deadly heresy, was of the sons of the fisherfolk, afterwards a low caste, and even then an occupation, on account of its cruelty, particularly abhorred. Nanda was a cowherd. The two Panthakas were born out of wedlock, to a girl of good family through intercourse with a slave (so that by the rule laid down in Manu 31, they were actually outcasts). Kâpâ was the daughter of a deer-stalker, Punnâ and Punnikâ had been slave girls. Sumangalamâtâ was daughter and wife to workers in rushes, and Subhâ was the daughter of a smith.   More instances could doubtless be quoted already, and others will become known when more texts are published.

It does not show much historical insight to sneer at the numbers as small, and to suggest that the supposed enlightenment or liberality was mere pretence.   The facts speak for themselves ; and the percentage of low-born members of the Order was probably in fair proportion to the percentage of persons belonging to the despised *gâtis* and *sippas* as compared with the rest of the population.   Thus of the Therîs mentioned in the Therî Gâthâ we know the social position of sixty, of whom five are mentioned above—that is, $8\frac{1}{2}$ per cent. of the whole number were base-born.   It is most likely that this is just about the proportion which persons in similar social rank bore to the rest of the population.

Whether the Buddhist Order differed in this respect from the other similar communities which are mentioned in the Buddhist books as having already existed when the Buddhist Order was founded, is still matter of controversy.   The Buddhist books are mostly silent on the matter.   But that very silence is valuable evidence.   It is scarcely likely that, if there had been much difference, there should be no allusion to it in the Pitakas.   And the few passages in print confirm this.   We have seen how in the Sâmañña-phala Sutta (above, p. 77) it is taken for granted that a slave could join an Order (that is any order, not the Buddhist). And in the Aggañña Sutta of the Dîgha, and the Madhura Sutta of the Magghima, there is express mention of Sûdras becoming Samaṇas, as if it were a recognised and common occurrence, long before the time of the rise of Buddhism. So in the Gâtaka (III, 381) we hear of a potter, and at IV, 392 of a Kandâla, who become Samaṇas (not Buddhist Samaṇas)[1].

On the other hand, it is just possible that in these passages the custom afterwards followed in the Buddhist Order is simply put back to earlier times, and is an anachronism. The low-born, however earnest in their search after truth, were no doubt excluded from any community of hermits or religious recluses in which Brahmans had the upper hand. But all the twice-born (the Dvigas, that is the Khattiyas, Brâhmaṇas, and Vessas) were certainly justified, by public opinion, in becoming Samaṇas. To what extent the Sûdras, and the tribes below the Sûdras, were accorded, in communities other than the Buddhist, a similar privilege, is at present doubtful. But the Buddha certainly adopted, and probably extended, the most rational view current at the time.

There is one point, however, in which he seems to have restricted (and for a valid reason) the existing custom. It is impossible to avoid the inference from the passage just referred to (in the Sâmañña-phala, above, p. 77), that the existing orders, or most of them, admitted slaves to their ranks. Now among a number of rules laid down to regulate admission to the Buddhist Order, in such wise that the existing rights of third parties should not be encroached upon, there is a rule (translated in 'Vinaya Texts,' S. B. E., I, 199) that no runaway slave shall be admitted. And in the form of words to be used at the chapter held for admitting new members, one of the questions asked of the candidate is: ' Are you a freeman[2]?' Whenever slaves were admitted to the Order, they must have previously obtained the consent of their masters, and also, I think, have been emancipated.

Secondly, as regards all such matters as we may now fairly call 'questions of caste' outside the Order, the Buddha adopted the only course then open to any man of sense ; that is to say, he strove to influence that public opinion, on which the observances depend, by a constant inculcation of reasonable views. Thus in the Âmagandha Sutta[3] of the Sutta

---

[1] See Fick, 'Sociale Gliederung im nordöstlichen Indien,' pp. 50, 51.
[2] 'Vinaya Texts,' I, 230.
[3] Translated by Fausböll, S. B. E., pp. 40–42.

Nipâta (certainly one of the very oldest of our documents) it is laid down, in eloquent words, that defilement does not come from eating this or that, prepared or given by this or that person, but from evil deeds and words and thoughts.

This is a particularly interesting passage, being one of the few in which sayings of previous Buddhas are recorded. In other words the Buddhists put forward this view as having been enunciated long ago—with the intended implication that it was a self-evident proposition which was common ground to the wise. No originality, no special insight, is claimed on account of a view that would have put an end to so many foolish prejudices based on superstition. The Buddha's position is again to adopt, in this matter, the sensible position already put forward by others.

As to other details also, which it would take too long to set out here, Gotama followed the same plan. On the general question, however, he had opinions, presumably his own. For they are not found elsewhere. And in the early Buddhist texts (always ready to give credit to others, and even anxious wherever possible to support their views by showing that others, especially in ancient times, had held them) these views are not referred to as part of the doctrine of either earlier or contemporary teachers.

We may class the utterances on this point under three heads—biological, ethical, and historical.

In the Vâse*tth*a Sutta of the Sutta Nipâta (several verses of which have been inserted also in the Dhammapada) the question, as in the So*n*ada*n*da Sutta, translated below, is as to what makes a man a Brahman. As his answer the Buddha reminds his questioners of the fact that whereas, in the case of plants (large or small), insects, quadrupeds, serpents, fish, and birds, there are many species and marks (due to the species) by which they can be distinguished—in the case of man there are no such species, and no such marks. ' Herein,' as pointed out by Mr. Chalmers [1], ' Gotama was in accord with the conclusion of modern biologists, that " the *Anthropidae* are represented by the single genus and species, Man"—a conclusion the more remarkable as the accident of colour did not mislead Gotama' as it did so many of his contemporaries then ; and even, within living memory, so many in the West. He goes on to draw the conclusion that distinctions made between different men are mere matters of prejudice and custom ; that it is wisdom and goodness that make the only valid distinction, that make a man a Brahman ; that the

---

[1] J. R. A. S., 1894, p. 396.

Arahat is therefore the true Brahman ; and that it is only the
ignorant who had, for so long, maintained that it was birth that
made a man a Brahman.

Similar arguments frequently recur. In the Madhura Sutta,
a dialogue, shortly after the Buddha's death, between the
king of Madhura and Kakkâna, the point raised is whether
the Brahmans are right in their exclusive claims. 'The
Brahmans say thus, Kakkâna :—" The Brahmans are the most
distinguished of the four divisions into which the people is
classified [1] ; every other division is inferior. The Brahmans
are the white division ; all the rest are black. The Brahmans
alone are accounted pure, not those who are not Brahmans.
The Brahmans are the legitimate sons of God (of Brahmâ),
born from His mouth, specially made by Him, heirs of
Brahmâ! What do you, Sir, say to this ? "'

The Buddhist answer is first to remind the king of the
actual facts of life—how a prosperous member of any one of
the four vannas would find members of each of the other
three to wait upon him and serve him. There was no
difference between them in this respect. Then, secondly, he
points out how a wicked man (whatever his vanna), in accordance with the doctrine of Karma acknowledged by all good
men (not only by Buddhists), will be reborn in some state of
woe ; and a good man in some state of bliss. Thirdly, a crim-
inal, whatever his vanna, would be equally subject to punishment for his crime. And lastly, a man, whatever his vanna,
would, on joining an order, on becoming a *religieux*, receive
equal respect and honour from the people [2].

A Brahman might object that all this ignores the important
point that the Brahmans were, originally, born of Brahmâ, and
are his legitimate heirs. It was this claim to especial connection with the mysterious powers of a supernatural kind, so
widely believed in, that formed their chief weapon in the
struggle. We find the Buddhist reply to that in the Aggañña
Sutta of the Dîgha, in many respects one of the most
interesting and instructive of all the Dialogues [3]. It is a kind

---

[1] Literally ' are the best colour' (vanna, with reference to the well-
known classification into four vannas, neither of which was a caste,
referred to above).

[2] This Madhura Sutta has now been edited and translated, with
valuable introduction and notes, by Mr. Robert Chalmers, in the
Journal of the Royal Asiatic Society, 1894.

[3] The larger portion of this Sutta (from the beginning of the genesis
part down to the election of the first king) is also preserved in the
Mahâvastu. See Senart's edition, vol. i, pp. 338–348. The reading
agninyam (p. 340, 17, &c.) represents the Pâli aggaññam.

of Buddhist book of Genesis. In it the pretensions of the
Brahmans are put forward in the same terms as those just
quoted above from the Madhura Sutta.

Gotama replies that they make these claims in forget-
fulness of the past. The claims have no basis in fact. It is
righteousness (dhamma) and not class distinction (va*nn*a)
that makes the real difference between man and man[1]. Do
we not daily see Brahman women with child and bearing
sons just like other folk? How can they then say that
they are born of God? And as to their origin, when the
evolution of the world began, beings were at first immaterial,
feeding on joy, giving light from themselves, passing through
the air. There was thick darkness round about them, and
neither sun nor moon, nor stars, nor sex, nor measures of time.
Then the earth rose in the midst of the waters, beautiful as
honey in taste and colour and smell, and the beings, eating
thereof, lost their brightness, and then sun and moon and
stars appeared, and time began to run. And then also their
bodies became more coarse and material, and differences of
complexion (va*nn*a) became manifest among them. Then
some prided themselves, and despised others, on the ground
of their finer complexion. And thereupon the fine-tasting
earth ceased to be so.

Then successively fine moss, and sweet creepers, and delicate
rice appeared, and each time the beings ate thereof with
a similar result. Then differences of sex appeared; and
households were formed; and the lazy stored up the rice,
instead of gathering it each evening and morning; and the
rights of property arose, and were infringed. And when lusts
were felt, and thefts committed, the beings, now become men,
met together, and chose certain men, differing from the others
in no wise except in virtue (dhamma), to restrain the evil
doers by blame or fines or banishment. These were the first
Kshatriyas. And others they chose to restrain the evil dispositions which led to the evil doing. And these were the first
Brahmans, differing from the others in no wise, except only in
virtue (dhamma).

Then certain others, to keep their households going, and
maintain their wives, started occupations of various kinds.
And these were the first vessas. And some abandoned their
homes and became the first recluses (sama*n*as). But all
were alike in origin, and the only distinction between them
was in virtue. And the highest of them all was acknowledged

---

[1] The words here are quoted in the Milinda, vol. i, p. 229 of my
translation.

to be the Arahat, who had made himself so by the destruction of the Four Mental Intoxications (the Âsavas) and by breaking the bonds that tied him to rebirths; the man who had laid aside every burden, who had lived the life, had accomplished all that had to be done, had gained his end, and by the highest knowledge was set free!

We may not accept the historical accuracy of this legend. Indeed a continual note of good-humoured irony runs through the whole story, with its fanciful etymologies of the names of the four vannâ; and the aroma of it would be lost on the hearer who took it *au grand sérieux*. But it reveals a sound and healthy insight, and is much nearer to the actual facts than the Brahman legend it was intended to replace.

Had the Buddha's views on the whole question won the day—and widely shared, as they were, by others, they very nearly prevailed—the evolution of social grades and distinctions would have gone on in India on lines similar to those it followed in the West, *and the caste system of India would never have been built up* [1].

---

[1] There is an admirable little book by M. Senart on the origin of caste, on the Brahman views about it, and on the present actual facts of caste in India, entitled ' Les Castes dans l'Inde.' Dr. Fick also in his ' Sociale Gliederung im nordöstlichen Indien zu Buddha's Zeit ' has collected the evidence found· in the Gâtaka book, and analysed it with great skill. Similar monographs on the Pitakas, and on the Epics, are much to be desired.

III. AMBA*TTH*A SUTTA.

[A YOUNG BRAHMAN'S RUDENESS AND AN OLD ONE'S
FAITH.]

I. 1. Thus have I heard. The Blessed One, when once on a tour through the Kosala country with a great company of the brethren, with about five hundred brethren, arrived at a Brahman village in Kosala named I*kkh*ânankala ; and while there he stayed in the I*kkh*ânankala Wood.

Now at that time the Brahman Pokkharasâdi was dwelling at Ukka*tth*a, a spot teeming with life, with much grassland and woodland and corn, on a royal domain, granted him by King Pasenadi of Kosala as a royal gift, with power over it as if he were the king[1].

2. Now the Brahman Pokkharasâdi[2] heard the news:

---

[1] So Buddhaghosa ; but he gives no further details as to the terms of the grant, or of the tenancy. The whole string of adjectives recurs below, pp. 111, 114, 127, 131 of the text, and râ*g*a-bhogga*m* at Vin. III, 222. Compare Divyâvadâna, p. 620.

The land revenue, payable of course in kind, would be a tithe. If the king had full proprietary (zemindary) rights as well, which is the probable meaning of râ*g*a-bhogga*m*, his share would be, either with or without the land tax, one half. The grant would be of his own rights only. The rights of the peasants to the other half, and to the use of the common and waste and woods, would remain to them. If Buddhaghosa's interpretation of brahmadeyya*m* is correct, then the grantee would also be the king's representative for all purposes judicial and executive. Elsewhere the word has only been found as applied to marriage ; and the first part of the compound (brahma) has always been interpreted by Brahmans as referring to themselves. But brahma as the first part of a compound never has that meaning in Pâli ; and the word in our passage means literally 'a full gift.'

[2] His full name was Pokkharasâdi Opama*ññ*o Subhagavaniko (M. II, 200) ; where the second is the gotta (*gens*) name and the third a local name. See the Introduction to the Mahâli Sutta.

' They say that the Samana Gotama, of the Sâkya clan,
who went out from a Sâkya family to adopt the religious
life, has now arrived, with a great company of the
brethren of his Order, at Ikkhânankala, and is staying
there in the Ikkhânankala Wood.   Now regarding that
venerable Gotama, such is the high reputation that has
been noised abroad :—That Blessed One is an Arahat,
a fully awakened one, abounding in wisdom and goodness, happy, with knowledge of the worlds, unsurpassed
as a guide to mortals willing to be led, a teacher for
gods and men, a Blessed One, a Buddha.   He, by himself, thoroughly knows and sees, as it were, face to face
this universe,—including the worlds above of the gods,
the Brahmas, and the Mâras, and the world below with
its recluses and Brahmans, its princes and peoples,—
and having known it, he makes his knowledge known
to others.   The truth, lovely in its origin, lovely in its
progress, lovely in its consummation, doth he proclaim,
both in the spirit and in the letter, the higher life doth
he make known, in all its fullness and in all its purity.

[88] 'And good is it to pay visits to Arahats like
that.'

3. Now at that time a young Brahman, an Ambattha [1], was a pupil under Pokkharasâdi the Brahman.
And he was a repeater (of the sacred words) knowing
the mystic verses by heart, one who had mastered the
Three Vedas, with the indices, the ritual, the phonology, and the exegesis (as a fourth) [2], and the legends

---

[1] According to Gât. IV, 363 (compare Gât. IV, 366) there were
also Ambatthas who were not Brahmans by birth, but farmers.

[2] The fourth is not expressly mentioned. Buddhaghosa (p. 247)
says we have to supply the fourth Veda, the Atharva. But the older
Pâli texts do not acknowledge the Atharva as a Veda. It only occurs,
as the Athabbana Veda, in the Atthakathâs and Tîkâs. And it is quite
unnecessary to suppose a silent reference to it here. The fourth place
is quite sufficiently filled as suggested in the translation. The Âthabbana,
given (in S. N, 927) as the name of a mystic art (together with
astrology, the interpretation of dreams and of lucky signs, and so
forth), is probably not the Veda, but witchcraft or sorcery. The
Pitakas always take three Vedas, and three only, for granted. And the
whole point of the Tevigga Sutta (translated in full in my ' Buddhist

as a fifth, learned in the idioms and the grammar, versed in Lokâyata sophistry, and in the theory of the signs on the body of a great man[1],—so recognised an authority in the system of the threefold Vedic knowledge as expounded by his master, that he could say of him : 'What I know that you know, and what you know that I know.'

4. And Pokkarasâdi told Amba*tth*a the news, and said : ' Come now, dear Amba*tth*a, go to the Sama*n*a Gotama, and find out whether the reputation so noised abroad regarding him is in accord with the facts or not, whether the Sama*n*a Gotama is such as they say or not.'

5. ' But how, Sir, shall I know whether that is so or not?'

' There have been handed down, Amba*tth*a, in our mystic verses thirty-two bodily signs of a great man,— signs which, if a man has, he will become one of two things, and no other[2]. If he dwells at home he will become a sovran of the world, a righteous king, bearing rule even to the shores of the four great oceans, a conqueror, the protector of his people, possessor of the seven royal treasures. [89] And these are the seven treasures that he has—the Wheel, the Elephant, the Horse, the Gem, the Woman, the Treasurer, and the

---

Suttas') is this three-, not four-, fold division. Four Vedas are referred to in the Milinda, at p. 3, and the Atharva-veda, at p. 117.

[1] This is the standing description in the Suttas of a learned Brahman. See below, pp. 114, 120 (of the text); A. I, 163; Mil. 10; Divyâvadâna 620, &c. One or two of the details are not quite certain, as yet.

[2] The knowledge of these thirty-two marks of a Great Being, (Mahâ-purusha) is one of the details in the often-recurring paragraph giving the points of Brahman wisdom, which we have just had at § 3. No such list has been found, so far as I know, in those portions of the pre-Buddhistic priestly literature that have survived. And the inference from both our passages is that the knowledge is scattered through the Brahman texts. Many of the details of the Buddhist list (see the note below on p. 106 of the text) are very obscure; and a collection of the older Brahman passages would probably throw light upon them, and upon a curious chapter in mythological superstition. Who will write us a monograph (historical of course) on the Mahâ-purusha theory as held in early times among the Aryans in India?

Adviser as a seventh[1]. And he has more than a thousand sons, heroes, mighty in frame, beating down the armies of the foe. And he dwells in complete ascendancy over the wide earth from sea to sea, ruling it in righteousness without the need of baton or of sword. But if he go forth from the household life into the houseless state, then he will become a Buddha who removes the veil from the eyes of the world. Now I, Ambattha, am a giver of the mystic verses; you have received them from me.'

6. 'Very good, Sir,' said Ambattha in reply; and rising from his seat and paying reverence to Pokkharasâdi, he mounted a chariot drawn by mares, and proceeded, with a retinue of young Brahmans, to the Ikkhânankala Wood. And when he had gone on in the chariot as far as the road was practicable for vehicles, he got down, and went on, into the park, on foot.

7. Now at that time a number of the brethren were walking up and down in the open air. And Ambattha went up to them, and said : 'Where may the venerable Gotama be lodging now? We have come hither to call upon him.'

8. Then the brethren thought: 'This young Brahman Ambattha is of distinguished family, and a pupil of the distinguished Brahman Pokkharasâdi. The Blessed One will not find it difficult to hold conversation with such.' And they said to Ambattha : 'There, Ambattha, is his lodging[2], where the door is shut, go quietly up and enter the porch gently, and give a cough, and knock on the cross-bar. The Blessed One will open the door for you.'

9. Then Ambattha did so. And the Blessed One opened the door, and Ambattha entered in. And the other young Brahmans also went in; and they exchanged with the Blessed One the greetings and

---

[1] For the details of these seven see further my 'Buddhist Suttas,' pp. 251–259.
[2] Vihâra; often rendered 'monastery,' a meaning the word never has in the older texts.

compliments of politeness and courtesy, and took their
seats.   But Amba*tth*a, walking about, said something
or other of a civil kind in an off-hand way, fidgeting
about the while, or standing up, to the Blessed One
sitting there.

[**90**] 10. And the Blessed One said to him : ' Is that
the way, Amba*tth*a, that you would hold converse
with aged teachers, and teachers of your teachers well
stricken in years, as you now do, moving about the
while or standing, with me thus seated ? '

11. 'Certainly not, Gotama. It is proper to speak
with a Brahman as one goes along only when the
Brahman himself is walking, and standing to a Brahman
who stands, and seated to a Brahman who has taken
his seat, or reclining to a Brahman who reclines. But
with shavelings, sham friars, menial black fellows, the
offscouring of our kinsman's heels [1]—with them I would
talk as I now do to you ! '

' But you must have been wanting something, Amba*tth*a, when you came here. Turn your thoughts
rather to the object you had in view when you came.
This young Brahman Amba*tth*a is ill bred, though he
prides himself on his culture ; what can this come from
except from want of training [2] ? '

12. Then Amba*tth*a was displeased and angry
with the Blessed One at being called rude ; and at the
thought that the Blessed One was vexed with him, he
said, scoffing, jeering, and sneering at the Blessed
One : ' Rough is this Sâkya breed of yours, Gotama,
and rude ; touchy is this Sâkya breed of yours and

---

[1] Bandhupâdâpa*kkâ*.   Neumann, *loc. cit.* p. 521, says 'treading
on one another's heels.'   Buddhaghosa refers the expression to the
Brahman theory that the *S*ûdras were born from Brahmâ's heels.   And
this may well have been the meaning.   For though Gotama and the
majority of his order were well born, still others, of low caste, were
admitted to it, and Amba*tth*a is certainly represented as giving vent to
caste prejudice when he calls the brethren ' black fellows.'   Compare
M. I, 334; S. IV, 117, and below, D. I, 103.

[2] And is therefore, after all, not so much his fault as that of his
teacher.   That this is the implication is clear from the text, pp. 90, 91
(§§ 10–13) below.

violent. [91] Menials, mere menials[1], they neither venerate, nor value, nor esteem, nor give gifts to, nor pay honour to Brahmans. That, Gotama, is neither fitting, nor is it seemly!'

Thus did the young Brahman Ambattha for the first time charge the Sâkyas with being menials.

13. 'But in what then, Ambattha, have the Sâkyas given you offence?'

'Once, Gotama, I had to go to Kapilavatthu on some business or other of Pokkharasâdi's, and went into the Sâkyas' Congress Hall[2]. Now at that time there were a number of Sâkyas, old and young, seated in the hall on grand seats, making merry and joking together, nudging one another with their fingers[3]; and for a truth, methinks, it was I myself that was the subject of their jokes; and not one of them even offered me a seat. That, Gotama, is neither fitting, nor is it seemly, that the Sâkyas, menials as they are, mere menials, should neither venerate, nor value, nor esteem, nor give gifts to, nor pay honour to Brahmans.'

Thus did the young Brahman Ambattha for the second time charge the Sâkyas with being menials.

---

[1] Ibbhâ. Chalmers (J. R. A. S., 1894, p. 343) renders this 'nought but men of substance,' and he has been followed by Frazer, 'Literature of India,' p. 118. But Buddhaghosa's interpretation is confirmed both by the context and by the derivation.

[2] Santhâgâra. Childers is quite wrong about this word. It is the hall where a clan mote was held, and is used exclusively of places for the assemblies of the householders in the free republics of Northern Kosala. It never means a royal rest house, which is râgâgâraka, as we had above (p. 1, § 2 of the Pâli text). Thus at M. I, 353, 4 and Gât. IV, 147 we have this identical hall of the Sâkyas at Kapilavatthu, and at M. I, 457 a similar one of the Sâkyas at Kâtumâya; at M. P. V, 56 (VI, 23 of the translation in my 'Buddhist Suttas') we have the congress hall of the Mallas of Kusinârâ, and at M. I, 228 and Vin. I, 233 that of the Likkhavis of Vesâlî—all of them called Santhâgâra, and all referred to in connection with a public meeting of the clan.

[3] Anguli-patodakena. The Introductory Story to the 52nd Pâkittiya (Vin. IV, 110=III, 84) tells how a Bhikshu was inadvertently done to death by being made to laugh immoderately in this way. It must there mean 'tickling.' Here, and at A. IV, 343, it seems to have the meaning given above.

14. 'Why a quail, Ambattha, little hen bird though she be, can say what she likes in her own nest. And there the Sâkyas are at their own home, in Kapilavatthu. It is not fitting for you to take offence at so trifling a thing.'

15. 'There are these four grades [1], Gotama,—the nobles, the Brahmans, the tradesfolk, and the work-people. And of these four, three—the nobles, the tradesfolk, and the work-people—are, verily, but attendants on the Brahmans. [92] So, Gotama, that is neither fitting, nor is it seemly, that the Sâkyas, menials as they are, mere menials, should neither venerate, nor value, nor esteem, nor give gifts to, nor pay honour to the Brahmans.'

Thus did the young Brahman Ambattha for the third time charge the Sâkyas with being menials.

16. Then the Blessed One thought thus: 'This Ambattha is very set on humbling the Sâkyas with his charge of servile origin. What if I were to ask him as to his own lineage.' And he said to him:

'And what family do you then, Ambattha, belong to?'

'I am a Kanhâyana.'

'Yes, but if one were to follow up your ancient name and lineage, Ambattha, on the father's and the mother's side, it would appear that the Sâkyas were once your masters, and that you are the offspring of one of their slave girls. But the Sâkyas trace their line back to Okkâka the king [2].

'Long ago, Ambattha, King Okkâka, wanting to divert the succession in favour of the son of his favourite queen, banished his elder children—Okkâmukha, Karanda, Hatthinika, and Sinipura—from the land. And being thus banished they took up their dwelling on the slopes of the Himâlaya, on the borders of a lake where a mighty oak tree grew

---

[1] Vannâ.
[2] On this famous old king see the legends preserved in the M. B. V, 13; Mahâvastu I, 348; Gât. II, 311; Sum. I, 258.

And through fear of injuring the purity of their
line they intermarried with their sisters.

'Now Okkâka the king asked the ministers at his
court: "Where, Sirs, are the children now[1]?"'

'There is a spot, Sire, on the slopes of the Himâlaya,
on the borders of a lake, where there grows a mighty
oak (sako). There do they dwell. And lest they
should injure the purity of their line they have
married their *own* (sakâhi) sisters.'

'Then did Okkâka the king burst forth in admira-
tion [93]: "Hearts of oak (sakyâ) are those young
fellows! Right well they hold their own (parama-
sakyâ)[2]!"

'That is the reason, Amba*tth*a, why they are
known as Sâkyas. Now Okkâka had a slave girl
called Disâ. She gave birth to a black baby. And
no sooner was it born than the little black thing said,
"Wash me, mother. Bathe me, mother. Set me free,
mother, of this dirt. So shall I be of use to you."

'Now just as now, Amba*tth*a, people call devils
"devils," so then they called devils "black fellows"
(ka*n*he). And they said: "This fellow spoke as
soon as he was born. 'Tis a black thing (ka*n*ha)
that is born, a devil has been born!" And that is
the origin, Amba*tth*a, of the Ka*n*hâyanas[3]. He was
the ancestor of the Ka*n*hâyanas[4]. And thus is it,
Amba*tth*a, that if one were to follow up your ancient
name and lineage, on the father's and on the mother's
side, it would appear that the Sâkyas were once
your masters, and that you are the offspring of one
of their slave girls.'

17. When he had thus spoken the young Brahmans
said to the Blessed One: 'Let not the venerable

---

[1] Sammanti, 'dwell,' not in Childers in this sense. But see S. I,
226=Sum. I, 125 and *G*ât. V, 396.

[2] The oak (which doesn't grow in the text, and could not grow
in the Terai) has been introduced to enable the word play to be
adequately rendered. The Pâli Sâka means a teak tree.

[3] Ka*n*hâyana is the regular form of patronymic from Ka*n*ha.

[4] Buddhaghosa gives further details as to his subsequent life.

Gotama humble Ambattha too sternly with this reproach of being descended from a slave girl. He
is well born, Gotama, and of good family; he is
versed in the sacred hymns, an able reciter, a learned
man. And he is able to give answer to the venerable
Gotama in these matters.'

18. Then the Blessed One said to them: 'Quite
so. If [94] you thought otherwise, then it would
be for you to carry on our discussion further. But
as you think so, let Ambattha himself speak [1].'

19. 'We do think so; and we will hold our peace.
Ambattha is able to give answer to the venerable
Gotama in these matters.'

20. Then the Blessed One said to Ambattha the
Brahman: 'Then this further question arises, Ambattha, a very reasonable one which, even though
unwillingly, you should answer. If you do not give
a clear reply, or go off upon another issue [2], or
remain silent, or go away, then your head will split
in pieces on the spot [3]. What have you heard, when
Brahmans old and well stricken in years, teachers of
yours or their teachers, were talking together, as to
whence the Kanhâyanas draw their origin, and who
the ancestor was to whom they trace themselves
back?'

And when he had thus spoken Ambattha remained
silent. And the Blessed One asked the same
question again. [95] And still Ambattha remained
silent. Then the Blessed One said to him: 'You

---

[1] Buddhaghosa (p. 263) says that Gotama's object was to confine
the discussion to a single opponent, since if all spoke at once, it could
not well be brought to a conclusion. In the text Gotama repeats the
whole speech of the Brahmans.

[2] Aññena aññam patikarasi. For this idiom, not in Childers,
see M. I, 250; Vin. I, 85; A. I, 187, 198; Mil. 94; Sum. I, 264.
It is answering one thing by alleging another.

[3] This curious threat—which never comes to anything, among the
Buddhists, and is apparently never meant to—is a frequent form of
expression in Indian books, and is pre-Buddhistic. Comp. Brihad Âr.
Up. III, 6. 2 and 9. 26. Buddhist passages are M. I, 231; Dhp. 72;
Dhp. A. 87, 140; Gât. I, 54; V, 21, 33, 87, 92, 493, &c.

had better answer, now, Amba*tth*a. This is no
time for you to hold your peace. For whosoever,
Amba*tth*a, does not, even up to the third time of
asking, answer a reasonable question put by a
Tathâgata (by one who has won the truth), his head
splits into pieces on the spot.'

21. Now at that time the spirit who bears the
thunderbolt [1] stood over above Amba*tth*a in the sky
with a mighty mass of iron, all fiery, dazzling, and
aglow, with the intention, if he did not answer, there
and then to split his head in pieces. And the Blessed
One perceived the spirit bearing the thunderbolt, and
so did Amba*tth*a the Brahman. And Amba*tth*a on
becoming aware of it, terrified, startled, and agitated,
seeking safety and protection and help from the
Blessed One, crouched down beside him in awe [2],
and said: 'What was it the Blessed One said?
Say it once again!'

'What do you think, Amba*tth*a? What have
you heard, when Brahmans old and well stricken in
years, teachers of yours or their teachers, were talking
together, as to whence the Ka*n*hâyanas draw their
origin, and who the ancestor was to whom they
trace themselves back?'

'Just so, Gotama, did I hear, even as the venerable
Gotama hath said. That is the origin of the Ka*n*-
hâyanas, and that the ancestor to whom they trace
themselves back.'

22. And when he had thus spoken the young
Brahmans fell into tumult, and uproar, and turmoil;
and said: 'Low born, they say, is Amba*tth*a the
Brahman; his family, they say, is not of good
standing; they say he is descended from a slave
girl; and the Sâkyas were his masters. We did
not suppose that the Sama*n*a Gotama, whose words
are righteousness itself, was not a man to be trusted!'

23. And the Blessed One thought: [96] 'They

---

[1] Va*g*ira-pâ*n*î: to wit, Indra, says Buddhaghosa.
[2] Upanisîdati; whence Upanishad, a mystery, secret, listened
to in awe.

K

go too far, these Brahmans, in their depreciation of Amba*tth*a as the offspring of a slave girl. Let me set him free from their reproach.' And he said to them: 'Be not too severe in disparaging Amba*tth*a the Brahman on the ground of his descent. That Ka*n*ha became a mighty seer[1]. He went into the Dekkan, there he learnt mystic verses, and returning to Okkâka the king, he demanded his daughter Madda-rûpî in marriage. To him the king in answer said: "Who forsooth is this fellow, who—son of my slave girl as he is—asks for my daughter in marriage;" and, angry and displeased, he fitted an arrow to his bow. But neither could he let the arrow fly, nor could he take it off the string again[2].

'Then the ministers and courtiers went to Ka*n*ha the seer, and said: "Let the king go safe, Sir; let the king go safe[3]."

"The king shall suffer no harm. But should he shoot the arrow downwards, then would the earth dry up as far as his realm extends."

"Let the king, Sir, go safe, and the country too."

"The king shall suffer no harm, nor his land. But should he shoot the arrow upwards, the god would not rain for seven years as far as his realm extends[4]."

"Let the king, Sir, go safe, and the country too; and let the god rain."

"The king shall suffer no harm, nor the land either, and the god shall rain. But let the king aim the arrow at his eldest son. The prince shall suffer no harm, not a hair of him shall be touched."

'Then, O Brahmans, the ministers told this to Okkâka,

---

[1] Rishi, mystic sage, magician being no doubt implied, as in B. V. II, 81 = *G*ât. I, 17 (verse 90). Compare Merlin.

[2] The effect of course of the charm which, Buddhaghosa tells us (p. 265), was known as the Amba*tth*a charm.

[3] Sotthi hotu. This is the old mystic word swasti. We have lost the use of such expressions, *Faustum fac regem.*

[4] All this, says Buddhaghosa, was *brutum fulmen.* The Amba*tth*a charm had only power to stop the arrow going off; not to work such results as these.

and said : " Let the king aim [1] at his eldest son. He will suffer neither harm nor terror." And the king did so, and no harm was done. But the king, terrified at the lesson given him, [97] gave the man his daughter Madda-rûpî to wife. You should not, O Brahmans, be too severe to disparage Amba*ttha* in the matter of his slave-girl ancestress. That Ka*n*ha was a mighty seer.'

24. Then the Blessed One said to Amba*ttha*: 'What think you, Amba*ttha*? Suppose a young Kshatriya should have connection with a Brahman maiden, and from their intercourse a son should be born. Now would the son thus come to the Brahman maiden through the Kshatriya youth receive a seat and water (as tokens of respect) from the Brahmans?'

'Yes, he would, Gotama.'

'But would the Brahmans allow him to partake of the feast offered to the dead, or of the food boiled in milk [2], or of the offerings to the gods, or of food sent as a present?'

'Yes, they would, Gotama.'

'But would the Brahmans teach him their verses or not?'

'They would, Gotama.'

'But would he be shut off, or not, from their women?'

'He would not be shut off.'

'But would the Kshatriyas allow him to receive the consecration ceremony of a Kshatriya?'

'Certainly not, Gotama.'

'Why not that?'

'Because he is not of pure descent on the mother's side.'

25. 'Then what think you, Amba*ttha*? Suppose a Brahman youth should have connection with a Kshatriya maiden, and from their intercourse a son should be born. Now would the son thus come to the Kshatriya maiden through the Brahman youth receive

---

[1] Literally ' place the arrow (which had a barb shaped like a horse-shoe) on his son.'

[2] Thâlipâka. See G*â*t. I, 186; Mil. 249. It is used in sacrifices, and also on special occasions.

a seat and water (as tokens of respect) from the Brahmans?'

'Yes, he would, Gotama.'

'But would the Brahmans allow him to partake of the feast offered to the dead, or of food boiled in milk, or of an offering to the gods, or of food sent as a present?'

'Yes, they would, Gotama.'

'But would the Brahmans teach him their verses or not?'

'They would, Gotama.'

[98] 'But would he be shut off, or not, from their women?'

'He would not, Gotama.'

'But would the Kshatriyas allow him to receive the consecration ceremony of a Kshatriya?'

'Certainly not, Gotama.'

'Why not that?'

'Because he is not of pure descent on the father's side.'

26. 'Then, Ambattha, whether one compares women with women, or men with men, the Kshatriyas are higher and the Brahmans inferior.

'And what think you, Ambattha? Suppose the Brahmans, for some offence [1] or other, were to outlaw a Brahman by shaving him and pouring ashes over his head [2], were to banish him from the land or from the township. Would he be offered a seat or water among the Brahmans?'

'Certainly not, Gotama.'

'Or would the Brahmans allow him to partake of the food offered to the dead, or of the food boiled in milk, or of the offerings to the gods, or of food sent as a present?'

'Certainly not, Gotama.'

---

[1] Pakarana. Perhaps 'in consequence of some regulation or other.' Buddhaghosa (p. 267) says 'offence,' but compare Mil. 189.

[2] Assa-putena vadhitvâ, literally 'killing him with (the proceeding called) the Ash-basket.' Compare the idiom 'cut him dead.' It is also mentioned at A. II, 242.

'Or would the Brahmans teach him their verses or not?'

'Certainly not, Gotama.'

'And would he be shut off, or not, from their women?'

'He would be shut off.'

27. 'But what think you, Amba*tth*a? If the Kshatriyas had in the same way outlawed a Kshatriya, and banished him from the land or the township, would he, among the Brahmans, be offered water and a seat?'

'Yes, he would, Gotama.'

'And would he be allowed to partake of the food offered to the dead, or of the food boiled in milk, or of the offerings to the gods, or of food sent as a present?'

'He would, Gotama.'

'And would the Brahmans teach him their verses?'

'They would, Gotama?'

'And would he be shut off, or not, from their women?'

'He would not, Gotama.'

[99] 'But thereby, Amba*tth*a, the Kshatriya would have fallen into the deepest degradation, shaven as to his head, cut dead with the ash-basket, banished from land and township. So that, even when a Kshatriya has fallen into the deepest degradation, still it holds good that the Kshatriyas are higher, and the Brahmans inferior.

28. 'Moreover it was one of the Brahmâ gods, Sana*m*-kumâra [1], who uttered this stanza [2]:

---

[1] Sana*m*-kumâra means 'ever virgin.' According to the legend—common ground to Brahmans and Buddhists—there were five 'mind born' sons of Brahmâ, who remained always pure and innocent, and this Brahmâ was one of the five. See the passages quoted by Chalmers in the J. R. A. S., 1894, p. 344.

Hofrath Bühler has pointed out that in the Mahâbhârata III, 185 (Bombay edition) there is an interesting passage where Sanat-kumâra (the Sanskrit form of the name Sana*m*-kumâra) is actually represented by the Brahmans themselves as having uttered, as referee in a dispute on a point similar to the one here discussed, not indeed the actual words here imputed to him, but others of a very similar import. See the whole article in the J. R. A. S., 1897, pp. 585–588. We either have in our

[2] For note 2 see next page.

" The Kshatriya is the best of those among this folk
    who put their trust in lineage.
But he who is perfect in wisdom and righteousness,
    he is the best among gods and men."

' Now this stanza, Ambattha, was well sung and not
ill sung by the Brahmâ Sanam-kumâra, well said and
not ill said, full of meaning and not void thereof.   And
I too approve it; I also, Ambattha, say :

" The Kshatriya is the best of those among this folk
    who put their trust in lineage [3].
But he who is perfect in wisdom and righteousness,
    he is the best among gods and men." '

Here ends the First Portion for Recitation [4].

---

text a quotation from an older recension of the same legend, or one
of the two—either the Brahman editors of the Mahâbhârata, or the
composers of our Sutta—have twisted the legend a little in their own
favour.

[2] The verse is a favourite one.   It occurs also at M. I, 358; S. I,
153; II, 284; and below in the Aggañña Sutta.

[3] Gotta-patisârino.   Either 'tracing back their gotras' or
'referring back to their gotras' according as we derive the word
with Childers from √sar, or with Bühler from √smar.   It occurs also
in the description (Mahâ Sudassana Sutta) of the ideal woman as
kimkâra-patisârinî.   Bühler, loc. cit., renders it 'record their
gotras.'

The next line might also be rendered ' when perfect,' &c., referring
to the Kshatriya.

[4] This question of caste, besides being often referred to in isolated
passages, is described at length also in the Assalâyana, Kannakathâla,
and Madhura Suttas, all in the Magghima.   The first has been
translated into German by Professor Pischel and the last into English
by Mr. Chalmers, J. R. A. S., 1894, p. 341 and foll.   On the facts of
caste as disclosed in the Gâtaka book see Fick's 'Sociale Gliederung
in Indien zu Buddha's Zeit,' Kiel, 1897; and on the general history of
caste in India see Senart's 'Les Castes dans l'Inde,' Paris, 1896.

CHAPTER II.

II. 1. ' But what, Gotama, is the righteousness, and what the wisdom spoken of in that verse?'

' In the supreme perfection in wisdom and righteousness, Amba*ttha*, there is no reference to the question either of birth, or of lineage, or of the pride which says : " You are held as worthy as I," or " You are not held as worthy as I." It is where the talk is of marrying, or of giving in marriage, that reference is made to such things as that. For whosoever, Amba*ttha*, are in bondage to the notions of birth or of lineage, or to the pride of social position, or of connection by marriage, they are far from the best wisdom and righteousness. It is only by having got rid of all such bondage that one can realise for himself [100] that supreme perfection in wisdom and in conduct.'

2. ' But what, Gotama, is that conduct, and what that wisdom?'

[*Here follow, under Morality* (Sîla) [1],

The introductory paragraphs (§§ 40-42 *of the Sâ-mañña-phala, pp.* 62, 63 *of the text*) *on the appearance of a Buddha, his preaching, the conversion of a hearer, and his renunciation of the world : then come*

1. *The Sîlas, above, pp.* 4-12 (§§ 8-27) *of the text. Only the refrain differs. It runs here, at the end of each clause, through the whole of this repeated passage :* ' *This is reckoned in him as morality.*'

---

[1] Buddhaghosa, p. 268, seems to have had a different reading— idam p'assa hoti sîlasmi*m*—from that preserved in our text. It comes to much the same result, but is better, as omitting the word bhikkhu.

Then under Conduct (Karana),

2. *The paragraph on Confidence, above, p.* 69 *of the text,* § 63. *The refrain from here onwards is: ' This is reckoned to him as conduct.'*

3. *The paragraph on ' Guarded is the door of his senses,' above, p.* 70 *of the text,* § 64.

4. *The paragraph on ' Mindful and self-possessed,' above, p.* 70 *of the text,* § 65.

5. *The paragraph on Content, above, p.* 71 *of the text,* § 66.

6. *The paragraph on Solitude, above, p.* 71 *of the text,* § 67.

7. *The paragraphs on the Five Hindrances, above, pp.* 71–2 *of the text,* §§ 68–74.

8. *The paragraphs on the Four Rapt Contemplations*[1], *above, pp.* 73–76, §§ 75–82. *The refrain at the end of each of them (' higher and better than the last') is here, of course, to be read not as higher fruit of the life of a recluse, but as higher conduct.*

Under Wisdom (Viggâ),

9. *The paragraphs on Insight arising from Knowledge (*Nâna-dassanam*), above, p.* 76 *of the text,* §§ 83, 84. *The refrain from here onwards is: ' This is reckoned in him as wisdom, and it is higher and sweeter than the last.'*

10. *The paragraphs on the Mental Image, above, p.* 77 *of the text,* §§ 85, 86.

11. *The paragraphs on Mystic Gifts (*Iddhi*), above, p.* 77 *of the text,* § 87, 88.

12. *The paragraphs on the Heavenly Ear (*Dibbasota*), above, p.* 79 *of the text,* §§ 89, 90.

13. *The paragraphs on Knowledge of the hearts of others (*Keto-pariya-ñânam*), above, p.* 79 *of the text,* §§ 91, 92.

14. *The paragraphs on Memory of one's own previous*

---

[1] It is important to notice that these are put, not under wisdom, but under conduct.

births (Pubbe-nivâsa-anussati-ñâna), *above, p.* 81 *of the text,* §§ 93, 94.

15. *The paragraph on the Divine Eye* (Dibba*k*akkhu), *above, /.* 82 *of the text,* § 95, 96.

16. *The paragraphs on the Destruction of the Deadly Floods* (Âsavâna*m* khaya-ñâna*m*), *above, p.* 83 *of the text,* §§ 97, 98 [1].]

'Such a man, Amba*tth*a, is said to be perfect in wisdom, perfect in conduct, perfect in wisdom and conduct. And there is no other perfection in wisdom and conduct higher and sweeter than this.'

3. 'Now, Amba*tth*a, to this supreme perfection in wisdom and goodness [101] there are Four Leakages [2]. And what are the four?'

'In case, Amba*tth*a, any recluse or Brahman, without having thoroughly attained unto this supreme perfection in wisdom and conduct, with his yoke on his shoulder (to carry fire-sticks, a water-pot, needles, and the rest of a mendicant friar's outfit), should plunge into the depths of the forest, vowing to himself: "I will henceforth be one of those who live only on fruits that have fallen of themselves"—then, verily, he turns out worthy only to be a servant unto him that hath attained to wisdom and righteousness.

'And again, Amba*tth*a, in case any recluse or Brahman, without having thoroughly attained unto this supreme perfection in wisdom and conduct, and without having attained to living only on fruits fallen of themselves, taking a hoe and a basket with him, should plunge into the depths of the forest, vowing to himself: "I will henceforth be one of those who live only on bulbs and roots and fruits"—then, verily, he turns out worthy only to be a servant unto him who hath attained to wisdom and righteousness.

---

[1] There are therefore eight divisions of conduct, and eight of the higher wisdom.

[2] Apâya-mukhâni, 'outlets, leakages, so that it cannot fill up.' The word aya-mukha*m*, inlet, is used in its concrete sense at D. I, 74, and both words at A. II, 166; and 'outlet' occurs figuratively, in a secondary sense, as in this passage, in the Sigâlovâda Sutta, p. 299.

'And again, Ambattha, in case any recluse or Brahman, without having thoroughly attained unto this supreme perfection in wisdom and conduct, and without having attained to living only on fruits fallen of themselves, and without having attained to living only on bulbs and roots and fruits, should build himself a fire-shrine near the boundaries of some village or some town, and there dwell serving the fire-god [1]—then, verily, he turns out worthy only to be a servant unto him that hath attained to wisdom and righteousness.

'And again, Ambattha, in case any recluse or Brahman, without having thoroughly attained unto this supreme perfection in wisdom and conduct, and without having attained to living only on fruits fallen of themselves, and without having attained to living only on bulbs and roots and fruits, and without having attained to serving the fire-god, [102] should build himself a four-doored almshouse at a crossing where four high roads meet, and dwell there, saying to himself: "Whosoever, whether recluse or Brahman, shall pass here, from either of these four directions, him will I entertain according to my ability and according to my power"—then, verily, he turns out worthy only to be a servant unto him who hath attained to wisdom and righteousness.

'These are the Four Leakages, Ambattha, to supreme perfection in righteousness and conduct [2].

4. 'Now what think you, Ambattha? Have you, as one of a class of pupils under the same teacher, been instructed in this supreme perfection of wisdom and conduct [3]?'

'Not that, Gotama. How little is it that I can pro-

---

[1] For instances of this see Gât. I, 285, 494; II, 43. Such service paid to a god has already been condemned in the tract on the Sîlas, the minor details of mere morality (above, pp. 24, 25).

[2] Buddhaghosa here (p. 270) says that all sorts of Brahman ascetics are here intended to be included, and he gives further details of eight different sorts (discussed in the Journal of the P. T. S. for 1891, pp. 34 foll.).

[3] Sandissasi sâkariyako. Compare M. P. S. 6, 7, 8, 9, 24, 25.

fess to have learnt! How supreme this perfection of
wisdom and conduct! Far is it from me to have been
trained therein?'

'Then what think you, Amba*ttha*? Although you
have not thoroughly attained unto this supreme perfection of wisdom and goodness, have you been trained
to take the yoke upon your shoulders, and plunge into
the depths of the forest as one who would fain observe
the vow of living only on fruits fallen of themselves?'

'Not even that, Gotama.'

'Then what think you, Amba*ttha*? Although you
have not attained unto this supreme perfection of
wisdom and goodness, nor have attained to living on
fruits fallen of themselves, have you been trained to
take hoe and basket, and plunge into the depths of the
forest as one who would fain observe the vow of living
only on bulbs and roots and fruits?'

'Not even that, Gotama.'

'Then what think you, Amba*ttha*? Although you
have not attained unto this supreme perfection of
wisdom and goodness, and have not attained to living
on fruits fallen of themselves, and have not attained
to living on bulbs and roots and fruits, have you been
taught to build yourself a fire-shrine on the borders of
some village or some town, and dwell there as one who
would fain serve the fire-god?'

[103] 'Not even that, Gotama.'

'Then what think you, Amba*ttha*? Although you
have not attained unto this supreme perfection of
wisdom and goodness, and have not attained to living
on fruits fallen of themselves, and have not attained
to living on bulbs and roots and fruits, and have not
attained to serving the fire-god, have you been taught
to build yourself a four-doored almshouse at a spot
where four high roads cross, and dwell there as one
who would fain observe the vow to entertain whosoever might pass that way, from any of the four
directions, according to your ability and according
to your power?'

'Not even that, Gotama.'

5. 'So then you, Amba*tth*a, as a pupil, have fallen short[1] of due training, not only in the supreme wisdom and conduct, but even in any one of the Four Leakages by which the complete attainment thereof is debarred. And your teacher too, the Brahman Pokkharasâdi, has told you this saying: "Who are these shavelings, sham friars, menial black fellows, the offscouring of our kinsman's heels, that they should claim converse with Brahmans versed in the threefold Vedic lore!"—he himself not having even fulfilled any one even of these lesser duties (which lead men to neglect the higher ones). See, Amba*tth*a, how deeply your teacher, the Brahman Pokkharasâdi, has herein done you wrong.'

6. 'And the Brahman Pokkharasâdi, Amba*tth*a, is in the enjoyment of a grant from Pasenadi, the king of Kosala. But the king does not allow him to come into his presence. When he consults with him he speaks to him only from behind a curtain. How is it, Amba*tth*a, that the very king, from whom he accepts this pure and lawful maintenance, King Pasenadi of Kosala, does not admit him to his presence? See, Amba*tth*a, how deeply your teacher, the Brahman Pokkharasâdi, has herein done you wrong[2].'

7. 'Now what think you, Amba*tth*a? Suppose a king, either seated on the neck of his elephant or on the back of his horse, or standing on the footrug of his chariot [104], should discuss some resolution of state with his chiefs or princes. And suppose as he left the spot and stepped on one side, a workman (*Sû*dra) or the slave of a workman should come up and, standing there, should discuss

---

[1] Parihînako sâ*k*ariyako. 'Have been done out of, neglected in the matter of, defrauded of, this wisdom,' &c.

[2] By concealing this suggestive fact, and thereby leaving you ignorant that the king, a Kshatriya, looked down on a Brahman, even one whom he considered, as a Brahman, of great merit. So at *G*ât. V, 257 a king calls a Brahman 'low born' (hîna-*g*a*kk*o) compared with himself.

the matter, saying: "Thus and thus said Pasenadi the king." Although he should speak as the king might have spoken, or discuss as the king might have done, would he thereby be the king, or even as one of his officers?'

'Certainly not, Gotama.'

8. 'But just so, Amba*tth*a, those ancient poets (Rishis) of the Brahmans, the authors of the verses, the utterers of the verses, whose ancient form of words so chanted, uttered, or composed, the Brahmans of to-day chant over again and rehearse, intoning or reciting exactly as has been intoned or recited—to wit, A*tth*aka, Vâmaka, Vâmadeva, Vessâmitta, Yamataggi, Angirasa, Bhâradva*g*a, Vâse*tth*a, Kassapa, and Bhagu [1] —though you can say: "I, as a pupil, know by heart their verses," that you should on that account be a Rishi, or have attained to the state of a Rishi— such a condition of things has no existence!'

9. 'Now what think you, Amba*tth*a? What have you heard when Brahmans, old and well stricken in years, teachers of yours or their teachers, were talking together—did those ancient Rishis, whose verses you so chant over and repeat, parade about well groomed, perfumed, trimmed as to their hair and beard, adorned with garlands and gems, clad in white garments, in the full possession and enjoyment of the five pleasures of sense, as you, and your teacher too, do now?'

[105] 'Not that, Gotama.'

'Or did they live, as their food, on boiled rice of the best sorts, from which all the black specks had been sought out and removed, and flavoured with sauces and curries of various kinds, as you, and your teacher too, do now?'

'Not that, Gotama.'

'Or were they waited upon by women with fringes

---

[1] On these names see Tevi*gg*a Sutta I, 13 (p. 172 of my 'Buddhist Suttas') and 'Vinaya Texts,' II, 130.

and furbelows [1] round their loins, as you, and your teacher too, do now?'

'Or did they go about driving chariots, drawn by mares with plaited manes and tails [2], using long wands and goads the while, as you, and your teacher too, do now?'

'Not that, Gotama.'

'Or did they have themselves guarded in fortified towns, with moats dug out round them [3] and cross-bars let down before the gates [4], by men girt with long swords, as you, and your teacher too, do now?'

'Not that, Gotama.'

10. 'So then, Ambattha, neither are you a Rishi, nor your teacher, nor do you live under the conditions under which the Rishis lived. But whatever it may be, Ambattha, concerning which you are in doubt or perplexity about me, ask me as to that. I will make it clear by explanation.'

11. Then the Blessed One went forth from his chamber, and began to walk up and down. And Ambattha did the same. And as he thus walked

---

[1] Ve*th*aka-nata-passâhi. We have here probably the ancient name of the very elaborate girdles which all the fashionable women and goddesses wear on the old bas reliefs. Cunningham, 'Stûpa of Bharhut,' Pl. LI, gives figures and details of them. To judge from the bas reliefs—and I cannot call to mind any Pi*t*aka passage contradicting them—the women (lay women of course, the Sisterhood wore robes from the shoulders downwards) have only very elaborate headdresses and necklaces, a skirt from the waist to the ankles, and a very broad and handsome girdle worn over the top of the skirt. They were unclothed from the neck to the waist.

[2] Kutta-vâlehi. The chariot of the time, as represented on the bas reliefs, had standing room for four passengers, the steeds wore plumes on their heads, and had their manes and tails elaborately plaited. 'Stûpa of Bharhut,' Pl. XII, shows us the chariot of Pasenadi, king of Kosala (see ibid. pp. 124, 125). Kutta is not in Childers. But it occurs frequently. See *G*ât. I, 296, 433; II, 127, 128; IV, 219; Asl. 321.

[3] Compare *G*ât. IV, 106; Mil. 330.

[4] Okkhitta-palighâsu. Childers says (following the Sanskrit dictionaries) bars ' of iron.' But where does the iron come in? This is surely a modern improvement. Unfortunately the word is found elsewhere (M. I, 139; A. III, 84; Dhp. 398) only in an ethical sense.

up and down, following the Blessed One, he took stock of the thirty-two signs of a great man, whether they appeared on the body of the Blessed One or not. And he perceived them all save only two. [106] With respect to those two—the concealed member and the extent of tongue [1]—he was in doubt and perplexity, not satisfied, not sure.

12. And the Blessed One knew that he was so in doubt. And he so arranged matters by his Wondrous Gift that Ambattha the Brahman saw how that part of the Blessed One that ought to be hidden by clothes was enclosed in a sheath. And the Blessed One so bent round his tongue that he touched and stroked both his ears, touched and stroked both his nostrils, and the whole circumference of his forehead he covered with his tongue [2].

---

[1] Neither text nor commentary make it clear what these two marks really quite meant. The first, says Buddhaghosa, is 'like an elephant's,' and the second seems, from what follows, to be the power of extending the tongue, like a snake's, to a great length. This last is possibly derived from poetical descriptions of the tongues of flame or light playing round the disk of the sun.

As to the means by which the Buddha made the first visible to Ambattha, Buddhaghosa simply quotes Nâgasena (at Mil. 169) to show that he made a visible image of himself fully dressed in his robes. And the difficulty is to see how that would have helped matters. Only an historical explanation of the meaning of the marks can here guide us to what is inferred.

[2] These are two of the thirty-two bodily marks of a Great Being (Mahâ-purisa), as handed down among the Brahmans (see note above, p. 88 of the text, § 5) and adopted by the Buddhists. They are in part adaptations to a man of poetical epithets applied to the sun, or to the personification of the mystic human sacrifice; partly characteristics of personal beauty such as any man might have; and one or two of them—the little wart, for instance, between the eyes with white hair on it, and the protuberance at the top of the head—may possibly be added in reminiscence of personal bodily peculiarities which Gotama actually had.

One of the Dialogues in the Dîgha, the Lakhana Sutta, is devoted to these thirty-two marks. They are also enumerated, with slight differences, in the Mahâpadhâna Sutta; and later books give other lists differing from each other, and from the old lists, in many small points.

The story told here in §§ 11, 12 recurs in identical words in the

And Amba*tth*a, the young Brahman, thought:
'The Sama*n*a Gotama is endowed with the thirty-
two signs of a great man, with them all, not only
with some of them.' And he said to the Blessed
One: 'And now, Gotama, we would fain depart.
We are busy, and have much to do.'

'Do, Amba*tth*a, what seemeth to you fit.'

And Amba*tth*a mounted his chariot drawn by
mares, and departed thence.

13. Now at that time the Brahman Pokkharasâdi
had gone forth from Ukka*tth*a with a great retinue
of Brahmans, and was seated in his own pleasaunce
waiting there for Amba*tth*a. And Amba*tth*a came
on to the pleasaunce. And when he had come in
his chariot as far as the path was practicable for
chariots, he descended from it, and came on foot
to where Pokkharasâdi was, and saluted him, and
took his seat respectfully on one side. And when
he was so seated, Pokkharasâdi said to him:

14. 'Well, Amba*tth*a! Did you see the Blessed
One?'

'Yes, Sir, we saw him.'

'Well! is the venerable Gotama so as the reputation [107] about him I told you of declares; and not
otherwise. Is he such a one, or is he not?'

'He is so, Sir, as his reputation declares, and not
otherwise. Such is he, not different. And he is
endowed with the thirty-two signs of a great man,
with all of them, not only with some.'

'And did you have any talk, Amba*tth*a, with the
Sama*n*a Gotama?'

'Yes, Sir, I had.'

'And how did the talk go?'

Then Amba*tth*a told the Brahman Pokkharasâdi
all the talk that he had had with the Blessed One.

15. When he had thus spoken, Pokkharasâdi said to
him: 'Oh! you wiseacre! Oh! you dullard! Oh! you

Sela Sutta (S. N. No. 33 = M. No. 92) and forms the subject of one of
the dilemmas put by King Milinda to Nâgasena (Mil. 167).

expert, forsooth, in our threefold Vedic lore!   A man,
they say, who should carry out his business thus, must,
on the dissolution of the body, after death, be reborn
into some dismal state of misery and woe.   What
could the very points you pressed in your insolent
words lead up to, if not to the very disclosures the
venerable Gotama made[1]?   What a wiseacre; what
a dullard; what an expert, forsooth, in our threefold
Vedic lore.'   And angry and displeased, he struck
out with his foot, and rolled Amba*tth*a over.   And
he wanted, there and then, himself, to go and call
on the Blessed One.

[108] 16. But the Brahmans there spake thus to
Pokkharasâdi : ' It is much too late, Sir, to-day to
go to call on the Sama*n*a Gotama.   The venerable
Pokkharasâdi can do so to-morrow.'

So Pokkharasâdi had sweet food, both hard and
soft, made ready at his own house, and taken on
wagons, by the light of blazing torches, out to
Ukka*tth*a.   And he himself went on to the I*kkh*â-
nankala Wood, driving in his chariot as far as the
road was practicable for vehicles, and then going
on, on foot, to where the Blessed One was.   And
when he had exchanged with the Blessed One the
greetings and compliments of politeness and courtesy,
he took his seat on one side, and said to the Blessed
One :

17. ' Has our pupil, Gotama, the young Brahman
Amba*tth*a, been here ? '

' Yes, Brahman, he has.'

' And did you, Gotama, have any talk with him ? '

' Yes, Brahman, I had.'

' And on what wise was the talk that you had
with him.'

18. Then the Blessed One told the Brahman Pokkharasâdi all the talk that had taken place.   And when

---

[1] Âsa*gg*a âsa*gg*a . . . upanîyya upanîyya. Buddhaghosa is
somewhat ambiguous in his interpretation of this idiomatic phrase, on
which compare M. I, 250, 251 ; A. I, 172.

L

he had thus spoken Pokkharasâdi said to the Blessed One:

'He is young and foolish, Gotama, that young Brahman Ambattha. Forgive him, Gotama.'

'Let him be quite happy, Brahman, that young Brahman Ambattha.'

[109] 19. And the Brahman Pokkharasâdi took stock, on the body of the Blessed One, of the thirty-two marks of a Great Being. And he saw them all plainly, save only two. As to two of them—the sheath-concealed member and the extensive tongue—he was still in doubt and undecided. But the Blessed One showed them to Pokkharasâdi, even as he had shown them to Ambattha[1]. And Pokkharasâdi perceived that the Blessed One was endowed with the thirty-two marks of a Great Being, with all of them, not only with some. And he said to the Blessed One: 'May the venerable Gotama grant me the favour of taking his to-morrow's meal with me, and also the members of the Order with him.' And the Blessed One accepted, by silence, his request.

20. Then the Brahman Pokkharasâdi, seeing that the Blessed One had accepted, had (on the morrow) the time announced to him: 'It is time, oh Gotama, the meal is ready.' And the Blessed One, who had dressed in the early morning, put on his outer robe, and taking his bowl with him, went, with the brethren, to Pokkharasâdi's house, and sat down on the seat prepared for him. And Pokkharasâdi, the Brahman, satisfied the Blessed One, with his own hand, with sweet food, both hard and soft, until he refused any more, and the young Brahmans the members of the Order. And when the Blessed One had finished his meal, and cleansed the bowl and his[2] hands, Pokkharasâdi took a low seat, and sat down beside him.

21. Then to him thus seated [110] the Blessed One

---

[1] Above, p. 106 of the text, § 12 repeated.
[2] Onîta-patta-pânim. See the note at 'Vinaya Texts,' I, 83.

discoursed in due order; that is to say, he spake to him of generosity, of right conduct, of heaven, of the danger, the vanity, and the defilement of lusts, of the advantages of renunciation. And when the Blessed One saw that Pokkharasâdi, the Brahman, had become prepared, softened, unprejudiced, upraised, and believing in heart, then he proclaimed the doctrine the Buddhas alone have won; that is to say, the doctrine of sorrow, of its origin, of its cessation, and of the Path. And just as a clean cloth from which all stain has been washed away will readily take the dye, just even so did Pokkharasâdi, the Brahman, obtain, even while sitting there, the pure and spotless Eye for the Truth, and he knew: 'Whatsoever has a beginning in that is inherent also the necessity of dissolution.'

22. And then the Brahman Pokkharasâdi, as one who had seen the Truth, had mastered it, understood it, dived deep down into it, who had passed beyond doubt and put away perplexity and gained full confidence, who had become dependent on no other man for his knowledge of the teaching of the Master, addressed the Blessed One, and said:

'Most excellent, oh Gotama (are the words of thy mouth), most excellent! Just as if a man were to set up that which has been thrown down, or were to reveal that which has been hidden away, or were to point out the right road to him who has gone astray, or were to bring a light into the darkness so that those who had eyes could see external forms, —just even so, Lord, has the truth been made known to me, in many a figure, by the venerable Gotama. And I, oh Gotama, with my sons, and my wife, and my people, and my companions, betake myself to the venerable Gotama as my guide, to the truth, and to the Order. May the venerable Gotama accept me as a disciple, as one who, from this day forth, as long as life endures, has taken him as his guide. And just as the venerable Gotama visits the families of others, his disciples, at Ukka*tth*a, so let him visit mine. Whosoever there may be there, of Brahmans or their wives, who shall pay reverence to the venerable Gotama, or stand up in his presence, or offer him a seat or water, or take delight in him, to him that will be, for long, a cause of weal and bliss.'

'It is well, Brahman, what you say.'

Here ends the Ambattha Sutta.

INTRODUCTION

SONADANDA SUTTA.

THIS Dialogue comes very appropriately immediately after the Ambaṭṭha. That dealt with the general question of pride of birth, or social position. This deals with the special question of what is the essential quality which makes a man a Brahman. The conclusion is, no doubt, substantially the same. But there is a difference, and the difference is instructive.

In trying to gain over Ambaṭṭha to his (the Buddha's) view of the essential distinction—rather than birth or social position—between man and man, Gotama includes the whole list as set out above in the thirteen divisions of the Sâmañña-phala[1]. In trying to gain over Sonadanda to his (the Buddha's) view of what is the essential quality that makes a man a Brahman, he gives the same details, but puts the Ghânas (the states of Ecstasy) not under Conduct, but under Paññâ (Intelligence).

The reason seems to be simply that the verse, on which the exposition in the Ambaṭṭha turns, mentions only Wisdom and Conduct (containing no word for Intelligence), and that it is not thought accurate to put the states of Ecstasy (which are Indian, not specially Buddhist) under Wisdom. It is true that the Buddhist position is that 'goodness is a function of intelligence, as beauty is of health' (to quote the words of Matthew Bassendine). But under Intelligence they always distinguish two phases—the enquiring, and necessarily therefore doubting, activity, of the mind; and the final stage of emancipation and peace when the laws of the universe are clearly seen, and firmly grasped, and cheerfully acquiesced in.

---

[1] See the summary above, pp. 57–59, in the Introduction to the Sâmañña-phala.

It is this latter phase which they call Wisdom (Vi*gg*â)[1]—the contrary of the Avi*gg*â, which is ignorance of the action of Karma, of the Four Noble Truths, and of the doctrine of the Âsavas or Intoxications. The man who knows these; who, finally and permanently out of the jungle and in the open, quite beyond the stage of 'wasting his wonder on the fabulous soul,' has attained to, and remains in this state of Nirvâ*n*a in Ara*h*atship, is not only, in Buddhist terminology, called a Brahman, but is, in fact, declared to be the only true Brahman.

It is amazing that So*n*ada*n*da, as learned as he is wealthy, does not see that this, the logical outcome of the Buddha's argument, and carefully led up to in the final paragraph of the exposition[2], is really incompatible with the supremacy of the Brahmans in the ordinary sense of that word. He is baffled by the skill with which he is gradually led on, by the usual Socratic method adopted in so many of the Dialogues, to accept one self-evident truth after another. There is indeed nothing, till we come to that last paragraph, which any intelligent Brahman could not, with safety, and with due regard to his own doctrine, fully accept. In other words, the doctrine of Brahman supremacy was intellectually indefensible. It was really quite inconsistent with the ethical standard of the times, which the Brahmans, in common with the rest of the people, fully accepted.

Our Sutta is by no means the only one in which the same, or a similar, argument leads up to the same, or a similar, conclusion. It will aid us in understanding the real gist of our Sutta to mention one or two of these.

In the Tika*nn*a and Gâ*n*usso*n*i Suttas of the A*n*guttara[3] the question put by the Buddha is: 'What sort of person do you Brahmans acknowledge to be a Tevi*gg*a Brahman (a Brahman with threefold lore)?'

The answer of each of the Brahmans is, in the words of our Sutta, § 4: 'A Brahman well born on both sides, of pure descent, through the father and through the mother, back through seven generations, with no slur put upon him, and no reproach, in respect of birth—a repeater (of the sacred words) knowing the mystic verses by heart, one who has mastered the Three Vedas, with the indices, the ritual, the phonology, and the exegesis (as a fourth), and with the

---

[1] The English equivalents do not exactly cover the corresponding Pâli terms, which are not, in the texts, used always with scrupulous distinctiveness.

[2] § 23 of the text, and of the translation below.

[3] Vol. i, pp. 163-168.

legends as a fifth—a man learned in the (etymologies of the) words and in the grammar, versed in Lokâyata (Nature-lore)[1] and in the theory of the signs on the body of a great man.'

Whereupon the Buddha rejoins that in the teaching of the Arahats the 'threefold lore' is different; and on being asked what it is, answers in the words of sections 93, 95, and 97 of the Sâmañña-phala Sutta, which are quoted as the last three paragraphs of his exposition in our Sutta, that is to say,

a. The knowledge of one's own previous births.

b. The knowledge of other people's previous births.

c. The knowledge of the Four Truths, and of the Four Intoxications (Âsavas), leading on to the emancipation of Arahatship.

The only difference is that at the end of each section, and after the words setting forth the emancipation, the following sentence is added:

'This first (or second, or third) lore hath he required. Ignorance is dispelled within him, and wisdom has been born. The darkness has been dissipated, the light has appeared. (And all this) inasmuch as he has continued in earnestness, in zeal, in mastery of himself.'

And at the end of the whole the following verses are also added:

' Him do they honour whose heart,—unswerving in goodness, and wise,
Given to earnest thought,—rests in his own control,
Pacified, stedfast.   And him resolute, able in method,
Threefold in knowledge, dispelling the darkness, the con-
queror of Death, who
Lived for the weal of gods and of men delivered from folly,
Him of the threefold lore, mindful and self-possessed,
Him do they honour, the Buddha, our Gotama, wearing
now,
Conqueror, too, of Birth, the last of his mortal frames!'

' 'Tis he who is a Brâhmana indeed
Who knows the births that he has lived before;
And sees (with Heavenly Eye) the states of bliss,
And states of woe, that other men pass through;
Has reached the end of all rebirths, become
A sage, perfect in insight, Arahat,
In these three modes of knowledge threefold wise.

---

[1] See below in the Introduction to the next Sutta.

Him do I call a Brahman, threefold wise,
And not the man who mutters o'er again
The mystic verse so often muttered through before.'

How important a place this doctrine occupied in early
Buddhism is made evident by the fact that this latter
stanza, with variations at the close, is so constantly repeated.
We find it in the 99th Sutta of the Iti-vuttaka (p. 100) and in
the 91st Sutta of the Ma*gghi*ma (the Brahmâyu Sutta). And
it is quoted also, not only in this Sutta in the A*ṅ*guttara, and
in another Sutta in the Sa*m*yutta (I, 167), but also in the
collection of verses from the Pi*t*akas called the Dhammapada
(verse 423); and also in the other collection of such verses
(probably belonging to some other school of Buddhists), now
preserved in the oldest MS. yet discovered in India, the
so-called Kharosh*thi* MS., portions of which have simultaneously found their way, last year, to both St. Petersburg
and Paris.

The whole section of the Dhammapada, which contains
this quotation, consists of no less than forty verses, each of
which, from one point of view or another, emphasise this
point of the identification, by the Buddhists, of the Arahat
with the Brahman. Twenty-seven of them are taken from
the Vâse*ttha* Sutta of the Sutta Nipâta, in which the question
raised is precisely the same as that raised in our Sutta, and
in which the reply, though different in details, amounts to
much the same as the reply given here.

Two conclusions force themselves upon us. It is, in the
first place, a striking proof of the high social esteem in which
the Brahmans, as such, and quite irrespective of character,
were held by the masses of the people. We have hitherto
only had the views which the Brahmans held about themselves. And very absurd they seem to readers whose own
vivid sense of superiority rests on a self-complacency quite
as inexpugnable as that of the Brahmans. Here we have
evidence from an independent source,—evidence all the
stronger because it is found in Suttas in which the exclusive
claims of the Brahmans by birth are vigorously contested.
When the Buddhists, in selecting a title of honour for those
they valued so highly, for the best of men, for the Arahats,
selected the name of Brahman, it is clear that that word,
in the opinion of the early Buddhists, conveyed to the minds
of the people an exalted meaning, a connotation of real
veneration and respect. And it is not likely that this would
have been the case unless the Brahmans had, at least as

a general rule, deserved it—and on other grounds than the mere prerogative of birth.

In the second place, if the contention of the Buddhists had been universally accepted—if the word Brahman had come to mean, not only a man of a certain descent, but exclusively a man of a certain character and insight— then the present caste system of India could never have grown up. But it was obviously impossible that the contention should succeed.

The method, adopted by all reformers, of pouring new wine into old bottles, putting new meanings into ancient words, can only succeed under conditions, that, in this case, were non-existent. And it is always open to the danger that, with the old and hallowed word, the old superstition associated with it will also survive. It was a method largely adopted by the Buddhists; and in numerous other cases, to which I have elsewhere called attention, adopted with success. The subsequent language of India is full of phrases and words which bear, not the meaning which they previously bore, but the new and higher meaning put into them by Buddhists. But in this case the two ideas were too widely apart, too contradictory. A physical meaning cannot be replaced by an ethical one. The actual facts of life, which they could not alter,—could not, indeed, attempt to alter,— were a constant influence, against their view, too strong to be overcome. Brahmans by birth, many of them, perhaps most of them, engaged in various worldly trades and occupations, and therefore Brahmans *only* by birth, were so constant and so important a factor in the daily and hourly life of the people, that the idea of birth could not be dissociated from the word. The Buddhists failed. And they not only failed, their very choice of the word as a title of honour, must (through the wide influence they exercised for so many centuries throughout and beyond the valley of the Ganges) have actually afforded a fresh strength to the veneration which the word inspired. The very means they adopted to lend weight to their doctrine of emancipation became a weapon to be turned against themselves.

It is unlikely that this really mattered much. The point was only one detail in a broad scheme which was doomed from the outset to failure—that is if failure to attain immediate and lasting acceptance can rightly be called the failure of a theory of life.

A theory which placed the ideal in Self-conquest, regarded final salvation as obtainable in this world, and in this world only, and only by self-conquest—a view of life that ignored the 'soul' and brought the very gods themselves under the domain of law—a religious movement which aimed its keenest shafts against all those forms of belief in the supernatural and mysterious, appealing most strongly alike to the hopes and to the fears of the people—a philosophy that confined itself to going back. step by step, from effect to cause, and poured scorn on speculations as to the ultimate origin and end of all things—might gain, by the powerful personality of its founder and the enthusiasm and zeal of his early followers, a certain measure of temporary success.   But it fought against too many vested interests at once, it raised up too many enemies, it tried in 'pouring new wine into the old bottles' to retain too much of the ancient phraseology, for lasting victory—at least at that time, and in an advancing country then assimilating to itself surrounding peoples at a lower grade of culture.   The end was inevitable. And it was actually brought about, not by persecution, but by the gradual weakening of the theory itself, the gradual creeping back, under new forms and new names, of the more popular beliefs.

The very event, which seemed, in the eyes of the world, to be the most striking proof of the success of the new movement, the conversion and strenuous support of Asoka, the most powerful ruler India had had—indeed the first real overlord over practically the whole of India—only hastened the decline.   The adhesion of large numbers of nominal converts, more especially from the newly incorporated and less advanced provinces, produced weakness, rather than strength, in the movement for reform.   The day of compromise had come.   Every relaxation of the old thoroughgoing position was widely supported by converts only half converted.   And the margin of difference between the Buddhists and their opponents gradually faded almost entirely away.   The soul theory, step by step, gained again the upper hand.   The caste system was gradually built up into a completely organised system.   The social supremacy of the Brahmans by birth became accepted as an incontrovertible fact.   And the inflood of popular superstition which overwhelmed the Buddhist movement, overwhelmed also the whole pantheon of the Vedic gods.   Buddhism and Brahmanism alike passed practically away, and modern Hinduism arose on the ruins of both.

The struggle is now being renewed under conditions perhaps, on the whole, more favourable.   The tone of worldliness and love of material comfort, the eager restlessness of modern social, and economic competition, the degradation of learning to a mere means of getting on and making money, are no doubt all unfavourable to any movement for the social and religious elevation of a people. But history shows, notably in the case of the Reformation in Europe, how powerfully the contact of two diverse views of life tends to widen the thoughts of men. Both India and Europe in the twentieth century may be fairly expected to afford fresh examples of the same influence. And in India the powerful aid of the new methods of science and of historical criticism will lend their invaluable aid to the party endeavouring, now once again, to place the ideal, not in birth, but in character and wisdom.

IV. SONADANDA SUTTA.

[CHARACTERISTICS OF THE TRUE BRAHMAN.]

[111] 1. Thus have I heard. The Blessed One once, when going on a tour through the Anga country with a great multitude of the brethren, with about five hundred brethren, arrived at Kampâ[1]. And there at Kampâ he lodged on the bank of the Gaggarâ Lake[2].

Now at that time the Brahman Sonadanda was dwelling at Kampâ, a place teeming with life[3], with much grassland and woodland and water and corn, on a royal domain granted him by Seniya Bimbisâra, the king of Magadhâ[4], as a royal fief, with power over it as if he were the king.

2. Now the Brahmans and householders of Kampâ heard the news: ' They say that the Samana Gotama of the Sâkya clan, who went out from a Sâkya family to adopt the religious life, has now arrived, with a great

---

[1] Kampâ, the capital of Angâ, was on the East bank of the river of the same name (Gât. IV, 454), which formed the Eastern boundary of Magadhâ. It was close to the modern Bagulpur, about Lat. 24° 10′ by Long. 87°. Like other names of famous places in India, it was used over again by colonists in the Far East, and there means what we now call Cochin China and Annam (I-Tsing, p. 58).

[2] So called after Queen Gaggarâ, who had had it excavated, says Buddhaghosa (Sum. I, 279). He adds that on its banks was a grove of champaka trees, so well known for the fragrance of their beautiful white flowers. It was under those trees that the wandering mendicants put up.

[3] Sattussada. The meaning is really quite settled, though Fausböll wrongly translates ussada 'desire,' and Oldenberg and myself ' uneven,' at S. N. 783 = Vin. I, 3. See No. 15 in the list of the thirty-two marks. Also Gât. IV, 188 = Dhp. A. 339; Gât. IV, 60 = Dhp. A. 95; Gât. IV, 4 ; P. G. D. 22–44; Asl. 307.

[4] In the Buddha's time Angâ was subject to Magadhâ.

company of the brethren at *K*ampâ, and is staying there
on the shore of the Gaggarâ Lake. Now regarding that
venerable Gotama, such is the high reputation that has
been noised abroad :—That Blessed One is an Arahat,
a fully awakened one, abounding in wisdom and goodness, happy, with knowledge of the worlds, unsurpassed
as a guide to mortals willing to be led, a teacher for
gods and men, a Blessed One, a Buddha. He, by himself, thoroughly knows and sees, as it were, face to face
this universe,—including the worlds above of the gods,
the Brahmas, and the Mâras, and the world below with
its recluses and Brahmans, its princes and peoples,—
and having known it, he makes his knowledge known
to others. The truth, lovely in its origin, lovely in its
progress, lovely in its consummation, doth he proclaim,
both in the spirit and in the letter, the higher life doth
he make known, in all its fullness and in all its purity.

'And good is it to pay visits to Arahats like that.'

[112] And the Brahmans and householders of
*K*ampâ began to leave *K*ampâ in companies and in
bands from each district [1], so that they could be
counted, to go to the Gaggarâ Lake.

3. Now at that time So*n*ada*n*da the Brahman had
gone apart to the upper terrace of his house for his
siesta, and seeing the people thus go by, he said to his
doorkeeper : ' Why are the people of *K*ampâ going
forth like this towards the Gaggarâ Lake ? '

Then the doorkeeper told him the news. And he
said : 'Then, good doorkeeper, go to the Brahmans
and householders of *K*ampâ, and say to them :
" So*n*ada*n*da the Brahman desires them to wait. He
will himself come to see the Sama*n*a Gotama." '

'Very well, Sir,' said the doorkeeper, and he did so.

[113] 4. Now at that time there were about five
hundred Brahmans from different kingdoms lodging at
*K*ampâ for some business or other. And when they
heard that So*n*ada*n*da was intending to visit the

---

[1] Perhaps in ' companies and separately '; but I follow Buddhaghosa. Comp. M. I, 231 ; A. II, 55.

Samana Gotama, they went to Sonadanda, and asked whether that was so.

'That is my intention, Sirs. I propose to call on the Samana Gotama.'

'Let not the venerable Sonadanda do that. It is not fitting for him to do so. If it were the venerable Sonadanda who went to call upon him, then the venerable Sonadanda's reputation would decrease and the Samana Gotama's would increase. This is the first reason why you, Sir, should not call upon him, but he upon you.'

5. And they laid before Sonadanda the Brahman in like manner also other considerations, to wit :

That he was well born on both sides, of pure descent through the mother and through the father back through seven generations, with no slur put upon him, and no reproach, in respect of birth—

That he was prosperous, well to do, and rich—

[114] That he was a repeater (of the sacred words), knowing the mystic verses by heart, one who had mastered the Three Vedas, with the indices, the ritual, the phonology, and the exegesis (as a fourth), and the legends as a fifth, learned in the words and in the grammar, versed in Lokâyata (Nature-lore), and in the theory of the signs on the body of a great man—

That he was handsome, pleasant to look upon, inspiring trust, gifted with great beauty of complexion, fair in colour, fine in presence [1], stately [2] to behold—

That he was virtuous, increased in virtue, gifted with virtue that had waxed great—

That he had a pleasant voice and pleasing delivery, and was gifted with polite address, distinct, not husky [3], suitable for making clear the matter in hand—

That he was the teacher of the teachers of many,

---

[1] Brahma-vakkasî. 'With a body like that of Mahâ Brahmâ,' says Buddhaghosa (p. 282). The Burmese and Siamese MSS. read vakkhasî.

[2] Akkhuddâvakâso, for which Buddhaghosa (pp. 282, 284) gives three contradictory explanations.

[3] Anelagalâya. 'Not slobbering,' says Buddhaghosa.

instructing three hundred Brahmans in the repetition of the mystic verses, and that many young Brahmans, from various directions and various counties, all craving for the verses, came to learn them by heart under him—

That he was aged, old, and well stricken in years, long-lived and full of days—

That he was honoured, held of weight, esteemed worthy, venerated and revered by Seniya Bimbisâra, the king of Magadhâ—

That he was honoured, held of weight, esteemed worthy, venerated and revered by Pokkharasâdi, the Brahman—

That he dwelt at *K*ampâ, a place teeming with life, with much grassland and woodland and corn, on a royal fief granted him by Seniya Bimbisâra, the king of Magadhâ, as a royal gift, with power over it as if he were the king—

For each of these reasons it was not fitting that he, So*n*ada*nd*a the Brahman, should call upon the Sama*n*a Gotama, but rather that the Sama*n*a Gotama should call upon him.

6. And when they had thus spoken, So*n*ada*nd*a said to them :

[115] 'Then, Sirs, listen, and hear why it is fitting that I should call upon the venerable Gotama, and not he should call upon me—

'Truly, Sirs, the venerable Gotama is well born on both sides, of pure descent through the mother and the father back through seven generations, with no slur put upon him, and no reproach in respect of birth—

'Truly, Sirs, the Sama*n*a Gotama has gone forth (into the religious life), giving up the great clan of his relations [1]—

'Truly, Sirs, the Sama*n*a Gotama has gone forth (into the religious life), giving up much money and gold, treasure both buried and above the ground—

---

[1] 'Eighty thousand families on the mother's, and eighty thousand on the father's side,' says Buddhaghosa—making a total for the Sâkya clan of 800,000, reckoning five to a family.

'Truly, Sirs, the Sama*n*a Gotama, while he was still a young man, without a grey hair on his head, in the beauty of his early manhood, has gone forth from the household life into the homeless state—

'Truly, Sirs, the Sama*n*a Gotama, though his father and mother were unwilling, and wept, their cheeks being wet with tears, nevertheless cut off his hair and beard, and donned the yellow robes, and went out from the household life into the homeless state—

'Truly, Sirs, the Sama*n*a Gotama is handsome, pleasant to look upon, inspiring trust, gifted with great beauty of complexion, fair in colour, fine in presence, stately to behold—

'Truly, Sirs, the Sama*n*a Gotama is virtuous with the virtue of the Arahats, good and virtuous, gifted with goodness and virtue—

'Truly, Sirs, the Sama*n*a Gotama hath a pleasant voice, and a pleasing delivery, he is gifted with polite address, distinct, not husky, suitable for making clear the matter in hand—

'Truly, Sirs, the Sama*n*a Gotama is the teacher of the teachers of many—

'Truly, Sirs, the Sama*n*a Gotama has no passion of lust left in him, and has put away all fickleness of mind—

'Truly, Sirs, the Sama*n*a Gotama believes in Karma, and in action [1], he is one who puts righteousness in the forefront (of his exhortations) to the Brahman race—

'Truly, Sirs, the Sama*n*a Gotama went forth from a distinguished family primeval [2] among the Kshatriya clans—

---

[1] Kamma-vâdî kiriya-vâdî. Compare 'Vinaya Texts,' II, 109, 112.

[2] Âdîna-khattiya-kulâ. The reading is doubtful, and the Burmese MSS., after their constant habit, have replaced it by an easy reading, abhinna-khattiya-kulâ, 'unbroken Kshatriya family.' But all the Sinhalese MSS. agree in reading either âdina or âdîna; and if the reading had once been abhinna, it is difficult to see how the alteration to the more difficult reading should have occurred.

'Truly, Sirs, the Samana Gotama went forth from a family prosperous, well to do, and rich—

[116] 'Truly, Sirs, people come right across the country from distant lands to ask questions of the Samana Gotama—

'Truly, Sirs, multitudes of heavenly beings put their trust in the Samana Gotama—

'Truly, Sirs, such is the high reputation noised abroad concerning the Samana Gotama, that he is said to be an Arahat, exalted, fully awakened, abounding in wisdom and righteousness, happy, with knowledge of the worlds, a Blessed One, a Buddha—

'Truly, Sirs, the Samana Gotama has all the thirty-two bodily marks of a Great Being—

'Truly, Sirs, the Samana Gotama bids all men welcome, is congenial, conciliatory, not supercilious, accessible to all, not backward in conversation—

'Truly, Sirs, the Samana Gotama is honoured, held of weight, esteemed and venerated and revered by the four classes (of his followers—the brethren and sisters of the Order, laymen and lay women)—

'Truly, Sirs, many gods and men believe in the Samana Gotama—

'Truly, Sirs, in whatsoever village or town the Samana Gotama stays, there the non-humans do the humans no harm—

'Truly, Sirs, the Samana Gotama as the head of an Order, of a school, as the teacher of a school, is the acknowledged chief of all the founders of sects. Whereas some Samanas and Brahmans have gained a reputation by all sorts of insignificant matters[1], not

---

Buddhaghosa skips the clause, which (if it was in the text before him) is suggestive. He would scarcely have done so unless the matter were really very simple. 'Autonomous' would make a good sense in the context; but I have taken the word, in the sense of 'primordial, aboriginal,' as being a derivative from âdi, in the same way as adhîna is from adhi. This is simple enough; the only difficulty being that the word occurs nowhere else.

[1] Literally 'anyhow'; 'such as by wearing no clothes' explains Buddhaghosa (p. 288).

M

so the Samaṇa Gotama.   His reputation comes from
perfection in conduct and righteousness—

' Truly, Sirs, the king of Magadhâ, Seniya Bimbisâra,
with his children and his wives, with his people and his
courtiers, has put his trust in the Samaṇa Gotama—

' Truly, Sirs, King Pasenadi of Kosala, with his
children and his wives, with his people and his
courtiers, has put his trust in the Samaṇa Gotama—

' Truly, Sirs, Pokkharasâdi the Brahman, with his
children and his wives, with his people and his inti-
mates, has put his trust in the Samaṇa Gotama—

' Truly, Sirs, the Samaṇa Gotama is honoured, held
of weight, esteemed, and venerated and revered alike
by Seniya Bimbisâra, the king of Magadhâ, by
Pasenadi the king of Kosala, and by Pokkharasâdi
the Brahman—

[117] ' Truly, Sirs, the Samaṇa Gotama has now
arrived at Kampâ, and is staying on the shores of the
Gaggarâ Lake.   But all Samaṇas and Brahmans who
come into our village borders are our guests.   And
guests we ought to esteem and honour, to venerate
and revere.   And as he is now so come, he ought to
be so treated, as a guest—

' For each and all of these considerations it is not
fitting that the Samaṇa Gotama should call upon us,
but rather does it behove us to call upon him.   And so
far only do I know the excellencies of the Samaṇa
Gotama, but these are not all of them, for his excellence is beyond measure.'

7. And when he had thus spoken, those Brahmans
said to him : ' The venerable Soṇadaṇda declares the
praises of the Samaṇa Gotama on such wise, that were
he to be dwelling even a hundred leagues from here, it
would be enough to make a believing man go thither
to call upon him, even had he to carry a bag (for the
provisions for the journey) on his back[1].   Let us then
all go to call on the Samaṇa Gotama together !'

---

[1] Puḷamsenâpi.   Compare A. II, 183, where a precisely similar
phrase occurs.

So Sonadanda the Brahman went out to the Gaggarâ Lake with a great company of Brahmans.

8. Now the following hesitation arose in Sonadanda's mind as he passed through the wood : ' Were I to ask the Samana Gotama a question, if he were to say : " The question ought not to be asked so, thus ought the question to be framed ; " the company might thereupon speak of me with disrespect, saying : " Foolish is this Sonadanda the Brahman, and inexpert. [118] He is not even able to ask a question rightly." But if they did so my reputation would decrease ; and with my reputation my incomings would grow less, for what we have to enjoy, that depends on our reputation. But if the Samana Gotama were to put a question to me, I might not be able to gain his approval [1] by my explanation of the problem. And if they were then to say to me : " The question ought not to be answered so ; thus ought the problem to be explained ; " the company might thereupon speak of me with disrespect, saying : " Foolish is this Sonadanda the Brahman, and inexpert. He is not even able to satisfy the Samana Gotama by his explanation of the problem put." But if they did so, my reputation would decrease ; and with my reputation my incomings would grow less, for what we have to enjoy, that depends upon our reputation. But on the other hand if, having come so far, I should turn back without calling upon the Samana Gotama, then might the company speak disrespectfully of me, saying : " Foolish is this Sonadanda the Brahman, and inexpert, though obstinate with pride, he is so afraid that he dare not call on the Samana Gotama. How can he turn back after having come so far ? " But if they did so, my reputation would decrease ; and with my reputation my incomings would grow less. For what we have to enjoy, that depends upon our reputation.'

9. So Sonadanda the Brahman went up to where the

---

[1] Kittam na ârâdheyyam, 'win over his mind.' Comp. M. I, 85, 341 ; II, 10 ; Mil. 25.

Blessed One was. And when he had come there he
exchanged with the Blessed One the greetings and
compliments of politeness and courtesy, and took his
seat on one side. And as to the Brahmans and householders of *K*ampâ, some of them bowed to the Blessed
One and took their seats on one side; some of them
exchanged with him the greetings and compliments of
politeness and courtesy, and then took their seats on
one side; some of them called out their name and
family, and then took their seats on one side; and some
of them took their seats on one side in silence.

[119] 10. Now as Soñadañda was seated there he
was still filled with hesitation, thinking as before set
out; and he added to himself: 'Oh! would that the
Samaña Gotama would but ask me some question on
my own subject, on the threefold Vedic lore. Verily,
I should then be able to gain his approval by my
exposition of the problem put!'

11. Now the Blessed One became aware in his own
mind of the hesitation in the mind of Soñadañda, and
he thought: 'This Soñadañda is afflicted in his heart.
I had better question him on his own doctrine.' And
he said to him: 'What are the things, Brahman, which
the Brahmans say a man ought to have in order to be
a Brahman, so that if he says: "I am a Brahman," he
speaks accurately and does not become guilty of falsehood?'

12. Then Soñadañda thought: [120] 'What I wished
and desired and had in my mind and hoped for—that
the Samaña Gotama should put to me some question
on my own subject, on the threefold Vedic lore—that
he now does. Oh! that I may be able to satisfy his
heart with my exposition thereof!'

13. And drawing his body up erect, and looking
round on the assembly, he said to the Blessed One:
'The Brahmans, Gotama, declare him to be a Brahman
who can accurately say "I am a Brahman" without
being guilty of falsehood, who. has five things. And
what are the five? In the first place, Sir, a Brahman is
well born on both sides, on the mother's side and on

the father's side, of pure descent back through seven generations, with no slur put upon him, and no reproach, in respect of birth—

'Then he is a repeater (of the sacred words), knowing the mystic verses by heart, one who has mastered the Three Vedas, with the indices, the ritual, the phonology, and the exegesis (as a fourth), and the legends as a fifth, learned in the phrases and in the grammar, versed in Lokâyata sophistry, and in the theory of the signs on the body of a great man—

'Then he is handsome, pleasant to look upon, inspiring trust, gifted with great beauty of complexion, fair in colour, fine in presence, stately to behold—

'Then he is virtuous, increased in virtue, gifted with virtue that has grown great—

'Then he is learned and wise, the first, or it may be the second, among those who hold out the ladle[1].'

14. 'But of these five things, oh Brahman, is it possible to leave one out, and to declare the man who has the other four to be a Brahman, to be one who can accurately, and without falling into falsehood, claim to be a Brahman?'

'Yes, Gotama, that can be done. We could leave out colour[2]. For what does colour matter? [121] If he have the other four—good birth, technical training, virtue, and wisdom, as just set forth[3]—Brahmans would still declare him to be a Brahman; and he could rightly, without danger of falsehood, claim to be one.'

15. 'But of these four things, oh Brahman, is it possible to leave one out, and to declare the man who has the other three to be a Brahman, to be one who can rightly, and without falling into falsehood, claim to be a Brahman?'

'Yes, Gotama, that could be done. We could leave out the verses. For what do the verses matter? If

---

[1] That is, 'officiate at a sacrifice by pouring out of a spoon a libation of butter, or of spirituous Soma, to the fire god.'

[2] Vanna, much the same as 'caste,' though that rendering is not strictly accurate. (See the Introduction to the Ambaṭṭha.)

[3] The full text is repeated, both here and in the following sections.

he have the other three—good birth, virtue, and wisdom—Brahmans would still declare him to be a Brahman; and he could rightly, without danger of falsehood, claim to be one.'

16. 'But of these three things, Brahman, is it possible to leave one out, and to declare the man who has the other two to be a Brahman, to be one who can accurately, and without falling into falsehood, claim to be a Brahman?'

'Yes, Gotama, that could be done. We could leave out birth. For what does birth matter? If he have the other two—virtue and wisdom—Brahmans would still declare him to be a Brahman; and he could rightly, without danger of falsehood, claim to be one.'

[122] 17. And when he had thus spoken the other Brahmans said to Sonadanda: 'Say not so, venerable Sonadanda, say not so! He depreciates not only our colour, but he depreciates our verses and our birth. Verily the venerable Sonadanda is going over to the doctrine of the Samana Gotama.'

18. Then the Blessed One said to those Brahmans: 'If you, oh Brahmans, think that Sonadanda is unlearned, that he speaks unfittingly, that he is unwise, that he is unable to hold his own with me in this matter, let him keep silence, and do you discuss with me. But if you think him learned, able in speech, wise, able to hold his own, then do you keep silence, and let him discuss with me.'

19. And when he had thus spoken, Sonadanda the Brahman said to those Brahmans: 'Let not the venerable ones say so. Say not so, Sirs. [123] I do not depreciate either our colour, nor our verses, nor our birth.'

20. Now at that time a young Brahman named Angaka[1], sister's son to Sonadanda the Brahman, was seated in that company. And Sonadanda said to those

---

[1] This name looks suspiciously like a kind of personification of the five Angas (the five characteristics) of the true Brahman as just above, § 13, set out.

Brahmans : ' Do the venerable ones see this Angaka, our nephew ? '

' Yes, Sir, we see him.'

' Well! Angaka, Sirs, is handsome, pleasant to look upon, inspiring trust, gifted with great beauty of complexion, fair in colour, fine in presence, stately to behold—none in this assembly is like unto him in colour, save only the Samana Gotama.

' And Angaka, Sirs, is a repeater (of the sacred words), knowing the mystic verses by heart, one who has mastered the Three Vedas, with the indices, the ritual, the phonology, and the exegesis (as a fourth), and the legends as a fifth, learned in the phrases and the grammar, versed in Lokâyata (Nature-lore), and in the theory of the signs on the body of a great man—I myself have taught him the verses.

' And Angaka, Sirs, is well born on both sides, on the mother's side and on the father's side, of pure descent back through seven generations, with no slur put upon him, and no reproach in respect of birth—I myself know his forebears, on the mother's side and on the father's.

' If Angaka, Sirs, should kill living things, and take what has not been given, and go the way of the adulterer, and speak lies, and drink strong drink, what then, Sirs, would his colour avail him ? what the verses ? what his birth ?

' It is in so far, Sirs, as a Brahman is virtuous, increased in virtue, gifted with virtue that has grown great ; in so far as he is learned and wise, the first, or it may be the second, among those who hold out the ladle, that Brahmans would declare him, as endowed with these two qualities, to be a Brahman, to be one who could rightly say " I am a Brahman " without falling into falsehood.'

21. ' But of these two things, oh Brahman, is it possible to leave one out, and to declare the man who has the other to be a Brahman, to be one who can rightly, and without falling into falsehood, claim to be a Brahman ? '

[124] ‘Not that, Gotama! For wisdom, oh Gotama, is purified by uprightness, and uprightness is purified by wisdom. Where there is uprightness, wisdom is there, and where there is wisdom, uprightness is there. To the upright there is wisdom, to the wise there is uprightness, and wisdom and goodness are declared to be the best thing in the world [1]. Just, oh Gotama, as one might wash hand with hand, or foot with foot, just even so, oh Gotama, is wisdom purified by uprightness, and uprightness is purified by wisdom. Where there is uprightness, wisdom is there, and where there is wisdom, uprightness is there. To the upright, there is wisdom, to the wise there is uprightness, and wisdom and goodness are declared to be the best thing in the world.’

22. ‘That is just so, oh Brahman. And I, too, say the same. But what, then, is that uprightness and what that wisdom?’

‘We only know, oh Gotama, the general statement in this matter. May the venerable Gotama be pleased to explain the meaning of the phrase.’

‘Well then, oh Brahman, give ear, and pay earnest attention, and I will speak.’

23. ‘Very well, Sir,’ said Sonadanda in assent to the Blessed One. And the Blessed One said:

[*Here follow the paragraphs 40–63 in the Sâmañña-phala Sutta above, pp. 62–70 of the text; that is, the paragraph on the appearance of a Buddha, his preaching, the conversion of the hearer, his renunciation of the world, all the Sîlas, and the paragraph on Confidence, § 63.*]

‘This also, oh Brahman, is that uprightness’ (*Sîla*).

[*Here follow the paragraphs on the Ghânas, begin-*

---

[1] Oldenberg renders this (‘Buddha,’ p. 283) as follows: ‘The wisdom of the upright and the uprightness of the wise have, of all uprightness and wisdom in the world, the highest value.’ I cannot see how this can be grammatically justified; though the sentiment is admirable enough, and would have somewhat relieved the monotony of the paragraph. On paññâna as nominative, not genitive, see, for instance, S. I, 41, 42; Sum. I, 171, 290; A. IV, 342.

ning at So vivi*kk'* eva kâmehi *in § 75 of the Sâmañña-
phala down to the end of § 82, then the paragraphs on
Insight arising from Knowledge, on the Mental Image,
on the Wondrous Gifts, on the Heavenly Ear, on Knowledge of the hearts of others, on Memory of one's own
previous births, on the Divine Eye, and on the Destruction of the Deadly Floods, all as in the Sâmañña-phala,
§§ 83–98 inclusive.*]

'This, oh Brahman, is that wisdom[1].'

24. When he had thus spoken, So*n*ada*n*d*a* the
Brahman said to the Blessed One:

[125] 'Most excellent, oh Gotama (are the words of
thy mouth), most excellent! Just as if a man were to
set up that which has been thrown down, or were to
reveal that which has been hidden away, or were to
point out the right road to him who has gone astray,
or were to bring a light into the darkness so that those
who had eyes could see external forms—just even so
has the truth been made known to me, in many a
figure, by the venerable Gotama. I, even I, betake
myself to the venerable Gotama as my guide, to the
truth, and to the Order. And may the venerable
Gotama accept me as a disciple, as one who, from this
day forth, as long as life endures, has taken him as his
guide. And may the venerable Gotama grant me the
favour of taking his to-morrow's meal with me, and
also the members of the Order with him.'

Then the Blessed One signified, by silence, his consent. And So*n*ada*n*d*a*, on seeing that he had done so,
arose from his seat and bowed down before the Blessed

---

[1] The repetition here is nearly the same as that in the Amba*ttha*
Sutta, summarised above at the translation of p. 100 of the text. The
only difference is that the paragraphs 64–74 of the Sâma*ññ*a-phala
there included as coming under *K*ara*n*a (Conduct) are here included
under Sîla (Uprightness). The *Gh*ânas, there put, not under Vi*gg*â
(Wisdom), but under *K*ara*n*a, are here put, not under Sîla, but
under Pa*ññ*â (Intelligence). In other words Pa*ññ*â includes all
that was there included under Vi*gg*â, and the Four *Gh*ânas besides.
But Sîla includes all that is put in the Amba*ttha* under Sîla—all
indeed of the eight divisions of Sîla as summarised above, pp. 57–59.
See Buddhaghosa's notes at pp. 219, 268, 292.

One, and walking round him with his right hand towards him, departed thence. And at early dawn he made ready at his house sweet food, both hard and soft, and had the time announced to the Blessed One: 'It is time, oh Gotama, and the meal is ready.'

25. Then the Blessed One, who had dressed in the early morning, put on his outer robe, and taking his bowl with him, went with the brethren to So*n*ada*n*da's house, and sat down on the seat prepared for him. And So*n*ada*n*da the Brahman satisfied the Blessed One, and the brethren, with his own hand, with sweet food, both hard and soft, until they refused any more. And when the Blessed One had finished his meal, and cleansed the bowl and his hands, So*n*ada*n*da took a low seat, and sat down beside him, and said:

26. 'If, oh Gotama, after I have entered the assembly, I should rise from my seat to bow down before the venerable Gotama, then the assembly would find fault with me [1]. Now he with whom the assembly should find fault, his reputation would grow less; and he who should lose his reputation, his income would grow less. For that which we have to enjoy, that depends upon our reputation. If then, when I am seated in the assembly, I stretch forth my joined palms in salutation, let the venerable Gotama accept that from me as a rising up from my seat. [120] And if when I am seated in the assembly I take off my turban, let the venerable Gotama accept that from me as a salutation with my head. So if, when I am in my chariot, I were to get down from the chariot to salute the venerable Gotama, the surrounders would find fault with me. If, then, when mounted on my chariot, I bend down low the staff of my goad, let the venerable Gotama accept that from me as if I had got down. And if, when mounted on my chariot, I should wave

---

[1] On the ground, says Buddhaghosa (p. 292), that he would be saluting a much younger man, one young enough to be his grandson. If this tradition be correct, it would follow that this Sutta must be describing events very early in the public ministry of the Buddha.

my hand, let the venerable Gotama accept that from me as if I had bowed low in salutation[1]!'

27. Then the Blessed One instructed and roused and incited and gladdened Soṇadaṇḍa the Brahman with religious discourse, and then rose from his seat and departed thence.

Here ends the Soṇadaṇḍa Sutta.

---

[1] It will be seen from this section that Soṇadaṇḍa is represented as being a convert only to a limited extent.   He still keeps on his school of Vedic studies, and is keenly anxious to retain the good opinion of his students, and of other Brahmans.   And if that part of the Buddha's doctrine put before him in this Sutta be examined, it will be found to be, with perhaps one or two exceptions, quite compatible with the best Brahman views.   No doubt if every detail were carried to its strict logical conclusion there would be no further need for Vedic studies, except from the historical standpoint.   But those details are, on the face of them, ethical.   They belong to a plane not touched on in the then Vedic studies.   They could be accepted by an adherent of the soul theory of life.   And the essential doctrines of Buddhism—the Path, the Truths, and Arahatship—are barely even referred to.

INTRODUCTION

KÛTADANTA SUTTA.

WHOEVER put this Sutta together must have been deeply imbued with the spirit of subtle irony that plays no less a part in the Suttas than it does in so many of the Gâtakas. I have already called attention to the great importance for the right understanding of early Buddhist teaching of a constant appreciation of this sort of subtle humour[1]. It has been hitherto, so far as I am aware, entirely overlooked—that is, in the Suttas; every one recognises it in the Gâtaka tales. The humour is not at all intended to raise a laugh, scarcely even a smile. And the aroma of it, pervading the whole of an exposition—none the less delightful because of the very serious earnestness of the narrator, all the while, as regards the ethical point at issue—is apt to be lost sight of precisely because of that earnestness. And just as a joke may be explained, but the point of it spoilt in the process, so in the attempt to write about this irony, much more delicate than any joke, one runs great danger of smothering it under the explanatory words.

The attempt, nevertheless, must be made. And it is most easy, perhaps, to do so by an example which no one will dispute. In the Râgovâda Gâtaka[2] we are told of the two kings, reigning over the famous lands of Benares and Kosala, who simultaneously determined to examine into their own faults! No courtier would tell them of any. So they each went, and went in vain, to the people in the city, outside the palace on a similar quest. Finding no fault-finders there, they each went on to the city gate, and then to the surrounding suburbs, all in vain. So they each made over the kingdom to their respective ministers, and with a single attendant as charioteer, sallied forth into the world,

---

[1] See, for instance, the notes above on p. 33; and the remarks, in the Introduction to the Ambattha, on the Aggañña Sutta.

[2] No. 1 in vol. ii of the Pâli text in Prof. Fausböll's edition, and of the Cambridge translation edited by Prof. Cowell.

to find some one to tell them of their faults. Bent on this, so serious, quest, the two came face to face in a low cart-track with precipitous sides. Each calls on the other to make way for a king. Both are kings! How to settle the point? 'I have it,' says one charioteer: 'Let the younger give way.' The kings turn out to be exactly of an age. 'Then let the lord of the lesser realm go back.' Their kingdoms are exactly equal in size. And so on, in succession, are found to be the strength of their two armies, the amount of their treasure, the glory of their renown, the fame of their realms, the distinction of their caste, and tribe, and family. Then at last comes the solution. The king of Kosala overcomes evil by evil. Of the other, the king of Benares, it is said:

> 'Anger he conquers by calmness,
> And by goodness the wicked,
> The stingy he conquers by gifts,
> And by truth the speaker of lies[1].'

And on this being proclaimed, the king of Kosala and his charioteer alighted from their chariot. And they took out the horses, and removed their chariot, and made way for the king of Benares.

There is not a word in the whole story, here told in abstract[2], to suggest that it is not all sober history. But of course the whole story is invented. The two kings are brought on to the stage merely to carry on their broad shoulders the moral of the tale, and the dry humour of the predicament in which they find themselves is there to attract attention to, to add emphasis to, the lesson taught.

What is the especial point in this fun—a kind of fun quite unknown in the West? It is the piquancy of the contrast between the mock seriousness of the extravagant, even impossible details, and the real serious earnestness of the ethical tone. The fun of the extravagance can be matched, easily enough, in European, and especially in American humour. The piquancy of this contrast is Indian, and especially Buddhist. Even the theosophic myth-makers of the Vedas had a sense of the humour in the incongruities, the half realities of their myths. One feels it occasionally even in the Brâhmaṇas. In the Upanishads it is very marked. The Liturgy of the Dogs, the Fable of the Senses, the War of the Devas and Asuras, and several other such episodes

---

[1] This verse is quoted in the Dhammapada (verse 223).

[2] The full version can also be seen in my 'Buddhist Birth Stories,' pp. xxii–xxvi.

have this mixture of unreality and earnestness, and it finds its perhaps most touching expression in the legend of Na*k*iketas. And the Buddhists, in their *G*âtaka stories, often adopted and developed old Indian tales of a similar sort.

But why should we think that this sort of humour is confined to the *G*âtakas? We have a *G*âtaka story of the Great King of Glory, certainly based on the Sutta of the same name, for it expressly quotes it, and embodies the numerous details which lead up to the sublime lesson at the end of it[1]. And those details are at least as extravagant as the details in the Râ*g*ovâda *G*âtaka. Allowing for all the earnestness undeniably animating both the story-teller and the hearers, it is clear that they enjoyed, all the time, the dry humour of the exaggeration and grotesqueness of the details of the story as it went along. Now the details are given only in the Sutta; and omitted, as well known, in the *G*âtaka. They build up a gorgeous fairy tale in which the ancient mythology of the sun-myth is brought into play in order to show how the greatest possible majesty and glory of the greatest and best of all possible kings is, after all, but vanity. And the details, here also, in the Sutta, are enlivened by an intentional exaggeration, a designed dry humour, similar to that in the Râ*g*ovâda *G*âtaka, above referred to.

A similar state of things is found in the Aggañña Sutta, as pointed out above in the Introduction to the Amba*tth*a; in the Keva*tt*a Sutta, translated below; and in many other Suttas. In all of them there is the same exaggeration, the same dry humour, the same restrained art of the story-teller. It is impossible not to see that to the early tellers and hearers of these legends, always striking, often with a special beauty of their own, the unreality of the whole thing was just as evident, and was meant to be as evident, as it is now to us. They knew quite well that the lesson taught was the principal matter, the main point compared with which all others were quite subservient. And it made no difference that, for instance, the Great King of Glory was expressly identified with the Buddha in a former birth. They accepted it all; and entered none the less into the spirit of the legend as legend, because they enjoyed both the lesson and the manner of the telling of it.

And so, I would submit, stands the case also with our present Sutta. The whole legend is obviously invented *ad hoc*. Its details are not meant to be taken seriously as

---

[1] Both *G*âtaka and Sutta are translated in full in my 'Buddhist Suttas' (vol. xi of the S. B. E., pp. 238–289).

historical fact. The forced twist given to the meaning of the words vidhâ and parikkhâro is not serious. The words could not be used in the new sense assigned. What we have is a sort of pun, a play upon the words, a piece of dialectic smartness, delightful to the hearers then, and unfortunately quite impossible to be rendered adequately, in English prose, for readers now.

And it is quite open to question whether this does not apply as much to the whole Sutta as to the legend of King Wide-realm. The Brahman Kûṭadanta (pointed-tooth) is mentioned nowhere else, and is very likely meant to be rather the hero of a tale than an historical character. In that case we should have before us a novelette, an historical romance, in which the Very Reverend Sir Goldstick Sharp-tooth, lord of the manor of Khânumata,—cruel enough, no doubt, and very keen on being sure that his 'soul' should be as comfortable in the next world as he was, now, in this,—makes up his mind to secure that most desirable end by the murder of a number of his fellow creatures, in honour of a god, or as he would put it, by celebrating a sacrifice.

In order to make certain that not one of the technical details—for to the accurate performance of all these the god was supposed to attach great weight—should be done wrong, the intending sacrificer is ironically represented as doing the very last thing any Brahman of position, under similar circumstances, would think of doing. He goes to the Samaṇa Gotama for advice about the modes of the ritual to be performed at the sacrifice; and about the requisite utensils, the altar-furniture, to be used in making it.

The Buddha's answer is to tell him a wonderful legend of a King Wide-realm, and of the sacrifice he offered— truly the most extraordinary sacrifice imaginable. All its marvellous details, each one settled, be it noted, on the advice of a Brahman, are described with a deliberate extravagance none the less delicious because of the evident earnestness of the moral to be inferred.

The Brahman of our Sutta wants to know the three modes in which the ritual is to be performed. The three 'modes' are declared in the legend (§ 15) to be simply three conditions of mind, or rather one condition of mind at three different times, the harbouring of no regret, either before or during or after the sacrifice, at the expenditure involved. And the material accessories required, the altar-furniture, the priest's outfit, what is that? It is the hearty co-operation with the king of four divisions of his people, the nobles, the officials, the Brahmans, and the householders. That makes four articles of furniture. And eight personal qualifications of the king himself. That makes other eight. And four personal qualifications of his advising Brahman make up the total of the sixteen articles required. No living thing, either animal or vegetable, is injured. All the labour is voluntary. And all the world co-operates in adding its share to the largesse of food, on strict vegetarian principles, in which, alone, the sacrifice consists. It is offered on behalf, not only of the king himself, but of all the good. And the king desires to propitiate, not any god, but living men. And the muttering of mystic verses over each article used and over mangled and bleeding bodies of unhappy victims, verses on which all the magic efficacy of a sacrifice had been supposed to depend, is quietly ignored.

It is all ironical, of course—just the very contrary, in every respect, of a typical Vedic sacrifice. And the evident unreality of the legend may be one explanation of the curious fact that the authors of the Gâtaka book (notwithstanding that King Wide-realm's Chaplain is actually identified in the Sutta with the Buddha himself in a previous birth) have not included this professedly Gâtaka story in their collection. This is the only case, so far discovered, in which a similar omission has been made.

Having thus laughed the Brahman ideal of sacrifice out of court with the gentle irony of a sarcastic travesty, the author or authors of the Sutta go on to say what they think a sacrifice ought to be. Far from exalting King Wide-realm's procedure, they put his sacrifice at the very bottom of a long list of sacrifices each better than the other, and leading up to the sweetest and highest of all, which is the attainment of Arahatship.

Here again, except in the last paragraph, there is nothing exclusively Buddhistic. That a sacrifice of the heart is better than a sacrifice of bullocks, the ethical more worthy than any physical sacrifice, is simply the sensible, rational, human view of the matter. The whole long history of the development of Indian thought, as carried on chiefly by Brahmans (however much it may have owed in the earliest period to the nobles and others), shows that they, the more enlightened and cultured of the Brahmans, were not only as fully alive to this truth as any Buddhist, but that they took it all along for granted.

Even in the Vedas themselves there is already the germ of this view in the mental attitude as regards Aditi and Varuna. And in the pre-Buddhistic Khândogya, in the mystic identification of the sacrifice with man[1], we find

---

[1] Khândogya Upanishad III, 16 and 17.

certain moral states placed on an equality with certain parts of the sacrificial procedure. And among these moral states, ahimsâ, the habit of causing no injury to any living thing, is especially mentioned. This comes very near to the Hebrew prophet's: 'I will have mercy, and not sacrifice [1].' The more characteristically Indian point of view is, no doubt, in the words of the old saying long afterwards taken up into the Mahâbhârata, that it is truth (not mercy) that outweighs a thousand sacrifices [2]. But there is a very great probability that the ahimsâ doctrine, foreshadowed in the Upanishad, and afterwards so extravagantly taken up by the Niganthas, the Gains of the Buddha's time, was also a part of the earlier Gain doctrine, and therefore not only in germ, but as a developed teaching, pre-Buddhistic. Though the Buddhists did not accept this extreme position, there would seem therefore to be no valid reason for doubting the accuracy of the Buddhist tradition that their view of sacrifice was based on a very ancient belief which was, in fact, common ground to the wise, whether inside or outside the ranks of the Brahmans.

Our Sutta is, then, merely the oldest extant expression, in so thorough and uncompromising a way, of an ancient and widely held trend of opinion. On this question, as on the question of caste or social privileges, the early Buddhists took up, and pushed to its logical conclusions, a rational view held also by others. And on this question of sacrifice their party won. The Vedic sacrifices, of animals, had practically been given up when the long struggle between Brahmanism and Buddhism reached its close. Isolated instances of such sacrifices are known even down to the Muhammadan invasion. But the battle was really won by the Buddhists and their allies. And the combined ridicule and earnestness of our Sutta will have had its share in bringing about the victory.

That they did win is a suggestive fact. How could they have done so if the Indians of that time had been, as is so often asserted of them by European writers, more deeply addicted to all manner of ritual than any other nation under heaven, more superstitious, more averse to change in religious ceremonial? There seems to me no reason to believe that they were very different, in these respects, from

---

[1] Hosea vi. 6; quoted Matt. ix. 13, and xii. 7. See also Micah vi. 6–8. Prov. xv. 8, and xxi. 13, are, of course, later.

[2] Mahâbhârata I, 3095 nearly = XIII, 1544. Compare XIII, 6073.

Greeks or Romans of the same period. On the contrary there was a well marked lay feeling, a wide-spread antagonism to the priests, a real sense of humour, a strong fund of common sense. Above all there was then the most complete and unquestioned freedom of thought and expression in religious matters that the world had yet witnessed. To regard the Indian peoples through Brahman spectacles, to judge them from the tone prevalent in the *S*rauta and Gr*i*hya Sûtras, it would seem impossible that this victory could have been won. But it was won. And our views of Indian history must be modified accordingly.

There is a curious expression in the stock phrase describing the learned Brahman, so often found in the Pi*t*akas, which I have left untranslated in this Sutta, being uncertain as to the meaning in which it was used at the time when our Sutta was composed. It will be instructive, in more ways than one, to collect and consider the other passages in which the word occurs.

Lokâyata is explained by Wilson as 'the system of atheistical philosophy taught by *K*ârvâka[1],' and by the Petersburg Dictionary as ' Materialism.' Now the description of the good Brahman as put, in the Buddhist Suttas, into the mouth of Brahmans themselves[2], mentions Lokâyata as one branch of his learning. The whole paragraph is complimentary. And though the exact connotation of one or two of the other terms is doubtful, they are all descriptive of just those things which a Brahman would have been rightly proud to be judged a master of. It is evident, therefore, that the Dictionary interpretations of the word are quite out of place in this connection.

Yet they are each of them, at least for a later period, well authenticated. Kumârila Bha*tt*a, in his Vârttika (verse 10), charges the Mîmâ*m*sâ system with having been, for the most part, converted into a Lokâyata system, and claims for his own book the merit of bringing it back to theistic lines[3]. Now of course the Mîmâ*m*sists would indignantly deny this. Kumârila, who seems to have been a good deal of a bigot, is here merely hurling at adversaries, who claimed to be as orthodox as himself, a term of abuse. But it is clear that he uses that term in the sense of ' atheistic.' The exact phrase

[1] He gives as his authority the Amara Ko*s*a; but the Ko*s*a merely mentions the word, in a list, without any explanation.

[2] A*n*guttara I, 163, and other passages.

[3] The passage is quoted in Muir's ' Sanskrit Texts,' III, 95.

would be nâstika, as opposed to his own âstika-patha: that is, the system or the man who says 'there is not,' an infidel. This is somewhat wider than atheist; it comes however, in Kumârila's mouth, to much the same thing.

Sankarâkârya uses the word Lokâyata several times[1], and always in the same specific sense as the view of those who look upon the soul as identical with the body, as existing only so long as the body exists, not continuing, after death, in a new condition and separate from the body. A very similar, if not indeed the very same view is also controverted in the Brahma-gâla Sutta (above, p. 46); and is constantly referred to throughout the Pitakas under the stock phrase tam gîvam tam sarîram[2]. But it is never called Lokâyata in the Pitakas. It seems to be the view that there is a soul; but that it is diffused through the body, and dies with it; and is not a separate unity, within the body but not of it, which flies away from the body after death. It is not necessary to suppose that either Sankara or the Buddhists had in their minds any book setting forth a philosophy based on this single proposition, or any actual school using such a book as a manual. It may have been so. But the expressions used point rather to an opinion held by certain thinkers, in union with other opinions, and not expounded in any special treatise. Nor do either the Buddhists or Sankara pretend to set out that opinion in full. They are dealing with it only so far as is necessary to enforce their own contrary positions. And though 'materialist,' as a rough and ready translation of Sankara's Lokâyatika, gives a good idea, to a European reader, of the sort of feeling conveyed to Sankara's Indian readers, yet it is not quite exact. European 'materialists' (and one or two may be discovered by careful search) do not hold the view which Sankara describes to his Lokâyatikas.

Buddhaghosa in our passage has: Lokâyatam vukkati vitanda-vâda-sattham, 'the Lokâyata is a text-book of the Vitandas (Sophists)[3].' This does not help us much; but previously, p. 91, he explains Lokakkhâyikâ as follows: 'Foolish talk according to the Lokâyata, that is the Vitanda, such as: "By whom was this world created? By

---

[1] For instance in his commentary on the Brahma-Sûtra, I, 1, 2; II, 2, 2; III, 3, 53.

[2] For instance in the Mahâli and Gâliya Suttas, both translated below.

[3] Sum. I, 247. The Vitandas are quoted and refuted in the Attha Sâlinî, pp. 3, 90, 92, 241 (where the word is wrongly spelt).

such a one. A crow is white from the whiteness of its bones; cranes are red from the redness of their blood."'

Other Pâli comments on the word are the Abhidhâna Padîpikâ (verse 112), which says simply, probably following Buddhaghosa: Vita*n*da-sattha*m* viññeyya*m* ya*m* ta*m* lokâyata*m*. The date of this work is the middle of the twelfth century A.D. Much clearer is Aggava*m*sa in the Sadda-nîti, which is a generation older. He says[1]:

Loko ti bâla-loko; ettha âyatanti ussâhanti vâyamanti vâdassâdenâti lokâyata*m*. Ayatati vâ tena loko, na yatati na îhati vâ, lokâyata*m*. Ta*m* hi gandha*m* nissâya sattâ puñña-kiriyâya *k*itta*m* *n*a uppâdenti. Lokâyata*m* nâma: sabba*m* u*kkh*ittha*m* sabbam anu*kkh*ittha*m* seto kâko kâ*l*o bako iminâ va iminâ va kâranenâti evam-âdi-niratthaka-kara*n*apa*t*isa*m*yutta*m* titthiya-sattham, ya*m* loke Vita*n*da-sattha*m* vu*kk*ati, ya*m* sandhâya Bodhisatto asamadhuro Vidhûra-pa*n*dito:

Na seve Lokâyatika*m*, n'eta*m* puññâya va*ddh*ana*m* ti âha.

'Loko means the common world. Lokâyata means: "on that they âyatanti;" that is, they exert themselves about it, strive about it, through the pleasure they take in discussion. Or perhaps it means: "the world does not yatati by it;" that is, does not depend on it, move on by it. For living beings do not stir up their hearts to right-doing by reason of that book[2]. Now the Lokâyata is the book of the unbelievers (of the Titthiyas) full of such useless disputations as the following: "All is impure; all is not impure; the crow is white, the crane is black; and for this reason or for that"—the book known in the world as the Vita*n*da-sattha, of which the Bodisat, the incomparable leader, Vidhûra the pandit, said:

"Follow not the Lokâ yạta, that works not for progress in merit."'

---

[1] Quoted *sub voce* in Subhûti's ' Abhidhânappadîpikâ Sû*k*i,' p. 310. According to the Sâsana Va*m*sa Dîpikâ (Dr. Mabel Bode's edition, p. 74), he lived at Arimaddana in Burma in 1127 A.D. See also Sâsana Va*m*sa Dîpo, verse 1238; Gandha Va*m*sa, pp. 63, 67; Forchammer, 'Jardine Prize Essay,' p. 34; J. P. T. S., 1882, p. 103.

[2] With this attempt at derivation may be compared Nîlaka*nth*a on the passage quoted below from the Mahâbhârata (as given in B. R.), Loka evâyatante te lokayatikâ. Also Prof. Cowell's suggestion (Sarvad. S., p. 2) that Lokâyata may be analysed etymologically as ' prevalent in the world.' The exact meaning of âyata is really very doubtful.

The verse quoted—certainly a very old one—is in the Vidhûra *G*âtaka[1], and the commentator there says: 'This means: Follow not Lokâyata disputation, Vita*nd*a chatter, concerned with useless matters which neither give paradise nor lead men on into the Path.'

*S*ankara says: 'There is thus, according to them, no soul, separate from the body, and capable of going to the heavenly world or obtaining release[2].' The unknown author of the *G*âtaka commentary, who certainly wrote however in the fifth century, gives the allied proposition as his own conclusion from the uselessness of their discussions, not as the opinion of the Lokâyatikas themselves. It would be an easy transition from the one expression to the other. And the difference is suggestive, especially in the light of other passages in both Sanskrit and Pâli books.

For while the Mahâbhârata has precisely the same use of the word as the Pi*t*akas, later works use it in a manner approximating more and more nearly to that of *S*ankara. The passage in the Mahâbhârata is at I, 2889 (= Hari Va*m*sa 14068), where, at the end of a list of the accomplishments of learned Brahmans, they are said to be masters of the Lokâyata. Being mentioned, as in our passage, at the end of the list, it is plain that this branch of learning is meant to be taken as of minor importance. But it is not yet considered unfavourably, much less opprobiously. And the Petersburg Dictionary, from which I take most of these references, points out that the word may possibly, in this passage, have some other meaning than 'Materialism.'

The Râmâya*n*a goes further. There the word is also in a list, but the Laukâyatikâ are blamed as 'clever in useless things[3].' So in the Saddharma Pu*nd*arîka the good Mahâyânist does not serve or court or wait upon (among other low people) 'the Lokâyatikas who know by heart the Lokâyata mantras (mystic verses)[4].' The date of

---

[1] Fausböll's edition, VI, 286. No less than four bas reliefs, illustrating this *G*âtaka, have been found at the Bharhut Tope. See my 'Buddhist Birth Stories,' p. cii. On the greater age of the verses, as compared with the prose, of the *G*âtakas, see ibid. lxxviii.

[2] *Loc. cit.* See Deussen, 'Vedânta-system,' 310; and Thibaut, 'Vedânta-Sutras,' II, 269.

[3] Gorresio's edition, II, 109, 29. Both these passages from the epics are from later portions of them.

[4] Chapter XIII, at the beginning. Burnouf (p. 168) reads tantras (instead of mantras), no doubt wrongly, and has a curious blunder in his note on the passage (p. 409). He says Lokâyata means in Pâli 'fabulous history, romance'; and quotes, as his authority, the passage

this may be a century or two after Christ. And in the Gain book, entitled the Bhagavatî, which Weber puts at about the same time, the Lokâyatikas occur in a similar list of blameworthy persons[1].

In the Milinda, which is probably somewhat earlier, the word is mentioned twice. One passage ascribes a knowledge of the Lokâyata (in a sentence expanded from the very clause in our Sutta) to the hero of the story, Nâgasena[2]. Here the Milinda is quite at the old standpoint. The other passage is in a parenthesis[3] in which the sub-hero, the king, is described as 'fond of wordy disputations, and in the habit of wrangling against the quibbles of Lokâyatas and Vitandas.' This may possibly be a gloss which has crept into the text. But in any case it is evidence that, at the time when it was written, the later view of the meaning of the word had become prevalent.

In the long list of various sorts of hermits given in the Harsha Karita the Lokâyatikas come among others who would be classed by Vedântists as heretics[4]. We cannot, unfortunately, draw any certain conclusion as to whether or not there were actually any Lokâyatikas living in Bâna's time. In expanding previous descriptions of the concourse of hermits in the forest, he may be merely including in his list all the sorts of such people he had ever heard or read of.

Lastly, the Lokâyata system is, in various works of the fourteenth century and later, appropriately fathered on Kârvâka, a mythical character in the Mahâbhârata, an ogre, who appears in the garb of a Brahman[5]. It is not certain whether this is due to the ingenuity of a friend or a foe. In either case, like the fathering of the later Sânkhya on the ancient sage Kapila; or the fathering of the collection of fables, made by Planudes in the fourteenth century A.D., upon Aesop the story-teller of the fifth century B.C., it has been eminently successful, has deceived many, and is still widely accepted.

Pending the discovery of other texts, and especially of

given above from the Abhidhâna Padîpikâ, in which Lokâyatam is simply explained as vitanda-sattham. This last expression cannot possibly mean anything of that sort.

[1] Weber, Ueber ein fragment der Bhagavatî, II, 248.
[2] My Milinda, I, 7.
[3] Ibid. I, 17.
[4] Cowell's Translation, p. 236.
[5] Madhusûdana Sarasvatî, Prabodhakandrodaya, Sarva-darsana-samgraha.

such as are not only the testimony of opponents, the best working hypothesis to explain the above facts seems to be that about 500 B.C. the word Lokâyata was used in a complimentary way as the name of a branch of Brahman learning, and probably meant *Nature-lore*—wise sayings, riddles, rhymes, and theories handed down by tradition as to cosmogony, the elements, the stars, the weather, scraps of astronomy, of elementary physics, even of anatomy, and knowledge of the nature of precious stones, and of birds and beasts and plants. To be a master of such lore was then considered by no means unbecoming to a learned Brahman, though it ranked, of course, below his other studies. At that time there was no school so called, and no special handbook of such knowledge. But portions of it trenched so closely upon, were so often useful as metaphor in discussing the higher and more especially priestly wisdom, that we find sayings that may well have belonged to it preserved in the pre-Buddhistic literature. Such passages, for instance, as Bri. Âr. Up. III, 8, 3, *K*hând. Up. IV, 17, 1, and VI, 2–7, on the worlds and on cosmogony; *K*hând. III. on the colour of the rays of the sun; Bri. Âr. Up. II, 1, 5–7, and III, 7, 3–7, on the elements; Ait. Âr. III, 2, 1, 4, and others, on the parts of the body; and many others of a similar kind on these and other subjects might be cited as examples.

The amount then existing of such lore was too small to make a fair proficiency in it incompatible with other knowledge. As the amount of it grew larger, and several branches of natural science were regularly studied, a too exclusive acquaintance with Lokâyata became looked upon with disfavour. Even before the Christian era masters of the dark sayings, the mysteries, of such mundane lore were marked with sophists and casuists. This feeling is increasingly vouched for in the early centuries of our era. In the fifth century we hear of a book, presumably on the riddles and mysteries of the craft, as it is called 'a book of quibbles.' Various branches of mundane science had been by that time fairly well worked out. Lokâyata was still the name for the old *Nature-lore*, on the same level as folk-lore, and in contradistinction, not only to theosophy on the one hand, but to such science as there was on the other.

In the first half of the eighth century Kumârila uses the word as a mere term of abuse, and in the sense of infidel, of his equally orthodox opponents, the Mîmâ*m*sists. And shortly afterwards *S*ankara, in setting forth his theory of the soul, controverts a curious opinion which he ascribes to Lokâyatikas,—possibly wrongly, as the very same opinion was controverted ages before in the Pi*t*akas, and not there called Lokâyata, though the word was in use in Pi*t*aka times.

Finally in the fourteenth century the great theologian Sâya*n*a-Mâdhava has a longish chapter in which he ascribes to the Lokâyatikas the most extreme forms of the let-us-eat-and-drink-for-to-morrow-we-die view of life; of Pyrrhonism in philosophy, and of atheism in theology. The Lokâyata had no doubt, at that time, long ceased to exist. His very able description has all the appearance of being drawn from his own imagination; and is chiefly based on certain infidel doggrel verses which cannot possibly have formed a part of the Lokâyata studied by the Brahmans of old [1]. It is the ideal of what will happen to the man of some intellect, but morally so depraved that he will not accept the theosophist position.

Throughout the whole story we have no evidence of any one who called himself a Lokâyatika, or his own knowledge Lokâyata. After the early use of the word in some such sense as Nature-lore, folk-lore, there is a tone of unreality over all the statements we have. And of the real existence of a school of thought, or of a system of philosophy that called itself by the name there is no trace. In the middle period the riddles and quibbles of the Nature-lorists are despised. In the last period the words Lokâyata, Lokâyatika, become mere hobby horses, pegs on which certain writers can hang the views that they impute to their adversaries, and give them, in doing so, an odious name.

---

[1] Sarva-dar*s*ana-sa*m*graha, Chapter I, translated by Prof. Cowell in the version published in 1882.

V. KÛṬADANTA SUTTA.

[THE WRONG SACRIFICE AND THE RIGHT.]

[127] 1. Thus have I heard. The Blessed One once, when going on a tour through Magadhâ, with a great multitude of the brethren, with about five hundred brethren, came to a Brahman village in Magadhâ called Khânumata. And there at Khânumata he lodged in the Ambalaṭṭhikâ pleasaunce [1].

Now at that time the Brahman Kûṭadanta was dwelling at Khânumata, a place teeming with life, with much grassland and woodland and water and corn, on a royal domain presented him by Seniya Bimbisâra the king of Magadhâ, as a royal gift, with power over it as if he were the king.

And just then a great sacrifice was being got ready on behalf of Kûṭadanta the Brahman. And a hundred bulls, and a hundred steers, and a hundred heifers, and a hundred goats, and a hundred rams had been brought to the post for the sacrifice.

2. Now the Brahmans and householders of Khânumata heard the news of the arrival of the Samaṇa Gotama [2]. [128] And they began to leave Khânumata in companies and in bands to go to the Ambalaṭṭhikâ pleasaunce.

3. And just then Kûṭadanta the Brahman had gone apart to the upper terrace of his house for his siesta; and seeing the people thus go by, he asked his door-keeper the reason. And the doorkeeper told him [3].

---

[1] Not the same as the one with the same name half way between Râgagaha and Nâlandâ (above, p. 1 of the text). Buddhaghosa (p. 294) says it was like it.

[2] The whole of § 2 of the Soṇadanda is here repeated.

[3] All given in the text in full, as in the Soṇadanda Sutta.

4. Then Kûtadanta thought: 'I have heard that the Samana Gotama understands about the successful performance of a sacrifice with its threefold method and its sixteen accessory instruments. Now I don't know all this, and yet I want to carry out a sacrifice. [129] It would be well for me to go to the Samana Gotama, and ask him about it.'

So he sent his doorkeeper to the Brahmans and householders of Khânumata, to ask them to wait till he could go with them to call upon the Blessed One.

5. But there were at that time a number of Brahmans staying at Khânumata to take part in the great sacrifice. And when they heard this they went to Kûtadanta, and persuaded him, on the same grounds as the Brahmans had laid before Sonadanda. not to go. But he answered them in the same terms as Sonadanda had used to those Brahmans. [134] Then they were satisfied, and went with him to call upon the Blessed One [1].

9. And when he was seated there Kûtadanta the Brahman told the Blessed One what he had heard [2], and requested him to tell him about success in performing a sacrifice in its three modes [3] and with its accessory articles of furniture of sixteen kinds [4].

---

[1] §§ 3–7 inclusive of the Sonadanda are here repeated in full in the text.

[2] As in § 4.

[3] Vidhâ. Childers gives 'pride' as the only meaning of this word. But he has made a strange muddle between it and vidho. All that he has under both words should be struck out. All that he has under vidho should be entered under vidhâ, which has always the one meaning 'mode, manner, way.' Used ethically of the Arahats it refers, no doubt, to divers 'modes' of pride or delusion (as for instance in vidhâsu na vikampanti at S. I, 84, and in the passage quoted in Childers). He makes vidhâ a very rare word, and vidho a common one. It is just the contrary. Vidhâ is frequent, especially at the end of adjectival compounds. Vidho is most rare. It is given doubtfully by Buddhaghosa, in discussing a doubtful reading at Sum. I, 269, in the sense of 'yoke'; and is a possible reading at Vin. II, 136, 319; IV, 168, 363 in the sense of 'brooch' or 'buckle.'

Here vidhâ in Kûtadanta's mouth means, of course, mode of rite or ritual. Gotama lays hold of the ambiguity of the word, and twists it round to his ethical teaching in the sense of mode of generosity.

[4] Parikkhârâ, 'accessories, fillings, equipments, appurtenances,'

'Well then, O Brahman, give ear and listen attentively and I will speak.'

'Very well, Sir,' said ·Kûṭadanta in reply; and the Blessed One spake as follows :—

10. 'Long ago, O Brahman, there was a king by name Wide-realm (Mahâ Viǵita) [1], mighty with great wealth and large property; with stores of silver and gold, of aids to enjoyment [2], of goods and corn ; with his treasure-houses and his garners full.   Now when King Wide-realm was once sitting alone in meditation he became anxious at the thought: " I have in abundance all the good things a mortal can enjoy. The whole wide circle of the earth is mine by conquest to possess.   'Twere well if I were to offer a great sacrifice that should ensure me weal and welfare for many days."

'And he had the Brahman, his chaplain, called; and telling him all that he had thought, [135] he said: " So I would fain, O Brahman, offer a great sacrifice—let the venerable one instruct me how—for my weal and my welfare for many days."

11. 'Thereupon the Brahman who was chaplain said to the king : " The king's country, Sire, is harassed and harried.   There are dacoits abroad who pillage the villages and townships, and who make the roads unsafe.   Were the king, so long as that is so, to levy a fresh tax, verily his majesty would be acting wrongly. But perchance his majesty might think : ' I'll soon put a stop to these scoundrels' game by degradation and banishment, and fines and bonds and death !' But their licence cannot be satisfactorily put a stop to so. The remnant left unpunished would still go on harassing the realm.   Now there is one method to adopt to

---

—the furniture of a room, the smallest things one wears, the few objects a wandering mendicant carries about with him, and so on. Here again the word is turned into a riddle, the solution of which is the basis of the dialogue.

[1] Literally ' he who has a great realm '—just as we might say Lord Broadacres.

[2] ' Such as jewels and plate,' says Buddhaghosa (p. 295).

put a thorough end to this disorder. Whosoever there be in the king's realm who devote themselves to keeping cattle and the farm, to them let his majesty the king give food and seed-corn. Whosoever there be in the king's realm who devote themselves to trade, to them let his majesty the king give capital. Whosoever there be in the king's realm who devote themselves to government service [1], to them let his majesty the king give wages and food. Then those men, following each his own business, will no longer harass the realm; the king's revenue will go up; the country will be quiet and at peace; and the populace, pleased one with another and happy, dancing their children in their arms, will dwell with open doors."

'Then King Wide-realm, O Brahman, accepted the word of his chaplain, [136] and did as he had said. And those men, following each his business, harassed the realm no more. And the king's revenue went up. And the country became quiet and at peace. And the populace, pleased one with another and happy, dancing their children in their arms, dwelt with open doors.

12. 'So King Wide-realm had his chaplain called, and said: "The disorder is at an end. The country is at peace. I want to offer that great sacrifice—let the venerable one instruct me how—for my weal and my welfare for many days."

'Then let his majesty the king send invitations to whomsoever there may be in his realm who are Kshatriyas, vassals of his, either in the country or the towns; or who are ministers and officials of his, either in the country or the towns; or who are Brahmans of position, either in the country or the towns; or who are householders of substance, either in the country or the towns, saying: "I intend to offer a great sacrifice. Let the venerable ones give their sanction to what will be to me for weal and welfare for many days."

'Then King Wide-realm, O Brahman, accepted the

---

[1] Râga-porise. On this word, the locative singular of a neuter abstract form, compare M. I, 85.

word of his chaplain, [137] and did as he had said. And they each—Kshatriyas and ministers and Brahmans and householders—made alike reply : " Let his majesty the king celebrate the sacrifice. The time is suitable, O king[1] ! "

'Thus did these four, as colleagues by consent, become wherewithal to furnish forth that sacrifice[2].

13. 'King Wide-realm was gifted in the following eight ways :—

' He was well born on both sides, on the mother's side and on the father's, of pure descent back through seven generations, and no slur was cast upon him, and no reproach, in respect of birth—

' He was handsome, pleasant in appearance, inspiring trust, gifted with great beauty of complexion, fair in colour, fine in presence, stately to behold—

' He was mighty, with great wealth, and large property, with stores of silver and gold, of aids to enjoyment, of goods and corn, with his treasure-houses and his garners full—

' He was powerful, in command of an army, loyal and disciplined, in four divisions (of elephants, cavalry, chariots, and bowmen), burning up, methinks, his enemies by his very glory—

' He was a believer, and generous, a noble giver, keeping open house, a welling spring[3] whence Samanas and Brahmans, the poor and the wayfarers, beggars, and petitioners might draw, a doer of good deeds—

' He was learned in all kinds of knowledge—

' He knew the meaning of what had been said, and could explain : " This saying has such and such a meaning, and that such and such "—

---

[1] 'Because it was right and fit to do such deeds when one was young and rich. To spend one's days in selfishness, and then, in old age to give gifts would be no good,' says Buddhaghosa (p. 297).

[2] Yaññassa parikkhârâ. The latter word is here twisted round to a new sense.

[3] Opâna = udapâna. Compare M. I, 379; Vin. I, 236; Mil. 411; Sum. I, 298; and the note at ' Vinaya Texts,' II, 115.

'He was intelligent, expert and wise, and able to think out things present or past or future [1]—

'And these eight gifts of his, too, became wherewithal to furnish forth that sacrifice.

[138] 14. 'The Brahman his chaplain was gifted in the following four ways :—

'He was well born on both sides, on the mother's and on the father's, of pure descent back through seven generations, with no slur cast upon him, and no reproach in respect of birth—

'He was a student repeater who knew the mystic verses by heart, master of the Three Vedas, with the indices, the ritual, the phonology, and the exegesis (as a fourth), and the legends as a fifth, learned in the idioms and the grammar, versed in Lokâyata (Nature-lore) and in the thirty marks on the body of a great man—

'He was virtuous, established in virtue, gifted with virtue that had grown great—

'He was intelligent, expert, and wise ; foremost, or at most the second, among those who hold out the ladle.'

'Thus these four gifts of his, too, became wherewithal to furnish forth that sacrifice.

15. 'And further, O Brahman, the chaplain, before the sacrifice had begun, explained to King Wide-realm the three modes :

'Should his majesty the king, before starting on the great sacrifice, feel any such regret as : "Great, alas, will be the portion of my wealth used up herein," let not the king harbour such regret. Should his majesty the king, whilst he is offering the great sacrifice, feel any such regret as : "Great, alas, will be the portion of my wealth used up herein," let not the king harbour such regret. Should his majesty the king, when the great sacrifice has been offered, feel any such regret as : "Great, alas, has been the portion of my wealth used up herein," let not the king harbour such regret.'

---

[1] Buddhaghosa explains this as meaning that he knew the result of Karma, he knew that his present prosperity was a gift to him by the good deeds done to others in the past, and that there would be a similar result in future for his good deeds done now.

'Thus did the chaplain, O Brahman, before the sacrifice had begun, explain to King Wide-realm the three modes.

16. 'And further, O Brahman, the chaplain, before the sacrifice had begun, in order to prevent any compunction that might afterwards, in ten ways, arise as regards those who had taken part therein, said: " Now there will come to your sacrifice, Sire, men who destroy the life of living things, and men who refrain therefrom —men who take what has not been given, and men who refrain therefrom—men who act evilly in respect of lusts, and men who refrain therefrom—men who speak lies, and men who do not—men who slander, and men who do not—men who speak rudely, and men who do not—men who chatter vain things, and men who refrain therefrom—[139, 140] men who covet, and men who covet not—men who harbour illwill, and men who harbour it not—men whose views are wrong, and men whose views are right. Of each of these let them, who do evil, alone with their evil. For them who do well let your majesty offer, for them, Sire, arrange the rites, them let the king gratify, in them shall your heart within find peace."

17. 'And further, O Brahman, the chaplain, whilst the king was carrying out the sacrifice, instructed and aroused and incited and gladdened his heart in sixteen ways: " Should there be people who should say of the king, as he is offering the sacrifice: 'King Wide-realm is celebrating sacrifice without having invited the four classes of his subjects, without himself having the eight personal gifts, without the assistance of a Brahman who has the four personal gifts;' then would they speak not according to the fact. For the consent of the four classes has been obtained, the king has the eight, and his Brahman has the four, personal gifts. With regard to each and every one of these sixteen conditions the king may rest assured that it has been fulfilled. He can sacrifice, and be glad, and possess his heart in peace[1]."

---

[1] This whole closing sentence is repeated, in the text, of each of the sixteen.

[141] 18. 'And further, O Brahman, at that sacrifice neither were any oxen slain, neither goats, nor fowls, nor fatted pigs, nor were any kinds of living creatures put to death. No trees were cut down to be used as posts, no Dabbha grasses mown to strew around the sacrificial spot. And the slaves and messengers and workmeñ there employed were driven neither by rods nor fear, nor carried on their work weeping with tears upon their faces. Whoso chose to help, he worked; whoso chose not to help, worked not. What each chose to do, he did; what they chose not to do, that was left undone. With ghee, and oil, and butter, and milk, and honey, and sugar only was that sacrifice accomplished.

[142] 19. 'And further, O Brahman, the Kshatriya vassals, and the ministers and officials, and the Brahmans of position, and the householders of substance, whether of the country or of the towns, went to King Wide-realm, taking with them much wealth, and said: "This abundant wealth, Sire, have we brought hither for the king's use. Let his majesty accept it at our hands!"

'"Sufficient wealth have I, my friends, laid up, the produce of taxation that is just. Do you keep yours, and take away more with you!"

'When they had thus been refused by the king, they went aside, and considered thus one with the other: "It would not beseem us now, were we to take this wealth away again to our own homes. King Wide-realm is offering a great sacrifice. Let us too make an after-sacrifice!"

20. 'So the Kshatriyas established a continual largesse to the east of the king's sacrificial pit, and the officials to the south thereof, and the Brahmans to the west thereof, and the householders to the north thereof. And the things given, and the manner of their gift, was in all respects like unto the great sacrifice of King Wide-realm himself.

[143] 'Thus, O Brahman, there was a fourfold co-operation, and King Wide-realm was gifted with

eight personal gifts, and his officiating Brahman with four.   And there were three modes of the giving of that sacrifice.   This, O Brahman, is what is called the due celebration of a sacrifice in its threefold mode and with its furniture of sixteen kinds!'

21.   And when he had thus spoken, those Brahmans lifted up their voices in tumult, and said: 'How glorious the sacrifice, how pure its accomplishment!' But Kûṭadanta the Brahman sat there in silence.

Then those Brahmans said to Kûṭadanta: 'Why do you not approve the good words of the Samaṇa Gotama as well-said?'

'I do not fail to approve: for he who approves not as well-said that which has been well spoken by the Samaṇa Gotama, verily his head would split in twain. But I was considering that the Samaṇa Gotama does not say: "Thus have I heard," nor "Thus behoves it to be," but says only "Thus it was then," or "It was like that then." So I thought: "For a certainty the Samaṇa Gotama himself must at that time have been King Wide-realm, or the Brahman who officiated for him at that sacrifice. Does the venerable Gotama admit that he who celebrates such a sacrifice, or causes it to be celebrated, is reborn at the dissolution of the body, after death, into some state of happiness in heaven?'

'Yes, O Brahman, that I admit. And at that time I was the Brahman who, as chaplain, had that sacrifice performed.'

22.   'Is there, O Gotama, any other sacrifice less difficult and less troublesome, with more fruit and more advantage still than this?'

[144] 'Yes, O Brahman, there is.'

'And what, O Gotama, may that be?'

'The perpetual gifts kept up in a family where they are given specifically to virtuous recluses.

23.   'But what is the reason, O Gotama, and what the cause, why such perpetual givings specifically to virtuous recluses, and kept up in a family, are less difficult and troublesome, of greater fruit and greater

o

advantage than that other sacrifice with its three modes and its accessories of sixteen kinds ?'

'To the latter sort of sacrifice, O Brahman, neither will the Arahats go, nor such as have entered on the Arahat way. And why not? Because at it beating with sticks takes place, and seizing by the throat[1]. But they will go to the former, where such things are not. And therefore are such perpetual gifts above the other sort of sacrifice.'

24. 'And is there, O Gotama, any other sacrifice less difficult and less troublesome, of greater fruit and of greater advantage than either of these ?'

[145] 'Yes, O Brahman, there is.'

'And what, O Gotama, may that be ?'

'The putting up of a dwelling place (Vihâra) on behalf of the Order in all the four directions.'

25. 'And is there, O Gotama, any other sacrifice less difficult and less troublesome, of greater fruit and of greater advantage than each and all of these three?'

'Yes, O Brahman, there is.'

'And what, O Gotama, may that be ?'

'He who with trusting heart takes a Buddha as his guide, and the Truth, and the Order—that is a sacrifice better than open largesse, better than perpetual alms, better than the gift of a dwelling place.'

[146] 26. 'And is there, O Gotama, any other sacrifice less difficult and less troublesome, of greater fruit and of greater advantage than all these four ?'

'When a man with trusting heart takes upon himself the precepts—abstinence from destroying life ; abstinence from taking what has not been given , abstinence from evil conduct in respect of lusts ; abstinence from lying words ; abstinence from strong, intoxicating, maddening drinks, the root of carelessness—that is a sacrifice better than open largesse, better than perpetual alms, better than the gift of dwelling places, better than accepting guidance.'

---

[1] The attendants, at such a general largesse, says Buddhaghosa (p. 303), push the recipients about, make them stand in a queue, and use violence in doing so.

27. 'And is there, O Gotama, any other sacrifice less difficult and less troublesome, of greater fruit and of greater advantage than all these five ?'

'Yes, O Brahman, there is.'

[147] 'And what, O Gotama, may that be ?'

[The answer is the long passage from the Sâmañña-phala, § 40, p. 62 (of the text), down to § 75 (p. 74), on the First Ghâna, as follows :—

1. The Introductory paragraphs on the appearance of a Buddha, his preaching, the conversion of a hearer, and his renunciation of the world.

2. The Sîlas (minor morality).

3. The paragraph on Confidence.

4. The paragraph on 'Guarded is the door of his senses.'

5. The paragraph on 'Mindful and self-possessed.'

6. The paragraph on Content.

7. The paragraph on Solitude.

8. The paragraphs on the Five Hindrances.

9. The description of the First Ghâna.]

'This, O Brahman, is a sacrifice less difficult and less troublesome, of greater fruit and greater advantage than the previous sacrifices.'

[The same is then said of the Second, Third, and Fourth Ghânas, in succession (as in the Sâmañña-phala, §§ 77–82), and of the Insight arising from knowledge (ibid. §§ 83, 84), and further (omitting direct mention either way of §§ 85–96 inclusive) of the knowledge of the destruction of the Âsavas, the deadly intoxications or floods (ibid. §§ 97–98).]

'And there is no sacrifice man can celebrate, O Brahman, higher and sweeter than this.'

28. And when he had thus spoken, Kûtadanta the Brahman said to the Blessed One :

'Most excellent, O Gotama, are the words of thy mouth, most excellent ! Just as if a man were to set up what has been thrown down, or were to reveal that which has been hidden away, or were to point out the right road to him who has gone astray, or were to bring a light into the darkness so that those who had eyes could see external forms—just even so has the truth been made known to me in many a figure by the venerable Gotama. I, even I, betake myself to the venerable Gotama as my guide, to the Doctrine and the Order. May the venerable One accept me as a disciple, as one who, from this day forth, as long as life endures, has taken him as his guide. And I [148] myself, O Gotama, will have the seven hundred bulls, and the seven hundred steers, and the seven hundred heifers, and the seven hundred goats, and the seven hundred rams set free. To them I grant their life. Let them eat green grass and drink fresh water, and may cool breezes waft around them.'

29. Then the Blessed One discoursed to Kûṭadanta the Brahman in due order; that is to say, he spake to him of generosity, of right conduct, of heaven, of the danger, the vanity, and the defilement of lusts, of the advantages of renunciation. And when the Blessed One became aware that Kûṭadanta the Brahman had become prepared, softened, unprejudiced, upraised, and believing in heart, then did he proclaim the doctrine the Buddhas alone have won; that is to say, the doctrine of sorrow, of its origin, of its cessation, and of the Path. And just as a clean cloth, with all stains in it washed away, will readily take the dye, just even so did Kûṭadanta the Brahman, even while seated there, obtain the pure and spotless Eye for the Truth, and he knew : 'Whatsoever has a beginning, in that is inherent also the necessity of dissolution.'

30. And then the Brahman Kûṭadanta, as one who had seen the Truth, had mastered it, understood it, dived deep down into it, who had passed beyond doubt, and put away perplexity and gained full confidence, who had become dependent on no other for his knowledge of the teaching of the Master, addressed the Blessed One and said :

'May the venerable Gotama grant me the favour of taking his to-morrow's meal with me, and also the members of the Order with him.'

And the Blessed One signified, by silence, his consent. Then the Brahman Kûṭadanta, seeing that the Blessed One had accepted, rose from his seat, and keeping his right towards him as he passed, he departed thence. And at daybreak he had sweet food, both hard and soft, made ready at the pit prepared for his sacrifice, and had the time announced to the Blessed One : 'It is time, O Gotama ; and the meal is ready.' And the Blessed One, who had dressed early in the morning, put on his outer robe, and taking his bowl with him, went with the brethren to Kûṭadanta's sacrificial pit, and sat down there on the seat prepared for him. And Kûṭadanta the Brahman [149] satisfied the brethren with the Buddha at their head, with his own hand, with sweet food, both hard and soft, till they refused any more. And when the Blessed One had finished his meal, and cleansed the bowl and his hands, Kûṭadanta the Brahman took a low seat and seated himself beside him. And when he was thus seated the Blessed One instructed and aroused and incited and gladdened Kûṭadanta the Brahman with religious discourse ; and then arose from his seat and departed thence.

Kûṭadanta Sutta is ended.

INTRODUCTION

MAHÂLI SUTTA.

THE form of this Sutta is remarkable We have two distinct subjects discussed. First the question of the ability to see heavenly sights and hear heavenly sounds being raised, the Buddha says that it is not for the sake of acquiring such powers that people join the Order under him. And being asked what their object then is, he gradually leads the questioner on to Arahatship, as the aim, along the Eight-fold Path. There the Sutta might appropriately have ended. But the Buddha himself then raises a totally different question—whether the soul and the body are the same. And though, for the reason stated below, he gives no answer, he leads the discourse again up to Arahatship along the series of mental states set out in the Sâmañña-phala.

This second part of our Dialogue might form a separate Sutta, and it is in fact added, as a Sutta by itself, to the present division of the Dialogues. Why then is it also included here? Buddhaghosa's answer is that the young noble Mahâli, who raises the first point, was known to harbour the heresy that there is a soul, and that it has form. (The words the commentator uses are very short, and the context must, I think, be supplied from the passage translated above, § 10 on p. 46.) It was to clear his mind of this notion that the Buddha specially raised the second point.

However this may be, the Sutta must have been already a double one, must have had its present form, before it received a place in that division of the Buddhist scriptures where it now stands. Each Sutta in that division incorporates the whole of the very ancient tract called the Sîlas. The division is therefore called the Sîla Vagga. And no Sutta not containing the Sîlas can belong to it. Our Sutta only contains the Sîlas in the second part. That part, therefore, must have belonged to it when the dialogues were arranged as they now stand.

The question raised in that second part is one of a group of questions on which primitive Buddhism expresses no

opinion. They are called the Ten Avyâkatâni, the Indeterminates, points not determined. Besides being often mentioned
in the Dialogues translated in the present work and elsewhere,
they form the subject of the Avyâkata Saɱyutta (No. 44
in vol. iv of the Saɱyutta Nikâya), and they are as
follows[1]:—

1, 2. Whether the world is eternal or not.
3, 4. Whether the world is infinite or not.
5, 6. Whether the soul is the same as the body, or distinct
    from it[2].
7-10. Whether a man who has attained to the truth
    (a Tathâgata) exists, or not, and in any way, after
    death.

There are others mentioned occasionally by themselves;
but these form the usual group. Of them, those numbered
1-4 and 7-10 are speculations already condemned in the
Brahma-gâla (above, pp. 27 foll., pp. 35 foll., and p. 40
respectively). The remaining two, those numbered 5 and 6,
form the subject of the Gâliya, incorporated in our present
Sutta.

The position taken by the primitive Buddhists as to these
Indeterminates is so often referred to that it undoubtedly was
an important item in the Buddha's actual belief. It is
rendered very clear by the old legend put into the Buddha's
mouth in the Udâna just quoted. There the various non-
Buddhist teachers of the time are represented as expressing
strong opinions one way or the other on these questions;
and as getting so excited about them that they came to
blows. Gotama thereupon tells a story how, in ancient days,
a similar riot having taken place, the king had all the blind
men in the city brought together, and had an elephant
brought in. Each of the blind men touches a different
part of the elephant. The king then asks them to explain
what an elephant is like. He who had felt the head said
it was like a water-pot. He who had felt the ear said it was
like a winnowing basket. He who had felt the tusk said
it was like a plough-share. He who had felt the trunk
said it was like a plough-handle. He who had felt the
body said it was like a granary. He who had felt its legs
said it was like a pillar. He who had felt its back said it

---

[1] Poʈʈhapâda Sutta (translated below) Saɱyutta IV, 393; Udâna
VI, 4; M. I, 484, &c.
[2] Taɱ gîvaɱ taɱ sarîraɱ. Childers (sub voce pañho) renders
this: 'Is this the life? is this the body?' but that must be wrong.
See Sum. I, 319.

was like a mortar. He who had felt its tail said it was like a pestle. He who had felt its bristles said it was like a broom. And each one was so sure he was right that they clamoured one against the other, and came to blows, to the amusement of the king. Then comes the moral :—

> ' In such points Brahmans and recluses stick
> Wrangling on them, they violently discuss—
> Poor folk ! they see but one side of the shield ! '

The inference is obvious. To discuss such questions is mere speculation, useless, because it is based on insufficient evidence. This is the philosophic position; and it resembles very closely the position taken up, in the West, many centuries afterwards, by Hume and his followers. And, as usual in primitive Buddhism, the ethical corollary is very emphatically insisted upon. It is several times pointed out in the Dialogues[1] of these ten speculations that they—

> ' The jungle, the desert, the puppet show, the writhing, the entanglement, of speculation—are accompanied by sorrow, by wrangling, by resentment, by the fever of excitement; they conduce neither to detachment of heart, nor to freedom from lusts, nor to tranquillity, nor to peace, nor to wisdom, nor to the insight of the higher stages of the Path, nor to Arahatship.'

In other words the speculations, being based on insufficient evidence, are not only useless—they are also, therefore, wrong ; that is, from the Buddhist point of view, a disadvantage in the struggle towards the only aim worth striving for—the perfection and emancipation of Arahatship.

As for the special point of our Sutta—the lesson that no wise man will condescend to discuss the question whether the soul is, or is not, the same as the body—it must be remembered that the negative is the view now known to be so widely, indeed universally prevalent among unthinking people throughout the world that it was almost certainly held also in India. The general opinion about the soul in the pre-Buddhistic Upanishads is somewhat different. There (to judge by the passages set out in my article in the J. R. A. S. for January 1899) it is looked upon as being, at least during life, smaller than the body, though after death, when it flies away from the body through an aperture in the top of the head, it was apparently regarded as a subtle and very impalpable, but still material, double of the body of the deceased.

It was the refusal to allow any place for this universal

---

[1] For instance, M. I, 485.

belief in a semi-material soul in his own system that is the most striking, and perhaps the most original. feature in Gotama's teaching. No other religion of which we have sufficient records to enable us to form an opinion on the point has been constructed without the 'soul.' Where the others said 'soul,' Gotama said usually 'Action,' which comes to much the same as character.

In this respect he came very near to our modern use of the word in such expressions as 'a high-souled man' or 'a soul for music.' And it is worth calling attention to the fact that even in Shakspere more than half the times the word is used it is in this secondary, ethical, emotional sense. Even in the old authorised translation of our Bible, in which the word occurs altogether 449 times, it is used 55 times merely in the sense of person [1], only 85 times in the animistic sense, and 3c6 times in the sense of emotional or intellectual qualities or disposition [2].

This will make Gotama's position, which is really very simple, more clear. He rejected entirely the use of the word in the old animistic sense. He retained it in a personal sense, in the meaning of 'oneself, himself,' &c. [3] And though, of course, he acknowledged the reality of the emotional and intellectual dispositions, he refused absolutely to look upon them as a unity.

The position is so absolute, so often insisted on, so fundamental to the right understanding of primitive Buddhism, that it is essential there should be no mistake about it. Yet the position is also so original, so fundamentally opposed to what is usually understood as religious belief, both in India and elsewhere, that there is great temptation to attempt to find a loophole through which at least a covert or esoteric belief in the soul, and in future life (that is of course of a soul), can be recognised. in some sort of way, as part of so widely accepted a religious system. There is no loophole, and the efforts to find one have always met with unswerving opposition, both in the Pi/akas themselves and in extra-canonical works [4].

---

[1] 'We were in the ship two hundred and seventy-six souls,' Acts xxvii. 37.

[2] There are about a score of ambiguous passages; but a different decision as to them would not change the proportion to any substantial extent.

[3] Attano, attanâ, &c., in all the oblique cases. But for the nominative attâ, the use of which might have been misunderstood, sa y a m is almost always, if not indeed always, substituted.

[4] See the quotations in my 'American Lectures' (London, 1896), pp. 39–42, and the notes above, pp. 81, 87.

Our available records are not at present sufficient to enable us to judge either of the numbers, or of the importance, of those Buddhists who made such attempts. But it is clear from the tone of the first .chapter of the Kathâ Vatthu, and from the express statements of the commentary on it, that there were such Buddhists as early as the time of Asoka. They belonged to two out of the eighteen schools of thought which had then arisen. The names of these schools are the Sammitiyâ and the Vaggi-puttakâ[1]. We may yet hope to recover a work which will contain their arguments in their own words. But if the opinion condemned at pp. 14–19 of the Kathâ Vatthu be really theirs, as the commentator declares it is, then it would seem that they held a view practically the same as that opinion of Mahâli, which the Buddha, in our Sutta, goes out of his way to raise in the form of a question, and to put aside as unworthy of discussion.

The expression sambodhi-parâyano used in this Sutta, § 13, has been hitherto misunderstood.

The Buddhist ideal is a subjective state to be reached, in this world, by going along an eightfold path, so called because of the eight good qualities or characteristics which make up its eight parts. Progress along this path is divided into four stages in which certain evil dispositions, the ten so-called Bonds, are got rid of. The Sambodhi is the insight, wisdom, intelligence, awakening, which is essential to the three higher stages of this state of Arahatship. And what is connoted by the term can best, perhaps, be understood by bearing in mind its seven constituent parts, the Sambogghangâ — self-possession, investigation into the truth, energy, calm, joy, concentration, and magnanimity.

In describing the first and lowest of the four stages of the Path, it is always stated (Dîgha I, 156; M. P. S. II, 27; A. II, 238, &c.) of the disciple—not that he has then attained the sambodhi, he has only attained abhisamaya—but that he is sambodhi-parâyano. Childers (*sub voce* parâyano) explains this as 'having the Four Truths as his support.' But Buddhaghosa (Sum. I, 313) says: 'He has the sambodhi—by which is meant that of the three higher stages—as his furthermost aim; in other words, he will attain to that.'

Buddhaghosa's explanation is the only one possible in

---

[1] Kathâ-vatthu-ppakara*n*a-a*tth*akathâ, p. 8 (in the Journal of the Pâli· Text Society for 1889).

the context, and is confirmed by every other passage in the Pâli Pi*t*akas where the word sambodhi has been traced. It never means the wisdom of a Buddha, but always the insight of the higher stages of the path to Arahatship. But it is necessary to point this out because the distinction is of the first importance for the history of Buddhism; and also because the erroneous rendering of Burnouf has been followed by Childers in the Dictionary, *sub voce* sambodhi ('attainment of Buddhaship, Buddhahood'), and has not been corrected by any of the distinguished scholars who have discussed the meaning of Asoka's eighth edict in which the word occurs[1]. The king there says that he 'set out for the sambodhi.' If this means that he had started, in his own opinion, along the line of the Pâramitâs, towards the attainment, in some future birth, of Buddhahood, then it is most interesting and important as giving us the earliest mention of a doctrine not found in the Pâli Pi*t*akas, and entirely opposed to their view of Buddhism. But the word does not necessarily imply this, nor does the context require it. The doctrine spoken of with contempt, by the Mahâyânist doctors, as the 'Lesser Vehicle' is quite possible here, and more in accordance with all the rest of the Asoka expressions. There would seem to be no sufficient reason why we should not understand Asoka to mean that he had started, in his own opinion, along the Eightfold Path, towards the attainment, doubtless in some future birth, of Arahatship. Whether this be so or not, this is the only meaning of the word so far found in the Pi*t*akas.

And further, this entering on the Path—the Eightfold Path to the wisdom of the Arahat—is a quite different thing from becoming a Buddhist. There are numerous passages where the very nature of the discourse held not only to laymen (upâsakas), but even to members of the Order (bhikkhus), shows that they were not supposed to have attained as yet to the state of mind described as 'entering upon the Path.' Both the rules of the Order, and the precepts laid down for laymen, are, from the Pi*t*aka point of view, on a different plane altogether, lower than, apart from, that of the Path. Acting up to those rules, carrying out those precepts, can never even result in 'conversion' without the awakening of the new life. It is therefore very doubtful whether the word 'conversion' should be used, in English translations of Buddhist texts, to express a man's

---

[1] See Senart, 'Inscriptions de Piyadasi,' I, 186, and the other authorities referred to at I, 182 and II, 223.

becoming an upâsaka or a bhikkhu. For though the word
'conversion' is used in English in two senses—either that
of joining the outward organisation of a new faith, or that of
having one's eyes opened to the higher life—the second is
the more accurate use of the word, and ought always to
be implied in the first.

The word sambodhi-parâyano occurs in the passage
first above quoted (Dîgha I, 156) in the answer to the
question, 'What is the aim of the life of the recluse (that
is, of the member of the Buddhist Order)?' Opponents and
controversialists are fond of asking this question, and it is
interesting to notice how it is answered. It is never the
attainment of Buddhahood, but always (though the phraseology differs) the attainment of Arahatship. Thus, in the
standing phrase used to state that so and so has become
an Arahat (M. P. S., p. 60, at the end of Chapter V, and often
elsewhere), it is said he has realised the aim of the higher
life (brahmakariya-pariyosânam). The Ratha-vinîta and
the Kulla Sakuludâyi Dialogues (Nos. 24 and 79 of the
Magghima Collection) lead up to the same conclusion. In
the Samyutta IV, 51, the aim is said to be the complete
understanding of sorrow (dukkhassa pariññâ), and the
same reply is expanded further on in the same book (IV, 233)
by the explanation that the way of gaining this understanding is to follow out the whole of the Eightfold Path
to Arahatship. And this is repeated further on (S. V, 6:
compare Mil. 49, 101). In the Aṅguttara (IV, 7) the object
is said to be the destruction of the seven bonds, the destruction of which is precisely Arahatship.

So sambodhi-patto is used in the Sutta Nipâta, 478, 503,
to describe the Arahat, of whom it is said (Itivuttaka, No 47,
p. 42 : compare ibid. p. 117 = A. II, 14, and also A. II, 200,
202 ; S. N. 765) that even here, in this world, he will reach
up to the sambodhi, the way to which is said to be the
Eightfold Path (M. I, 431 and the Dhamma-kakka-ppavattana
Sutta, &c.). And sambodhi-parâyano, with which we
started, is only another way of stating what is expressed by
amata-parâyano ('having the ambrosia of Arahatship as
his aim') in a Sutta, not yet traced, but quoted by Moggallî-
putta Tissa at Kathâ Vatthu XXII, 7 [1].

Of course the above is not intended to imply that the
Buddha had not attained the sambodhi. He was an Arahat,
and, as such, had all the graces an Arahat should have [2].

---

[1] Compare brahma-parâyano at Mil. 234, brahmakariya-
parâyano at A. III, 75, and danda-parâyano at M. I, 88.

[2] Childers thinks sambodho is merely another form of sambodhi.

On the same page of this Sutta we have two instances of
a curious manner of address not infrequent in the Pi*t*akas,
but as yet very imperfectly understood. After being told
that Nâgita was the name of the Buddha's personal attendant,
we find him suddenly, and without any explanation, addressed
as Kassapa. And the young Li*kkh*avi, introduced to us at the
beginning of the Sutta by the name 'Hare-lip' (O*tth*addha),
is addressed both by Nâgita and by the Buddha, neither by
his name O*tth*addha, nor as Li*kkh*avi, but (and again without
any explanation) as Mahâli.

There are several points in this question of address which
cannot yet be solved, but several others are already pretty
clear. There are at least eight different modes of speaking
of or to a person :—

1. *A nickname* arising out of some personal peculiarity. Such
are Lambaka*nn*a (Hanging-eared), Kû*t*adanta (with a pro-
truding tooth), O*tth*addha (Hare-lipped), Anâthapi*nd*ika
(the beggars' friend), Dârupattika (the man with the wooden
bowl). All these are used in a quite friendly, but familiar way.
And such names occur so often that it would seem as if
nearly everybody was known by a nickname.

2. *A personal name*, called in Pâli the mûla-nâma. This,
like our own so-called Christian names, is not connected with
any personal peculiarity. Some of these names (like similar
ones among ourselves) are of very obscure derivation, but
others are clear enough as adjectives with a good or lucky
meaning. Such are Tissa (after the lucky star of that name),
Devadatta (our Theodore), Bhaddiya (nearly the same as
our Frederick), Nanda or Ânanda (Joy), Abhaya (Fear-
less), and many others.

3. *The name of the Gotta or gens*, what we should call
a surname or family name. These are usually patronymic in
form ; such as Opama*ññ*a, Ka*nh*âyana, Moggallâna,
Kassapa, Ka*nd*arâyana, Konda*ññ*a, Vâse*tth*a, Vessâ-
yana, Bhâradvâga, Va*kkh*âyana.

4. *The name of the clan*, called in Pâli Kula-nâma, such
as Sakka, Kâlâma, Buli, Koliya, Li*kkh*avi, Va*gg*i,
Malla, &c.

5. *The name of the mother*, with putta (son) added to it;
such as Sâri-putta (the more usual name by which the
famous disciple Upatissa is called), Vedehi-putta (a name
of A*g*âtasattu king of Magadhâ), Ma*nd*ikâ-putta (= Upaka),

As the former is only found as yet in one ambiguous phrase (M. I, 17;
II, 211; S. IV, 6, 8, 97, 233, &c.), the discussion of its meaning
would be premature.

Mantâni-putta (=Punna), Godhi-putta (=Devadatta), Moggali-putta (=Tissa, author of the Kathâ Vatthu). Less frequently the reverse is the case, and a mother or father, whose child has become famous, is simply referred to as the mother, or father, of so and so.

It is noteworthy that the name of the father is never used in this way, and that the mother's name is never a personal name; but always taken either from the clan, or from the family, to which she belonged. Occasionally the root-form of the name of the clan, or of the trade, has -putto added to it in a similar way (Vanganta-putto, Todeyya-putto[1], rathakâra-putto). But these cases, which are rare, should rather be classified under the next division.

6. *The name of the position in society*, or the occupation, of the person addressed. Such are brâhmana, gahapati, mahârâga, thapati, &c.

7. A mere *general term of courtesy* or respect, not containing any special application to the person addressed—such as bhante, âvuso, ayye, &c.

8. Lastly there is the *local name*, never used in addressing a person, but prefixed or added to the mûla or gotta name, in narrative sentences, to distinguish between two or more people of the same name. Thus of the eighteen different Kassapas mentioned in the books, three are distinguished, in narrative, as Uruvela-Nadî- and Gayâ-Kassapa respectively; of the eight different Kittas one is distinguished as Makkhikâsandika; of the seventeen different Bhâradvâgas one is distinguished as Kâpathika. Other instances are probably Hatthako Âlavako, Bâhiyo Dârukiriyo, Pokkharasâdi Subhagavaniko, &c.

On the rules regulating the choice as to which one of these various sorts of names should, under the circumstances, be used in any particular case, the following observations may be made.

It is not considered courteous among equals, except in the case of close familiarity, to use either of the two sorts of personal names, that is, either the nickname or the mûla-nâma.

The Buddha addresses Brahmans as Brâhmana (for instance Sonadanda and Kûtadanta above in the Suttas so called; Gânussoni at M. I, 16, 178; A. I, 56, 159, 166; II, 173; IV, 54; Sangaya at M. II, 127, 132, though his gotta name is

---

[1] Todeyya-putto may be rendered either 'son of the man of Tudi' or 'of the sons of the dwellers in Tudi' (a well-known village), or lastly 'of the Todeyya clan,' 'the Todeyyan.'

given, Âkâsa-gotta; Sikha at A. II, 232, though his gotta name is given, Moggallâna). But we have had one instance above where he addresses a young Brahman as Amba*ttha*, apparently a clan name (his gotta was Ka*nh*âya*na*). This solitary exception may be because of his youth.

On the other hand the Buddha usually addresses ascetics, not as paribbâ*g*aka, but by their gotta name. Thus at M. I, 228–250 he calls Sa*kk*ako, the Niga*ntha*, by his gotta name Aggi-vessâyana. At M. I, 497–500 he calls Dîgha-nakho (so called, no doubt, because he kept his nails long) by his gotta name, which is again Aggi-vessâyana. And at M. II, 40 he calls Vekha*na*so by his gotta name of Ka*kk*âna. This is only in accord with the usage followed by others besides the Buddha. Thus *G*ânusso*n*i, a Brahman, at M. I, 175, addresses the ascetic Pilotika by his gotta name of Va*kkh*âyana, and Assa*g*i, a member of the Buddhist order, also calls Sa*kk*ako by his gotta name (*loc. cit.*), and every-body, not a Buddhist, addresses the Buddha by his gotta name, as Gotama. When therefore we find other ascetics addressed by the Buddha by the same name as has been used in the introductory narrative (as, for instance, in the case of Sarabha, A. I, 186; Potaliya, A. II, 100; Po*tth*apâda, D. I, 178 foll.), one may conclude that these also are probably gotta names. This custom of addressing people by their gotta name, no doubt a common one in certain cases, was expressly forbidden to Niga*ntha*s (Jacobi, 'Gaina-Sûtras,' II, 305). They called their own Order a gotra (ibid. 321, 327), and apparently thought it worldly to recognise the existence of any other.

The Buddha addresses members of his own clan, whether members of his Order or not, by their personal names (so of Vappa, A. II, 197; of Mahânâma, M. I, 91, 354; A. I, 220; III, 284). The same holds good of the junior members of the Order, but some at least of the more distinguished among them are always addressed by him either by their gotta, or by their mother's, name (compare Moggallâna, Ka*kk*âna, Kassapa, Gotamî, Sâriputta). Nâgita, for instance, though he is addressed as Kassapa by his nephew, the novice Sîha, is addressed by the Buddha simply as Nâgita.

Probably every Brahman, and every member of each of the free clans, had a gotta name. We have no certain instance of such a name in any other case. The gotta names used in the clans are the same as those given in Brahman books to Brahmans. It has been concluded that they are Brahman names, and that the clans must have adopted them from the Brahmans, each family or *gens* taking the gotta name of

their private chaplain, their purohita priest. But in that
case we should surely expect to find some evidence that such
priests were usually maintained in such clans. There is no
evidence of the kind. All that we can fairly conclude is that
the clans claimed, by the very use of these names, to be
descended from the same ancestors as the Brahmans, who
also bore the names: and that the claim was admitted to be
well founded. As shown above, even Brahmans use these
gotta names of non-Brahmans. It would seem that the nickname, when once generally known, tended, in *speaking of*
a person, to drive the others out of use. But it is never used
in *speaking to* the person referred to by it.

From the usage referred to, as followed by the Buddha and
others, it would seem that the gotta name was considered as
more honourable than either of the personal names, and also
than the descriptive general name or title of paribbâ*g*aka
(wandering mendicant, recluse). Even the title Brâhma*n*a
was dropped for the gotta name in the case of a recluse.

There are a number of problems, both as to general principles and as to details, that still remain, in this matter of
names, unsolved. Is Â*l*âra, for instance, a nickname or
a mûla-nâma; is Kâlâmo a gotta name or a clan name[1]?
To what classes of the people was the use of gotta names
limited, and what is the historical explanation of this limitation? Were there as many as a dozen clan names in Magadhâ
and Kosalâ combined? What was exactly implied by the
clan-name, the Kula-nâma? The word gotta probably
had the same meaning, when the Pi*t*akas were composed, as
gotra has in the later law books written by the priests. How
comes it then that the number of gottas referred to is so
very small? Are there much more than a score altogether?
What light does the meaning of the mûla and gotta names
throw on the religious conceptions and social customs of the
people?

I hope to return to these and similar questions when I can
find time to publish my Pâli *Onomasticon*, of the names in
the Pi*t*akas and in the older inscriptions. What has here
been said is probably sufficient to make the use of the names
in this Sutta clear[2].

---

[1] See my note at ' Buddhist Suttas,' p. 75, and compare *contra*
A. I, 188, 278.

[2] Eva*m*-nâmo eva*m*-gotto at M. II, 33; S. III, 25; D. I, 242
is followed at D. I, 13 by eva*m*-va*nn*o; but evidence of any effect of
social distinctions on names is at present very slight.

VI. MAHÂLI SUTTA.

[THE AIM OF THE BRETHREN.]

[150] 1. Thus have I heard. The Blessed One was once staying at Vesâlî at the Gabled Hall in the Great Wood[1]. Now at that time a number of Brahmans, who had been sent on pressing business of one kind or another from Kosalâ and Magadhâ, were lodging at Vesâlî.

And they heard the news: 'They say that the Samana Gotama of the Sâkya clan, who went out from a Sâkya family to adopt the religious life, is now staying at Vesâlî at the Gabled Hall in the Great Wood. Now regarding that venerable Gotama, such is the high reputation that has been noised abroad: "That Blessed One is an Arahat, a fully awakened one, abounding in wisdom and goodness, happy, who knows all worlds, unsurpassed as a guide to mortals willing to be led, a teacher for gods and men, a Blessed One, a Buddha. He, by himself, thoroughly knows and sees, as it were, face to face this universe,—including the worlds above of the gods, the Brahmâs, and the Mâras, and the world below with its recluses and Brahmans, its princes and peoples,—and having known it, he makes his knowledge known to others. The truth, lovely in its origin, lovely in its progress, lovely in its

---

[1] The Great Wood stretched from Vesâlî northwards to the Himâlaya range. In it they had laid out a pleasaunce for the Order, and made there a storied house, with a hall below surrounded by pillars only, and facing the west, and above it the gabled apartments in which the Buddha so often stayed.

consummation, doth he proclaim, both in the spirit and
in the letter, the higher life doth he make known, in
all its fullness and in all its purity.   And good is it to
pay visits to Arahats like that."'

2. So those Brahmans from Kosalâ and Magadhâ
went out to the Great Wood, and to the Gabled Hall.
Now at that time the venerable Nâgita was acting as
the personal attendant on the Blessed One.   And they
went to him, and said: 'Where is it, Nâgita, that that
venerable Gotama is lodging now, for we wish to see
him.'

[151] ' It is not a fitting time, Sirs, to call upon the
Blessed One.   He has retired into solitude.'

Then they sat down round about, saying, 'We will
not go away without seeing the venerable Gotama.'

3. And Hare-lip the Li*kkh*avi, too, came to the
Great Wood, and to the Gabled Hall, with a retinue of
his clan;· and going up to the venerable Nâgita, he
saluted him, and reverently standing apart, he said to
him : 'Where, venerable Nâgita, is the Blessed One
now lodging, the Arahat, the Buddha ; for we wish to
see him?'   And on receiving a similar reply he, too, sat
down apart, saying : 'I will not go till I have seen the
August One, the Arahat, the Buddha.'

4. But Sîha, a novice [1], came up to the venerable
Nâgita, and saluted him, and standing reverently
apart, he said to him : 'These envoys of the Brahmans
from Kosalâ and Magadhâ, many of them, have come,
O Kassapa [2], to call upon the Blessed One; and Hare-
lip the Li*kkh*avi, too, with a retinue of his clan, has
come to do the same. 'Twere best, O Kassapa, that all
this folk should be allowed to see the Blessed One.'

---

[1] He was the son of Nâgita's sister. He had joined the Order as
a novice when only seven years old, and shown so much intelligence
as a learner that he was a favourite with all, even with the Buddha
himself. He must therefore be different from the other Sîha, also
a Li*kkh*avi, who is the hero of the story told at Vin. I, 233–238 = A. IV,
179–188, as the latter is not a member of the Order at all.
Professor Edward Müller (J. P. T. S., 1888, p. 97) confounds
the two.

[2] This is the gotta, the *gens*, to which Nâgita belonged.

'Very well, then, Sîha. Tell the Blessed One yourself.'

'Very good, Sir,' said Sîha the novice in assent to the venerable Nâgita. And he went where the Blessed One was, and saluted him, and standing reverently apart, he said to him even as he had said to Nâgita.

[152] 'Very well, Sîha. Spread out a mat for me in the shade in front of the house.'

5. And Sîha did so. And the Blessed One came out from the house, and sat down. And the Brahmans from Kosalâ and Magadhâ exchanged with him the greetings and compliments of politeness and courtesy, and took their seats on one side. And Hare-lip the Li*kkh*avi also, with the retinue of his clan, bowed down to the Blessed One, and seated himself on one side. And when he was thus seated he addressed the Blessed One, and said :

'Some few days ago, Sir, Sunakkhatta of the Li*kkh*avis [1] came to me, and said: "It is only three years, Mahâli [2], since I first came under the Blessed One, and I can see heavenly forms, pleasant to behold, fitted to satisfy all one's desires, exciting longing in one's heart. But I cannot hear heavenly sounds like that." Now, Sir, are there such heavenly sounds, which he could not hear, or have they no existence?'

'They are real, those heavenly sounds, pleasant, fitted to satisfy one's desires, exciting longing in one's heart, which he could not hear. They are not things of nought.'

---

[1] This young man became the Buddha's personal attendant; but afterwards, when the Buddha was in extreme old age (M. I, 68), he went over to the creed of Kora the Kshatriya, and left the Buddhist Order. Kora's doctrine was the efficacy of asceticism, of rigid self-mortification. And it was to show how wrong this doctrine, as put forth by Sunakkhatta, was, that the Buddha told the story (*G*ât. I, 398) of the uselessness of the efforts he himself had made when

'Now scorched, now frozen, lone in fearsome woods,
Naked, without a fire, afire within,
He, as a hermit, sought the crown of faith.'

But we do not hear that Sunakkhatta ever came back to the fold.

[2] This is again the name of the gotta, the *gens*. Buddhaghosa (p. 316) calls him a râ*g*a.

6. 'But what then is the proximate, and what the
ultimate cause, why he could not hear them, they
being thus real and not things of nought?'

[153] 7. 'Suppose a recluse, Mahâli, to have practised one-sided concentration of mind with the object of
seeing such heavenly forms in any one direction,—in the
East, or the South, or the West, or the North, or above,
or below, or across,—and not with the object of hearing
such heavenly sounds. Then since he has practised
one-sided concentration, with the one object only in
view, he only sees the sights, he hears not the sounds.
And why not? Because of the nature of his self-
concentration [samâdhi].

[154] 8, 9. 'And so also, Mahâli, if he have practised
one-sided concentration with the object of hearing, in
any one direction, the heavenly sounds. Then, and
for the same reason, he hears the sounds, but he sees
not the sights.

[155] 10, 11. 'But suppose, Mahâli, he has practised
self-concentration with the double object in view of
seeing and hearing, in any one direction, those
heavenly sights and those heavenly sounds. Then
since he has practised self-concentration with the
double object in view, he both sees the sights and
hears the sounds. And why so? Because of the
nature of his self-concentration.'

12. 'Then, Sir, is it for the sake of attaining to the
practice of such self-concentration that the brethren
lead the religious life under the Blessed One?'

'No, Mahâli. There are things, higher and sweeter
than that, for the sake of which they do so.'

[156] 13. 'And what, Sir, may those other things be?'

'In the first place, Mahâli, a brother by the complete
destruction of the Three Bonds (the Delusions of self,
Doubt, and Trust in the efficacy of good works and
ceremonies)[1] becomes a converted man, one who cannot be reborn in any state of woe, and is assured of

---

[1] See my 'American Lectures' (London, 1896, pp. 142–149) for
the full meaning of these three, and of the following Bonds.

attaining to the Insight (of the stages higher still)[1]. That, Mahâli, is a condition, higher and sweeter, for the sake of which the brethren lead the religious life under me.

'And then further, Mahâli, a brother by the complete destruction of those Three Bonds, and by reducing to a minimum lust, illwill, and dullness, becomes a Once-returner, one who on his first return to this world shall make an end of pain. That, Mahâli, is a condition higher still and sweeter, for the sake of which the brethren lead the religious life under me.

'And then further, Mahâli, a brother by the complete destruction of the Five Bonds that bind people to this world [2] becomes an inheritor of the highest heavens [3], there to pass away, thence never to return [4]. That, Mahâli, is a condition higher still and sweeter, for the sake of which the brethren lead the religious life under me.

'And then further, Mahâli, when a brother by the destruction of the Deadly Floods (or Intoxications—Lusts, Becomings, Delusion, and Ignorance) has, by himself, known and realised and continues to abide here, in this visible world, in that emancipation of mind, that emancipation of heart, which is Arahatship—that, Mahâli, is a condition higher still and sweeter still, for the sake of which the brethren lead the religious life under me.

'Such, Mahâli, are the conditions higher and sweeter

---

[1] Sambodhi-parâyano. So Buddhaghosa on this (p. 313) and my Introduction to this Sutta.

[2] The above three, and Sensuality and Illwill.

[3] Opapâtiko, literally 'accidental'; but the use of such a word would only mislead the reader, the real connotation of the word being that of the words I have chosen. Those who gain the highest heavens are so called because there is no birth there in the ordinary way. Each being, who is there, has appeared there suddenly, accidentally as it were, without generation, conception, gestation or any of the other means attending the birth of beings in the world.

[4] It is impossible to ignore a reference here to the view expressed in the Bri′had Âra*n*yaka Upanishad (VI, 2, 15). 'There do they dwell far away, beyond, in the Brahmâ-worlds. And for them there is no return.'

(than seeing heavenly sights and hearing heavenly sounds), for the sake of which the brethren lead the religious life under me.'

14. 'But is there, Sir, a path, is there a method, for the realisation of these conditions?'

'Yes, Mahâli, there is.'

[157] 'And what, Sir, may be that path, what that method?'

'Verily it is this Noble Eightfold Path, that is to say: Right views, right aspirations, right speech, right action, a right means of livelihood, right effort, right mindfulness, and right ecstasy in self-concentration [1]. This, Mahâli, is the path, and this the method, for the realisation of these conditions.

15. 'One day, Mahâli, I was staying at Kosambî, in the Ghosita pleasaunce. There two recluses, Ma*nd*issa the wandering mendicant, and *G*âliya the pupil of Dârupattika (the man with the wooden bowl), came to me, and exchanged with me the greetings and compliments of politeness and courtesy, and stood reverently apart. And so standing they said to me:

'How is it then, O venerable Gotama, is the soul the same thing as the body? Or is the soul one thing and the body another?'

'Listen then, Sirs, and give heed attentively, and I will speak.'

'Very good, Sir,' said those two mendicants in assent, and I spake as follows:—

[*Here follows the whole of the exposition given in the Sâma*nn*a-phala Sutta, §§ 40–75, that is to say:*

1. *The appearance of a Buddha and his preaching.*

2. *The awakening of a hearer, and his entry into the Order.*

3. *His self-training in act, word, and speech.*

4. *The minor details of morality which he observes.*

5. *The absence of fear, confidence of heart thence resulting.*

---

[1] See my 'American Lectures,' pp. 136–141; and Sum. I, 314–316.

6. *The way in which he learns to guard the door of his senses.*

7. *The constant self-possession he thus gains.*

8. *The power of being content with little, with simplicity of life.*

9. *The emancipation of heart from the five hindrances —covetousness, illwill, sloth of body and mind, excitement and worry, and perplexity.*

10. *The resulting joy and peace that he gains.*]

16. 'Then estranged from lusts, aloof from evil states, he enters into and remains in the First Rapture—a state of joy and ease, born of detachment, reasoning and investigation going on the while. Now, Sirs, when a Bhikshu knows thus and sees thus, would that make him ready to take up the subject: " Is the soul the same thing as the body, or is the soul one thing and the body another ? " '

' Yes, it would, Sir[1].'

' But I, Sirs, know thus and see thus. And nevertheless I do not say either the one or the other.'

[158] 17, 18. [*The cases are then put of a Bhikshu who has acquired the second, third, and fourth Raptures* (D. II, 77–81) *and the knowledge arising from insight* (*N*âna-dassana; D. II, 83, 84); *and the same question, reply, and rejoinder are given in each case.*]

19. 'With his heart thus serene (&c. above, p. 85), he directs and bends down his mind to the knowledge of the destruction of the Deadly Floods. He knows as it really is: " This is pain." He knows as it really is: " This is the origin of pain." He knows as it really is : " This is the cessation of pain." He knows as it really is: " This is the Path that leads to the cessation of pain." He knows as they really are: "These are the Deadly Floods." He knows as it really is: " This is the origin of the Deadly Floods." He knows as it really is: " This is the cessation of the Deadly Floods." He knows as it really is: "This is the

---

[1] The Siamese edition reads: ' No, it would not, Sir.' On the idiom kalla*m* eta*m* va*k*anâya compare A. I, 144; M. II, 211.

Path that leads to the cessation of the Deadly Floods."
To him, thus knowing, thus seeing, the heart is set free
from the Deadly Taint of Lusts, is set free from the
Deadly Taint of Becomings, is set free from the Deadly
Taint of Ignorance. In him, thus set free, there arises
the knowledge of his emancipation, and he knows:
"Rebirth has been destroyed. The higher life has been
fulfilled. What had to be done has been accomplished.
After this present life there will be no beyond!"'

'When a Bhikshu, Sirs, knows thus and sees thus,
would that make him ready to take up the question:
"Is the soul the same as the body, or is the soul one
thing and the body another?"'

'No, Sir, it would not [1].'

'And I, Sirs, know thus and see thus. And nevertheless I do not say either the one or the other.'

Thus spake the Blessed One; and Hare-lip the
Li*kkh*avi, pleased at heart, exalted the word of the
Blessed One.

———

Here ends the Mahâli Sutta.

———

[1] So three Sinhalese and two Burmese MSS. and the Siamese
edition. Two Sinhalese MSS. read: 'Yes, Sir, it would.' But
Buddhaghosa had clearly, both here and above, § 16, the reading we
have followed. And he gives a characteristic explanation—that whereas
the Arahat (in § 19) would have too much wisdom to be led astray,
following the false trail of the soul theory, the Bhikshu who had only
reached up to the *Gh*ânas might, being still a puthu*gg*ana, an
unconverted man, have leanings that way.

To hold that the soul *is* the same as the body is the heresy referred
to in the Brahma-*g*âla (above, p. 46). See also the Introduction to the
Kû*t*adanta (above, p. 167).

VII. *GÂLIYA SUTTA.*

[IS THE SOUL DISTINCT FROM THE BODY ?]

[*This Sutta having been incorporated, word for word, as §§ 15–19, inclusive, in the last Sutta, the reader is referred to the translation given there.*

The Mahâli Sutta must have already included, when the Dîgha was put together, this *Gâliya* episode. For there would otherwise be no reason for the Mahâli Sutta being put into the Sîlakkhanda Vagga, the Sîlas being contained only in that episode.

Why then should the episode appear also again, in full, as a separate Sutta? Is it merely because of the importance of the question? We have another instance of a similar kind, where the episode of Nigrodha's question, only referred to at § 23 of the Kassapa-Sîhanâda Sutta, is set out afterwards, in full, in the Udumbarîka Sîhanâda Sutta (No. 25 in the Dîgha). But there the whole episode is not given twice in full. Such cross-references are fairly frequent in the Piṭakas, and are of importance for the history of the literature. One of the most striking cases is where the Samyutta quotes a Sutta, now contained in the Dîgha, by name. (Sakka-pañha Sutta, S.III,13; compare Sum. I,51; Mil. 350.)]

INTRODUCTION

KASSAPA-SÎHANÂDA SUTTA.

IN this Sutta the Buddha, in conversation with a naked ascetic, explains his position as regards asceticism—so far, that is, as is compatible with his invariable method (as represented in the Dialogues) when discussing a point on which he differs from his interlocutor.

When speaking on sacrifice to a sacrificial priest, on union with God to an adherent of the current theology, on Brahman claims to superior social rank to a proud Brahman, on mystic insight to a man who trusts in it, on the soul to one who believes in the soul theory, the method followed is always the same. Gotama puts himself as far as possible in the mental position of the questioner. He attacks none of his cherished convictions. He accepts as the starting-point of his own exposition the desirability of the act or condition prized by his opponent—of the union with God (as in the Tevigga), or of sacrifice (as in the Kûtadanta), or of social rank (as in the Ambattha), or of seeing heavenly sights, &c. (as in the Mahâli), or of the soul theory (as in the Potthapâda). He even adopts the very phraseology of his questioner. And then, partly by putting a new and (from the Buddhist point of view) a higher meaning into the words ; partly by an appeal to such ethical conceptions as are common ground between them ; he gradually leads his opponent up to his conclusion. This is, of course, always Arahatship—that is the sweetest fruit of the life of a recluse, that is the best sacrifice, that the highest social rank, that the best means of seeing heavenly sights, and a more worthy object ; and so on. In our Sutta it is the path to Arahatship which is the best asceticism.

There is both courtesy and dignity in the method employed. But no little dialectic skill, and an easy mastery of the ethical points involved, are required to bring about the result. On the hypothesis that the Buddha is a sun myth, and his principal disciples personifications of the stars, the facts seem difficult to explain. One would expect, then, something quite different. How is it that the other disciples who must, in that case, have concocted these Dialogues, refrain so entirely from astrological and mythological details? How is it they attribute to their hero qualities of courtesy and sympathy, and a grasp of ethical problems, all quite foreign, even antagonistic, to those usually ascribed to sun-heroes—mostly somewhat truculent and very un-ethical personages?

On the hypothesis that he was an historical person, of that training and character he is represented in the Pi*t*akas to have had, the method is precisely that which it is most probable he would have actually followed.

Whoever put the Dialogues together may have had a sufficiently clear memory of the way he conversed, may well have even remembered particular occasions and persons. To the mental vision of the compiler, the doctrine taught loomed so much larger than anything else, that he was necessarily more concerned with that, than with any historical accuracy in the details of the story. He was, in this respect, in much the same position as Plato when recording the dialogues of Socrates. But he was not, like Plato, giving his own opinions. We ought, no doubt, to think of compilers, rather than of a compiler. The memory of co-disciples had to be respected, and kept in mind. And so far as the actual doctrine is concerned our Dialogues are probably a more exact reproduction of the thoughts of the teacher than the dialogues of Plato.

However this may be, the method followed in all these Dialogues has one disadvantage. In accepting the position of the adversary, and adopting his language, the authors compel us, in order to follow what they give us as Gotama's view, to read a good deal between the lines. The *argumentum ad hominem* can never be the same as a statement of opinion given without reference to any particular person. That is strikingly the case with our present Sutta.

When addressing his five hearers—the Pañ*k*avaggiyâ, the first five converts, and the first Arahats—in the Deer-park at Benares, on the occasion of his first discourse, the Buddha is represented to have spoken of asceticism in a very different way. He there calls it one of 'two extremes which are to be avoided'; and describes it as 'painful, unworthy, and unprofitable[1].' So in the Puggala Pañ*ñ*atti (IV, 24) the very practices set out in our Sutta, by Kassapa the ascetic,

---

[1] 'Buddhist Suttas' (S. B. E.), p. 147.

as desirable and praiseworthy, are set out as the actions by
which a man injures himself. There is nothing of this sort
in our Sutta. To judge from it alone one might fairly
conclude that the Buddha approved of asceticism, only insisting
that the self-mastery and self-control of the Path were the
highest and best forms of it. There is really no inconsistency
in these three Suttas. But while the first discourse and the
Puggala passage were both addressed to disciples, our Sutta
is addressed to an ascetic, and the language used is modified
accordingly. The conclusion in all is exactly the same.

It is clear that at the time when our Sutta was put together
the practice of self-mortification had already been carried out
to a considerable extent in India. And further details, in
some of which the self-imposed penances are even more
extreme, are given in other Dialogues of the same date,
notably in the twelfth Sutta of the Magghima. This is oddly
enough also called a Sîhanâda Sutta, and the reason is not
far to seek.

The carrying out of such practices, in all countries, wins for
the ascetic a very high reputation. Those who despise earthly
comforts, and even submit themselves to voluntary torture,
are looked upon, with a kind of fearsome wonder, as more
holy than other men. And no doubt, in most cases, the
ascetics laid claim to special virtue. In the Suttas dealing
with the practices of the ascetics, Gotama, in laying stress
on the more moderate view, takes occasion also to dispute this
claim. He maintains, as in our Sutta, that the insight and
self-control and self-mastery of the Path, or of the system
of intellectual and moral self-training laid down for the
Bhikkhu, are really harder than the merely physical practices
so much more evident to the eye of the vulgar. It was
a point that had to be made. And the Suttas in which it
is made are designated as Sîhanâdas, literally 'the lion's
roars'—the proud claim by the Arahat to a dignity and
veneration greater than that allowed by the people to the
self-torturer, or even to the man who

> 'Bescorched, befrozen, lone in fearsome woods,
> Naked, without a fire, afire within,
> Struggled, in awful silence, towards the goal[1]!'

And the boast goes really even further. Not only were the
ascetics no better than the Arahats, they were even not so
practical. The self-mortification was an actual hindrance.
It turned men's minds from more essential matters. Diogenes
was not only not superior to other men, no nearer to the

---

[1] M. I, 79 = Gât. I, 390.

truth than they, by reason of his tub and of his physical renunciation; he was their ethical inferior, and was intellectually wrong. So hard, so very hard, was the struggle[1] that the Arahat, or the man striving towards Arahatship, should be always sufficiently clothed, and take regular baths, regular exercise, regular food. The line was to be drawn at another point. He was to avoid, not what was necessary to maintain himself in full bodily vigour and power, but all undue luxury, and all worry about personal comfort. It was his duty to keep himself in health.

It is open to question whether the earnest and unworldly would now draw the line at the precise point at which Gotama drew it; either as regards what they would think proper for themselves now, or what they would have thought most proper for those living in India then. Probably they would think rather that he erred on the side of austerity. His contemporaries the Niganthas thought the other way. And the most serious schism in the Buddhist Order, that raised by Devadatta, was especially defended on the ground that Gotama would not, as regards various points, adopt ascetic practices which Devadatta held to be then necessary.

It is probable that Gotama was largely guided by the opinions and practice of previous recluses. For we have already seen that in other matters, important it is true but not essential, Gotama adopted and extended, so far as it agreed with the rest of his system, what had already been put forward by others. But we cannot, as yet, speak on this point with as much certainty as we could in the other cases of the ethical view of sacrifice, of the ethical connotation attached to the word Brahman[2], and of the reasonable view as to social distinctions and questions of impurity. Our available texts are only sufficient, at present, to suggest the probability.

The technical term tapas is already found in the Rig-veda, though only in the latest hymns included in the collection. It is literally 'glow, burning,' and very early acquired the secondary sense of retirement into solitude, and of the attempted conquest of one's lower nature by the burning heat of bodily austerity. And this must have been a common practice, for the time of the year most favourable to such

---

[1] So also Kâthaka Upanishad II, 7–13.
[2] See Brihad. III, 5, 1; 8, 10; IV, 4, 21–23; Khând. IV, 1, 7. Compare Âpastamba I, 8, 23, 6; Vas. VI, 3, 23, 25; XXVI, 11 = Manu II, 87 = Vishnu LV, 21; the passages quoted from the Mahâbhârata by Muir, 'Metrical Translations,' pp. 263–4, and Deussen, 'Vedânta-system,' p. 155.

tapas came to be known as the month tapas. There was no association with the word of what we call 'penance,' a conception arising out of an entirely different order of religious ideas. There was no idea of atonement for, punishment of, making amends for sin. But just as the sacrificer was supposed, by a sort of charm that he worked by his sacrifice, to attain ends desirable for himself, so there was supposed to be a sort of charm in tapas producing mystic and marvellous results. The distinction seems to have been that it was rather power, worldly success, wealth, children, and heaven that were attained by sacrifice ; and mystic, extraordinary, superhuman faculties that were attained by tapas.

By a natural anthropomorphism the gods too were supposed, for like ends, to offer sacrifice and to perform tapas. Thus it is sometimes by sacrifice, but more often by tapas, that in the different cosmological legends one god or the other is supposed to bring forth creation[1]. In the latter case an expression often used on such occasions is tapas atapasyata, literally 'he glowed a glow,' and the exact meaning of this enigmatic phrase is by no means certain. It may have been meant to convey that he glowed with fierce resolve, or that he glowed with deep thought, or that he glowed with strong desire, or that he carried out each or some or all of the practices given in Kassapa's three lists of self-mortifications in our Sutta. All these various ideas may possibly be meant to be inferred together, and before they were ascribed to gods similar actions must have been well known among men.

There were some, as one would expect, who therefore placed austerity above sacrifice, or held that it could take the place of sacrifice[2]. The more conservative view of the learned Brahman—that it is repeating by heart to oneself, and teaching others, the Vedic verses, that is the chief thing (with which twelve other qualities or practices should always be associated)—is only given with the interesting note that one teacher thinks 'the true' only, another thinks austerity only to be necessary, and yet a third thinks that learning and teaching the Veda is enough by itself, 'for that is tapas, that is tapas[3].' There are several passages making similar comparisons. Thus one text says : ' There are three branches of duty—sacrifice study of the Veda and charity are the first, austerity (tapas) is the second, to dwell as a learner one's life

---

[1] Satapatha-Br. VI, 1, 1, 13, and several times in the early Upanishads.
[2] So Khând. Up. III, 17, 2 and 4.
[3] Tait. I, 9. Compare, on the ethics, Manu VI, 92 and the Ten Pâramitâs. The idea that Veda-learning is tapas is a common one.

long in the house of one's teacher is the third. All these have as reward heavenly worlds. But he who stands firm in Brahman obtains deathlessness [1].'

So in the passages which explain (by no means consistently) where the soul goes to after it leaves the body, we have a somewhat corresponding division [2]. According to the *Kh*ândogya, those who know a certain mystical doctrine about five fires, and those who in the forest follow faith and austerity (tapas), go along the path of the gods to the Brahma worlds. On the other hand, they who sacrifice, and give alms go to the moon, and thence return to earth, and are reborn in high or low positions according to their deeds. But the bad become insects.

According to the Br*i*hadâra*n*yaka, those who know the mystic doctrine of the five fires, and those who in the woods practise faith and truth (not tapas) go to the Brahma worlds. On the other hand, those who practise sacrifice, charity, and austerity (tapas) go to the moon, and are thence reborn on earth. But those who follow neither of these two paths become insects.

Here austerity is put into a lower grade than it occupies in the last extract. Other later passages are Mu*nd*aka II, 7; III, 2, 4, 6; Pra*s*na I, 9; V, 4. Though the details differ there is a general consensus that above both sacrifice and austerity, which are themselves meritorious, there is a something higher, a certain kind of truth or faith or wisdom.

This is the exact analogue, from the Upanishad point of view, to the doctrine of the Buddhists that Arahatship is better than austerity. And though the Upanishad belief is not worked out with the same consistency, nor carried so far to its logical conclusion, as the Buddhist, that is simply to be explained by the facts that it is not only earlier, belonging to a time when thought was less matured, but is also not the work of one mind, but of several. There can be but little doubt that Gotama, during his years of study and austerity before he attained Nirvâ*n*a under the Tree of Wisdom, had come into contact with the very beliefs, or at least with beliefs similar to those, now preserved in the Upanishads; and that his general conclusion was based upon them. That he practically condemns physical tapas (austerity) altogether is no argument against his indebtedness, so far as the superiority of wisdom to austerity is concerned, to the older theory.

In the passages in which that older theory is set forth we

---

[1] *Kh*ând. Up. II, 23, 1.
[2] *Kh*ând. Up. V, 10; Br*i*had. VI, 2; Pra*s*na I, 9; V, 4. 5.

have the germs—indistinct statements, no doubt, and inconsistent, but still the first source—of the well-known theory
of the Âsramas; the Efforts (or perhaps Trainings), four
stages into which the life of each member of the ranks of the
twice-born (the Dvigas) should be divided. In later times
these are (1) the student, (2) the householder, (3) the hermit,
and (4) the wandering ascetic; that is, the Brahmakârin,
the Grihastha, the Vânaprastha, and the Yati[1]. And
stress was laid on the order in which the stages of effort were
taken up, it being held improper for a man to enter the latter
without having passed through the former.

The Upanishad passages know nothing of the curious
technical term of Effort (Âsrama) applied to these stages.
And they have really only two divisions (and these not
regarded as consecutive stages), that of the sacrificer and of
the hermit (not the Bhikshu). Of course studentship is
understood as preliminary to both. But we are here at
a standpoint really quite apart from the Âsrama theory, and
Sankara and other commentators are obliged to resort to
curious and irreconcilable shifts when they try to read back
into these old texts the later and more developed doctrine[2].

Even the names of the several Âsramas do not occur, as
such, in the older Upanishads. Brahmakârin is frequently
used for pupil, Yati in two or three passages means ascetic;
but Grihastha, Vânaprastha, and Bhikshu do not even
occur[3]. The earliest mention of the Four Efforts is in the
old law books. Gautama (III, 2) gives them as Brahmakârin,
Grihastha, Bhikshu, and Vaikhânasa (student, householder, wandering beggar, and hermit). Âpastamba (II, 9,
21, 1) has a different order, and different names for the four
stages — Gârhasthyam, Âkâryakulam, Maunam, and
Vânaprasthyam[4].

Hofrath Bühler dated these works (very hypothetically)
in the fifth and third, or possibly in the sixth and fourth
centuries B.C.[5] The theory of the Four Efforts was then

---

[1] So Manu V, 137; VI, 87. Compare VIII, 390, and VI, 97.

[2] See Max Müller's interesting note in his translation of the
Upanishads (Part I, pp. 82–84).

[3] See Jacob's Concordance under the words.

[4] Comp. Baudhâyana II, 10, 17, 6, and Âpastamba II, 4, 9, 13.

[5] He ventures on a conjecture as to possible date in the case of
Âpastamba only. Him he places on linguistic grounds not later than
the third century B.C.; and, if the argument resting on the mention of
Svetaketu hold good, then a century or two older. Burnell, whom
Bühler (Baudh. p. xxx) calls 'the first authority on the literature of
the Schools of the Taittirîya Veda,' to which Âpastamba belonged,

already current, but by no means settled as to detail. It must evidently have taken shape between the date of the Upanishads just quoted and that of the law books ; that is to say, either just before or some time after the rise of Buddhism. We can, I think, go safely further, and say that it must have been, in all probability, after Buddha, and even after the time when the Pi*t*akas were put together. For neither the technical term Âsrama, nor any of the four stages of it, are mentioned in the Pi*t*akas.

The theory has become finally formulated, in the order as to detail which has permanently survived, in the later law books from Vasish*th*a onwards. He gives the Four Efforts or stages in the life of an orthodox person, as (1) Student, (2) Householder, (3) Hermit, (4) Wandering Mendicant—Brahma-*k*ârin, G*ri*hastha, Vânaprastha, and Parivrâ*g*aka [1].

It will be noticed that this final arrangement differs in two respects—and both of them of importance—from the earliest. In the first place the wandering beggar is put in the last, that is in the highest, place. He is not subordinated, as he was at first, to the hermit. In the second place the expression Bhikshu, applied in Gautama to the wandering mendicant, is dropped in the later books.

The commentators are at great pains to harmonise the divergent order. And they do so by suggesting that the earlier arrangement (which, of course, is, in their eyes, the strange one) is meant to infer exactly the same as does the contrary later arrangement so familiar to them. To them the wandering mendicant had become the last, in order of time and importance, of the Four Efforts ; and they try to put back their own view into the words of the ancient writer they are dealing with. But if the order they were familiar with implies one thing, the older order, which is exactly the reverse, can scarcely imply the same. Or if it does, then the question arises, why should it ? In either case the explanation may be sought for in the history of the two ideas.

Now the distinction between the two is quite clear, though the ambiguity of the English word 'ascetic,' often applied to both, may tend to hide it from view [2]. Gautama starts his

---

was not convinced by the arguments leading up to the above conclusion. He only ventured, after reading them, to put Âpastamba 'at least B.C.' (Manu, p. xxvii). Baudhâyana was some generations older than Âpastamba (see Bühler, Âp. pp. xxi-xxii). And Gautama was older still.

[1] Vas. VII, 2.

[2] Thus Bühler uses the one term 'ascetic' to render a number of Sanskrit words—for sa*m*nyâsin at Baudh. II, 10, 17 ; for bhikshu

description of the hermit by saying that he is to feed on roots and fruits, and practise tapas. And all the later books lay stress on the same point ; often giving, as instances of the tapas, one or other of the very practices detailed by Kassapa the tâpasa, in his three lists, in our Sutta[1]. On the other hand, the wandering mendicant does not practise these severe physical self-mortifications. He is never called tâpasa, and though he has abandoned the world, and wanders without a home, simply clad, and begging his food, his self-restraint is mental rather than physical. Of the fifteen rules laid down for him by Gautama, who calls him the Bhikshu (in X, 11–25), four or five are precisely equivalent to rules the Buddhist Bhikshu has to observe. There is one significant rule in Baudhâyana, however, which is quite contrary to the corresponding Buddhist rule. According to it the twice-born mendicant of the priestly books is, in begging for food, to observe the rules of ceremonial purity, what we call now the rules of caste[2].

Now while the belief in the special efficacy and holiness of austerity, self-torture, tapas; is a world-wide phenomenon, and the practice of it was, no doubt, very early in India too, the idea of the wandering mendicant is peculiar to India. And though the origin and early history of this institution are at present obscure, we have no reason to believe that it was of ancient date.

It was older than the Buddha's time. Both Buddhist and Gain records agree on this point. And they are confirmed by an isolated passage in an Upanishad which, as a whole, is pre-Buddhistic[3]. There it is said that he who desires to see

---

at Gaut. III, 2, 11; for parivrâgaka at Vâs. X, 1; for yati at Manu VI, 54, 56, 69, 86; for tâpasa at Manu VI, 27; for muni at Manu VI, 11. Of these the last two refer to the hermit in the woods (the tâpasa), the others to the wandering mendicant (the bhikshu). Even for the old Brahman who remains at home under the protection of his son (the Veda-samnyâsin), he has 'become an ascetic' (samnyased in the Sanskrit, Manu VI, 94).

This rendering can, in each case, be easily justified. Each of the Sanskrit words means one or other form, one or other degree, of what may be called asceticism. But the differences might be made clear by variety of rendering.

[1] Gautama has altogether ten rules for the hermit, none of which were applicable to the Buddhist Bhikshu (Gaut. III, 26–35).

[2] Baudhâyana II, 10, 18, 4, 5. Manu VI, 27 (of the hermit). So also Vas. X, 31, according to the commentator. But Bühler thinks otherwise; and Manu VI, 94 confirms Bühler's view.

[3] Brihadâranyaka Upanishad III, 5, 1.

the god Brahman cannot attain his end by speculation; he must put away learning and become childlike, put away childishness and become a muni (a silent one)[1], put away silence and become a Brâhmana (that is, of course, not a Brahmana by birth, but one in a sense nearly the same as Gotama attaches to the word in the Sonadanda Sutta). This is to explain why it is that 'Brâhmanas' (in the ethical sense) give up cravings for children and wealth and the world and adopt begging as a regular habit (bhikshâkaryam karanti). Another recension of the same passage, also preserved in the same Upanishad[2], but in a connection which Deussen thinks is a later interpolation[3], ascribes this habit to 'men of old.' The statement is no doubt ambiguous. It might be taken to apply to the hermit (the tâpasa) who also begged. But I think on the whole that the wandering mendicant is more probably referred to, and referred to as belonging to a higher sphere than the muni, the ascetic. If that be so, this is the earliest passage in which any one of these three ideas (the wandering mendicant, his superiority to the ascetic, and the special ethical sense of the word Brâhmana[4]) have, as yet, been found.

The oldest reference in the priestly literature to unorthodox Bhikshus (not necessarily Buddhists) is probably the Maitrî Upanishad VII, 8, which is much later. There is a custom, often referred to in the law books, of students begging their food. This was doubtless of long standing. But it is a conception altogether different from that of the wandering mendicant. The word Bhikshu does not occur in any of these passages. And indeed of all the Upanishads indexed in Colonel Jacob's 'Concordance' the word only occurs in one—in the little tract called the Parama-hamsa Upanishad.

Whenever it may have arisen, the peculiar institution of the Bhikshu is quite as likely, if not more likely, to have originated in Kshatriya circles than among the learned Brahmans. All our authorities—Brahman Upanishads, Buddhist Pitakas, Gain Angas—agree in ascribing to Kshatriyas a most important, not to say predominant, part in such religious activity as lay apart from sacrifice. To take for granted that

---

[1] Afterwards an epithet often used, in the priestly literature of the hermit (the tâpasa), in the Buddhist books of the Arahat.

[2] Brihad. IV, 4, 22.

[3] 'Sechzig Upanishads,' p. 465.

[4] Perhaps, on this third notion, Khând. IV, 1, 7 is another passage of about the same date. A wise Sûdra is apparently there called a Brâhmana. But the application is by no means certain.

the Brahmans must have originated the idea, or the practice, is to ignore all these authorities. And it is only in the Kshatriya books—those of the Buddhists and *G*ains—that the details of the practice receive much weight, or are dealt with in full detail.

The oldest law book has barely a page on the rules for Bhikshus, whereas the regulations, of about the same age, preserved in the Buddhist texts, fill the three volumes translated, under the title 'Vinaya Texts,' in the 'Sacred Books of the East.' And as time goes on the priestly literature continues to treat the life of a Bhikshu as entirely subordinate, and in the curtest manner. Even Manu has only three or four pages on the subject. The inconsistency, brevity, and incompleteness of the regulations in the priestly books lead one to suppose that, at the time when they were written, there were not enough Bhikshus, belonging to those circles, to make the regulations intended for them alone a matter of much practical importance. In other words, the development also of the Bhikshu idea was due rather to the Kshatriyas than to the sacrificing priests.

The latter were naturally half-hearted in the matter. Even after they had invented the Âsrama theory, they did not seem to be very keen about it. On the contrary, there are several passages the other way. Âpastamba closes his exposition of them with a remark that upsets the whole theory: 'There is no reason to place one Âsrama before another[1].' And just before that he quotes a saying of Pra*g*âpati from which it follows that those who become Bhikshus do not gain salvation·at all, 'they become dust and perish.'

This was no doubt the real inmost opinion of the more narrow-minded of the priests. But the first maker of the phrase did not quite like to put this forward in his own name—the idea of the Bhikshu as a man worthy of special esteem had already become too strong for that. So he makes the god his stalking-horse; and tries, by using his name, to gain respectability and acceptance for his view. And it survives accordingly as late as the earlier portion of Manu (II, 230), where mention is made of 'the Three Âsramas,' omitting the Bhikshu. We ought not to be surprised to find that, though the whole passage is reproduced, in other respects, in the Institutes of Vish*n*u (XXXI, 7), this very curious and interesting phrase is replaced by another which avoids the difficulty.

---

[1] Âp. II, 9, 24, 15.

Baudhâyana also actually quotes with approval another old saying: 'There was forsooth an Asura, Kapila by name, the son of Prahlâda. Striving against the gods he made these divisions (the Âsramas). A wise man should not take heed of them [1].

If the priests, when the custom of 'going forth' as a Bhikshu was becoming prevalent, had wished to counteract it, to put obstacles in the way, and especially to prevent any one doing so without first having become thoroughly saturated with the priestly view of things, they could scarcely have taken a more efficacious step than the establishment of this theory. And so far as it served this purpose, and so far only, do they seem to have cared much for it. We have no evidence that the theory had, at any time, become a practical reality—that is, that any considerable number of the twice-born, or even of the Brahmans, did actually carry out all the four Âsramas. Among the circles led by the opinion of learned and orthodox priests it was, no doubt, really held improper for any man to become a *religieux* until he was getting old, or without having first gone through a regular course of Vedic study. And whenever he did renounce the world he was expected to follow such of the ancient customs (now preserved in the priestly books under the three heads of Vânaprastha, Parivrâgaka, and Vedasamnyâsin) as he chose to follow. But even then he need not observe a clear distinction between these various heads. The percentage of elderly Brahmans who followed any of the three at all must always have been very small indeed, and of these a good many probably became Veda-samnyâsins, a group which lies outside of the Âsramas The rules are admitted to be obsolete now. Sankara says they were not observed in his time [2]. And the theory seems to be little more than a priestly protest against the doctrine, acted upon by Buddhists, Gains, and others, and laid down in the Madhura Sutta, that even youths might 'go forth' without any previous Vedic study [3].

There were, in other words, in the Indian community of that time, a number of people—very small, no doubt, compared with the total population, but still amounting to some thousands—who estimated the mystic power of tapas above that of sacrifice; who gave up the latter, and devoted themselves, in the woods, to those kinds of bodily austerity and

---

[1] Baudh. II, 6, 11, 28.
[2] See the passage quoted by Deussen, 'Vedânta-system,' p. 40.
[3] See the full text in Chalmers's paper in the J. R. A. S. for 1894.

self-torture of which our Sutta gives the earliest detailed account. There were others who rejected both, and preferred the life of the wandering mendicant. In both classes there were unworthy men who used their religious professions for the 'low aims' set out in the tract on the Sîlas incorporated in our Sutta, whose very words, in not a few instances, recur in the old law books.

But there was also no little earnestness, no little 'plain living and high thinking' among these 'irregular friars.' And there was a great deal of sympathy, both with their aims and with their practice (provided always they keep to the priestly view of things), among the official class, the regular sacrificing priests. Instead of condemning them, the priests tried, therefore, rather to regulate them. One Vikhanas compiled a special book on Tapas, called either after the author the Vaikhânasa Sûtra, or after the subject the Srâmanaka Sûtra, which is several times referred to as an authority in the law books whose precepts are doubtless, in part, taken from it [1]. Tapas was then, in accordance with the general view in the circles in which the law books were composed, regarded as the higher of the two, and put therefore at the end in the list of Âsramas.

But there was also another view which had already made itself felt in the Upanishads, which is the basis of our Sutta, and which no doubt became more widely spread in consequence of its having been the view taken up by the progressive party we now call Buddhists. According to this view the life of the Bhikshu, of the wandering mendicant, was the higher. This view, disliked by the more narrow-minded, but regarded with favour by the more spiritually-minded of the Brahmans, gradually attained so unquestionably the upper hand, that the order of the last two of the Âsramas had to be changed. Tapas became then a preliminary stage to, instead of the final crown of, the religious life.

But the other view continued to be held by a large and influential minority. The strong leaning of the human heart to impute a singular efficacy to physical self-mortifications

---

[1] See Bühler's 'Manu,' XXVII, and the commentators referred to in Bühler's notes, pp. 202 and 203. Also Vas. IX, 10; Gaut. III, 27; Baudh. II, 6, 11, 14, 15 (which proves the identity of the two); III, 3, 15–18. Haradatta on Âpastamba II, 9, 21, 21 (where he also says they are the same). Dr. Burnell had in his possession fragments of this work, or what, in his opinion, seemed to be so. He says it was used by followers of the Black Yagur-veda. Bühler also (Âp. p. 154, note) says the Sûtra is in existence, and procurable in Gugarât.

of all kinds could not be eradicated. Many of the laity still looked on those who carried out such practices with peculiar favour. The tendency made itself felt even in Buddhism, in spite of our present Sutta, and of many other passages to a similar effect. There is a special name for the 'extra vows,' the dhutangas, carried out by such of the brethren as were inclined that way. And these receive special glorification in a whole book at the end of the Milinda[1]. It is true that, even in these 'extra vows,' all the extreme forms of tapas are omitted. But this is only a matter of degree. In the priestly law books, also, though they go somewhat further than the dhutangas, the most extreme forms are omitted, especially in the rules for hermits and mendicants contained in the earlier books. This is another point in which the early Buddhists and the more advanced of the learned Brahmans of their time are found to be acting in sympathy. But the discussion of the details would take us too far from our subject.

The Niganthas, Âgîvakas, and others went to the other extreme, and like the Buddhists, they never admitted any theory like that of the distinction in time between the Four Âsramas[2]. It is even doubtful how far that distinction became a really valid and practical reality among the learned priests. They alone, as we have seen, always laid stress on the importance of not 'going forth,' either as ascetic or as wandering mendicant (tâpasa or bhikshu), unless first the years of studentship, and then the life as a sacrificing householder, had been fulfilled. They spoke occasionally of *Three Efforts* only. And as we have seen the lawyers differed in the order in which they mention the two classes of *religieux*[3].

---

[1] My 'Milinda,' II, 244–274.

[2] The Buddhists admitted a distinction in class as between tâpasas and bhikkhus. They often distinguish between the simple pabbaggâ of the latter and the tâpasa-pabbaggâ of the former. See for instance *G*ât. III, 119 (of non-Buddhists).

[3] When the warrior hero of the Râmâyana brutally murders a peaceful hermit, it is not necessary to call in the Âsrama rules to justify the foul deed. The offence (in the view of the poet on the part of the hermit, in the view of most Westerns on the part of the hero) is simply social insolence. Would public opinion, in Kosala, have sanctioned such an act, or enjoyed such a story, in the time of the Pi*t*akas? The original Râmâyana probably arose, as Professor Jacobi has shown, in Kosala; but this episode (VII, 76) is not in the oldest part. The doctrine for which the poet claims the approval of the gods (and which,

By the time that the later order was settled the word Bhikshu had come to mean so specially a Buddhist mendicant that the learned Brahmans no longer thought it fitting to apply the term to their own mendicants. This at least may be the explanation of the fact that it is used in Gautama's law book, and not afterwards.

The history of the word is somewhat doubtful. It is not found as yet, as we have seen above, in any pre-Buddhistic text. Perhaps the Gains or the Buddhists first used it. But it was more probably a term common before their time, though not long before, to all mendicants. The form is sufficiently curious for Pânini to take special notice of it in the rule for the formation from desideratives of nouns in u[1]. In another rule[2] he mentions two Bhikshu Sûtras—manuals for mendicants, as the Vaikhânasa Sûtra was for the hermits (tâpasas). These are used by the Pârâsarinas and the Karmandinas, two groups or corporations, doubtless, of Brahmanical mendicants. Professor Weber refers to this in his History of Indian Literature, p. 305, and Professor Kielhorn has been kind enough to inform me that nothing more has been since discovered on the matter. These Sûtras are not mentioned elsewhere. And they can never have acquired so much importance as the Vaikhânasa Sûtra, or they would almost certainly have been referred to in the sections in the later law books on mendicants, just as the Vaikhânasa is in the sections on the tâpasas.

It is also very curious to find Brâhmana Bhikshus with special class names as if they belonged to an Order like those of the Buddhists and the Gains. No such Brahmanical Orders of recluses (pabbagitâ) are mentioned in the Pitakas. When Brâhmana Bhikshus are referred to, it is either as isolated recluses, or by a generic name not implying any separate Order. Thus in an important passage of the Anguttara we have the following list of *religieux*, contemporaries of the Buddha :—

1. Âgivikâ.
2. Niganthâ.
3. Munda-sâvakâ.
4. Gatilakâ.
5. Paribbâgakâ.
6. Magandikâ.
7. Tedandikâ.
8. Aviruddhakâ.
9. Gotamakâ.
10. Devadhammikâ.

No. 1. *The men of the livelihood*, among whom Makkhali Gosâla was a recognised leader, were especially addicted to

---

therefore, was not unquestioned among men, or he need not have done so) is that a Sûdra may not become a tâpasa.

[1] II, 3, 54. [2] IV, 3, 110.

tapas of all kinds, and went always quite naked. The name probably means : ' Those who claimed to be especially strict in their rules as to means of livelihood.' The Buddhists also laid special stress on this. The fifth of the eight divisions of the Eightfold Path is sammâ âgîvo[1].

No. 2. *The Unfettered* are the sect we now call *G*ains, then under the leadership of the Nâtaputta. They were also addicted, but to a somewhat less degree, to tapas ; and Buddhaghosa here adds that they wore a loin cloth.

No. 3. *The disciples of the Shaveling* are stated by Buddha-ghosa to be the same as No. 2. The reading is doubtful, and his explanation requires explanation. Perhaps some special subdivision of the *G*ains is intended.

No. 4. *Those who wear their hair in braids.* To do so was the rule for the orthodox hermits (the Vânaprasthas or Tâpasas, Gautama III, 34). The Brâhma*n*a Bhikshu, on the other hand, was either to be bald, or to have only a forelock (ibid. 22).

No. 5. *The wanderers.* This is a generic term for wander-ing mendicants. They went, according to Buddhaghosa, fully clad.

Nos. 6–10 are said by Buddhaghosa to be followers of the Titthiyâ, that is the leaders of all schools that were non-Buddhist. It is precisely here that the list becomes most interesting, the first five names being otherwise known. And it is much to be regretted that the tradition had not preserved any better explanation of the terms than the vague phrase repeated by Buddhaghosa.

No. 6 is quite unintelligible at present.

No. 7. *The Bearers of the triple staff* have not been found elsewhere, as yet, earlier than the latest part of Manu (XII, 10). It is very possibly the name given in the Buddhist com-munity to the Brâhma*n*a Bhikshus (not Tâpasas). They carried three staves bound up as one, as a sign, it is sup-posed, of their self-restraint in thought, word, and deed. This explanation may possibly hold good for so early a date. But it may also be nothing more than an edifying gloss on an old word whose original meaning had been forgotten. In that case the gloss would be founded on such passages as Gaut. III, 17[2], where the idea of this threefold division of conduct recurs in the law books. But the technical term trida*nd*in is not mentioned in them.

---

[1] See on this Order the passages quoted above in the note at p. 71 ; and Leumann in the ' Vienna Oriental Journal,' III, 128.

[2] Comp. Baudhâyana XI, 6, 11, 23 ; Manu V, 165 ; IX, 29.

No. 8. *The not opposing ones, the Friends,* are not mentioned elsewhere.

No. 9. *The followers of Gotama* means, almost certainly, the followers of some other member of the Sâkya clan, distinct from our Gotama. who also founded an Order. We only know of one who did so, Devadatta. The only alternative is that some Brâhma*n*a, belonging to the Gotama gotra, is here referred to as having had a community of Bhikshus named after him. But we know nothing of any such person.

No. 10. *Those who follow the religion of the God* are not mentioned elsewhere. Who is 'the God'? Is it Sakka (Indra) or *S*iva? The Deva of the names Devadatta, Devase*tth*i, Devadaha, &c., is probably the same.

We find in this suggestive list several names, used technically as the designation of particular sects, but in meaning applicable quite as much to most of the others. They all claimed to be pure as regards means of livelihood, to be unfettered, to be friends; they all wandered from place to place, they were all mendicants. And the names can only gradually have come to have the special meaning of the member of one school, or order, only. We should not, therefore, be surprised if the name Bhikshu, also, has had a similar history [1].

---

[1] There is a similar list, also full of interesting puzzles, but applicable of course to a date later by some centuries than the above, in the Milinda, p. 191. Worshippers of *S*iva are there expressly mentioned.

VIII. KASSAPA-SÎHANÂDA SUTTA.

[THE NAKED ASCETIC.]

[**161**] 1. Thus have I heard. The Blessed One was once dwelling at U*gu*ññâ, in the Ka*nn*akatthala deer-park[1]. Now Kassapa, a naked ascetic, came to where the Exalted One was, and exchanged with him the greetings and compliments of civility and courtesy, and stood respectfully aside. And, so standing, he said to the Exalted One:

2. 'I have heard it said, O Gotama, thus: "The Sama*na* Gotama disparages all penance; verily he reviles and finds fault with every ascetic, with every one who lives a hard life." Now those, O Gotama, who said this, were they therein repeating Gotama's words, and not reporting him falsely? Are they announcing, as a minor tenet of his, a matter really following from his Dhamma (his system)? Is there nothing in this opinion of his, so put forward as wrapt up with his system, or as a corollary from it, that could meet with objection[2]? For we would fain bring no false accusation against the venerable Gotama.'

3. 'No, Kassapa. Those who said so were not

---

[1] Miga-dâye. That is, a place set apart for deer to roam in in safety, a public park in which no hunting was allowed.

[2] It would, perhaps, be more agreeable to the context if one could render this idiomatic phrase: 'Is there anything in this opinion of theirs as to his system, or as to this corollary they have drawn from it, which amounts to being a matter he would object to?' But I do not see how this could be reconciled with the syntax of the Pâli sentence. And Buddhaghosa takes it as rendered above, summarising it in the words: 'Is your opinion herein altogether free from blame?'

following my words. On the contrary, they were reporting me falsely, and at variance with the fact.

[162] ' Herein, O Kassapa, I am wont to be aware, with vision bright and purified, seeing beyond what men can see, how some men given to asceticism, living a hard life, are reborn, on the dissolution of the body, after death, into some unhappy, fallen state of misery and woe ; while others, living just so, are reborn into some happy state, or into a heavenly world—how some men given to asceticism, but living a life less hard, are equally reborn, on the dissolution of the body, after death into some unhappy, fallen state of misery and woe ; while others, living just so, are reborn in some happy state, or into a heavenly world. How then could I, O Kassapa, who am thus aware, as they really are, of the states whence men have come, and whither they will go, as they pass away from one form of existence, and take shape in another,—how could I disparage all penance ; or bluntly revile and find fault with every ascetic, with every one who lives a life that is hard ?

4. ' Now there are, O Kassapa, certain recluses and Brahmans who are clever, subtle, experienced in controversy, hair splitters, who go about, one would think, breaking into pieces by their wisdom the speculations of their adversaries. And as between them and me there is, as to some points, agreement, and as to some points, not. As to some of those things they approve, we also approve thereof. As to some of those things they disapprove, we also disapprove thereof. As to some of the things they approve, we disapprove thereof. As to some of the things they disapprove, we approve thereof. And some things we approve of, so do they. And some things we disapprove of, so do they. [163] And some things we approve, they do not. And some things we disapprove of, they approve thereof.

5. ' And I went to them, and said : " As for those things, my friends, on which we do not agree, let us leave them alone. As to those things on which we

agree, let the wise put questions about them, ask for
reasons as to them, talk them over, with or to their
teacher, with or to their fellow disciples, saying : 'Those
conditions of heart, Sirs, which are evil or accounted
as evil among you, which are blameworthy or accounted
as such among you, which are insufficient for the
attainment of Arahatship, or accounted as such among
you, depraved or accounted as such among you—who
is it who conducts himself as one who has more
absolutely put them away from him, the Samana
Gotama, or the other venerable ones, the teachers of
schools ? ' "

6. ' Then it may well be, O Kassapa, that the wise,
so putting questions one to the other, asking for
reasons, talking the matter over, should say : " The
Samana Gotama conducts himself as one who has
absolutely put those conditions away from him ;
whereas the venerable ones, the other teachers of
schools, have done so only partially." Thus is it,
O Kassapa, that the wise, so putting questions one to
the other, asking for reasons, talking the matter over,
would, for the most part, speak in praise of us
therein.

7. ' And again, O Kassapa, let the wise put questions
one to another, ask for reasons, talk the matter over,
with or to their teacher, with or to their fellow disciples,
saying : " Those conditions of heart, Sirs, which are
good or accounted as such among you, which are
blameless or accounted as such among you, which
suffice to lead a man to Arahatship or are accounted as
sufficient among you, which are pure or accounted
as such among you—who is it who conducts himself as
one who has more completely taken them upon him,
the Samana Gotama, or the other venerable ones, the
teachers of schools ? "

8. ' Then it may well be, O Kassapa, that the wise,
so putting questions one to the other, asking for reasons,
talking the matter over, should say : " The Samana
Gotama conducts himself as one who has completely
taken these conditions upon him, whereas the venerable

ones, the other teachers of schools, have done so only partially." Thus it is, O Kassapa, that the wise, so putting questions one to the other, asking for reasons, talking the matter over, would, for the most part, speak in praise of us therein.

[164] 9–12. '[And further, also, O Kassapa, the wise would, for the most part, acknowledge that the body of my disciples were more addicted to that which is generally acknowledged to be good, refrain themselves more completely from that which is generally acknowledged to be evil, than the venerable ones, the disciples of other teachers [1].]

[165] 13. ' Now there is, O Kassapa, a way, there is a method which if a man follow he will of himself, both see and know that : " The Samana Gotama is one who speaks in due season, speaks that which is, that which redounds to advantage, that which is the Norm (the Dhamma), that which is the law of self-restraint (the Vinaya)."

' And what, Kassapa, is that way, what that method, which if a man follow, he will, of himself, know that, and see that. Verily it is this Noble Eightfold Path, that is to say : Right Views, Right Aspirations, Right Speech, Right Action, Right Mode of Livelihood, Right Effort, Right Mindfulness, and Right Rapture.

' This, Kassapa, is that way, this that method, which if a man follow, he will of himself, both know and see that : " The Samana Gotama is one who speaks in due season, speaks that which is, that which redounds to profit, that which is the Norm, that which is the law of self-restraint." '

14. And when he had spoken thus, Kassapa, the naked ascetic, said to the Exalted One :

' And so also, Gotama, are the following ascetic practices accounted, in the opinion of some Samanas

---

[1] The four paragraphs 5, 6, 7 and 8 are here repeated in full in the text with the change only of reading ' *the body of the disciples of the Samana Gotama* ' instead of ' *the Samana Gotama*,' and similarly for the other teachers.

and Brâhma*n*as, as Sama*n*a-ship and Brâhma*n*a-ship[1].—
[166]

'He goes naked :—

'He is of loose habits (performing his bodily functions, and eating food, in a standing posture, not crouching down, or sitting down, as well-bred people do) :—

'He licks his hands clean (after eating, instead of washing them, as others do) [2] :—

'(When on his rounds for alms, if politely requested to step nearer, or to wait a moment, in order that food may be put into his bowl), he passes stolidly on (lest he should incur the guilt of following another person's word) :—

'He refuses to accept food brought (to him, before he has started on his daily round for alms) :—

'He refuses to accept (food, if told that it has been prepared) especially for him :—

'He refuses to accept any invitation (to call on his rounds at any particular house, or to pass along any particular street, or to go to any particular place) :—

'He will not accept (food taken direct) from the mouth of the pot or pan[3] (in which it is cooked ; lest

---

[1] The following description of the naked ascetic recurs in the Mag*gh*ima I, 77, 238, 342, II, 161, and in the Puggala Pa*ññ*atti IV, 24. It consists of a string of enigmatic phrases which are interpreted in my translation, according to Buddhaghosa here, and the unknown commentator on the Puggala. These two are very nearly word for word the same. The differences are just such as would arise when two authors are drawing upon one uniform tradition.

It would seem from M. I, 238, if compared with I, 524, that it was the Âgîvakas (see note above on p. 71) who were more especially known for the practice of these forms of asceticism : and from M. I, 77 that it was these forms that had been followed by Gotama himself before his eyes were opened, before he attained to Nirvâ*n*a. (M. I, 167.)

[2] Hatthâpalekhano. The tradition was in doubt about this word. Both commentators give an alternative rendering : 'He scratched himself clean with his hand after stooling.' And the Puggala Pa*ññ*atti commentator adds a very curious piece of old folklore as his reason for this explanation.

[3] Ka*l*opi; not in Childers. It no doubt means some cooking vessel of a particular shape, but the exact signification, and the deriva-

those vessels should be struck or scraped, on his account, with the spoon) :—

' (He will) not (accept food placed) within the threshold (lest it should have been placed there specially for him) :—

' (He will) not (accept food placed) among the sticks[1] (lest it should have been placed there specially for him):—

' (He will) not (accept food placed) among the pestles (lest it should have been placed there specially for him) :—

' When two persons are eating together he will not accept (food, taken from what they are eating, if offered to him by only one of the two) :—

' He will not accept food from a woman with child (lest the child should suffer want) :—

' He will not accept food from a woman giving suck (lest the milk should grow less) :—

' He will not accept food from a woman in intercourse with a man [2] (lest their intercourse be hindered):—

---

tion of it are both unknown. It may possibly be a Kolarian or Dravidian word. Many centuries afterwards karo*t*a and karo*t*i were included in the Vyutpatti, and the Amara Kosa, as meaning ' vessel.' It is of course out of the question that a word of the fifth century B.C. can be derived from either of them; but they are evidently the descendants of allied forms. Childers gives another form khalopî on the authority of the Abhidhâna Padîpikâ (twelfth century), verse 456, where it occurs in a list of names of pots. Another—kha*l*opi—is put in his text by Trenckner at Milinda, p. 107, from one MS., but the other two differ. Both commentators paraphrase it here by ukkhali pa*kkh*i vâ.

[1] Na Da*nd*a-m-antara*m*. That is, perhaps, among the firewood; but the expression is not clear. The Commentaries only give the reason. Dr. Neumann (on Ma*ggh*ima I, 77) has, ' he does not spy beyond the lattice' or perhaps ' beyond the bars of the grate' (spähte nicht über das Gitter), but this seems putting a great deal of meaning into the sticks, and not sufficiently reproducing the force of antara*m*. And how can pa*t*iga*nh*âti mean 'spy'? We have, no doubt, to fill out an elliptical phrase. But it is just such cases as those in this paragraph where we are more likely to go right if we follow the ancient tradition.

[2] Na purisantara-gatâya. The commentators only give the reason. On the meaning of the word compare *G*ât. I, 290.

' He will not accept food collected (by the faithful in time of drought) [1] :—

' He will not accept food where a dog is standing by (lest the dog should lose a meal) :—

' He will not accept food where flies are swarming round (lest the flies should suffer) :—

' He will not accept fish, nor meat, nor strong drink, nor intoxicants, nor gruel [2] :—

' He is a "One-houser" (turning back from his round as soon as he has received an alms at any one house), a " One-mouthful-man " :—

' Or he is a " Two-houser," a " Two-mouthful-man " :—

' Or he is a " Seven-houser," a " Seven-mouthful-man " :—

' He keeps himself going on only one alms [3], or only two, or so on up to only seven :—

' He takes food only once a day, or once every two days, or so on up to once every seven days. Thus does he dwell addicted to the practice of taking food according to rule, at regular intervals, up to even half a month.

' And so also, Gotama, are the following ascetic practices accounted, in the opinion of some Samanas and Brâhmanas, as Samanaship and Brâhmanaship :—

---

[1] Na samkhittisu. Both meaning and derivation are uncertain. Dr. Neumann has ' not from the dirty.'

[2] Thusodaka. It is not fermented. The traditional interpretation here is : ' a drink called Suvîrakam (after the country Suvîra) made of the constituents, especially the husk, of all cereals.' The use of salt Sovîraka as a cure for wind in the stomach is mentioned at Mahâ Vagga VI, 16. 3; and it was allowed, as a beverage, if mixed with water, to the Buddhist Bhikkhus. In Vimâna Vatthu XIX, 8 it is mentioned in a list of drinks given to them. Childers calls it ' sour gruel' following Subhûti in the first edition (1865) of the Abhidhâna Padîpikâ (verse 460), but in the Abh. Pad. Sûki (published in 1893) Subhûti renders it 'kongey'; something of the same sort as barley water. Buddhaghosa adds : ' Every one agrees that it is wrong to drink intoxicants. These ascetics see sin even in this.' The corresponding Sanskrit word, tusodaka, is found only in Susruta.

[3] Datti. ' A small pot,' says Buddhaghosa, ' in which special titbits are put aside, and kept.'

'He feeds on potherbs, on wild rice [1], on Nivâra seeds, on leather parings [2], on the water-plant called Ha*t*a, on the fine powder which adheres to the grains of rice beneath the husk, on the discarded scum of boiling rice, on the flour of oil-seeds [3], on grasses, on cow-dung, on fruits and roots from the woods, on fruits that have fallen of themselves.

'And so also, Gotama, are the following ascetic practices accounted, in the opinion of some Sama*n*as and Brâhma*n*as, as Sama*n*aship and Brâhma*n*aship :—

'He wears coarse hempen cloth :—
'He wears coarse cloth of interwoven hemp and other materials :—
'He wears cloths taken from corpses and thrown away [4] :—
'He wears clothing made of rags picked up from a dust heap :—
'He wears clothing made of the bark of the Tirî*t*aka tree [5] :—
[167] 'He wears the natural hide of a black antelope :—
'He wears a dress made of a network of strips of a black antelope's hide [6] :—
'He wears a dress made of Kusa grass fibre :—
'He wears a garment of bark :—

---

[1] Sâmâka, not in Childers. See M. I, 156. *G*ât.' II, 365, III, 144.

[2] Daddula, not in Childers. See M. I, 78, 156, 188.

[3] Pi*ññ*aka, not in Childers. See Vin. IV, 341. The commentators here merely say: 'This is plain.'

[4] *Kh*ava-dussâni pi dhâreti. The commentators give an alternative explanation: 'Clothing made of Eraka grass tied together.' Was such clothing then used to wrap dead bodies in?

[5] Tirîtâni pi dhâreti. This custom is referred to at Mahâ Vagga VIII, 29, as having been there followed by ascetics. The use of such garments is there forbidden to the Bhikkhus.

[6] A*g*inakkhipam pi dhâreti. Buddhaghosa gives here an explanation different from that given by him on Vin. III, 34 (quoted 'Vinaya Texts,' II, 247), where the word also occurs. The Puggala Pa*ññ*atti gives both explanations as possible. Khipa at A. I, 33 means some sort of net. A*g*inakkhipa is referred to at S. I, 117 as the characteristic dress of an old Brahman.

'He wears a garment made of small slips or slabs of wood (shingle) pieced together [1]:—

'He wears, as a garment, a blanket of human hair [2]:—

'He wears, as a garment, a blanket made of horses' tails [3]:—

'He wears, as a garment, a blanket made of the feathers of owls :—

'He is a "plucker-out-of-hair-and-beard," addicted to the practice of plucking out both hair and beard :—

'He is a "stander-up," rejecting the use of a seat:—

'He is a "croucher-down-on-the-heels," addicted to exerting himself when crouching down on his heels [4]:—

'He is a "bed-of-thorns-man," putting iron spikes or natural thorns under the skin on which he sleeps [5]:—

'He uses a plank bed :—

'He sleeps on the bare ground [6]:—

'He sleeps always on one side :—

'He is a "dust-and-dirt-wearer," (smearing his body with oil he stands where dust clouds blow, and lets the dust adhere to his body):—

'He lives and sleeps in the open air [7]:—

'Whatsoever seat is offered to him, that he accepts

---

[1] Phalaka-*k*îram pi dhâreti. See Mahâ Vagga VIII, 28. 2; *K*ulla Vagga V, 29. 3.

[2] So of A*g*ita of the garment of hair, above, p. 73. Both commentators say the hair is human hair.

[3] Vâla-kambalam pi dhâreti. So the commentators here. The alternative rendering given by us at 'Vinaya Texts,' II, 247, 'skin of a wild beast,' should be corrected accordingly. That would be vâ*l*a, and all the passages where our word occurs read vâla. Comp. A. I, 240.

[4] Ukku*t*ikappadhâna. Compare Dhp. 141, 2 = Divy. 339. The commentator says he progressed in this posture by a series of hops. The posture is impossible to Europeans, who, if they crouch down on their heels, cannot keep their balance when the heels touch the ground. But natives of India will sit so for hours without fatigue.

[5] Both commentators add : 'or stands, or walks up and down.'

[6] Tha*nd*ila-seyyam pi kappeti. The Burmese MSS. and Buddhaghosa, but not the Siamese edition, read ta*nd*ila. So does my MS. at Dhp. 141. The Puggala omits the word. S. IV, 118, and Mil. 351 have the *th*.

[7] Abbhokâsiko *k*a hoti. There is no comment on this. But compare G*â*t. IV, 8 ; Mil. 342.

(without being offended at its being not dignified enough) :—

'He is a "filth-eater," addicted to the practice of feeding on the four kinds of filth (cow-dung, cow's urine, ashes, and clay) [1] :—

'He is a "non-drinker," addicted to the practice of never drinking cold water (lest he should injure the souls in it) [2] :—

'He is an "evening-third-man," addicted to the practice of going down into water thrice a day (to wash away his sins).

15. 'If a man, O Kassapa, should go naked, and be of loose habits, and lick his hands clean with his tongue, and do and be all those other things you gave in detail, down to his being addicted to the practice of taking food, according to rule, at regular intervals up to even half a month—if he does all this, and the state of blissful attainment in conduct, in heart, in intellect, have not been practised by him, realised by him, then is he far from Samanaship, far from Brâhmanaship. But from the time, O Kassapa, when a Bhikkhu has cultivated the heart of love that knows no anger, that knows no illwill—from the time when, by the destruction of the deadly intoxications (the lusts of the flesh, the lust after future life, and the defilements of delusion and ignorance), he dwells in that emancipation of heart, that emancipation of mind, that is free from those intoxications, and that he, while yet in this visible world, has come to realise and know—from that time, O Kassapa, is it that the Bhikkhu is called a Samana, is called a Brâhmana [3]!

---

[1] Vekaṅiko. So of an Âgîvaka at Gât. I, 390, and compare 'Vinaya Texts,' II, 59. My rendering of the word at Mil. 259 ought, I think, to be corrected accordingly. But why was not this entered among the foods above, where one of them was already mentioned? It looks like an afterthought, or a gloss.

[2] Apânako. Compare my Milinda II, 85 foll. on this curious belief.

[3] That is, of course, a true recluse, an actual Arahat. Throughout these sections Gotama is purposely at cross purposes with his questioner. Kassapa uses the word Brâhmana in his own sense; that is,

'And if a man, O Kassapa, feed on potherbs, on wild rice, on Nivâra seeds, or on any of those other things you gave in detail down to fruits that have fallen of themselves, and the state of blissful attainment in conduct, in heart, in intellect, have not been practised by him, realised by him, then is he far from Samanaship, far from Brâhmanaship. But from the time, O Kassapa, when a Bhikkhu has cultivated the heart of love that knows no anger, that knows no ill-will—from the time when, by the destruction of the deadly intoxications (the lusts of the flesh, the lust after future life, and the defilements of delusion and ignorance), he dwells in that emancipation of heart, that emancipation of mind, that is free from those intoxications, and that he, while yet in this visible world, has come to realise and know—from that time, O Kassapa, is it that the Bhikkhu is called a Samana, is called a Brâhmana!

[168] 'And if a man, O Kassapa, wear coarse hempen cloth, or carry out all or any of those other practices you gave in detail down to bathing in water three times a day, and the state of blissful attainment in conduct, in heart, in intellect, have not been practised by him, realised by him, then is he far from Samanaship, far from Brâhmanaship. But from the time, O Kassapa, when a Bhikkhu has cultivated the heart of love that knows no anger, that knows no illwill—from the time when, by the destruction of the deadly intoxications (the lusts of the flesh, the lust after future life, and the defilements of delusion and ignorance), he dwells in that emancipation of heart, that emancipation of mind, that is free from those intoxications, and that he, while yet in this visible world, has come to realise and know—from that time, O Kassapa, is it that the Bhikkhu is called a Samana, is called a Brâhmana!'

---

not in the ordinary sense, but of the ideal *religieux*. Gotama, in his answer, keeps the word; but he means something quite different, he means an Arahat. On the persistent way in which the Pitaka texts try to put this new meaning into the word, see above, in the Introduction to the Kûtadanta.

[169] 16. And when he had thus spoken, Kassapa, the naked ascetic, said to the Blessed One: 'How hard then, Gotama, must Samanaship be to gain, how hard must Brâhmanaship be!'

'That, Kassapa, is a common saying in the world that the life of a Samana and of a Brâhmana is hard to lead. But if the hardness, the very great hardness, of that life depended merely on this ascetism, on the carrying out of any or all of those practices you have detailed, then it would not be fitting to say that the life of the Samana, of the Brâhmana, was hard to lead. It would be quite possible for a householder, or for the son of a householder, or for any one, down to the slave girl who carries the water-jar, to say: "Let me now go naked, let me become of low habits," and so on through all the items of those three lists of yours. But since, Kassapa, quite apart from these matters, quite apart from all kinds of penance, the life is hard, very hard to lead; therefore is it that it is fitting to say: "How hard must Samanaship be to gain, how hard must Brâhmanaship be!" For from the time, O Kassapa, when a Bhikkhu has cultivated the heart of love that knows no anger, that knows no illwill—from the time when, by the destruction of the deadly intoxications (the lusts of the flesh, the lust after future life, and the defilements of delusion and ignorance), he dwells in that emancipation of heart, in that emancipation of mind, that is free from those intoxications, and that he, while yet in this visible world, has come to realise and know—from that time, O Kassapa, is it that the Bhikkhu is called a Samana, is called a Brâhmana[1]!'

[170] 17. And when he had thus spoken, Kassapa, the naked ascetic, said to the Blessed One : 'Hard is it, Gotama, to know when a man is a Samana, hard to know when a man is a Brâhmana!'

'That, Kassapa, is a common saying in the world

---

[1] This paragraph, like the last and like the next, is, in the Pâli, broken up into three sections, one for each of the three lists of penances.

that it is hard to know a Samana, hard to know a Brâhmana. But if being a Samana, if being a Brâhmana, depended merely on this asceticism, on the carrying out of any or each of those practices you have detailed, then it would not be fitting to say that a Samana is hard to recognise, a Brâhmana is hard to recognise. It would be quite possible for a house-holder, or for the son of a householder, or for any one down to the slave girl who carries the water-jar, to know: " This man goes naked, or is of loose habits, or licks his fingers with his tongue," and so on through all the items of those three lists of yours. But since, Kassapa, quite apart from these matters, quite apart from all kinds of penance, it is hard to recognise a Samana, hard to recognise a Brâhmana, therefore is it fitting to say : " Hard is it to know when a man is a Samana, to know when a man is a Brâhmana!" For from the time, O Kassapa, when a Bhikkhu has culti-vated the heart of love that knows no anger, that knows no illwill—from the time when, by the destruc-tion of the deadly intoxications (the lusts of the flesh, the lust after future life, and the defilements of delusion and ignorance), he dwells in that emancipation of heart, in that emancipation of mind, that is free from those intoxications, and that he, while yet in this visible world, has come to realise and know—from that time, O Kassapa, is it that the Bhikkhu is called a Samana, is called a Brâhmana !'

[171] 18. And when he had thus spoken, Kassapa, the naked ascetic, said to the Blessed One : 'What then, Gotama, is that blissful attainment in conduct, in heart, and in mind?'

[The answer [171–173] is all the paragraphs in the Sâmañña-phala translated above, and here divided as follows :—

Under Conduct (Sîla).

1. The paragraphs on the appearance of a Buddha, the conversion of a layman, his entry into the Order (§§ 40–42 above, pp. 78–79).

2. The Sîlas, as in the Brahma-*g*âla, §§ 8–27. See above, pp. 57, 58.

3. The paragraph on Confidence (§ 63 above, p. 79).

Under the heart (*K*itta).

4. The paragraph on 'Guarded is the door of his senses' (§ 64 above, pp. 79, 80).

5. The paragraph on 'Mindful and Self-possessed' (§ 65 above, pp. 80, 81).

6. The paragraph on Simplicity of Life, being content with little (§ 66 above, p. 81).

7. The paragraphs on Emancipation from the Five Hindrances—covetousness, ill-temper, laziness, worry, and perplexity (§§ 67–74 above, pp. 82-84).

8. The paragraph on the Joy and Peace, that, as a result of this emancipation, fills his whole being (§ 75 above, p. 84).

9. The paragraphs on the Four Ecstasies (*Gh*ânas,—§§ 75–82 above, pp. 84–86).

Under Intelligence (Pa*ññ*â).

10. The paragraphs on the Insight arising from Knowledge (*Ñâ*na-dassana,—§§ 83, 84 above, pp. 86, 87.)

11. The paragraphs on the power of projecting mental images (§§ 85, 86 above, p. 87).

12. The paragraphs on the five modes of special intuition (abhi*ññ*â):—

a. The practice of Iddhi.

b. Hearing heavenly sounds.

c. Knowledge of other people's thoughts.

d. Knowledge of one's own previous births.

e. Knowledge of other people's previous births.

13. The realisation of the Four Noble Truths, the destruction of the Intoxications, and the attainment of Arahatship.]

'And there is no other state of blissful attainment

in conduct and heart and mind which is, Kassapa, higher and sweeter than this [1].

[174] 21. 'Now there are some recluses and Brahmans, Kassapa, who lay emphasis on conduct. They speak, in various ways, in praise of morality. But so far as regards the really noble, the highest conduct, I am aware of no one who is equal to myself, much less superior. And it is I who have gone the furthest therein ; that is, in the highest conduct (of the Path).

'There are some recluses and Brahmans, Kassapa, who lay emphasis on self-mortification, and scrupulous care of others. They speak in various ways in praise of self-torture and of austere scrupulousness. But so far as regards the really noblest, the highest sort of self-mortification and scrupulous regard for others, I am aware of no one else who is equal to myself, much less superior. And it is I who have gone the furthest therein ; that is, in the highest sort of scrupulous regard for others [2].

'There are some recluses and Brahmans, Kassapa, who lay emphasis on intelligence. They speak, in various ways, in praise of intelligence. But so far as regards the really noblest, the highest intelligence, I am aware of no one else who is equal to myself, much less superior. And it is I who have gone the furthest therein ; that is, in the highest Wisdom [3] (of the Path).

---

[1] 'And by this,' says Buddhaghosa, 'he means Arahatship. For the doctrine of the Exalted One has Arahatship as its end.'

[2] At Aṅguttara II, 200 (compare M. I, 240-242) it is said that those addicted to tapo-*gigukkhâ* are incapable of Arahatship. Gotama must either, therefore, be here referring to his years of penance before he attained Nirvâṇa under the Tree of Wisdom ; or he must be putting a new meaning into the expression, and taking 'the higher scrupulousness' in the sense of the self-control of the Path. Probably both are implied.

Gigukkhâ is translated by Childers as 'disgust, loathing,' following the Sanskrit dictionaries. The example of it given at M. I, 78 is 'being so mindful, in going out or coming in, that pity is stirred up in one even towards a drop of water, to the effect that: "may I not bring injury on the minute creatures therein."' It comes therefore to very nearly the same thing as ahiṃsâ.

[3] Adhipaññâ. From Aṅguttara II, 93 it is clear that this is the

'There are some recluses and Brahmans, Kassapa, who lay emphasis on emancipation. They speak, in various ways, in praise of emancipation. But so far as regards the really noblest, the highest emancipation, I am aware of no one else who is equal to myself, much less superior. And it is I who have gone the furthest therein; that is, in the most complete emancipation (of the Path).

[175] 22. 'Now it may well be, Kassapa, that the recluses of adverse schools may say: " The Samana Gotama utters forth a lion's roar ; but it is in solitude that he roars, not where men are assembled." Then should they be answered: " Say not so. The Samana Gotama utters his lion's roar, and that too in the assemblies where men congregate."

'And it may well be, Kassapa, that the recluses of adverse schools should thus, in succession, raise each of the following objections :—

" But it is not in full confidence that he roars :—

" But men put no questions to him :—

" But even when questioned, he cannot answer :—

" But even when he answers, he gives no satisfaction by his exposition of the problem put :—

" But men do not hold his opinion worthy to be listened to :—

" But even when men listen to his word, they experience no conviction therefrom :—

" But even when convinced, men give no outward sign of their faith :—

" But even when they give such outward sign, they arrive not at the truth :—

" But even when they arrive at the truth they cannot carry it out : "—

'Then in each such case, Kassapa, they should be answered as before, until the answer runs :—" Say not so. For the Samana Gotama both utters forth his

---

wisdom of the higher stages only of the Path, not of Arahatship. For the man who has adhipaññâ has then to strive on till he attains to Arahatship. Puggala Paññatti IV, 26 is not really inconsistent with this.

lion's roar, and that too in assemblies where men congregate, and in full confidence in the justice of his claim, and men put their questions to him on that, and on being questioned he expounds the problem put, and by his exposition thereof satisfaction arises in their hearts, and they hold it worthy to listen to his word, and in listening to it they experience conviction, and being convinced they give outward signs thereof, and they penetrate even to the truth, and having grasped it they are able also to carry the truth out!

23. 'I was staying once, Kassapa, at Râgagaha, on the hill called the Vulture's Peak. And there a follower of the same mode of life as yours, by name [176] Nigrodha, asked me a question about the higher forms of austere scrupulousness of life. And having been thus questioned I expounded the problem put. And when I had thus answered what he asked, he was well pleased, as if with a great joy [1].'

'And who, Sir, on hearing the doctrine of the Exalted One, would not be well pleased, as if with a great joy. I also, who have now heard the doctrine of the Exalted One, am thus well pleased, even as if with a great joy. Most excellent, Lord, are the words of thy mouth, most excellent, just as if a man were to set up what has been thrown down, or were to reveal that which has been hidden away, or were to point out the right road to him who has gone astray, or were to bring a lamp into the darkness, so that those who have eyes could see external forms—just even so, Lord, has the truth been made known to me, in many a figure, by the Exalted One. And I, even I, betake myself as my guide to the Exalted One, and to the Doctrine; and to the Brotherhood. I would fain, Lord, renounce the world under the Exalted One; I would fain be admitted to his Order.'

24. 'Whosoever, Kassapa, having formerly been a member of another school, wishes to renounce the world and receive initiation in this doctrine and

---

[1] The whole conversation will be translated below. It forms the subject of the Udumbarika Sîhanâda Suttanta, No. 25 in the Dîgha.

discipline, he remains in probation for four months [1].
And at the end of the four months the brethren,
exalted in spirit, give him initiation, and receive him
into the Order, raising him up into the state of a Bhikkhu.   But nevertheless I recognise, in such cases, the
distinction there may be between individuals.'

'Since, Lord, the four months' probation is the
regular custom, I too, then, will remain on probation
for that time.   Then let the brethren, exalted in spirit,
give me initiation and raise me up into the state of
a Bhikkhu.'   [177]

So Kassapa, the naked ascetic, received initiation,
and was admitted to membership of the Order under
the Exalted One.   And from immediately after his
initiation the venerable Kassapa remained alone and
separate, earnest, zealous, and master of himself.
And e'er long he attained to that supreme goal [2] for
the sake of which clansmen go forth from the household
life into the homeless state : yea, that supreme goal
did he, by himself, and while yet in this visible world,
bring himself to the knowledge of, and continue to
realise, and to see face to face.   And he became sure
that rebirth was at an end for him, that the higher life
had been fulfilled, that everything that should be done
had been accomplished, and that after this present life
there would be no beyond!

And so the venerable Kassapa became yet another
among the Arahats.

Here ends the Kassapa-Sîhanâda Suttanta [3].

[1] According to the rule laid down in Vinaya I, 69.

[2] That is, Arahatship, Nirvâna.

[3] The Burmese MSS. call it the Mahâ Sîhanâda Sutta, which is
also the name given in the MSS. to the Twelfth Sutta in the Magghima—called there in the text (p. 83), and in the Milinda (p. 396), the
Lomahamsana Pariyâya.   We have had an instance above (p. 55) of
several different names being given, in the text itself, to the same
Sutta.   And I had already, in 1880, called attention in my 'Buddhist
Birth Stories' (pp. lx, lxi) to the numerous instances in the Gâtaka
Book of the same Gâtaka being known, in the collection itself, by
different names.   It is evident that the titles were considered a very
secondary matter.

INTRODUCTION

PO*TTH*APÂDA SUTTA.

THIS Sutta, beginning with a discussion on the mystery of trance, passes over, by a natural transition, or association of ideas, to the question of soul. For trance (as is pointed out by Po*tth*apâda in § 6) had been explained by adherents of the soul theory as produced by the supposed fact of a 'soul' having gone away out of the body.

As is well known, this hypothesis of a soul inside the body has been adopted, and no doubt quite independently, among so many different peoples in all parts of the world that it may fairly be described as almost universal. It is even by no means certain that it has not been quite universal; in which case its adoption is probably a necessary result of the methods of thought possible to men in early times. But it is, unfortunately, very easy for us, who now no longer use the word 'soul' exclusively in its original sense, to misunderstand the ancient view, and to import into it modern conceptions[1]. The oldest and simplest form of the hypothesis was frankly materialistic. The notion was that of a double—shadowy, no doubt, and impalpable—but still a physical double of the physical body; and made up, like the body, of the four elements.

When the 'soul' was away the body lay still, without moving, apparently without life, in trance, or disease, or sleep. When the 'soul' came back, motion began again, and life. Endless were the corollaries of a theory which, however devoid of the essential marks of a sound scientific hypothesis, underlies every variety of early speculation in India, as elsewhere.

Long before the date of the earliest records of Indian belief this theory, among the ancestors of the men to whom we owe those records, had gone through a whole course of development of which the Vedas show us only the results. They take the theory so completely for granted that the

---

[1] See above, p. 189.

details of it, as they held it, are nowhere set out in full, or in any detail. The hypothesis having been handed down from time immemorial, and being accepted by all, it was considered amply sufficient to refer to it in vague and indirect phraseology [1]. And the stage which the theory had reached before the time when our Sutta was composed can only be pieced together imperfectly from incidental references in the Upanishads.

I have collected these references together in the article already referred to (J. R. A. S., 1899), and need here only state the result. This is that the Upanishads show how the whole theory of the priests, as there set out, is throughout based on this old theory of a soul inside the body. The numerous details are full of inconsistencies, more especially on the point, so important to theologians, as to what happens to the soul after it flies away from the body. But not one of these inconsistent views leaves for a moment the basis of the soul theory. That is always taken for granted. And the different views set out in these priestly manuals by no means exhaust the list of speculations about the soul that must have been current in India when Buddhism arose, and when our Sutta was composed. There were almost certainly other views, allied to one or other of the thirty-two theories controverted above (pp. 44, 45). A careful search would no doubt reveal passages, even in the later priestly literature itself, acknowledging views which do not happen to be referred to in the Upanishads, but which bear the stamp of great anti-quity—such passages as Mahâbhârata XII, 11704, where we are told that if the soul, in departing from the body, goes out by way of the knees, it will go to the Sâdhyas.

However, that may be, it is certain that all the religions, and all the philosophies, the existing records show to have existed in India, in the time when Buddhism arose, are based on this belief in a subtle but material 'soul' inside the body, and in shape like the body. It would scarcely be going too far to say that all religions, and all philosophies, then existing in the world, were based upon it. Buddhism stands alone among the religions of India in ignoring the soul. The vigour and originality of this new departure are evident from the complete isolation in which Buddhism stands, in this respect, from all other religious systems then existing in the world. And the very great difficulty which those European writers, who are still steeped in animistic

---

[1] For souls inside animals, see Rig-veda I, 163, 6; for souls inside plants, Atharva-veda V, 5, 7.

preconceptions, find in appreciating, or even understanding the doctrine, may help us to realise how difficult it must have been for the originator of it to take so decisive and so far-reaching a step in religion and philosophy, at so early a period in the history of human thought.

Nearly a quarter of a century ago I put this in the fore-front of my first exposition of Buddhism. The publication, since then, of numerous texts has shown how the early Buddhist writers had previously followed precisely the same method [1]. They reserve, as is only natural, the enthusiasm of their poetry and eloquence for the positive side of their doctrine, for Arahatship. But the doctrine of the imperma-nence of each and every condition, physical or mental; the absence of any abiding principle, any entity, any *sub-stance*, any 'soul' (ani*kk*atâ, nissattatâ, ni*gg*îvatâ, anattalakkha-*n*atâ, na h'ettha sassato bhâvo attâ vâ upalabbhati) is treated, from the numerous points of view from which it can be approached, in as many different Suttas.

For the most part, one point only is dealt with in each text. In our Sutta it is, in the first place, the gradual change of mental conditions, of states of consciousness: and then, secondly, the point that personality, individuality (atta-pa*t*ilâbho) is only a convenient expression in common use in the world, and therefore made use of also by the Tathâgata, but only in such a manner that he is not led astray by its ambiguity, by its apparent implication of some permanent entity.

---

[1] See the authorities quoted in my 'American Lectures,' pp. 64, 65.

IX. PO*TTH*APÂDA SUTTA.

[The Soul Theory.]

[178] 1. Thus have I heard. The Exalted One was once staying at Sâvatthi in Anâtha Pi*nd*ika's pleasaunce in the *G*eta Wood. Now at that time Po*tth*apâda[1], the wandering mendicant, was dwelling at the hall put up in Queen Mallikâ's Park for the discussion of systems of opinion—the hall set round with a row of Tinduka trees, and known by the name of 'The Hall[2].' And there was with him a great following of mendicants; to wit, three hundred mendicants.

2[3]. Now the Exalted One, who had put on his under garment in the early morning, proceeded in his robes, and with his bowl in his hand, into Sâvatthi for alms.

---

[1] This, for the reasons given above at p. 195, is probably a gotta name; and, as such, a patronymic from the personal name, also Po*tth*apâda, meaning 'born under Po*tth*apadâ (the old name for the 25th lunar asterism, afterwards called Bhadrapadâ). Buddhaghosa says that as a layman he had been a wealthy man of the Brahman Va*nn*a. If so, it is noteworthy that he addresses the Buddha, not as Gotama, but as bhante.

[2] The very fact of the erection of such a place is another proof of the freedom of thought prevalent in the Eastern valley of the Ganges in the sixth century B.C. Buddhaghosa tells us that after 'The Hall' had been established, others near it had been built in honour of various famous teachers; but the group of buildings continued to be known as 'The Hall.' There Brahmans, Niga*nth*as, A*k*elas, Paribbâ*g*akas, and other teachers met and expounded, or discussed, their views.

It is mentioned elsewhere. See M. II, 22; Sum. I, 32.

Mallikâ was one of the queens of Pasenadi, king of Kosala. See *G*ât. III, 405; IV, 437.

[3] §§ 2–6 recur, nearly, at M. I, 513; II, 1, 2; S. IV, 398.

And he thought: ' It is too early now to enter Sâvatthi for alms. Let me go to the Hall, the debating hall in the Mallikâ Park, where Po*tth*apâda is.' And he did so.

3. Now at that time Po*tth*apâda was seated with the company of the mendicants all talking with loud voices, with shouts and tumult, all sorts of worldly talk: to wit, tales of kings, of robbers, of ministers of state; tales of war, of terrors, of battles; talks about foods and drinks, about clothes and beds and garlands and perfumes; talks about relationships; talks about equipages, villages, towns, cities, and countries; tales about women and heroes; gossip such as that at street corners, and places whence water is fetched; ghost stories; desultory chatter; legends about the creation of the land or sea; and speculations about existence and non-existence [1].

[**179**] 4. And Po*tth*apâda, the mendicant, caught sight of the Exalted One approaching in the distance. And at the sight of him he called the assembly to order, saying: ' Be still, venerable Sirs, and make no noise. Here is the Sama*n*a Gotama coming. Now that venerable one delights in quiet, and speaks in praise of quietude. How well it were if, seeing how quiet the assembly is, he should see fit to join us!' And when he spake thus, the mendicants kept silence.

5. Now the Exalted One came on to where Po*tth*apâda, the mendicant was. And the latter said to him: ' May the Exalted One come near. We bid him welcome. It is long since the Exalted One took the departure [2] of coming our way. Let him take a seat. Here is a place spread ready.'

And the Exalted One sat down. And Po*tth*apâda, the mendicant, brought a low stool, and sat down beside him. And to him thus seated the Exalted One said :

---

[1] For notes on this list, see above, p. 14, § 17.

[2] Idhâgamanâya pariyâya*m* akâsi. So M. I, 252, 326, 481, 514, &c. Perhaps 'since you made this change in your regular habits.'

S

'What was the subject, Po*tth*apâda, that you were
seated here together to discuss; and what was the talk
among you that has been interrupted?'

6. And when he had thus spoken, Po*tth*apâda said:
'Never mind, Sir, the subject we were seated together
to discuss. There will be no difficulty in the Exalted
One hearing afterwards about that. But long ago, Sir,
on several occasions, when various teachers, Sama*n*as
and Brahmans, had met together, and were seated in
the debating hall, the talk fell on trance[1], and the
question was: [180] "How then, Sirs, is the cessation
of consciousness brought about?"

'Now on that some said thus: "Ideas come to a man
without a reason and without a cause, and so also do
they pass away. At the time when they spring up
within him, then he becomes conscious; when they
pass away, then he becomes unconscious." Thus did
they explain the cessation of consciousness.

'On that another said: "That, Sirs, will never be so
as you say. Consciousness, Sirs, is a man's soul. It is
the soul that comes and goes. When the soul comes
into a man then he becomes conscious, when the
soul goes away out of a man then he becomes unconscious." Thus do others explain the cessation of
consciousness[2].

'On that another said: "That, Sirs, will never be as
you say. But there are certain Sama*n*as and Brahmans
of great power and influence. It is they who infuse
consciousness into a man, and draw it away out of him.
When they infuse it into him he becomes conscious,
when they draw it away he becomes unconscious." Thus
do others explain the cessation of consciousness[3].

---

[1] Abhisa*ññ*â-nirodho, 'the cessation of consciousness.'

[2] Buddhaghosa explains that they came to this conclusion on the
ground of such instances as that of the Rishi Migasingî, who, through
love of the celestial nymph Alambusâ, fell into a trance that lasted for
three years. This must be a different tale from that of the Rishi
Isisinga of *G*âtaka No. 523, whom Alambusâ tries in vain to seduce.
Compare Vimâna Vatthu XVIII, 11; L, 26.

[3] Buddhaghosa explains that the ground for this view is the way in
which sorcerers work charms (Athabbanikâ athabbana*m* payo-

'Then, Sir, the memory of the Exalted One arose in me, and I thought: "Would that the Exalted One, would that the Happy One were here, he who is so skilled in these psychical states." For the Exalted One would know how trance is brought about [1]. How, then, Sir, is there cessation of consciousness?'

7. 'Well, as to that, Po*tth*apâda, those Sama*n*as and Brahmans who said that ideas come to a man and pass away without a reason, and without a cause, are wrong from the very commencement. For it is precisely through a reason, by means of a cause, that ideas come and go. [181] By training some ideas arise. By training others pass away.

'And what is that training?' continued the Exalted One.

[*He then sets out the first part of the system of self-training for the* Bhikkhu, *as translated above,* pp. 78–84, *from the* Sâmañña-phala, *as follows :—*

1. *The introductory paragraphs on the appearance of a* Buddha, *his preaching, the convi*c*tion of a hearer and his renunciation of the world.*

2. *The tract on the* Silas, *the minor details of mere morality.*

3. *The paragraphs on Confidence.*

4. *The paragraphs on 'Guarded is the door of his senses.'*

5. *The paragraphs on 'Mindful and Self-possessed.'*

6. *The paragraphs on Solitude.*

7. *The paragraphs on the conquest of the Five Hindrances.*

And goes on :]

[182] 10. 'But when he has realised that these Five Hindrances have been put away from within him, a gladness springs up within him, and joy arises to him thus gladdened, and so rejoicing all his frame

---

genti—perhaps 'Atharva priests work out an Atharva charm') which make a man appear as dead as if his head had been cut off; and then bring him back to his natural condition.

[1] Sa*ññ*â-nirodhassa pakata*ññ*û. So Buddhaghosa. Compare Vin. II, 199.

becomes at ease, and being thus at ease he is filled
with a sense of peace, and in that peace his heart is
stayed. Then estranged from lusts, aloof from evil
dispositions, he enters into and remains in the First
Rapture (the First *Gh*âna)—a state of joy and ease
born of detachment, reasoning and investigation going
on the while. Then that idea, (that consciousness)[1], of
lusts, that he had before, passes away. And thereupon
there arises within him a subtle, but actual, consciousness of the joy and peace arising from detachment, and
he becomes a person to whom that idea is consciously
present.

'Thus is it that through training one idea, one sort
of consciousness, arises; and through training another
passes away. This is the training I spoke of,' said the
Exalted One.

11. 'And again, Po*tth*apâda, the Bhikkhu, suppressing all reasoning and investigation, enters into
and abides in the Second Rapture (the Second *Gh*âna)
—a state of joy and ease, born of the serenity of concentration, when no reasoning or investigation goes
on, a state of elevation of mind, a tranquillisation of
the heart within. Then that subtle, but actual, consciousness of the joy and peace arising from detachment, that he just had, passes away. And thereupon
there arises a subtle, but actual, consciousness of the
joy and peace born of concentration. And he becomes
a person conscious of that.

[183] 'Thus also is it that through training one idea,
one sort of consciousness, arises; and through training
another passes away. This is the training I spoke
of,' said the Exalted One.

12. 'And again, Po*tth*apâda, the Bhikkhu, holding
aloof from joy, becomes equable; and, mindful and self-
possessed, he experiences in his body that ease which
the Arahats talk of when they say: "The man serene
and self-possessed is well at ease." And so he enters

---

[1] Sa*ññ*â which is used in a sense covering both 'idea' and 'consciousness.' Ekâ 'sa*ññ*â is therefore rendered below, in the refrain,
'one idea, one sort of consciousness.'

into and abides in the Third Rapture (the Third
*Gh*âna). Then that subtle, but yet actual, consciousness, that he just had, of the joy and peace born of
concentration, passes away. And thereupon there
arises a subtle, but yet actual, consciousness of the
bliss of equanimity. And he becomes a person conscious of that.

'Thus also is it that through training one idea, one
sort of consciousness, arises; and through training
another passes away. This is the training I spoke
of,' said the Exalted One.

13. 'And again, Po*tth*apâda, the Bhikkhu, by the
putting away alike of ease and of pain, by the passing
away of any joy, any elation, he had previously felt,
enters into and abides in the Fourth Rapture (the
Fourth *Gh*âna)—a state of pure self-possession and
equanimity, without pain and without ease. Then
that subtle, but yet actual, consciousness, that he just
had, of the bliss of equanimity, passes away. And
thereupon there arises to him a subtle, but yet actual,
consciousness of the absence of pain, and of the
absence of ease[1]. And he becomes a person conscious of that.

'Thus also is it that through training one idea, one
sort of consciousness, arises; and through training
another passes away. This is the training I spoke of,'
said the Exalted One.

14. 'And again, Po*tth*apâda, the Bhikkhu, by passing
beyond the consciousness of form, by putting an end
to the sense of resistance, by paying no heed to the
idea of distinction, thinking: "The space is infinite,"
reaches up to and remains in the mental state in which

---

[1] Sukha and dukkha. Well-fare and ill-fare, well-being and ill-
being, ease and dis-ease, uneasiness, discomfort. 'Pain' is both too
strong a word, and has too frequently an exclusively physical sense,
to be a good rendering of dukkha. It is unfortunate that dis-ease
has acquired a special connotation which prevents the word being
used here; and that we have no pair of correlative words corresponding to those in the Pâli. For pain we have vedanâ often
(M. I, 10; M. P. S., chapters 2 and 4; Mil. 134), and sometimes
dukkha-vedanâ (Mil. 112).

the mind is concerned only with the consciousness of
the infinity of space. Then the consciousness, that
he previously had, of form passes away, and there
arises in him the blissful consciousness, subtle but yet
actual, of his being concerned only with the infinity
of space. And he becomes a person conscious of
that.

'Thus also is it that through training one idea, one
sort of consciousness, arises; and through training
another passes away. This is the training I spoke
of,' said the Exalted One.

[184] 15. 'And again, Potthapâda, the Bhikkhu, by
passing quite beyond the consciousness of space as
infinite, thinking: "Cognition[1] is infinite," reaches up
to and remains in the mental state in which the mind
is concerned only with the infinity of cognition. Then
the subtle, but yet actual, consciousness, that he just
had, of the infinity of space, passes away. And there
arises in him a consciousness, subtle but yet actual,
of everything being within the sphere of the infinity of
cognition. And he becomes a person conscious of
that.

'Thus also is it that through training one idea, one
sort of consciousness, arises; and through training
another passes away. This is the training I spoke of,'
said the Exalted One.

16. 'And again, Potthapâda, the Bhikkhu, by passing quite beyond the consciousness of the infinity of
cognition, thinking: "There is nothing that really is,"
reaches up to and remains in the mental state in
which the mind is concerned only with the unreality of
things. Then that sense of everything being within
the sphere of infinite cognition, that he just had, passes
away. And there arises in him a consciousness,
subtle but yet actual, of unreality as the object of his
thought[2]. And he becomes a person conscious of that.

---

[1] Viññâna; the exact translation of this word is still uncertain.
Perhaps 'mind' is meant.

[2] On these last three sections, which set out the fourth, fifth, and
sixth stages of Deliverance (the Vimokkhas), see my former transla-

'Thus also is it that through training one idea, one sort of consciousness, arises; and through training another passes away. This is the training I spoke of,' said the Exalted One.

17. 'So from the time, Po*tth*apâda, that the Bhikkhu is thus conscious in a way brought about by himself (from the time of the First Rapture), he goes on from one stage to the next, and from that to the next until he reaches the summit of consciousness. And when he is on the summit it may occur to him : " To be thinking at all is the inferior state. 'Twere better not to be thinking. Were I to go on thinking and fancying[1], these ideas, these states of consciousness, I have reached to, would pass away, but others, coarser ones, might arise. So I will neither think nor fancy any more." And he does not. And to him neither thinking any more, nor fancying, the ideas, the states of consciousness, he had, pass away; and no others, coarser than they, arise. So he touches cessation. Thus is it, Po*tth*apâda, that the attainment of the cessation of conscious ideas takes place step by step.

18. 'Now what do you think, Po*tth*apâda? Have you ever heard, before this, of this gradual attainment of the cessation of conscious ideas?'

'No, Sir, I have not. But I now understand what you say as follows: [and he repeated the words of section 17.]'

'That is right, Po*tth*apâda[2].'

[185] 19. 'And does the Exalted One teach that there is one summit of consciousness, or that there are several?'

---

tion at p. 52 of my 'Buddhist Suttas' (S. B. E.) and the notes on pp. 50, 51. These stages are almost exactly the same as the views controverted above at pp. 47, 48. And the doctrine of the sixth Vimokkha, as we see from M. I, 164, formed part of the teaching of Gotama's teacher, Â*l*âra Kâlâma.

[1] Abhisa*m*khareyya*m*, perhaps 'perfecting' or 'planning out.'

[2] The foregoing discussion on trance is the earliest one on that subject in Indian literature. Trance is not mentioned in the pre-Buddhistic Upanishads.

'In my opinion, Potthapâda, there is one, and there are also several.'

'But how can the Exalted teach that there both is one, and that there are also several?'

'As he attains to the cessation (of one idea, one state of consciousness) after another, so does he reach, one after another, to different summits up to the last. So is it, Potthapâda, that I put forward both one summit and several.'

20. 'Now is it, Sir, the idea, the state of consciousness, that arises first, and then knowledge; or does knowledge arise first, and then the idea, the state of consciousness; or do both arise simultaneously, neither of them before or after the other?'

'It is the idea, Potthapâda, the state of consciousness, that arises first, and after that knowledge. And the springing up of knowledge is dependent on the springing up of the idea, of the state of consciousness [1]. And this may be understood from the fact that a man recognises: "It is from this cause or that that knowledge has arisen to me."'

21. 'Is then, Sir, the consciousness identical with a man's soul, or is consciousness one thing, and the soul another [2]?'

'But what then, Potthapâda? Do you really fall back on the soul?'

[186] 'I take for granted [3], Sir, a material soul, having

---

[1] *Ñâna* depends on sa*ññ*â; that is, I take it, that the mass of knowledge a man has, his insight, his power of judgment, depends on the ideas, the states of consciousness (here, in this connection, those that arise in the *Gh*ânas, &c.) that are themselves due to the action on his sense organs of the outside world; but are in so far under his own control that he can shut out some, and give play to others.

[2] Buddhaghosa says that as a village pig, even if you bathe it in scented water, and anoint it with perfumes, and deck it with garlands, and lay it to rest on the best bed, will not feel happy there, but will go straight back to the dung-heap to take its ease; so Potthapâda, having tasted the sweet taste of the doctrine of the Three Signs (of the impermanence, the pain, and the absence of any abiding principle) found in everything, harks back to the superstition of the 'soul.'

[3] Pa*kk*emi. This is another of the words the exact sense of which, in Pi*t*aka times, is still doubtful. It means primarily 'to go

form, built up of the four elements, nourished by solid food[1].'

'And if there were such a soul, Po*tth*apâda, then, even so, your consciousness would be one thing, and your soul another. That, Po*tth*apâda, you may know by the following considerations. Granting, Po*tth*apâda, a material soul, having form, built up of the four elements, nourished by solid food; still some ideas, some states of consciousness, would arise to the man, and others would pass away. On this account also, Po*tth*apâda, you can see how consciousness must be one thing, and soul another.'

22. 'Then, Sir, I fall back on a soul made of mind, with all its major and minor parts complete, not deficient in any organ[2].'

'And granting, Po*tth*apâda, you had such a soul, the same argument would apply[3].'

[187] 23. 'Then, Sir, I fall back on a soul without form, and made of consciousness.'

'And granting, Po*tth*apâda, you had such a soul, still the same argument would apply[3].'

---

back towards, to revert,' and is so used in the Pi*t*akas. So in G. V, 196 and in S N. 662 (quoted as verse 125 in the Dhammapada, and recurring also G. III, 203; S. I, 13, 164). But somewhat in the same way as to go back home is to go to a place of security; so in a secondary sense, of opinions or reasons, it means apparently to revert to them, fall back on them, harp on them, with the connotation of regarding them as certain. At S. N. 803 it can be taken either way. At S. N. 788, 803, 840 = 908; M. I, 309, 445, and in the question and answer here, the latter seems to be the sense.

[1] Buddhaghosa says this was not his real opinion. He held to that set out below in § 23. But he advances this, more elementary, proposition, just to see how the Buddha would meet it. It is nearly the same as the first of the seven propositions about the soul controverted in the Brahma-*g*âla (above, pp. 46–48).

[2] This sort of soul is nearly the same as the one referred to above, in the Brahma-*g*âla (§ 12, p. 47); and in the Sâma*ññ*a-phala (§ 85, p. 87). It is a soul the exact copy, in every respect, of the body, and material, but so subtle that it can be described as 'made of mind.'

[3] The text repeats the answer given in § 21, with the necessary alterations. The supposition in § 23 is quoted at Asl. 360. The argument is of course that, even if Po*tth*apâda had any one of these

24. 'But is it possible, Sir, for me to understand whether consciousness is the man's soul, or the one is different from the other?'

'Hard is it for you, Potthapâda, holding, as you do, different views, other things approving themselves to you, setting different aims before yourself, striving after a different perfection, trained in a different system of doctrine, to grasp this matter!'

25–27. 'Then, Sir, if that be so, tell me at least: "Is the world eternal? Is this alone the truth, and any other view mere folly?"'

'That, Potthapâda, is a matter on which I have expressed no opinion.'

[Then, in the same terms, Potthapâda asked each of the following questions:—

2. Is the world not eternal?—

3. Is the world finite?—

4. Is the world infinite?—

[188] 5. Is the soul the same as the body?—

6. Is the soul one thing, and the body another?—

7. Does one who has gained the truth live again after death?—

8. Does he not live again after death?—

9. Does he both live again, and not live again, after death?—

10. Does he neither live again, nor not live again, after death?—

And to each question the Exalted One made the same reply:—][1]

'That too, Potthapâda, is a matter on which I have expressed no opinion.'

28. 'But why has the Exalted One expressed no opinion on that?'

'This question is not calculated to profit, it is not

---

three sorts of soul, then he would regard each of them, in the given case, as a permanent entity. But the consciousness is not an entity. It is a 'becoming' only; subject, as he must (and would) admit, to constant change. On his own showing then, it is not 'soul.'

[1] On these Ten Indeterminates see above, in the Introduction to the Mahâli Sutta.

concerned with the Norm (the Dhamma), it does not redound even to the elements of right conduct, nor to detachment, nor to purification from lusts, nor to quietude, nor to tranquillisation of heart, nor to real knowledge, nor to the insight (of the higher stages of the Path), nor to Nirvâna. Therefore is it that I express no opinion upon it.'

[189] 29. 'Then what is it that the Exalted One *has* determined?'

'I have expounded, Po*tth*apâda, what pain[1] is; I have expounded what is the origin of pain; I have expounded what is the cessation of pain; I have expounded what is the method by which one may reach the cessation of pain[2].'

30. 'And why has the Exalted One put forth a statement as to that?'

'Because that question, Po*tth*apâda, is calculated to profit, is concerned with the Norm, redounds to the beginnings of right conduct, to detachment, to purification from lusts, to quietude, to tranquillisation of heart, to real knowledge, to the insight of the higher stages of the Path, and to Nirvâna. Therefore is it, Po*tth*apâda, that I have put forward a statement as to that.'

'That is so, O Exalted One. That is so, O Happy One. And now let the Exalted One do what seemeth to him fit.'

And the Exalted One rose from his seat, and departed thence.

31. Now no sooner had the Exalted One gone away than those mendicants bore down upon Po*tth*apâda, the mendicant, from all sides with a torrent of jeering and biting words[3], saying: 'Just so, forsooth, this Po*tth*apâda gives vent to approval of whatsoever the Sama*n*a

---

[1] Dukkha. See the note above on §˙13.

[2] These are the Four Truths, set out more fully in my 'Buddhist Suttas' (S. B. E.), pp. 148–150.

[3] Vâ*k*âya sannitodakena sa*ñ*gambhari*m* aka*m*su. So also at S. II, 282 and A. I, 187. Probably from the roots tud and *g*ambh.

Gotama says, with his: "That is so, O Exalted One. That is so, O Happy One." Now we, on the other hand, fail to see that the Sama*n*a Gotama has put forward any doctrine that is distinct with regard to any one of the ten points raised.' And they went through them all in detail.

[190] But when they spake thus Po*tth*apâda, the mendicant, replied: 'Neither do I see that he puts forward, as certain, any proposition with respect to those points. But the Sama*n*a Gotama propounds a method in accordance with the nature of things, true and fit, based on the Norm, and certain by reason of the Norm. And how could I refuse to approve, as well said, what has been so well said by the Sama*n*a Gotama as he propounded that?'

32. Now after the lapse of two or three day*s K*itta, the son of the elephant trainer[1], and Po*tth*apâda, the mendicant, came to the place where the Exalted One was staying. And on their arrival *K*itta, the son of the elephant trainer, bowed low to the Exalted One, and took his seat on one side. And Po*tth*apâda, the mendicant, exchanged with the Exalted One the greetings and compliments of courtesy and friendship, and took his seat on one side, and when he was so seated he told the Exalted One how the mendicants had jeered at him, and how he had replied.

[191] 33. 'All those mendicants, Po*tth*apâda, are blind, and see not. You are the only one, with eyes to see, among them. Some things, Po*tth*apâda, I have laid down as certain, other things I have declared un-

---

[1] There are seven or eight *K*ittas in the books, one of whom, a layman, was placed by the Buddha at the head of the expounders of the Norm. The *K*itta of our passage was famous for the fact that he joined the Buddha's Order, and then, on one pretext or another, left it again, no less than seven times. (The same thing is related by I-Tsing of Bhart*ri*hari.) He prided himself on his keenness in distinguishing subtle differences in the meanings of words. And his last revolt was owing to a discussion of that sort he had had with Mahâ Ko*tth*ita. He took refuge with his friend Po*tth*apâda, who, says Buddhaghosa, brought him along with him, on this occasion, with the express purpose of bringing about a reconciliation.

certain. The latter are those ten questions that you raised, and for the reasons given I hold them matters of uncertainty. The former are the Four Truths I expounded, and for the reasons given I hold them to be matters of certainty.

[192] 34. 'There are some Samaṇas and Brahmans, Poṭṭhapâda, who hold the following opinion, indulge in the following speculation: " The soul is perfectly happy and healthy after death." And I went to them, and asked them whether that was their view or not. And they acknowledged that it was[1]. And I asked them whether, so far as they were in the habit of knowing or perceiving it[2], the world (that is, the people in the world) was perfectly happy, and they answered: " No."

'Then I asked them: " Or further, Sirs, can you maintain that you yourselves for a whole night, or for a whole day, or even for half a night or day, have ever been perfectly happy?" And they answered: " No."

'Then I said to them: " Or further, Sirs, do you know a way, or a method, by which you can realise a state that is altogether happy?" And still to that question they answered: " No."

'And then I said: " Or have you, Sirs, ever heard the voices of gods who had realised rebirth in a perfectly happy world, saying: ' Be earnest, O men, and direct in effort, towards the realisation of (rebirth in) a world of perfect happiness. For we, in consequence of similar effort, have been reborn in such a world.'" And still they answered: " No."

'Now what think you as to that, Poṭṭhapâda? That being so, does not the talk of those Samaṇas and Brahmans turn out to be without good ground[3]?'

---

[1] Compare above, pp. 44–47.

[2] Buddhaghosa takes ganaṃ passaṃ as plurals.

[3] Appâṭihîrakataṃ. Buddhaghosa explains this as 'witless' (paṭibhâna-virahitaṃ). It isthe contrary of sappâṭi hîrakataṃ which he explains (on § 45 below) by sappaṭiviharaṇaṃ. Perhaps the meaning of the two words is 'apposite' and 'not apposite' (compare B. R. on pratiharaṇa).

There is a closely-allied expression at M. P. S., pp. 26, 32, where the talk is of disciples who, when a discussion on a wrong opinion has

[193] 35[1]. 'Just as if a man should say: "How I long for, how I love the most beautiful woman in the land!"

'And people should ask him: "Well! good friend! this most beautiful woman in the land, whom you so love and long for, do you know whether that beautiful woman is a noble lady, or of priestly rank, or of the trader class, or of menial birth?"

'And when so asked, he should answer: "No."

'And people should ask him: "Well! good friend! This most beautiful woman in the land, whom you so love and long for, do you know what her name is, or her family name, or whether she be tall, or short, or of medium height; whether she be dark or brunette or golden in colour[2]; or in what village, or town, or city she dwells?"

'And when so asked, he should answer: "No."

'And people should say to him: "So then, good friend, whom you know not, neither have seen, her do you love and long for?"

'And when so asked, he should answer: "Yes."

'Now what think you of that, Potthapâda? Would it not turn out, that being so, that the talk of that man was witless talk?'

---

arisen, know how to refute it according to the doctrine (Dharma), and to preach, on the other hand, a doctrine that is sappâtihâriyam; that is, a doctrine which, in contra-distinction to the heresy advanced, is the apposite explanation from the Buddhist point of view. The Pâli word for miracle comes from the same root (prati-har); but to render here 'unmiraculous' would make nonsense of the passage, and both my own and Windisch's rendering of the word in the M. P. S. ('Buddhist Suttas,' p. 43; 'Mâra und Buddha,' p. 71) must be also modified accordingly.

On the form compare anuhîramâne, quoted at Sum. I, 61 from the Mahâ-padhâna Suttanta (No. 14 in the Dîgha).

[1] This simile recurs in the Tevigga Sutta (translated in my 'Buddhist Suttas,' S. B. E., XI, 175) and in the Magghima II, 33.

[2] Mangura-kkhavî. Perhaps 'of sallow complexion.' Compare M. I, 246 where all these three words for complexion are used. Mangulî itthî at V. III, 107 = S. II, 260 is an allied form. In all these cases an unhealthy complexion is inferred. Here it must evidently be taken in a favourable sense.

[194] 36, 37. 'Then just so also, Potthapâda, with the Samanas and Brahmans who talk about the soul being perfectly happy and healthy after death[1]. It is just, Potthapâda, as if a man were to put up a staircase in a place where four cross roads meet, to mount up thereby on to the upper storey of a mansion. And people should say to him : "Well! good friend! this mansion, to mount up into which you are making this staircase, do you know whether it is in the East, or in the West, or in the South, or in the North? whether it is high, or low, or of medium size?"'

'And when so asked, he should answer : "No."'

'And people should say to him : "But then, good friend, you are making a staircase to mount up into a mansion you know not of, neither have seen!"'

'And when so asked, he should answer : "Yes."'

'Now what think you of that, Potthapâda? Would it not turn out, that being so, that the talk of that man was witless talk?'

'For a truth, Sir, that being so, his talk would turn out to be witless talk.'

38. '[Then surely just so, Potthapâda, with those Samanas and Brahmans who postulate a soul happy and healthy after death. For they acknowledge that they know no such state in this world now. They acknowledge that they cannot say their own souls have been happy here even for half a day. And they acknowledge that they know no way, no method, of ensuring such a result[2].] Now what think you of that, Potthapâda. That being so, does not their talk, too, turn out to be without good ground?'

[195] 'For a truth, Sir, that being so, their talk would turn out to be without good ground.'

39. 'The following three modes of personality, Potthapâda, (are commonly acknowledged in the world):—material, immaterial, and formless[3]. The

---

[1] § 34 is here repeated in the text.

[2] § 34 repeated.

[3] Olâriko, manomayo, and arûpo atta-patilâbho. Buddhaghosa here explains atta-patilâbho by attabhâva-patilâbho;

first has form, is made up of the four elements, and is
nourished by solid food. The second has no form, is
made up of mind, has all its greater and lesser limbs complete, and all the organs perfect. The third is without
form, and is made up of consciousness only.

40-42. 'Now I teach a doctrine, Potthapâda, with
respect to each of these[1], that leads to the putting
off of that personality; so that, if you walk according
to that doctrine, the evil dispositions one has acquired
may be put away[2]; the dispositions which tend to
purification[3] may increase; and one may continue to see
face to face, and by himself come to realise, the full
perfection and grandeur of wisdom.

[196] 'Now it may well be, Potthapâda, that you
think: "Evil dispositions may be put away, the dis-

and on attabhâva he says (Asl. 308) that it is used for the body,
or the five Skandhas, because the fool jumps to the conclusion:
'This is my soul.'

These three forms of personality correspond nearly to the planes,
or divisions, into which the worlds are divided in the later Buddhist
theory—(1) the eleven kâmâvakara worlds, from purgatory below to
the deva heavens above, both inclusive: (2) the rûpâvakara worlds,
which are the sixteen worlds of the Brahma gods, and are attained to
by the practice of the Four Raptures (the Four Ghânas): (3) the
four arûpâvakara worlds, attained to by the practice of four of the
Vimokkhas (Nos. 4-7)

It will be noticed that the lowest of these three planes includes all
the forms of existence known in the West, from hell beneath to
heaven above. And that the others are connected with the pre-
Buddhistic idea of ecstatic meditation leading to special forms of
re-existence.

But it is clear from § 58 below that the opinion here put forward is
intended to represent, not any Buddhist theory, but a view commonly
entertained in the world, such as Potthapâda himself would admit,
and indeed has admitted (above, §§ 21-23). In either case, of course,
these modes of existence would be, from the Buddhist point of view,
purely temporary. They are the fleeting union of qualities that make
up, for a time only, an unstable individuality.

[1] The whole paragraph is repeated for each of the three modes of
personality.

[2] These samkilesikâ dhammâ are identified by Buddhaghosa
with the twelve kâmâvakara-akusala-kittappâdâ of Dhamma
Samgani 365-430. But compare, contra, Dh. S. 1241 (where, of
course, the word apariyâpannâ must be struck out).

[3] Buddhaghosa explains these as 'tranquillity and insight.'

positions that tend to purification may increase, one may continue to see face to face, and by himself come to realise, the full perfection and grandeur of wisdom, but one may continue sad." Now that, Po*tth*apâda, would not be accurate judgment. When such conditions are fulfilled, then there will be joy, and happiness, and peace, and in continual mindfulness and self-mastery, one will dwell at ease.

[197] 43-45. 'And outsiders, Po*tth*apâda, might question us thus: "What then, Sir, is that material (or that mental, or that formless) mode of personality for the putting away of which you preach such a doctrine as will lead him who walks according to it to get free from the evil dispositions he has acquired, to increase in the dispositions that tend to purification, so that he may continue to see face to face, and by himself come to realise, the full perfection and grandeur of wisdom?" And to that I should reply (describing it in the words I have now used to you[1]): "Why this very personality that you see before you is what I mean."

[198] 'Now what think you of that, Po*tth*apâda. That being so, would not the talk turn out to be well grounded?'

'For a truth, Sir, it would.'

46. 'Just, Po*tth*apâda, as if a man should construct a staircase, to mount up into the upper storey of a palace, at the foot of the very palace itself. And men should say to him[2]:

'"Well! good friend! that palace, to mount up into which you are constructing this staircase, do you know whether it is in the East, or in the West, or in the

---

[1] In the words of §§ 39, 40; that is, that whatever the mode of existence, of temporary individuality, there is happiness obtainable; but only in one way, by getting rid, namely, of certain evil dispositions, and by the increase of certain good dispositions. Buddhaghosa thinks this is said in protest against those who, seeking for happiness beyond the grave, do not admit that happiness can be reached here (as above, in § 34).

The above rendering of the elliptical phrase Aya*m* vâ so is confirmed by the simile in § 46.

[2] See above, § 37.

T

South, or in the North? whether it is high or low òr of medium size?"

'And when so asked, he should answer: "Why! here is the very palace itself! It is at the very foot of it I am constructing my staircase with the object of mounting up into it."

'What would you think, Potthapâda, of that? Would not his talk, that being so, turn out to be well grounded?'

'For a truth, Sir it would.'

[199] 47. 'Then just so, Potthapâda, when I answer thus [1] to the questions put to me.'

48. Now when he had thus spoken, Kitta, the son of the elephant trainer, said to the Exalted One:

'At that time, Sir, when a man is in possession of any one of the three modes of personality, are the other two unreal to him then? Is it only the one he has that is real [2]?'

49. 'At the time, Kitta, when any one of the three modes of personality is going on, then it does not come under the category of either of the other two. It is known only by the name of the mode going on.

[200] 'If people should ask you, Kitta, thus: "Were you in the past, or not? Will you be in the future, or not? Are you now, or not?"—How would you answer?'

'I should say that I was in the past, and not not; that I shall be in the future, and not not; that I am now, and not not.'

50. 'Then if they rejoined: "Well! that past personality that you had, is that real to you; and the future personality, and the present, unreal? The future personality that you will have, is that real to you; and the past personality, and the present, unreal? The personality that you have now, in the present, is that real to you; and the past personality, and the future, unreal?"—How would you answer?'

---

[1] §§ 42–45 repeated in full.
[2] Each of the three cases is given in full.

[201] 'I should say that the past personality that I had was real to me at the time when I had it; and the others unreal. And so also in the other two cases.'

51. 'Well! Just so, *K*itta, when any one of the three modes of personality is going on, then it does not come under the category of either of the other two.

52. 'Just, *K*itta, as from a cow comes milk, and from the milk curds, and from the curds butter, and from the butter ghee, and from the ghee junket; but when it is milk it is not called curds, or butter, or ghee, or junket; and when it is curds it is not called by any of the other names; and so on—

[202] 53. 'Just so, *K*itta, when any one of the three modes of personality is going on, it is not called by the name of the other. For these, *K*itta, are merely names, expressions, turns of speech, designations in common use in the world. And of these a Tathâgata (one who has won the truth) makes use indeed, but is not led astray by them[1].'

54. And when he had thus spoken, Po*tth*apâda, the mendicant, said to the Exalted One:

'Most excellent, Sir, are the words of thy mouth; most excellent! Just as if a man were to set up that which has been thrown down, or were to reveal that which has been hidden away, or were to point out the right road to him who has gone astray, or were to bring a light into the darkness so that those who had eyes could see external forms,—just even so has the truth

---

[1] The point is, of course, that just as there is no *substratum* in the products of the cow, so in man there is no *ego*, no constant unity, no 'soul' (in the animistic sense of the word, as used by savages). There are a number of qualities that, when united, make up a personality—always changing. When the change has reached a certain point, it is convenient to change the designation, the name, by which the personality is known—just as in the case of the products of the cow. But the abstract term is only a convenient *form of expression*. There never was any personality, *as a separate entity*, all the time.

The author of the Milinda (pp. 25, 27) has a precisely similar argument.

been made known, in many a figure, by the Exalted
One.   And I, Sir, betake myself to the Exalted One
as my guide, to his Doctrine, and to his Order.   May
the Exalted One accept me as an adherent; as one
who, from this day forth as long as life endures, has
taken him as his guide.'

55. But *K*itta, the son of the elephant trainer,
though he made use of the same words, concluded with
the request: 'And may I be permitted to go forth
from the world under the Exalted One; may I receive
admission into his Order.'   [203]

56. And his request was granted, and he was
received into the Order.   And from immediately after
his initiation *K*itta, the son of the elephant trainer,
remained alone and separate, earnest, zealous, and
resolved.   And e'er long he attained to that supreme
goal of the higher life for the sake of which the clansmen go forth utterly from the household life to become
houseless wanderers—yea! that supreme goal did he,
by himself, and while yet in this visible world, bring
himself to the knowledge of, and continue to realise,
and to see face to face!   And he became conscious
that rebirth was at an end; that the higher life had
been fulfilled; that all that should be done had been
accomplished; and that, after this present life, there
would be no beyond!

So the venerable *K*itta, the son of the elephant
trainer, became yet another among the Arahats.

_____

Here ends the Po*tth*apâda Suttanta.

INTRODUCTION

SUBHA SUTTA.

As this Sutta is almost word for word the same as the Sâmañña-phala, the question arises why it was considered advisable to include it in our collection as a separate Sutta. The chief difference is that the states of mind enumerated in the Sâmañña-phala as fruits of the life of a recluse are here divided under the three heads of Sîla, Samâdhi, and Paññâ (Conduct, Concentration, and Intelligence).

Samâdhi has not yet been found in any Indian book older than the Piṭakas. And, as in them, it is used exclusively of a mental state, never in a concrete sense, its meaning is not easy to fix exactly. It is not the same as Ghâna, which is a pre-Buddhistic term applied to four special forms of meditation, culminating in self-induced ecstasy. Samâdhi on the other hand is a constant habit, or faculty, of mind. The oldest Sanskrit text in which it occurs is the Maitrî Upanishad; and it probably has there the same meaning as it has in the Piṭakas.

In our present Sutta—and the principal reason for its existence as a separate Sutta is that it points out just this— it is pointed out that Samâdhi includes, it is true, the Ghânas, but also other, and very different things. These are the habit of guarding the doors of one's senses; constant mindfulness and self-possession; and the faculty of being content with little. From the negative point of view it is said to include emancipation from ill-temper, inertness of mind and body, worry, and perplexity; from the positive point of view it is said to include a constant state of joy and peace.

Wilson's Sanskrit Dictionary (1819) gives the meaning 'devout meditation'; and the rendering 'meditation' has been used for it in subsequent works in English by Western scholars. It is quite clear that this would be a very inadequate and misleading rendering in our Sutta. But exigencies of space preclude the discussion here, either of the meaning, or of the very interesting and suggestive history of the word in India.

How far was the word (literally 'allocation') invented or adopted by the Buddhists, or by their immediate spiritual forerunners, to express 'self-concentration' with implied co-ordination, harmonisation, of the mental faculties—an idea they wanted, in the statement of their most essential and ethical doctrines, to be used in preference to the more limited, more physical, notion of Ghâna? (It is Samâdhi, and not Ghâna, that we find in the Four Truths, in the Noble Path, and in the thirty-seven constituent parts of Arahatship.) How far, through the constant association of the two ideas, did the larger, as ethical feeling died away, become swallowed up by the smaller? At what date, in what circles, and under what reservations, did the word Samâdhi come to mean nothing more than meditation? The history of the two ideas, Samâdhi and Ghâna, has constant analogies with the history of the two similarly related ideas of Tâpasa and Bhikshu, and, like it, is of the first importance in following the evolution of philosophical and religious thought in India.

I have made some detailed contributions to the discussion of such questions in my 'Yogâvacara Manual' (Pâli Text Society, 1896, pp. xiv–xxviii); and must confine myself, here, to referring to those pages.

X. SUBHA SUTTA.

[CONDUCT, CONCENTRATION, AND INTELLECT.]

[204] I. 1. Thus have I heard. The venerable Ânanda was once staying at Sâvatthi in the *G*eta Wood, in Anâtha Pi*nd*ika's pleasaunce, shortly after the Exalted One had died away[1]. Now at that time the young Brahman Subha, the son of the man of Tudi[2], was dwelling at Sâvatthi on some business or other.

2. Now Subha, the young Brahman, addressed a certain young man, and said:

'Come now, young man. Go to the Sama*n*a Ânanda, and ask in my name as to whether his sickness and indisposition has abated, as to his health and vigour and condition of ease; and say: "'Twere well if the venerable Ânanda would be so kind as to pay a visit to Subha, the young Brahman, the son of the man of Tudi."'

3. 'Very well, Sir,' said that young man in reply. And he went to the place where the venerable Ânanda was staying, and exchanged with him the greetings and compliments of politeness and courtesy, and took his seat apart. And, so seated, he delivered to the venerable. Ânanda the message with which he had been charged.

[205] 4. On hearing that message, the venerable Ânanda said to him:

'It is not just now, young man, convenient, for I have just taken medicine. But perhaps I may be able to go on the morrow, if so be that conditions and opportunity seem fit.'

---

[1] The full details are given in Sumangala Vilâsinî, p. 7.
[2] A village near Sâvatthi, now in Nepal territory.

Then that young man arose from his seat, and went to Subha, and told him all, and added:

'So, Sir, the matter has been so far accomplished that perhaps the venerable Ânanda may be able to come on the morrow, if so be that conditions and opportunity seem fit.'

5. And the venerable Ânanda, when the night had passed away, dressed himself early in the morning, and went, in his robes and carrying his bowl, with a Bhikkhu from the *K*etiya country as his attendant, to Subha's house, and took his seat on the mat spread out for him. And Subha, the young Brahman, the son of the man of Tudi, came there where he sat, and exchanged with the venerable Ânanda the greetings and compliments of politeness and courtesy, and took his seat on one side. And, so seated, he said to the venerable Ânanda:

[206] 'You, Sir, have waited long on the venerable Gotama, constantly near him, continually in his company. You, Sir, will know what were the things the venerable Gotama was wont to praise; to which he used to incite the folk, in which he established them, and made them firm. What were they, Ânanda?'

6. 'Three are the bodies of doctrine, O Brahman, which the Exalted One was wont to praise; to which he used to incite the folk, in which he established them, and made them firm. And what are the three? The so noble body of doctrine regarding right conduct, the so noble body of doctrine regarding self-concentration, the so noble body of doctrine regarding intelligence[1].'

'And what, Ânanda, is this so noble body of doctrine regarding right conduct (Sîla) in praise of which the venerable Gotama was wont to speak; to which he used to incite the folk, in which he established them, and made them firm?'

7. [The reply §§ 7–29 is §§ 40–63 of the Sâma*ññ*aphala Sutta, including:

---

[1] On these three Skandhas of doctrine, see above, p. 82, and A. I, 125, &c.

1. The appearance of a Buddha, and his preaching.

2. The awakening of a hearer, and his entry into the Order.

3. His self-training in act, word, and speech.

4. The minor details of morality he observes.

5. The absence of fear, confidence of heart thence resulting.

And the answer concludes the enumeration with the words :—]

30. 'And there is yet something further, according to this system, still to be done.'

'Wonderful is this, Ânanda, and mysterious—both that this so noble group of conduct is well-rounded, not incomplete ; and that I perceive no other, like unto it, among the other Samaṇas and Brâhmaṇas outside of this communion. [207] And were they also to perceive such in themselves, then would they be satisfied with thus much, and would say : "So far is enough. We have done thus much. The aim of our Samaṇaship has been reached." But you, Ânanda, on the other hand, say : "There is yet something further, according to your system, still to be done."'

Here ends the First Portion for Recitation in the Subha Sutta.

II. 1. 'And what, Ânanda, is this so noble body of doctrine regarding self-concentration (Samâdhi) in praise of which the venerable Gotama was wont to speak; to which he used to incite the folk, in which he established them, and made them firm ?'

[The answer §§ 2–18 is §§ 64–82 of the Sâmaññaphala Sutta, that is to say :

1. The way in which he learns to guard the door of his senses.

2. The constant mindfulness and self-possession that he gains.

3. The power of being content with little, with simplicity of life.

4. The emancipation of heart from the Five Hindrances—covetousness, ill-temper, sloth of body and mind, excitement and worry, and perplexity.

5. The resulting joy and peace that pervades his bodily frame, and fills his heart.

6–9. The Four Raptures (*Gh*ânas).

And the answer is followed by the same injunction as to something further to be done, and the same rejoinder as above in Chapter I, § 30.]

[208] 20. 'And what, Ânanda, is this so noble body of doctrine regarding intellect (Pa*ññ*â) in praise of which the venerable Gotama was wont to speak; to which he used to incite the folk, in which he established them, and made them firm ?'

[The answer §§ 20–26 is §§ 83, 85, and 97 of the Sâma*ññ*a-phala Sutta, that is to say:

1. The *N*â*n*a-dassana—the insight which sees that the body is impermanent, and that mind (Vi*ññ*â*n*a) is bound up with it, has no existence independent of it.

2. The power of calling up mental images.

3. The perception of the Four Truths as to sorrow and the Eightfold Path; the rooting out of one's mind of the Intoxicants (the Asâvas); and the final assurance, consequent thereon, of Emancipation gained.]

[209] 27. 'This, young Brahman, is that so noble body of doctrine regarding intellect, of which that Exalted One was wont to speak in praise; to which he used to incite the folk, in which he established them, and made them firm.'

[210] 'Wonderful is this, Ânanda, and mysterious— both that this so noble group of doctrine regarding intellect is well-rounded, not incomplete; and that I perceive no other, like unto it, among the other Sama*n*as and Brâhma*n*as outside of this communion. And

there is not, in this matter, anything further to be accomplished. Most excellent, Ânanda, are the words of thy mouth, most excellent! Just as if a man were to set up that which has been thrown down, or were to reveal that which has been hidden away, or were to point out the right road to him who has gone astray, or were to bring a light into the darkness so that those who have eyes could see external forms —just even so has the truth been made known to me, in many a figure, by the venerable Ânanda. And I, even I, betake myself to that venerable Gotama as my guide, to the truth, and to the Order. May the venerable Ânanda receive me as an adherent, as one who, from this day forth, as long as life endures, has taken them as his guide.'

Here ends the Subha Suttanta.

INTRODUCTION

KEVADDHA SUTTA.

IN this Sutta we have the position taken up by the early Buddhists, and no doubt by Gotama himself, as to the practice of the wonders or miracles, in which there was then universal belief.

They were not, however, miracles in our Western sense. There was no interference by an outside power with the laws of nature. It was supposed that certain people, by reason of special (but quite natural) powers, could accomplish certain special acts beyond the power of ordinary men. These acts are eight in number: and as set forth in detail (above, pp. 88, 89) remind us of some (not of all) the powers now attributed to mediums. The belief is not Buddhist. It is pre-Buddhistic, and common to all schools of thought in India.

As usual[1] the Buddha is represented as not taking the trouble to doubt or dispute the fact of the existence of such powers. He simply says that he loathes the practice of them; and that a greater and better wonder than any or all of them is education in the system of self-training which culminates in Arahatship. There is no evidence of a similarly reasonable view of this question of wonders having been put forward by any Indian teacher before the Buddha.

It is very strange that Childers should have stated (Dict. p. 157) that 'Iddhi is the peculiar attribute of the Arahats.' He gives no authority for the statement. Devadatta, who was the very reverse of an Arahat, was noted for his power of Iddhi. And of the many Arahats mentioned in the books, only one or two, notably Moggallâna, were famed for this acquirement. They could have it, of course; just as they could have any craft or skill of the unconverted. But the eight powers referred to above are called the pothugganikâ- or puthugganikâ-iddhi[2] or âmisâ-iddhi[3]; that is, pre-

---

[1] See for other instances above, p. 206.
[2] Vin. II, 183; Gât. I, 360.   [3] A. I, 93.

cisely *not* an attribute of the Arahats, or even of men in the lower stages of the Path, but of the worldly, the unconverted, a practice carried out for worldly gain.

We have the Iddhi, the majestic movement, of animals[1]— the Iddhi, the glory and majesty and potency, of a king[2] —the Iddhi, the prosperity and splendour, of a rich young man[3]—the Iddhi, the craft and power, of a hunter[4]—the Iddhi, in the technical sense just explained, of the unconverted wonder-worker. The Iddhi of the Arahats, as such, was the majesty and potency of their victory, of their emancipation[5].

In illustration of his position Gotama is represented to have told a wonderful legend—how a Bhikshu, seeking the answer to a deep problem in religion and philosophy, goes up and up, by the power of his Iddhi, from world to world, appealing to the gods. In each heaven, as he mounts ever higher, the gods confess their ignorance, and send him on to the gods above, more potent and more glorious than they. And so he comes at last to the great god of gods, the Mahâ Brahmâ himself, only to be taken discreetly aside, and told in confidence, so that the gods may not hear it, that he too, the Mahâ Brahmâ, does not know the answer!

All the details of the story are worked out with persistent humour, characteristic of such legends in the Buddhist books, in order to bring out the two lessons—in the first place how, in all such matters, to trust to the gods is to lean on a broken reed; and secondly, how perfectly useless is the power of such Iddhi, which, even at its best, can give no better help than that to one in earnest about higher things.

The problem put is of great interest; and goes to the very core of the Buddhist *Welt-anschauung*, of Buddhist philosophy. *The world, as we know it, is within each of us.*

'Verily, I declare to you, my friend, that within this very body, mortal as it is and only a fathom high, but conscious and endowed with mind[6], is, the world, and the waxing thereof, and the waning thereof, and the way that leads to the passing away thereof[7]!'

On this Dr. Karl Neumann, whose illustrations of Buddhist

---

[1] Dhp. 175.   [2] Above, p. 88, and *G*ât. III, 454.
[3] A. I, 145.   [4] M. I, 152.
[5] That is, in the Pi*t*akas. In some passages of the fifth century A.D. it seems to be implied that, in certain cases, Iddhi was then considered to be a consequence of the Arahatta.

[6] Samanake, perhaps 'with the representative faculty.' Compare savi*nnân*ake kâye (A. I, 132). Morris here has, wrongly, sama-*n*aka.

[7] A*n*guttara II, 48 — Sa*m*yutta I, 62.

texts from passages in Western literature, old and new, are so happy, appropriately compares Schopenhauer's saying (W. W. V. I, 538), 'One can also say that Kant's teaching leads to the view that the beginning and end of the world are not to be sought without, but within, us.'

The problem, as put by the Bhikshu to the gods, is : 'Where do the elements pass away r' The Buddha, in giving his solution, first says that that is not the right way to put the question. It ought to be : 'Where do the elements find no foothold ; where does that union of qualities that make a person (nâma and rûpa) pass away?'

The alteration is suggestive. The person should be introduced ; a thinking being. We only know of the elements and their derivatives, as reflected in, constructed by, human intelligence. To the question, as thus altered, the answer is : 'They find no foothold in the mind of the Arahat, and when intellection (with special reference to the representative faculty) ceases, then they, and the person with them, cease.'

So in the Bâhiya story (Ud. I, 10) we are told :

'There, where earth, water, fire, and wind no footing find,
There are the nights not bright, nor suns resplendent,
  No moon shines there, there is no darkness seen.
And then, when he, the Arahat hath, in his wisdom, seen ;
From well and ill, from form and formless, is he freed !'

This is a striking, and in all probability intentional, contrast to the Upanishad passages where the same kind of language is used of the Great Soul, the corollary of the human soul. It is one of many instances (as has been pointed out by Father Dahlmann) where the same expressions, used in the Pitakas of the Arahat, are used in the older or later priestly speculation of God.

We have another reference to the view that the Four Elements find no foothold in the Arahat at Samyutta I, 15. And we see what is meant by this from verse 1111 in the Sutta Nipâta : 'To him who harbours no delight in feelings that arise, either from within or without, cognition (Viññâna) tends to wane.' That is, of course, not that his mental activity grows less—the mental alertness of the Arahat is laid stress upon throughout the books. The picture drawn of the Arahat *par excellence*, the Buddha himself, is a standing example of what the early Buddhists considered a man to be in whom the Viññâna had waned. Whatever else it is, it is the very reverse of a man intellectually asleep, unconscious of what is said to him, dull to ideas. But it is the picture of a man to whom the Four Elements, and all that follows from them, material things, and the ways in which they affect him, have ceased to have the paramount importance they have to the thoughtless[1].

---

[1] On Viññānassa nirodho, see further Ud. VIII, 9; S. III, 54–58; A. II, 45; and compare Asl. 350; A. IV, 39; and above. p. 87.

XI. KEVADDHA SUTTA.

[THE THREE WONDERS, AND THE GODS.]

[211] 1. Thus have I heard. The Exalted One was once staying at Nâlandâ in the Pâvârika's mango grove[1]. Now Kevaddha[2], a young householder, came where the Exalted One was, and bowed down in salutation to him, and took a seat on one side. And, so seated, he said to the Exalted One:

'This Nâlandâ of ours, Sir, is influential and prosperous, full of folk, crowded with people devoted to the Exalted One. It were well if the Exalted One were to give command to some brother to perform, by power surpassing that of ordinary men, a mystic wonder. Thus would this Nâlandâ of ours become even so much the more devoted to the Exalted One.'

On his speaking thus the Exalted One said to him:

'But, Kevaddha, it is not thus that I am wont to give instruction to the brethren: "Come now, my brethren; perform ye a mystic wonder, by power surpassing that of ordinary men, for the lay folk clad in their garments of white!"'

2. And a second time Kevaddha made the same request to the Exalted One, and received a second time the same reply.

---

[1] Afterwards the site of the famous Buddhist University.

[2] The MSS. differ as to the spelling of this name. It is improbable that a wealthy and distinguished man, of high social position, should have been called Kevatta, 'fisherman.' However, Dr. Neumann, who has translated this Suttanta in his 'Buddhistische Anthropologie,' pp. 62–100, has adopted this form; and it may turn out to be the better of the two.

[212] 3. And a third time Kevaddha, the young householder, addressed the Exalted One, and said:

'I would fain do no injury to the Exalted One. I only say that this Nâlandâ of ours is influential and prosperous, full of folk, crowded with people devoted to the Exalted One. It were well if the Exalted One were to give command to some brother to perform, by power surpassing that of ordinary men, a mystic wonder. Thus would this Nâlandâ of ours become even so much the more devoted to the Exalted One.'

'There are three sorts of wonders, Kevaddha, which I, having myself understood and realised them, have made known to others. And what are the three? The mystic wonder, the wonder of manifestation, and the wonder of education[1].

4. 'And what, Kevaddha, is the mystic wonder?

'In this case, Kevaddha, suppose that a brother enjoys the possession, in various ways, of mystic power—from being one he becomes multiform, from being multiform he becomes one: from being visible he becomes invisible: he passes without hindrance to the further side of a wall or a battlement or a mountain, as if through air: he penetrates up and down through solid ground, as if through water: he walks on water without dividing it, as if on solid ground: he travels cross-legged through the sky, like the birds on wing: he touches and feels with the hand even the Moon and the Sun, beings of mystic power and potency though they be: he reaches, even in the body, up to the heaven of Brahmâ. And some believer, of trusting heart, should behold him doing so.

[213] 5. 'Then that believer should announce the fact to an unbeliever, saying: "Wonderful, Sir, and marvellous is the mystic power and potency of that recluse. For verily I saw him indulging himself, in various ways, in mystic power:—from being one becoming multiform (&c., as before, down to) reaching, even in the body, up to the heaven of Brahmâ."'

---

[1] These are explained at length in the Saṃgârava Sutta, A. I, 168–173.

U

'Then that unbeliever should say to him: "Well, Sir! there is a certain charm called the Gandhâra Charm. It is by the efficacy thereof that he performs all this ¹."'

'Now what think you, Kevaddha? Might not the unbeliever so say?'

'Yes, Sir; he might.'

'Well, Kevaddha! It is because I perceive danger in the practice of mystic wonders, that I loathe, and abhor, and am ashamed thereof.

6. 'And what, Kevaddha, is the wonder of manifestation?

'Suppose, in this case, Kevaddha, that a brother can make manifest the heart and the feelings, the reasonings and the thoughts, of other beings, of other individuals, saying: "So and so is in your mind. You are thinking of such and such a matter. Thus and thus are your emotions." And some believer, of trusting heart, should see him doing so ².

[214] 7. 'Then that believer should announce the fact to an unbeliever, saying: "Wonderful, Sir, and marvellous is the mystic power and potency of that recluse. For verily I saw him making manifest the heart and the feelings, the reasonings and the thoughts, of other beings, of other individuals, saying: "So and so is in your mind. You are thinking of such and such a matter. Thus and thus are your emotions."

'Then that unbeliever should say to him: "Well, Sir! there is a charm called the Jewel Charm ³. It is by the efficacy thereof that he performs all this."

---

¹ The Gandhâra Charm is mentioned at *Gât.* IV, 498, 499, as a well-known charm for the single purpose only of making oneself invisible.

² The Sa*m*gârava Sutta (*loc. cit.*) tells us how—either by omens, or by interpreting exterior sounds, or by hearing the actual sound of the man's mental operations, or by knowing, in his own heart, the heart of the other.

³ Identified here, by Buddhaghosa, with the *K*intâma*n*î Vi*gg*â, which, according to *Gât.* III, 504, is only for following up trails. Compare Sum. 265, 267, 271.

It is most probable that the *G*âtaka is right in both cases as to the

'Now what think you, Kevaddha?   Might not the unbeliever so say?'

'Yes, Sir; he might.'

'Well, Kevaddha! It is because I perceive danger in the practice of the wonder of manifestation, that I loathe, and abhor, and am ashamed thereof.

8. 'And what, Kevaddha, is the wonder of education?

'Suppose, Kevaddha, that a brother teaches thus: "Reason in this way, do not reason in that way. Consider thus, and not thus. Get rid of this disposition, train yourself, and remain, in that." This, Kevaddha, is what is called "The wonder of education."

'And further, Kevaddha, suppose that a Tathâgata is born into the world, &c.'

[The text repeats the Sâmaññ̃a-phala Suttanta, §§ 40 to 84, and § 97, that is to say:

1. The preaching of the Buddha.

2. The awakening of a hearer, and his renunciation of the world.

3. His self-training in act, word, and speech.

4. The minor details of mere morality (summarised above at p. 58) which he observes.

5. The absence of fear, confidence of heart thence arising.

6. The way in which he learns to guard the doors of his senses.

7. The constant self-possession he thus gains.

8. The power of being content with little, of simplicity of life.

9. The emancipation of the heart from the Five Hindrances — covetousness, ill-temper, sloth of body and mind, excitement and worry, and perplexity.

10. The resulting joy and peace that he gains.

11. The training in the Four Raptures.

meaning of these charm-names, and that the objector is intentionally represented, like Ka*n*ha in the Amba*tth*a Suttanta, to be 'drawing the long bow.'

12. The insight arising from the knowledge of the nature of the body, and its impermanence, and of the fact that consciousness is bound up with it.

13. The realisation of the Four Truths, the destruction of the Intoxicants, and the final assurance of the emancipation of Arahatship.

The refrain throughout is: 'This, Kevaddha, is what is called the wonder of education.']

[215] 67. 'So these, Kevaddha, are the three wonders I have understood and realised myself, and made known to others.

'[1] Once upon a time, Kevaddha, there occurred to a certain brother in this very company of the brethren, a doubt on the following point: "Where now do these four great elements—earth, water, fire, and wind—pass away, leaving no trace behind?" So that brother, Kevaddha, worked himself up into such a state of ecstasy that the way leading to the world of the Gods became clear to his ecstatic vision.

68. 'Then that brother, Kevaddha, went up to the realm of the Four Great Kings; and said to the gods thereof: "Where, my friends, do the four great elements—earth, water, fire, and wind—cease, leaving no trace behind?"

'And when he had thus spoken the gods in the heaven of the Four Great Kings said to him: "We, brother, do not know that. But there are the Four Great Kings, more potent and more glorious than we. They will know it."

[216-219] 69-79. 'Then that brother, Kevaddha, went to the Four Great Kings, [and put the same question, and was sent on, by a similar reply, to the Thirty-three, who sent him on to their king, Sakka; who sent him on to the Yâma gods, who sent him on to their king, Suyâma; who sent him on to the Tusita gods, who sent him on to their king, Santusita; who sent him on

---

[1] From here to the end has been translated by the late Henry C. Warren in his 'Buddhism in Translations,' pp. 308 foll.

to the Nimmâna-rati gods, who sent him on to their king, Sunimmita; who sent him on to the Para-nimmita Vasavatti gods, who sent him on to their king, Vasavatti; who sent him on to the gods of the Brahmâ-world[1].']

[220] 80. 'Then that brother, Kevaddha, became so absorbed by self-concentration that the way to the Brahmâ-world became clear to his mind thus pacified. And he drew near to the gods of the retinue of Brahmâ, and said: "Where, my friends, do the four great elements—earth, water, fire, and wind—cease, leaving no trace behind?"

'And when he had thus spoken the gods of the retinue of Brahmâ replied: "We, brother, do not know that. But there is Brahmâ, the Great Brahmâ, the Supreme One, the Mighty One, the All-seeing One, the Ruler, the Lord of all, the Controller, the Creator, the Chief of all, appointing to each his place, the Ancient of days, the Father of all that are and are to be[2]! He is more potent and more glorious than we. He will know it."

'"Where then is that Great Brahmâ now?"

'"We, brother, know not where Brahmâ is, nor why Brahmâ is, nor whence. But, brother, when the signs of his coming appear, when the light ariseth, and the glory shineth, then will He be manifest. For that is the portent of the manifestation of Brahmâ when the light ariseth, and the glory shineth."

[221] 81. 'And it was not long, Kevaddha, before that Great Brahmâ became manifest. And that brother drew near to him, and said: "Where, my friend, do the four great elements—earth, water, fire, and wind—cease, leaving no trace behind?"'

And when he had thus spoken that Great Brahmâ said to him: "I, brother, am the Great Brahmâ, the Supreme, the Mighty, the All-seeing, the Ruler, the

---

[1] The question and answer in § 68 is repeated, in the text, in each case.

[2] So also above, p. 31.

Lord of all, the Controller, the Creator, the Chief
of all, appointing to each his place, the Ancient of
days, the Father of all that are and are to be!"

82. 'Then that brother answered Brahmâ, and said:
"I did not ask you, friend, as to whether you were
indeed all that you now say. But I ask you where
the four great elements—earth, water, fire, and wind—
cease, leaving no trace behind?"

83. 'Then again, Kevaddha, Brahmâ gave the
same reply. And that brother, yet a third time, put
to Brahmâ his question as before.

'Then, Kevaddha, the Great Brahmâ took that
brother by the arm and led him aside, and said:

[222] '"These gods, the retinue of Brahmâ, hold
me, brother, to be such that there is nothing I cannot
see, nothing I have not understood, nothing I have
not realised. Therefore I gave no answer in their
presence. I do not know, brother, where those four
great elements—earth, water, fire, and wind—cease,
leaving no trace behind. Therefore you, brother,
have done wrong, have acted ill, in that, ignoring[1] the
Exalted One, you have undertaken this long search,
among others, for an answer to this question. Go you
now, return to the Exalted One, ask him the question,
and accept the answer according as he shall make
reply."

84. 'Then, Kevaddha, that Bhikkhu, as quickly
as one could stretch forth his bended arm, or draw it
in when stretched forth, vanished from the Brahmâ-
world, and appeared before me. And he bowed in
salutation to me, and took his seat on one side; and,
so seated, he said to me: "Where is it, Sir, that these
four great elements—earth, water, fire, and wind—
cease, leaving no trace behind?"

85. 'And when he had thus spoken, Kevaddha,
I answered him thus: "Long, long ago, brother,

---

[1] Atisitvâ. The Siamese edition has abhisi*m*sitvâ. On
atisitvâ see Morris in the J. P. T. S., 1886, and Fausböll at
S. N. II, 366.

sea-faring traders were wont, when they were setting
sail on an ocean voyage, to take with them a land-
sighting bird. And when the ship got out of sight
of the shore they would let the land-sighting bird free.
Such a bird would fly to the East, and to the South,
and to the West, and to the North, to the zenith, and
to the intermediate points of the compass. And if
anywhere on the horizon it caught sight of land,
thither would it fly. But if no land, all round about,
were visible, it would come back even to the ship.
Just so, brother, do you, having sought an answer to
this question, and sought it in vain, even up to the
Brahmâ-world, come back therefore to me. [223]
Now the question, brother, should not be put as you
have put it. Instead of asking where the four great
elements cease, leaving no trace behind, you should
have asked :

"Where do earth, water, fire, and wind,
And long and short, and fine and coarse,
Pure and impure, no footing find?
Where is it that both name and form [1]
Die out, leaving no trace behind?"

'On that the answer is :

'The intellect of Arahatship, the invisible, the
endless, accessible from every side [2]—

---

[1] Nâmañ ka rûpañ ka; that is, the mental and the physical.
Dr. Neumann puts this into nineteenth-century language by translat-
ing 'subject and object.' And however un-Buddhistic the phrase
may be—for no Buddhist would use an expression apparently implying a unity in the subject—it really, if by subject be understood an
ever-changing group of impermanent faculties or qualities, comes
very near to the Buddhist meaning.

[2] Paham. Buddhaghosa takes this in the sense of tittha; that is,
ghat, flight of steps or shelving beach from which to step down into
water. James d'Alwis, who usually gives the view of Ba/uwan Tudâwa,
took it as = pabham, shining—which Buddhaghosa, who gives it as
an alternative explanation, had rejected ('Buddhist Nirvâna,' p. 39).
Dr. Neumann, the only European writer who has discussed the point,
thinks it is put by the poet, metri causâ, for pagaham, 'rejecting.'
But an English poet, if he wanted to save a syllable, would scarcely
write 'recting' for 'rejecting.' And the Pâli poet, had he wished to

'There is it that earth, water, fire, and wind,
And long and short, and fine and coarse,
Pure and impure, no footing find.
There is it that both name and form
Die out, leaving no trace behind.
When intellection ceases they all also cease.'

Thus spake the Exalted One. And Kevaddha, the young householder, pleased at heart, rejoiced at the spoken word.

Here ends the Kevaddha Suttanta.

give that meaning, could easily have found other means. He need have gone no further afield than adopting simply *g*aha*m*. That vi*ññ*âna, when qualified by such adjectives as those here used, can be meant for the vi*ññ*âna of a man who has attained to Nirvâna, could be supported by other passages from the Pi*t*akas.

INTRODUCTION

TO THE

LOHI*KK*A SUTTA.

IT is not easy to put ourselves in the mental position suitable for appreciating the kind of idea that underlies the argument in this Suttanta. The social view against which it is directed lies too remote from the social views universally admitted now in the West. But in the sixth century B.C., in the Eastern valley of the Ganges, the question as to the ethics of teachers and teaching was one of wide interest and of great importance.

*S*ankara quotes with approval the rules of the priestly law books which lay down that the ears of a *S*ûdra who hears the Veda (including of course the theosophy of the Upanishads) are to be filled with molten lead and lac. His tongue is to be split if he recites it; his body is to be cut through if he preserves it in his memory[1]. God himself has bestowed the exclusive right of teaching upon the hereditary priests[2]; who indeed claim to be, each of them, great divinities[3], even to the gods[4]. And it would be a danger to social order if they taught women, or any males not twice-born, or any twice-born males who would not share their views as to the ethics of teaching, and as to the privileges and prerogatives of the priest as teacher.

These passages are much later than the Pi*t*akas. But they, and the many others like them, give a fair idea of the spirit animating one section at least of the priests, and of a trend of opinion that doubtless had its supporters also in Pi*t*aka times. When Asoka thought he had brought about such a change in public opinion that those who had been very gods upon the earth had come to be gods no longer, he was very far from thinking right. That is a battle that is not so easily won. But the expression of his belief is sufficient to show that the striking idea he thought he had killed was far older than our existing text of Manu.

On the other hand one may be permitted to doubt whether the gentle measures approved by *S*ankara for keeping people in that state of life into which their evil deeds in a previous birth had brought them, were ever actually, in practice, carried

---

[1] Commentary on the Vedânta-Sûtras I, 3, 38.
[2] Manu I, 88.   [3] Ibid. IX, 317, 319.   [4] Ibid. XI, 85.

out. The Pi*t*akas themselves give ample proof that, in spite
of the priests, there were not a few base-born people who
succeeded, in that time at least, not only in getting taught,
but in becoming teachers. And this was not the case only
among the despised Buddhists. The numerous passages
collected by Dr. Muir in his article in the ' Indian Antiquary'
for 1877 show that the priestly literature itself—the law books
and the epics—has preserved evidence of the lax way in which
the strict rules as to exclusion from teaching or being taught
were really carried out. And that is especially the case,
according to the priestly tradition, in ancient times, as old, or
older, than the rise of Buddhism.

The fact doubtless is that, though there were bigots among
the Brahmans, and though they were strong enough to establish,
before the time to which our present Sutta refers, rules as to
restriction of teaching which no one in priestly circles could
venture formally to dispute—yet that there was also always
a strong party in India, to which many of the more liberal
minded of the Brahmans themselves belonged, who looked
with sympathy on relaxations of these rules. The general
practice must have been that the hereditary priests kept the
magic of the sacrifice, and the emoluments and privileges that
went with the knowledge of it, in their own hands. Even the
higher teaching of the mysteries of theosophy was to be handed
down only from priest-father to son, or from priestly teacher
to pupil. But there were many exceptions. The numerous
Brahmans who were not priests were wont, of course, to
emphasise the importance rather of birth than of knowledge.
We have enough evidence, even in the pre-Buddhistic Upanishads, of others, besides the priests, being teachers of the
higher wisdom. The four powerful kings, and the still important free clans, though they gave support to the Brahmans,
gave also equal support to other teachers—just as, in later
times, Hindu and Buddhist sovereigns are found supporting
Buddhists and Hindus alike.

Our knowledge of Indian views of life having been hitherto
derived almost exclusively from the priestly books, scholars
have inevitably tended to attach too great a degree of
importance to what the priests describe as the proper state
of things. As a matter of fact it never really prevailed.
Even now the Brahmans, or those who in the census returns
claim to be such, form only about five per cent. of the population. And of these the vast majority are not priests at all ;
they are engaged in all sorts of worldly occupations[1]. We

[1] Baines, ' General Report on the Census of 1891,' pp. 190, 202.
The census shows that out of 261 millions only fifteen millions could

must not judge India at any time, much less in the time of the Buddha, through the yellow spectacles of Sankara, or even of the priestly compilers of Manu. As M. Barth said, already in 1873, in protesting against Lassen for falling into this mistake [1]: 'We must distinguish, more than Lassen does, between different epochs, as well as between the pretensions of a caste and the real state of things. The Brahmans had not yet monopolised the intellectual life. Certain testimonies of the epics, applicable to this very period, as also the very nature of the Vedic books, show for example that there existed alongside of them an entire profane literature of great extent . . . which was certainly, at first, in other hands. . . . Their teaching (that of the Brahmans), it is true, appears to have been in a high degree esoteric and exclusive.'

The position taken up by the Buddha on this question, as appears from our present Sutta (and such other passages as M. I, 513-524; A. I, 277; III, 123-127; M. P. S. II, 32 = A. III, 69 = V, 56 = Mil. 144), is that every one should be allowed to learn; that every one, having certain abilities, should be allowed to teach; and that, if he does teach, he should teach all and to all; keeping nothing back, shutting no one out. But no man should take upon himself to teach others unless and until he have first taught himself, and have also acquired the faculty of imparting to others the truth he has gained himself.

There can, I think, be very little doubt but that the great teacher is here voicing the opinion of many others of liberal views, his contemporaries and predecessors. He lays no claim, either in our Sutta or elsewhere, to any special peculiarity in this respect. It is taken for granted that the arguments put into his mouth in our Sutta will appeal to the Brahman to whom they are addressed. And they are based not on any distinctively Buddhist doctrine but on general ethical principles accepted, or rather acceptable, by all.

---

read or write. On this striking fact Mr. Baines comments (p. 211): 'The second influence antagonistic to a more general spread of literacy is the long continued existence of a hereditary class whose object it has been to maintain their own monopoly of book learning as the chief buttress of their social supremacy. The opposition of the Brahmins to the rise of the writer class has been already mentioned; and the repugnance of both, in the present day, to the diffusion of learning amongst the masses, can only be appreciated after long experience.'

[1] 'Revue Critique,' June, 1873, translated by Dr. Muir in the 'Indian Antiquary,' 1874.

XII. LOHI*KK*A SUTTA.

[SOME POINTS IN THE ETHICS OF TEACHING.]

[**224**] 1. Thus have I heard. The Exalted One, when once passing on a tour through the Kosala districts with a great multitude of the members of the Order, with about five hundred Bhikshus, arrived at Sâlavatikâ (a village surrounded by a row of Sâla trees). Now at that time Lohi*kk*a [1] the Brahman was established at Sâlavatikâ, a spot teeming with life, with much grassland and woodland and corn, on a royal domain granted him by King Pasenadi of Kosala, as a royal gift, with power over it as if he were the king [2].

2. Now at that time Lohi*kk*a the Brahman was thinking of harbouring the following wicked view: 'Suppose that a Sama*n*a or a Brâhma*n*a have reached up to some good state (of mind), then he should tell no one else about it. For what can one man do for another? To tell others would be like the man who, having broken through an old bond, should entangle himself in a new one. Like that, I say, is this (desire to declare to others); it is a form of lust. For what can one man do for another [3]?'

---

[1] This is, I think, a local name; the name of the place from which he had come. If that be so, the better rendering throughout would be 'the Lohi*kk*a Brahman.'

[2] See above, pp. 108, 144.

[3] This is open to two interpretations: 'What can the teacher gain from a disciple?' or 'What can a disciple gain from a teacher?' 'Why should you trouble about others? they cannot help you!' or 'Why should you trouble about others? you cannot help them!' But in either case the implied ground of the argument is the proposition that a man's rise or fall, progress or defeat, in intellectual and religious matters, lies in himself. He must work out his own salvation.

3. Now Lohikka the Brahman heard the news:
'They say that the Samana Gotama, of the sons of
the Sâkyas, who went out from the Sâkya clan to
adopt the religious life, has now arrived, with a great
company of the brethren of his Order, on his tour
through the Kosala districts, at Sâlavatikâ. Now
regarding that venerable Gotama, such is the high
reputation that has been noised abroad:—that Exalted
One is an Arahat, fully awakened, abounding in wisdom
and goodness, happy, with knowledge of the worlds,
unsurpassed as a guide to mortals willing to be led, a
teacher for gods and men, an exalted one, a Buddha.
He, by himself, thoroughly knows, and sees as it were
face to face, this universe—including the worlds above
of the gods, the Brahmâs, and the Mâras; and the
world below with its Samanas and Brâhmanas, its
princes and peoples—and having known it, he makes
his knowledge known to others. The truth, lovely in
its origin, lovely in its progress, lovely in its consummation, doth he proclaim both in the spirit and in the
letter. The higher life doth he make known in all its
fullness, and in all its purity. And good is it to pay
visits to Arahats like that.'

[225] 4. Then Lohikka the Brahman said to Bhesikâ
the barber: 'Come now, good Bhesikâ, go where the
Samana Gotama is staying, and, on your arrival, ask in
my name as to whether his sickness and indisposition
has abated, as to his health and vigour and condition of
ease; and speak thus: "May the venerable Gotama,
and with him the brethren of the Order, accept the
to-morrow's meal from Lohikka the Brahman."'

5. 'Very well, Sir,' said Bhesikâ the barber, acqui-
escing in the word of Lohikka the Brahman, and did so
even as he had been enjoined. And the Exalted One
consented, by silence, to his request.

6. And when Bhesikâ the barber perceived that
the Exalted One had consented, he rose from his seat,
and passing the Exalted One with his right hand
towards him, went to Lohikka the Brahman, and on
his arrival spake to him thus:

'We addressed that Exalted One[1], Sir, in your name, even as you commanded. And the Exalted One hath consented to come.'

[226] 7. Then Lohikka the Brahman, when the night had passed, made ready at his own dwelling-place sweet food, both hard and soft, and said to Bhesikâ the barber: 'Come now, good Bhesikâ, go where the Samana Gotama is staying, and on your arrival, announce the time to him, saying: " It is time, O Gotama, and the meal is ready."'

'Very well, Sir,' said Bhesikâ the barber in assent to the words of Lohikka the Brahman; and did so even as he had been enjoined.

And the Exalted One, who had robed himself early in the early morning, went robed, and carrying his bowl with him, with the brethren of the Order, towards Sâlavatikâ.

8. Now, as he went, Bhesikâ the barber walked, step by step, behind the Exalted One. And he said to him:

'The following wicked opinion has occurred to Lohikka the Brahman: "Suppose that a Samana or a Brâhmana have reached up to some good state (of mind), then he should tell no one else about it. For what can one man do for another? To tell others would be like the man who, having broken through an old bond, should entangle himself in a new one. Like that, I say, is this (desire to declare to others); it is a form of lust." 'Twere well, Sir, if the Exalted One would disabuse his mind thereof. For what can one man do for another?'

'That may well be, Bhesikâ, that may well be.'

[227] 9. And the Exalted One went on to the dwelling-place of Lohikka the Brahman, and sat down on the seat prepared for him. And Lohikka the Brahman satisfied the Order, with the Buddha at its head, with his own hand, with sweet food both hard

---

[1] It is clear from this expression that Bhesikâ was already a follower of the new teaching.

and soft, until they refused any more. And when the Exalted One had finished his meal, and had cleansed the bowl and his hands, Lohi*kk*a the Brahman brought a low seat and sat down beside him. And to him, thus seated, the Exalted One spake as follows :

' Is it true, what they say, Lohi*kk*a, that the following wicked opinion has arisen in your mind : [and he set forth the opinion as above set forth]?'

' That is so, Gotama.'

10. ' Now what think you, Lohi*kk*a ? Are you not established at Sâlavatikâ ?'

' Yes, that is so, Gotama.'

' Then suppose, Lohi*kk*a, one were to speak thus : "Lohi*kk*a the Brahman has a domain at Sâlavatikâ. Let him alone enjoy all the revenue and all the produce of Sâlavatikâ, allowing nothing to anybody else!" Would the utterer of that speech be a danger-maker as touching the men who live in dependence upon you, or not ?'

' He would be a danger-maker, Gotama ?'

' And making that danger, would he be a person who sympathised with their welfare, or not ?'

' He would not be considering their welfare, Gotama.'

' And not considering their welfare, would his heart stand fast in love toward them, or in enmity ?'

' In enmity, Gotama.'

' But when one's heart stands fast in enmity, is that unsound doctrine, or sound ?'

' It is unsound doctrine, Gotama.'

' Now if a man hold unsound doctrine, Lohi*kk*a, I declare that one of two future births will be his lot, either purgatory or rebirth as an animal.'

[228] 11. ' Now what think you, Lohi*kk*a ? Is not King Pasenadi of Kosala in possession of Kâsi and Kosala ?'

' Yes, that is so, Gotama.'

' Then suppose, Lohi*kk*a, one were to speak thus : "King Pasenadi of Kosala is in possession of Kâsi and Kosala. Let him enjoy all the revenue and all the produce of Kâsi and Kosala, allowing nothing to

anybody else." Would the utterer of that speech be a
danger-maker as touching the men who live in dependence on King Pasenadi of Kosala—both you yourself
and others—or not?'

'He would be a danger-maker, Gotama.'

'And making that danger, would he be a person
who sympathised with their welfare, or not?'

'He would not be considering their welfare, Gotama.'

'And not considering their welfare, would his heart
stand fast in love toward them, or in enmity?'

'In enmity, Gotama.'

'But when one's heart stands fast in enmity, is that
unsound doctrine, or sound?'

'It is unsound doctrine, Gotama.'

'Now if a man hold unsound doctrine, Lohikka, I
declare that one of two future births will be his lot,
either purgatory or rebirth as an animal.

12 and 14. 'So then, Lohikka, you admit that he who
should say that you, being in occupation of Sâlavatikâ,
should therefore yourself enjoy all the revenue and
produce thereof, bestowing nothing on any one else;
and he who should say that King Pasenadi of Kosala,
being in power over Kâsi and Kosala, should therefore
himself enjoy all the revenue and produce thereof,
bestowing nothing on any one else—would be making
danger for those living in dependence on you; or for
those, you and others, living in dependence upon the
King. And that those who thus make danger for
others, must be wanting in sympathy for them. And
that the man wanting in sympathy has his heart set
fast in enmity. And that to have one's heart set fast
in enmity is unsound doctrine :—

13 and 15. 'Then just so, Lohikka, he who should say:
"Suppose a Samana or a Brâhmana to have reached
up to some good state (of mind), then should he tell
no one else about it. For what can one man do for
another? To tell others would be like the man who,
having broken through an old bond, should entangle
himself in a new one. Like that, I say, is this desire
to declare to others, it is a form of lust;"—[229] just

so he, who should say thus, would be putting obstacles
in the way of those clansman who, having taken upon
themselves the Doctrine and Discipline set forth by
Him-who-has-won-the-Truth, have attained to great
distinction therein—to the fruit of conversion, for
instance, or to the fruit of once returning, or to the
fruit of never returning, or even to Arahatship—he
would be putting obstacles in the way of those who
are bringing to fruition the course of conduct that will
lead to rebirth in states of bliss in heaven[1].   But
putting obstacles in their way he would be out of
sympathy for their welfare; being out of sympathy for
their welfare his heart would become established in
enmity; and when one's heart is established in enmity,
that is unsound doctrine.   Now if a man hold unsound
doctrine, Lohikka, I declare that one of two future
births will be his lot, either purgatory or rebirth as an
animal[2].

[230] 16. 'There are these three sorts of teachers
in the world, Lohikka, who are worthy of blame.   And
whosoever should blame such a one, his rebuke would
be justified, in accord with the facts and the truth, not
improper.   What are the three?

'In the first place, Lohikka, there is a sort of teacher
who has not himself attained to that aim of Samanaship
for the sake of which he left his home and adopted
the homeless life.   Without having himself attained to
it he teaches a doctrine (Dhamma) to his hearers, saying: "This is good for you, this will make you happy."
Then those hearers of his neither listen to him, nor
give ear to his words, nor become stedfast in heart
through their knowledge thereof; they go their own
way, apart from the teaching of the master.   Such
a teacher may be rebuked, setting out these facts, and

---

[1] Literally 'Who are making heavenly embryos ripe for rebirth in
heavenly states.'

[2] Paragraphs 12, 13 are repeated of the case put about Pasenadi,
king of Kosala.   In the translation both cases are included at the
beginning of § 12.

x

adding: "You are like one who should make advances
to her who keeps repulsing him, or should embrace her
who turns her face away from him.   Like that, do I
say, is this lust of yours (to go on posing as a teacher
of men, no one heeding, since they trust you not).
For what, then, can one man do for another?"

'This, Lohikka, is the first sort of teacher in the
world worthy of blame.   And whosoever should blame
such a one, his rebuke would be justified, in accord
with the facts and the truth, not improper.

17. 'In the second place, Lohikka, there is a sort of
teacher who has not himself attained to that aim of
Samanaship for the sake of which he left his home
and adopted the homeless life.   Without having himself attained to it he teaches a doctrine to his hearers,
saying: "This is good for you; that will make you
happy."   And to him his disciples listen; [231] they
give ear to his words; they become stedfast in heart
by their understanding what is said; and they go not
their own way, apart from the teaching of the master.
Such a teacher may be rebuked, setting out these facts
and adding : "You are like a man who, neglecting his
own field, should take thought to weed out his neigh-
bour's field.   Like that, do I say, is this lust of yours
(to go on teaching others when you have not taught
yourself).   For what, then, can one man do for
another?"

'This, Lohikka, is the second sort of teacher in the
world worthy of blame.   And whosoever should blame
such a one, his rebuke would be justified, in accord
with the facts and the truth, not improper.

18. 'And again, Lohikka, in the third place, there is
a sort of teacher who has himself attained to that
aim of Samanaship for the sake of which he left his
home and adopted the homeless life.   Having himself
attained it, he teaches the doctrine to his hearers, saying: "This is good for you, that will make you happy."
But those hearers of his neither listen to him, nor give
ear to his words, nor become stedfast in heart through
understanding thereof; they go their own way, apart

from the teaching of the master.   Such a teacher may
be rebuked, setting out these facts, and adding : "You
are like a man who, having broken through an old
bond, should entangle himself in a new one.   Like that,
do I say, is this lust of yours (to go on teaching when
you have not trained yourself to teach).   For what,
then, can one man do for another ?

' This, Lohi*kk*a, is the third sort of teacher in the
world worthy of blame.   And whosoever should blame
such a one, his rebuke would be justified, in accord
with the facts and the truth, not improper.   And these,
Lohi*kk*a, are the three sorts of teachers of which I
spoke.'

[232, 233] 19. And when he had thus spoken, Lohi*kk*a
the Brahman spake thus to the Exalted One :

' But is there, Gotama, any sort of teacher not
worthy of blame in the world ? '

' Yes, Lohi*kk*a, there is a teacher not worthy, in the
world, of blame.'

' And what sort of a teacher, Gotama, is so ? '

[The answer is in the words of the exposition set out above in the Sâma*ññ*a-phala, as
follows:—

1. The appearance of a Tathâgata (one who
won the truth), his preaching, the conversion of
a hearer, his adoption of the homeless state.
(Above, pp. 78, 79.)

2. The minor details of mere morality that he
practises.   (Above, pp. 57, 58.)

3. The Confidence of heart he gains from this
practice.   (Above, p. 79.)

4. The paragraph on ' Guarded is the door of
his Senses.'   (Above, pp. 79, 80.)

5. The paragraph on ' Mindful and Self-
possessed.'   (Above, pp. 80, 81.)

6. The paragraph on Simplicity of life,
being content with little.   (Above, p. 81.)

7. The paragraphs on Emancipation from the
Five Hindrances—covetousness, ill-temper, laziness, worry, and perplexity. (Above, pp. 82–84.)

8. The paragraph on the Joy and Peace that, as a result of this emancipation, fills his whole being. (Above, p. 84.)

9. The paragraphs on the Four Raptures (*Gh*ânas). (Above, pp. 84–86.)

10. The paragraphs on the Insight arising from Knowledge (the knowledge of the First Path). (Above, pp. 86, 87.)

11. The paragraphs on the Realisation of the Four Noble Truths, the destruction of the Intoxications—lust, delusions, becomings, and ignorance—and the attainment of Arahatship. (Above, pp. 92, 93.)

The refrain throughout and the closing paragraph is:]

'And whosoever the teacher be, Lohi*kk*a, under whom the disciple attains to distinction so excellent as that[1], that, Lohi*kk*a, is a teacher not open to blame in the world. And whosoever should blame such a one, his rebuke would be unjustifiable, not in accord either with the facts or with the truth, without good ground.'

[234] 78. And when he had thus spoken, Lohi*kk*a the Brahman said to the Exalted One :

'Just, Gotama, as if a man had caught hold of a man, falling over the precipitous edge of purgatory, by the hair of his head, and lifted him up safe back on the firm land—just so have I, on the point of falling into purgatory, been lifted back on to the land by the venerable Gotama. Most excellent, O Gotama, are the words of thy mouth, most excellent! Just as if a man were to set up what has been thrown down, or were to reveal what has been hidden away, or were to point out the right road to him who has gone astray, or were to bring a light into the darkness so that those who had eyes could see external forms—just even so has the truth been made known to me, in many a

---

[1] U*l*âra*m* v*i*sesa*m* adhiga*kkh*ati. See for instance Sa*m*yutta V, 154, 5.

figure, by the venerable Gotama. And I, even I, betake myself to the venerable Gotama as my guide, to the Doctrine, and to the Order. May the venerable Gotama accept me as a disciple; as one who, from this day forth as long as life endures, has taken him as his guide!'

Here ends the Lohikka Suttanta.

INTRODUCTION

TO THE

TEVIGGA SUTTA.

THIS is the only Suttanta, among the thirteen translated in this volume, in which the discourse does not lead up to Arahatship. It leads up only to the so-called *Brahma Vihâras*—the supreme conditions—four states of mind held to result, after death, in a rebirth in the heavenly worlds of Brahmâ. Why is it—the Buddhist ideal being Arahatship, which leads to no rebirth at all—that this lower ideal is thus suddenly introduced?

It would seem that the particular point here discussed was regarded as so important that it could scarcely be left out. And when we recollect that the highest teaching current before the Buddha, and still preserved in the pre-Buddhistic Upanishads, was precisely about union with Brahmâ; we may, without much danger of error, explain the position occupied in the series of dialogues by this Suttanta by the supposition that it was deliberately inserted here as the Buddhist answer to the Upanishad theory. In this respect it is noteworthy that the neuter Brahman is quietly ignored. That is quite in accordance with the method of the Suttantas. The Buddha is in them often represented as using, in his own sense, words familiar to his interlocutors in a different sense. The neuter Brahman is, so far as I am aware, entirely unknown in the Nikâyas, and of course the Buddha's idea of Brahmâ, in the masculine, really differs widely from that of the Upanishads.

There is nothing original in the Buddhist belief that a man's habit of mind at the time of his death would determine, save only in the one case of the Arahat, the nature of his rebirth. It is an Indian—not an exclusively Buddhist—theory. The Buddhist texts represent it as held by non-Buddhists, and already long before the Buddha's time, and as accepted by all as a matter of course. And it is even not exclusively Indian. As I have pointed out elsewhere, it is ascribed by Plato to Socrates[1]. The essentially Buddhist parts of the theory are three. In the first place, the choice of the particular details they held essential to such a habit of mind as would lead to rebirth in the Brahmâ-worlds ; secondly, their doctrine that there was not really any 'soul' to be reborn ; and thirdly, that the highest ideal was not to be reborn at all (even only once, and into union with Brahmâ).

The Gâtaka commentary in numerous passages states that the four Brahma Vihâras were practised, long before the time of the rise of Buddhism, by the sages of old. I have not found such a statement in the Nikâyas ; and it is most probable therefore that the Gâtaka commentator is ante-dating the particular meditations in question. However this may be, they remained, throughout the long history of Buddhism, an essential part of Buddhist practice. They are even mentioned in the Gâtaka Mâlâ, a work usually supposed to be Mahâyânist, and dated about a thousand years later than the Buddha[2]. They are well known to-day in Burma, Siam, and Ceylon. And it would be interesting to know whether they still form a part of the regulated meditations which are known to be practised by Buddhists in Thibet, China, and Japan. But they have not been found in any Indian book not a Buddhist work, and are therefore almost certainly exclusively Buddhist. Even the most determined anti-Buddhist must admit the beauty of the language (in spite of its repetitions §§ 76–78), the subtle depth of the ideas, and the great value of the practice from the point of view of ethical self-training. He would probably rejoin, and with truth, that similar sentiments are met with in other (post-Buddhistic) Indian books. But it is one thing to give expression in isolated passages to such views, and quite another to have selected just these four as the four corner-stones of habitual endeavour.

It should be recollected that the argument here is only an *argumentum ad hominem*. If you want union with Brahmâ — which you had much better not want—this is the way to attain to it[3].

---

[1] Phaedo 69. The full context is given in my 'Hibbert Lectures,' Appendix viii.

[2] In the well-known story of the Bodhisattva giving his body to feed a tigress (No. 1, verse 12).

[3] See the remarks above on p. 206.

XIII. TEVI*GG*A SUTTA.

[ON KNOWLEDGE OF THE VEDAS [1].]

1. Thus have I heard. When the Exalted One was once journeying through Kosala with a great company of the brethren, with about five hundred brethren, he came to the Brahman village in Kosala which is called Manasâka*t*a. And there at Manasâka*t*a the Exalted One stayed in the mango grove, on the bank of the river A*k*iravatî, to the north of Manasâka*t*a.

2. Now at that time many very distinguished and wealthy Brahmans were staying at Manasâka*t*a; to wit, Kaṅkî the Brahman, Târukkha the Brahman, Pokkharasâdi the Brahman, *G*ânusso*n*i the Brahman, Todeyya the Brahman, and other very distinguished and wealthy Brahmans [2].

---

[1] This Suttanta was translated from the MSS. in my 'Buddhist Suttas' (S. B. F., 1881). Since then the text has been published by the Pâli Text Society; and alterations and amendments in a number of details have been rendered necessary.

[2] Buddhaghosa says that—

    Kaṅkî lived at Opasâda,

    Târukkha lived at I*kkh*agala (so MSS., perhaps for I*kkh*â*n*angala),

    Pokkharasâdi (*sic* MS.) lived at Ukka*tth*a,

    *G*ânusso*n*i lived at Savatthi, and

    Todeyya lived at Tudigama.

*G*ânusso*n*i was converted by the Bhaya-bherava Sutta. On Pokkharasâdi, see above, pp. 108, 135, 147; and on Todeyya, see above, p. 267; and on all the names, see Ma*ggh*ima Nikâya, No. 98 = Sutta Nipâta III, 9.

Buddhaghosa adds that because Manasâka*t*a was a pleasant place the Brahmans had built huts there on the bank of the river and fenced them in, and used to go and stay there from time to time to repeat their mantras.

3. Now a conversation sprung up between Vâse*tth*a and Bhâradvâ*g*a, when they were taking exercise (after their bath) and walking up and down in thoughtful mood, as to which was the true path, and which the false [1].

4. The young Brahman Vâse*tth*a spake thus :
'This is the straight path, this the direct way which makes for salvation, and leads him, who acts according to it, into a state of union with Brahmâ. I mean that which has been announced by the Brahman Pokkharasâdi.'

5. The young Brahman Bhâradvâ*g*a spake thus :
'This is the straight path, this the direct way which makes for salvation, and leads him, who acts according to it, into a state of union with Brahmâ. I mean that which has been announced by the Brahman Târukkha.'

6. But neither was the young Brahman Vâse*tth*a able to convince the young Brahman Bhâradvâ*g*a, nor was the young Brahman Bhâradvâ*g*a able to convince the young Brahman Vâse*tth*a.

7. Then the young Brahman Vâse*tth*a said to the young Brahman Bhâradvâ*g*a :
'That Sama*n*a Gotama, Bhâradvâ*g*a, of the sons of the Sâkyas, who went out from the Sâkya clan to adopt the religious life, is now staying at Manasâka*t*a, in the mango grove, on the bank of the river A*k*iravatî, to the north of Manasâka*t*a. Now regarding that venerable Gotama, such is the high reputation that has been noised abroad : "That Exalted One is an Arahat, a fully enlightened one, abounding in wisdom and goodness, happy, with knowledge of the worlds, unsurpassed as a guide to mortals willing to be led, a teacher of gods and men, an Exalted One, a Buddha."

---

[1] *G*añghâvihâra*m* anu*k*añkamantâna*m* anuvi*k*arantâna*m*. *K*añkamati is to walk up and down thinking. I have added 'after their bath,' from Buddhaghosa, who says that this must be understood to have taken place when, after learning by heart and repeating all day, they went down in the evening to the riverside to bathe, and then walked up and down on the sand. Comp. Mil. 22; *G*ât. II, 240, 272.

Come, then, Bhâradvâ*g*a, let us go to the place where
the Sama*n*a Gotama is; and when we have come
there, let us ask the Sama*n*a Gotama touching this
matter. What the Sama*n*a Gotama shall declare unto
us, that let us bear in mind[1].'

'Very well, my friend!' said the young Brahman
Bhâradvâ*g*a, in assent, to the young Brahman Vâse*tth*a.

8. Then the young Brahman Vâse*tth*a and the young
Brahman Bhâradvâ*g*a went on to the place where the
Exalted One was.

And when they had come there, they exchanged
with the Exalted One the greetings and compliments
of politeness and courtesy, and sat down beside him.

And while they were thus seated the young Brahman
Vâse*tth*a said to the Exalted One:

'As we, Gotama, were taking exercise and walking
up and down, there sprung up a conversation between
us on which was the true path, and which the false.
I said thus :

'"This is the straight path, this the direct way
which makes for salvation, and leads him, who acts
according to it, into a state of union with Brahmâ.
I mean that which has been announced by the Brahman
Pokkharasâdi."'

'Bhâradvâ*g*a said thus :

'"This is the straight path, this the direct way
which makes for salvation, and leads him, who acts
according to it, into a state of union with Brahmâ.
I mean that which has been announced by the Brahman Târukkha."'

'Regarding this matter, Gotama, there is a strife,
a dispute, a difference of opinion between us.'

---

9. 'So you say, Vâse*tth*a, that you said thus :

'"This is the straight path, this the direct way
which makes for salvation, and leads him, who acts
according to it, into a state of union with Brahmâ.

---

[1] Comp. Divyâvadâna 196, 246; and Aṅguttara II, pp. 23, 24.

I mean that which has been announced by the Brahman Pokkharasâdi." '

'While Bhâradvâ*g*a said thus :

' " This is the straight path, this the direct way which makes for salvation, and leads him, who acts according to it, into a state of union with Brahmâ. I mean that which has been announced by the Brahman Târukkha." '

'Wherein, then, O Vâse*tth*a, is there a strife, a dispute, a difference of opinion between you [1] ? '

10. ' Concerning the true path and the false, Gotama. Various Brahmans, Gotama, teach various paths. The Addhariyâ Brahmans, the Tittiriyâ Brahmans, the *Kh*andokâ Brahmans [the *Kh*andavâ Brahmans], the Bavhari*g*â Brahmans [2]. Are all those saving paths ? Are they all paths which will lead him, who acts according to them, into a state of union with Brahmâ ?

' Just, Gotama, as near a village or a town there are many and various paths [3], yet they all meet together in the village—just in that way are all the various paths taught by various Brahmans—the Addhariyâ Brahmans, the Tittiriyâ Brahmans, the *Kh*andokâ Brahmans [the *Kh*andavâ Brahmans], the Bavhari*g*â Brahmans. Are all these saving paths ? Are they all paths which will lead him, who acts according to them, into a state of union with Brahmâ ? '

11. ' Do you say that they all lead aright, Vâse*tth*a?' ' I say so, Gotama.'

---

[1] This is either mildly sarcastic—as much as to say, 'that is six of one, and half a dozen of the other '—or is intended to lead on Vâse*tth*a to confess still more directly the fact that the different theologians held inconsistent opinions.

[2] The MSS. differ as to the last name, and some of them omit the last but one. The Adhvaryu, Taittirîya, *Kh*andoga, and Bahv*ri*ka priests—those skilled in liturgy generally, and in the Ya*g*ur, Sâma, and *R*ig Vedas respectively—are probably meant. If we adopt the other reading for the last in the list, then those priests who relied on liturgy, sacrifice, or chant would be contrasted with those who had ' gone forth ' as *religieux*, either as *Tâpasas* or as *Bhikshus*.

[3] Mag*g*âni, which is noteworthy as a curious change of gender.

'Do you really say that they all lead aright, Vâ-settha?'

'So I say, Gotama.'

12. 'But yet, Vâsettha, is there a single one of the Brahmans versed in the Three Vedas who has ever seen Brahmâ face to face?'

'No, indeed, Gotama.'

'Or is there then, Vâsettha, a single one of the teachers of the Brahmans versed in the Three Vedas who has seen Brahmâ face to face?'

'No, indeed, Gotama!'

'Or is there then, Vâsettha, a single one of the teachers of the teachers of the Brahmans versed in the Three Vedas who has seen Brahmâ face to face?'

'No, indeed, Gotama!'

'Or is there then, Vâsettha, a single one of the Brahmans up to the seventh generation who has seen Brahmâ face to face?'

'No, indeed, Gotama!'

13. 'Well then, Vâsettha, those ancient Rishis of the Brahmans versed in the Three Vedas, the authors of the verses, the utterers of the verses, whose ancient form of words so chanted, uttered, or composed, the Brahmans of to-day chant over again or repeat; intoning or reciting exactly as has been intoned or recited—to wit, Atthaka, Vâmaka, Vâmadeva, Vessâmitta, Yamataggi, Angirasa, Bhâradvâga, Vâsettha, Kassapa, and Bhagu [1]—did even they speak thus, saying: "We know it, we have seen it, where Brahmâ is, whence Brahmâ is, whither Brahmâ is?"'

'Not so, Gotama!'

14. 'Then you say, Vâsettha, that none of the Brahmans, or of their teachers, or of their pupils, even up to the seventh generation, has ever seen Brahmâ face to face. And that even the Rishis of old, the authors and utterers of the verses, of the ancient form of words which the Brahmans of to-day so carefully intone and recite precisely as they have

---

[1] See the note on these names at 'Vinaya Texts,' II, 130.

been handed down—even they did not pretend to know or to have seen where or whence or whither Brahmâ is[1]. So that the Brahmans versed in the Three Vedas have forsooth said thus: "What we know not, what we have not seen, to a state of union with that we can show the way, and can say: 'This is the straight path, this is the direct way which makes for salvation, and leads him, who acts according to it, into a state of union with Brahmâ!'"

'Now what think you, Vâse*tth*a? Does it not follow, this being so, that the talk of the Brahmans, versed though they be in the Three Vedas, turns out to be foolish talk?'

'In sooth, Gotama, that being so, it follows that the talk of the Brahmans versed in the Three Vedas is foolish talk!'

15. 'Verily, Vâse*tth*a, that Brahmans versed in the Three Vedas should be able to show the way to a state of union with that which they do not know, neither have seen—such a condition of things can in no wise be!

'Just, Vâse*tth*a, as when a string of blind men are clinging one to the other[2], neither can the foremost see, nor can the middle one see, nor can the hindmost see—just even so, methinks, Vâse*tth*a, is the talk of the Brahmans versed in the Three Vedas but blind talk: the first sees not, the middle one sees not, nor can the latest see. The talk then of these

---

[1] In the text §§ 12, 13 are repeated word for word.

[2] Andhave*n*î parampara*m* sa*m*satta. The Phayre MS. has replaced ve*n*î by pave*n*î, after the constant custom of the Burmese MSS. to improve away unusual or difficult expressions. Buddhaghosa explains andhave*n*i by andhapave*n*i; and tells a tale of a wicked wight, who meeting a company of blind men, told them of a certain village wherein plenty of good food was to be had. When they besought him for hire to lead them there, he took the money, made one blind man catch hold of his stick, the next of that one, and so on, and then led them on till they came to a wilderness. There he deserted them, and they all—still holding each the other, and vainly, and with tears, seeking both their guide and the path—came to a miserable end! Comp. M. II, 170.

Brahmans versed in the Three Vedas turns out to be ridiculous, mere words, a vain and empty thing!'

---

16. 'Now what think you, Vâse*tth*a? Can the Brahmans versed in the Three Vedas—like other, ordinary, folk—see the Moon and the Sun as they pray to, and praise, and worship them, turning round with clasped hands towards the place whence they rise and where they set?'

'Certainly, Gotama, they can [1].'

17. 'Now what think you, Vâse*tth*a? The Brahmans versed in the Three Vedas, who can very well—like other, ordinary, folk—see the Moon and the Sun as they pray to, and praise, and worship them, turning round with clasped hands to the place whence they rise and where they set—are those Brahmans, versed in the Three Vedas, able to point out the way to a state of union with the Moon or the Sun, saying: "This is the straight path, this the direct way which makes for salvation, and leads him, who acts according to it, to a state of union with the Moon or the Sun?"'

'Certainly, not, Gotama!'

18. 'So you say, Vâse*tth*a, that the Brahmans are not able to point out the way to union with that which they have seen, and you further say that neither any one of them, nor of their pupils, nor of their predecessors even to the seventh generation has ever seen Brahmâ And you further say that even the Rishis of old, whose words they hold in such deep respect, did not pretend to know, or to have seen where, or whence, or whither Brahmâ is. Yet these Brahmans versed in the Three Vedas say, forsooth, that they can point out the way to union with that which they know not, neither have seen [2]. Now what

---

[1] The words of the question are repeated in the text in this and the following answers. It must be remembered, for these sections, that the Sun and Moon were gods just as much as Brahmâ; and that the Moon always comes first in Nikâya and other ancient texts.

[2] The text repeats at length the words of §§ 12, 13, 14.

think you, Vâse*tth*a? Does it not follow that, this being so, the talk of the Brahmans, versed though they be in the Three Vedas, turns out to be foolish talk?'

'In sooth, Gotama, that being so, it follows that the talk of the Brahmans versed in the Three Vedas is foolish talk!'

19. 'Very good, Vâse*tth*a. Verily then, Vâse*tth*a, that Brahmans versed in the Three Vedas should be able to show the way to a state of union with that which they do not know, neither have seen—such a condition of things can in no wise be!'

'Just, Vâse*tth*a, as if a man should say, "How I long for, how I love the most beautiful woman in this land!"

'And people should ask him, "Well! good friend! this most beautiful woman in the land, whom you thus love and long for, do you know whether that beautiful woman is a noble lady or a Brahman woman, or of the trader class, or a *S*ûdra?"

'But when so asked, he should answer: "No."

'And when people should ask him, "Well! good friend! this most beautiful woman in all the land, whom you so love and long for, do you know what the name of that most beautiful woman is, or what is her family name, whether she be tall or short or of medium height, dark or brunette or golden in colour, or in what village or town or city she dwells?"

'But when so asked, he should answer: "No."

'And then people should say to him, "So then, good friend, whom you know not, neither have seen, her do you love and long for?"

'And then when so asked, he should answer: "Yes."

'Now what think you, Vâse*tth*a? Would it not turn out, that being so, that the talk of that man was foolish talk?'

'In sooth, Gotama, it would turn out, that being so, that the talk of that man was foolish talk!'

20. 'And just even so, Vâse*ttha*, though you say that the Brahmans are not able to point out the way to union with that which they have seen, and you further say that neither any one of them, nor of their pupils, nor of their predecessors even to the seventh generation has ever seen Brahmâ. And you further say that even the Rishis of old, whose words they hold in such deep respect, did not pretend to know, or to have seen where, or whence, or whither Brahmâ is. Yet these Brahmans versed in the Three Vedas say, forsooth, that they can point out the way to union with that which they know not, neither have seen! Now what think you, Vâse*ttha*? Does it not follow that, this being so, the talk of the Brahmans, versed though they be in the Three Vedas, is foolish talk?'

'In sooth, Gotama, that being so, it follows that the talk of the Brahmans versed in the Three Vedas is foolish talk!'

'Very good, Vâse*ttha*. Verily then, Vâse*ttha*, that Brahmans versed in the Three Vedas should be able to show the way to a state of union with that which they do not know, neither have seen—such a condition of things can in no wise be.'

————

21. 'Just, Vâse*ttha*, as if a man should make a staircase in the place where four roads cross, to mount up into a mansion. And people should say to him, "Well, good friend, this mansion, to mount up into which you are making this staircase, do you know whether it is in the east, or in the south, or in the west, or in the north? whether it is high or low or of medium size?

'And when so asked, he should answer: "No."

'And people should say to him, "But then, good friend, you are making a staircase to mount up into something—taking it for a mansion—which, all the while, you know not, neither have seen!"

'And when so asked, he should answer: "Yes."

'Now what think you, Vâse*ttha*? Would it not

turn out, that being so, that the talk of that man was foolish talk?'

'In sooth, Gotama, it would turn out, that being so, that the talk of that man was foolish talk!'

22. 'And just even so, Vâse*tth*a, though you say that the Brahmans are not able to point out the way to union with that which they have seen, and you further say that neither any one of them, nor of their pupils, nor of their predecessors even to the seventh generation has ever seen Brahmâ. And you further say that even the Rishis of old, whose words they hold in such deep respect, did not pretend to know, or to have seen where, or whence, or whither Brahmâ is. Yet these Brahmans versed in the Three Vedas say, forsooth, that they can point out the way to union with that which they know not, neither have seen! Now what think you, Vâse*tth*a? Does it not follow that, this being so, the talk of the Brahmans versed in the Three Vedas is foolish talk?'

'In sooth, Gotama, that being so, it follows that the talk of the Brahmans versed in the Three Vedas is foolish talk!'

23. 'Very good, Vâse*tth*a. Verily then, Vâse*tth*a, that Brahmans versed in the Three Vedas should be able to show the way to a state of union with that which they do not know, neither have seen—such a condition of things can in no wise be.'

24. 'Again, Vâse*tth*a, if this river A*k*iravatî were full of water even to the brim, and overflowing [1]. And a man with business on the other side, bound for the other side, making for the other side, should come up, and want to cross over. And he, standing on this bank, should invoke the further bank, and say, "Come hither, O further bank! come over to this side!"

'Now what think you, Vâse*tth*a? Would the further bank of the river A*k*iravatî, by reason of that man's

---

[1] Samatittika kâkapeyyâ. See on this phrase the note in my 'Buddhist Suttas' (S. B. E.), pp. 178, 179.

Y

invoking and praying and hoping and praising, come over to this side?'

'Certainly not, Gotama!'

25. 'In just the same way, Vâse*ttha*, do the Brahmans versed in the Three Vedas—omitting the practice of those qualities which really make a man a Brahman, and adopting the practice of those qualities which really make men non-Brahmans—say thus: "Indra we call upon, Soma we call upon, Varu*n*a we call upon, Îsâna we call upon, Pa*g*âpati we call upon, Brahmâ we call upon, [Mahiddhi we call upon, Yama we call upon [1]]" Verily, Vâse*tth*a, that those Brahmans versed in the Three Vedas, but omitting the practice of those qualities which really make a man a Brahman, and adopting the practice of those qualities which really make men non-Brahmans—that they, by reason of their invoking and praying and hoping and praising, should, after death and when the body is dissolved, become united with Brahmâ— verily such a condition of things can in no wise be [2]!'

---

26. 'Just, Vâse*tth*a, as if this river A*k*iravatî were full, even to the brim, and overflowing. And a man with business on the other side, making for the other side, bound for the other side, should come up, and want to cross over. And he, on this bank, were to be bound tightly, with his arms behind his back, by a strong chain. Now what think you, Vâse*tth*a, would that man be able to get over from this bank of the river A*k*iravatî to the further bank?'

'Certainly not, Gotama!'

27. 'In the same way, Vâse*tth*a, there are five things

---

[1] The Sinhalese MSS. omit Mahiddhi and Yama, but repeat the verb, 'we call upon,' three times after Brahmâ. It is possible that the Burmese copyist has wrongly inserted them to remove the strangeness of this repetition. The comment is silent.

[2] The Buddha, as usual, here takes the 'further bank' in the meaning attached to it by the theologians he is talking to, as union with Brahmâ. In his own system, of course, the 'further bank' is Arahatship. So Angúttara V, 232, 233, and elsewhere.

leading to lust, which are called, in the Discipline of the Arahats, a "chain" and a "bond."'

'What are the five?'

'Forms perceptible to the eye; desirable, agreeable, pleasant, attractive forms, that are accompanied by lust and cause delight. Sounds of the same kind perceptible to the ear. Odours of the same kind perceptible to the nose. Tastes of the same kind perceptible to the tongue. Substances of the same kind perceptible to the body by touch. These five things predisposing to passion are called, in the Discipline of the Arahats, a "chain" and a "bond." And these five things predisposing to lust, Vâse*tth*a, do the Brahmans versed in the Three Vedas cling to, they are infatuated by them, attached to them, see not the danger of them, know not how unreliable they are, and so enjoy them[1].'

28. 'And verily, Vâse*tth*a, that Brahmans versed in the Three Vedas, but omitting the practice of those qualities which really make a man a Brahman, and adopting the practice of those qualities which really make men non-Brahmans—clinging to these five things predisposing to passion, infatuated by them, attached to them, seeing not their danger, knowing not their unreliability, and so enjoying them—that these Brahmans should after death, on the dissolution of the body, become united to Brahmâ—such a condition of things can in no wise be!'

29. 'Again, Vâse*tth*a, if this river A*k*iravatî were full of water even to the brim, and overflowing. And a man with business on the other side, making for the other side, bound for the other side, should come up, and want to cross over. And if he covering himself up, even to his head, were to lie down, on this bank, to sleep.

'Now what think you, Vâse*tth*a? Would that man

---

[1] Gathitâ mu*kkh*itâ agg*h*opannâ. See A. I, 74, 274; Udâna VII, 3, 4; Sum. 59, &c.

be able to get over from this bank of the river A*k*iravatî to the further bank?'

'Certainly not, Gotama!'

30. 'And in the same way, Vâse*tth*a, there are these
Five Hindrances, in the Discipline of the Arahats [1],
which are called "veils," and are called "hindrances,"
and are called "obstacles," and are called "entanglements."'

'Which are the five?'

'The hindrance of worldly lusts,

'The hindrance of illwill,

'The hindrance of torpor and sloth of heart and
mind,

'The hindrance of flurry and worry,

'The hindrance of suspense.

'These are the Five Hindrances, Vâse*tth*a, which,
in the Discipline of the Arahats, are called veils, and
are called hindrances, and are called obstacles, and are
called entanglements [2].

'Now with these Five Hindrances, Vâse*tth*a, the
Brahmans versed in the Three Vedas are veiled,
hindered, obstructed, and entangled.

'And verily, Vâse*tth*a, that Brahmans versed in
the Three Vedas, but omitting the practice of those
qualities which really make a man a Brahman, and
adopting the practice of those qualities which really
make men non-Brahmans—veiled, hindered, obstructed,
and entangled by these Five Hindrances—that these
Brahmans should after death, on the dissolution of the
body, become united to Brahmâ—such a condition of
things can in no wise be!'

31. 'Now what think you, Vâse*tth*a, and what have
you heard from the Brahmans aged and well-stricken
in years, when the learners and teachers are talking

---

[1] Ariyassa vinaye. This may possibly mean 'in the disciple
recommended by *the* Arahat' (that is, by the Buddha). But the latter
is expressed rather by Sugata-vinaye. Comp. A*n*guttara V, 237–
239 with 234, 235.

[2] These Five Hindrances are more fully dealt with above, p. 82.

together? Is Brahmâ in possession of wives and wealth, or is he not[1]?'

'He is not, Gotama.'

'Is his mind full of anger, or free from anger?'

'Free from anger, Gotama.'

'Is his mind full of malice, or free from malice?'

'Free from malice, Gotama.'

'Is his mind tarnished, or is it pure[2]?'

'It is pure, Gotama.'

'Has he self-mastery, or has he not[3]?'

'He has, Gotama.'

32. 'Now what think you, Vâse*tth*a, are the Brahmans versed in the Vedas in the possession of wives and wealth, or are they not?'

'They are, Gotama.'

'Have they anger in their hearts, or have they not?'

'They have, Gotama.'

'Do they bear malice, or do they not?'

'They do, Gotama.'

'Are they pure in heart, or are they not?'

'They are not, Gotama.'

'Have they self-mastery, or have they not?'

'They have not, Gotama.'

33. 'Then you say, Vâse*tth*a, that the Brahmans are in possession of wives and wealth, and that Brahmâ is not. Can there, then, be agreement and likeness between the Brahmans with their wives and property, and Brahmâ, who has none of these things?'

---

[1] Sapariggaho vâ Brahmâ apariggaho vâ ti. Buddhaghosa says on Vâse*tth*a's reply, 'Kâma*kkh*andassa âbhavato itthipariggahena apariggaho,' thus restricting the 'possession' to women. But the reference is no doubt to the first 'hindrance'; and the word in the text, though doubtless alluding to possession of women also, includes more. Compare, on the general idea of the passage, the English expression, 'no encumbrances,' and Jacobi, 'Gaina-Sûtras' (S. B. E.) I, xxiii.

[2] Asaṅkili*tth*a-*k*itto. That is, says Buddhaghosa, 'free from mental torpor and idleness, worry and flurry.'

[3] Vasavattî vâ avasavattî vâ. Buddhaghosa says, in explanation of the answer, 'By the absence of wavering he has his mind under control (vase vatteti).'

'Certainly not, Gotama!'

34. 'Very good, Vâsettha. But, verily, that these Brahmans versed in the Vedas, who live married and wealthy, should after death, when the body is dissolved, become united with Brahmâ, who has none of these things—such a condition of things can in no wise be!'

35. 'Then you say, too, Vâsettha, that the Brahmans bear anger and malice in their hearts, and are tarnished in heart and uncontrolled, whilst Brahmâ is free from anger and malice, pure in heart, and has self-mastery. Now can there, then, be concord and likeness between the Brahmans and Brahmâ?'

'Certainly not, Gotama!'

36. 'Very good, Vâsettha. That these Brahmans versed in the Vedas and yet bearing anger and malice in their hearts, sinful, and uncontrolled, should after death, when the body is dissolved, become united to Brahmâ, who is free from anger and malice, pure in heart, and has self-mastery—such a condition of things can in no wise be!

'So that thus then, Vâsettha, the Brahmans, versed though they be in the Three Vedas, while they sit down (in confidence), are sinking down (in the mire)[1]; and so sinking they are arriving only at despair, thinking the while that they are crossing over into some happier land.

'Therefore is it that the threefold wisdom of the Brahmans, wise in their Three Vedas, is called a water-less desert, their threefold wisdom is called a pathless jungle, their threefold wisdom is called perdition!'

37. When he had thus spoken, the young Brahman Vâsettha said to the Blessed One:

---

[1] Âsîditva saṃsîdanti. I have no doubt the commentator is right in his explanation of these figurative expressions. Confident in their knowledge of the Vedas, and in their practice of Vedic ceremonies, they neglect higher things; and so, sinking into folly and superstition, 'they are arriving only at despair, thinking the while that they are crossing over into some happier land.'

'It has been told me, Gotama, that the Samana Gotama knows the way to the state of union with Brahmâ.'

'What do you think, Vâse*tt*ha, is not Manasâka*t*a near to this spot, not distant from this spot?'

'Just so, Gotama. Manasâka*t*a is near to, is not far from here.'

'Now what think you, Vâse*tt*ha, suppose there were a man born in Manasâka*t*a, and people should ask him, who never till that time had left Manasâka*t*a, which was the way to Manasâka*t*a. Would that man, born and brought up in Manasâka*t*a, be in any doubt or difficulty?'

'Certainly not, Gotama! And why? If the man had been born and brought up in Manasâka*t*a, every road that leads to Manasâka*t*a would be perfectly familiar to him.'

38. 'That man, Vâse*tt*ha, born and brought up at Manasâka*t*a might, if he were asked the way to Manasâka*t*a, fall into doubt and difficulty, but to the Tathâgata, when asked touching the path which leads to the world of Brahmâ, there can be neither doubt nor difficulty. For Brahmâ, I know, Vâse*tt*ha, and the world of Brahmâ, and the path which leadeth unto it. Yea, I know it even as one who has entered the Brahmâ-world, and has been born within it!'

---

39. When he had thus spoken, Vâse*tt*ha, the young Brahman, said to the Blessed One:

'Just so has it been told me, Gotama, even that the Samana Gotama knows the way to a state of union with Brahmâ. It is well! Let the venerable Gotama be pleased to show us the way to a state of union with Brahmâ, let the venerable Gotama save the Brahman race[1]!'

'Listen then, Vâse*tt*ha, and give ear attentively, and I will speak!'

---

[1] Buddhaghosa takes this to mean, 'Save *me* of the Brahman race.'

'So be it, Lord!' said the young Brahman Vâse*ttha*, in assent, to the Blessed One.

40. Then the Blessed One spake, and said:

'Know, Vâse*ttha*, that (from time to time) a Tathâgata is born into the world, an Arahat, a fully awakened one, abounding in wisdom and goodness, happy, with knowledge of the worlds, unsurpassed as a guide to mortals willing to be led, a teacher of gods and men, a Blessed One, a Buddha. He, by himself, thoroughly understands, and sees, as it were, face to face this universe—including the worlds above with the gods, the Mâras, and the Brahmâs; and the world below with its Sama*n*as and Brahmans, its princes and peoples;—and he then makes his knowledge known to others. The truth doth he proclaim both in the letter and in the spirit, lovely in its origin, lovely in its progress, lovely in its consummation: the higher life doth he make known, in all its purity and in all its perfectness.

41. 'A householder (gahapati), or one of his children, or a man of inferior birth in any class, listens to that truth[1]. On hearing the truth he has faith in the Tathâgata, and when he has acquired that faith he thus considers with himself:

'" Full of hindrances is household life, a path defiled by passion: free as the air is the life of him who has renounced all worldly things. How difficult it is for the man who dwells at home to live the higher life in all its fullness, in all its purity, in all its bright perfection! Let me then cut off my hair and beard, let me clothe myself in the orange-coloured robes, and let me go forth from a household life into the homeless state!"

'Then before long, forsaking his portion of wealth, be it great or be it small; forsaking his circle of relatives, be they many or be they few, he cuts off his hair and beard, he clothes himself in the orange-

---

[1] The point is, that the acceptance of this 'Doctrine and Discipline' is open to all; not of course that Brahmans never accept it.

coloured robes, and he goes forth from the household life into the homeless state.

42. 'When he has thus become a recluse he passes a life self-restrained by that restraint which should be binding on a recluse. Uprightness is his delight, and he sees danger in the least of those things he should avoid. He adopts and trains himself in the precepts. He encompasses himself with goodness in word and deed. He sustains his life by means that are quite pure; good is his conduct, guarded the door of his senses; mindful and self-possessed, he is altogether happy!'

43-75. 'And how, Vâse*tth*a, is his conduct good?'

[The answer is set forth in the words of the tract on the Sîlas, translated above, pp. 3–26, but with the refrain as in the Sâmañña-phala Suttanta above, p. 79. Then follow §§ 63–75, inclusive, of the Sâmañña-phala; setting forth :—

1. The confidence of heart that results from the sense of goodness.

2. The way in which he guards the doors of his senses.

3. The way in which he is mindful and self-possessed.

4. His habit of being content with little, of adopting simplicity of life.

5. His conquest of the Five Hindrances, each with the explanatory simile.

6. The joy and peace which, as a result of this conquest, fills his whole being.]

76. [1] 'And he lets his mind pervade one quarter of

---

[1] These paragraphs occur frequently; see, inter alia, Mahâ-Sudassana Sutta II, 8, in my 'Buddhist Suttas' (S. B. E.). It will be seen from 'Buddhism,' pp. 170, 171, that these meditations play a great part in later Buddhism, and occupy very much the place that prayer takes in Christianity. A fifth, the meditation on Impurity, has been added, at what time I do not know, before the last. These four (or five) are called the Brahma Vihâras, and the practice of them leads, not to Arahatship, but to rebirth in the Brahmâ-world.

the world with thoughts of Love, and so the second, and so the third, and so the fourth. And thus the whole wide world, above, below, around, and everywhere, does he continue to pervade with heart of Love, far-reaching, grown great, and beyond measure.

77. 'Just, Vâse*tth*a, as a mighty trumpeter makes himself heard—and that without difficulty—in all the four directions; even so of all things that have shape or life, there is not one that he passes by or leaves aside, but regards them all with mind set free, and deep-felt love.

'Verily this, Vâse*tth*a, is the way to a state of union with Brahmâ.

78. 'And he lets his mind pervade one quarter of the world with thoughts of pity[1], . . . sympathy[1], . . . equanimity[1], and so the second, and so the third, and so the fourth. And thus the whole wide world, above, below, around, and everywhere, does he continue to pervade with heart of pity, . . . sympathy, . . . equanimity, far-reaching, grown great, and beyond measure.

79. 'Just, Vâse*tth*a, as a mighty trumpeter makes himself heard—and that without difficulty—in all the four directions; even so of all things that have shape or life, there is not one that he passes by or leaves aside, but regards them all with mind set free, and deep-felt pity, . . . sympathy, . . . equanimity.

'Verily this, Vâse*tth*a, is the way to a state of union with Brahmâ.'

---

80. 'Now what think you, Vâse*tth*a, will the Bhikkhu who lives thus be in possession of women and of wealth, or will he not?'

'He will not, Gotama!'

'Will he be full of anger, or free from anger?'

'He will be free from anger, Gotama!'

'Will his mind be full of malice, or free from malice?'

---

[1] Paragraphs 76, 77 are supposed to be repeated of each.

'Free from malice, Gotama!'

'Will his mind be tarnished, or pure?'

'It will be pure, Gotama!'

'Will he have self-mastery, or will he not?'

'Surely he will, Gotama!'

81. 'Then you say, Vâse*tt*ha, that the Bhikkhu is free from household and worldly cares, and that Brahmâ is free from household and worldly cares. Is there then agreement and likeness between the Bhikkhu and Brahmâ?'

'There is, Gotama!'

'Very good, Vâse*tt*ha. Then in sooth, Vâse*tt*ha, that the Bhikkhu who is free from household cares should after death, when the body is dissolved, become united with Brahmâ, who is the same—such a condition of things is every way possible!

'And so you say, Vâse*tt*ha, that the Bhikkhu is free from anger, and free from malice, pure in mind, and master of himself; and that Brahmâ is free from anger, and free from malice, pure in mind, and master of himself. Then in sooth, Vâse*tt*ha, that the Bhikkhu who is free from anger, free from malice, pure in mind, and master of himself should after death, when the body is dissolved, become united with Brahmâ, who is the same—such a condition of things is every way possible!'

---

82. When he had thus spoken, the young Brahmans Vâse*tt*ha and Bhâradvâ*g*a addressed the Blessed One, and said:

'Most excellent, Lord, are the words of thy mouth, most excellent! Just as if a man were to set up that which is thrown down, or were to reveal that which is hidden away, or were to point out the right road to him who has gone astray, or were to bring a lamp into the darkness, so that those who have eyes can see external forms;—just even so, Lord, has the truth been made known to us, in many a figure, by the Exalted One. And we, even we, betake ourselves, Lord, to the Blessed One as our guide, to the Truth,

and to the Brotherhood. May the Blessed One accept
us as disciples, as true believers, from this day forth,
as long as life endures!'

Here ends the Tevigga Suttanta[1].

[1] Literally 'The Suttanta about those who have the knowledge of
the Three (Vedas).'   See p. 303, where the names of these 'doctors'
are given.

INDEX OF SUBJECTS AND PROPER NAMES.

INDEX OF PÂLI WORDS.

Kan*d*âla, 9.
Kariyâ, 64.
Kittaka, 10.
Kingulika*m*, 10.

Khandavâ, 303.
Khandokâ, 303.

Ganghâ-vihâra, 301.
Gâti, 100.
Gigu*kkh*â, 237.

*Ñâ*na, 252.
*Ñâ*na-dassana, 86.

Tapas, 209 foll.
Tittiriyâ, 303.
Tûlikâ, 12.

Than*d*ila, 231.
Thâlipâka, 119.
Thusodaka, 229.

Dan*d*amantara*m*, 228.
Datti, 229.
Daddula, 230.
Di*tth*i, xxvi, 26.
Disâ-dâho, 21.
Dukkha, 249.
Dosinâ, 66.

Dhutangas, 219.

Nakkhatta, 20.
Nâma-rûpa, 274, 283.
Nippesikâ, 16.
Nibuddha*m*, 9.
Nimm*itta*m gan*h*âti, 80.

Pakkhandino, 68.
Panga*k*iram, 10.
Pa*kk*attam, 29.
Pa*kk*emi, 252.
Pa*ññ*â, xxvi.
Pa*ññâ*na, 156.
Pa*t*alikâ, 12.
Pa*t*ikâ, 12.
Pa*t*i*k*arate, 116.
Pa*t*imokkha, 26.
Patha-gamana, 20.
Parikkhâro, 163, 174, 177.
Pariggaho, 313.
Pari*k*âreti, 50.
Paritassati, 53.
Parimaddana, 87.
Parihârapatha*m*, 10.
Palighâ, 130.

Pallanko, 11.
Paha*m*, 283.
Pâtikankhati, 4.
Pi*ññ*aka, 230.
Putam*s*ena, 150.
Pubbapetakathâ, 14.
Purisantara-gatâ, 228.
Pekkha*m*, 7.

Phalaka*k*iram, 231.

Bandhupâdapa*kk*â, 112.
Bahvarigâ, 303.
Brahma, 108.
Brahma-va*kkh*asî, 146.
Brahma-vihâra, 298-320.

Bhikkhu, 220 foll.

Maggâni, 303.
Mangura*kkh*avi, 258.
Mano-padosikâ, 33.
Muddâ, 21.
Mûla-nâma, 193.
Mokkha*k*ikâ, 10.

Râga-porise, 176.
Râga-bhogga, 108.

Lapakâ, 15.
Lokakkhâyikâ, 14.

Vankaka*m*, 10.
Van*n*a, 27, 99-101,114, 153.
Vatthu-vi*gg*â, 18.
Vasavattî, 313.
Vâda-pamokkhâya, 15.
Vâla-kambala*m*, 231.
Vikatikâ, 12.
Vi*ññâ*na, 87, 250, 274.
Vidhâ, 163, 174.
Vipphandita, 53.
Viva*tt*a, 28.
Viveka, 84.
Visikhâ-kathâ, 13.
Visûka-dassana*m*, 7.
Visesa, 296.
Vihâra, 111.
Veka*t*iko, 232.
Ve*th*aka, 130.
Vetâla*m*, 8.

Sa*ngh*ambhari, 255.
Sa*ññ*â, 252.
Sattussada, 144.
Santikâ, 10.
Santhâgâra, 113.
Sannitodaka, 255.

TRANSLITERATION OF ORIENTAL ALPHABETS ADOPTED FOR THE TRANSLATIONS OF THE SACRED BOOKS OF THE BUDDHISTS.

CONSONANTS.	MISSIONARY ALPHABET.			Sanskrit.	Zend.	Pehlevi.	Persian.	Arabic.	Hebrew.	Chinese.
	I Class.	II Class.	III Class.							
Gutturales.										
1 Tenuis	k	.	.	क	ﺝ	ﻦ	ﻚ	ﻚ	ב	k
2 „ aspirata	kh	.	.	ख	ﻉ	ﻰ	.	.	ה	kh
3 Media	g	.	.	ग	ﻉ	ﻦ	ﻚ	.	ר	.
4 „ aspirata	gh	.	.	घ	ﻚ	ﻋ	.	.	ר	.
5 Gutturo-labialis	q	.	.	.	ﻚ	.	ﺝ	ﺝ	ק	.
6 Nasalis	ḥ (ng)	.	.	ड़	{ ṅ (ng) ṅ (N) }	.	.	.	.	.
7 Spiritus asper	h	.	.	ह	ġ' (ɤ hv)	ə	.	.	ח	h, hs
8 „ lenis	’	.	.	.	.	.	—	—	ז	.
9 „ asper faucalis	’h	.	.	.	.	.	ﻮ	ﻮ	צ	.
10 „ lenis faucalis	’h	.	.	.	.	.	ﺝ	ﺝ	כ	.
11 „ asper fricatus	.	’h	.	.	.	.	ﻮ	ﻮ	כ	.
12 „ lenis fricatus	.	’h	.	.	.	.	.	.	.	.
Gutturales modificatae (palatales, &c.)										
13 Tenuis	.	k	.	च	.	ﺝ	ﻪ	.	.	k
14 „ aspirata	.	kh	.	छ	.	ﻉۇ	ﻮﻼ	ﻮﻼ	.	kh
15 Media	.	g	.	ज	.	.	.	.	.	.
16 „ aspirata	.	gh	.	झ	.	.	.	.	.	.
17 „ Nasalis	.	ñ	.	ञ	.	.	.	.	.	.

CONSONANTS (continued).	MISSIONARY ALPHABET.			Sanskrit.	Zend.	Pehlevi.	Persian.	Arabic.	Hebrew.	Chinese.
	I Class.	II Class.	III Class.							
18 Semivocalis	y			य	३ ʒ ु (init.)	ॐ	ى	ى	◌	y
19 Spiritus asper										
20 „ lenis		(y)								
21 „ asper assibilatus		s		श	ꝺ	?ᵹ	ج	ج		s
22 „ lenis assibilatus		z			ꝺ					
Dentales.										
23 Tenuis	t			त	ᵹ	ᵹ	ت	ت	ד ד	t
24 „ aspirata	th		TH	थ	ᵹᵹ		ث	ث	ת ת	th
25 „ assibilata		l								
26 Media	d			द	ꝺᵹ	ᵹ	د	د	נ ל	n
27 „ aspirata	dh		DH	ध			ذ	ذ		l
28 „ assibilata										
29 Nasalis	n	l		न			ن	ن	נ	
30 Semivocalis	l			ल						
31 „ mollis 1		l	L						ט ם	s
32 „ mollis 2										
33 Spiritus asper 1	s		s (S)		ᵹ	ᵹ	س	س	ס	s
34 „ asper 2										
35 „ lenis	z				ᵹ	ᵹ	ز	ز	ר	z
36 „ asperrimus 1		z	z (ž)				ژ	ژ	צ	ʒ, ʒh

Dentales modificatae (lingualos, &c.)		
38	Tenuis	*t*
39	„ aspirata	*th*
40	Media	*d*
41	„ aspirata	*dh*
42	Nasalis	*n*
43	Semivocalis	*r*
44	„ fricata	
45	„ diacritica	
46	Spiritus asper	*sh*
47	„ lenis	*zh*
Labiales.		
48	Tenuis	*p*
49	„ aspirata	*ph*
50	Media	*b*
51	„ aspirata	*bh*
52	Tenuissima	
53	Nasalis	*m*
54	Semivocalis	*w*
55	„ aspirata	*hw*
56	Spiritus asper	*f*
57	„ lenis	*v*
58	Anusvára	*m*
59	V.sarga	*h*

VOWELS	MISSIONARY ALPHABET. I Class	II Class	III Class	Sanskrit	Zend	Pehlevi	Persian	Arabic	Hebrew	Chinese
1 Neutralis	0								ı⎯	ǎ
2 Laryngo-palatalis	ə					) fin.				
3 " labialis	ɔ					ᴈ init.				
4 Gutturalis brevis	a	(a)		ब	ᴂ	ᴈ	ʌ	ʌ	ıl	ɑ
5 " longa	â			आ	ᴡ		ʋ	ʋ	l·ı	⎯
6 Palatalis brevis	i	(š)		wᴂr	ᴎ	ᴈ	ı'ı	ıّı	l·ı·l	⎯
7 " longa	ī			ᴦ						
8 Dentalis brevis	t			ᴩ						
9 " longa	ū			ᴪ						
10 Lingualis brevis	ri			ᴪ						
11 " longa	rī			ᴫ						
12 Labialis brevis	u	(u)		ᴫ	^ᴕ	⎯	·ı·ᴧ	·ı·ᴧ		u
13 " longa	û			ᴫ ᴫ	Ɛ(e) ᴧ(e)	ᴕ	ᴈ·b	ᴈ·b	l·ı	ᴖ
14 Gutturo-palatalis brevis	e	(e)			ᴧ ᴫ	ᴕ			·ı	e
15 " longa	è (ai)	(ai)								ᴖ
16 Diphthongus gutturo-palatalis	ai			ᴇ ᴇ	⇁ᴧ	⎯	·ᴧᴧ	·ᴧᴧ	l·ᴕ	ái
17 "	ei (ēi)									ei, ēi
18 "	oi (ōu)									
19 Gutturo-labialis brevis	o	(o)								o
20 " longa	ô (au)									
21 Diphthongus gutturo-labialis	âu	(au)		ᴥᴜ	ᴇᴜ (au)					áu
22 "	eu (ēu)									
23 "	ou (ōn)									
24 Gutturalis fracta	ä									
25 Palatalis fracta	ī									
26 Labialis fracta	ü									ü
27 Gutturo-labialis fracta	ŭ